Astrology Lessons
by Carl Payne Tobey

Edited, Annotated, Illustrated and Digitized by Naomi C Bennett

Written by Carl Payne Tobey 1955
Cover Art by David A. Smith
Copyright © 2015 Naomi C Bennett

All rights reserved. No part of this book may be reproduced or transmitted in any form or by any means, electronic or mechanical including photocopying or by any information storage and retrieval systems, without permission in writing from the publisher.

Paperback ISBN 978-1-892134-03-5

Publisher: BonAmi Publishing, Austin, Texas

Table of Contents

	Introduction	i
1.	A Mathematical Study of Biological and Psychological Dynamics	1
2.	The Unconscious Interpretive Apparatus and Three Survival Dynamics	17
3.	The Survival dynamic Reactors	31
4.	The Geometry of Time	47
5.	The Non-Survival Dynamics	63
6.	The Non-Survival Dynamic Guides, Part One	79
7.	The Non-Survival Dynamic Guides, Part Two	95
8.	Design in the Solar System	111
9.	The Astrological Houses and Planetary Aspects	129
10.	Erecting the Birth Chart	145
11.	The Natal Horoscope	159
12.	The Art of Interpretation	167
13.	Analytical Interpretation	171
14.	Survival or Non-Survival	199
15.	The Mysterious Social Survival Problems	213
16.	Seeds of Mental Illness	229
17.	Progressions, Transits and Horary Astrology	243
18.	The Statistical and the Analytical Approach	257
19.	Astrology at Work	271
20.	The Secondary Chart [Solar Parts Chart]	287
21.	Human Relationships	303
22.	A Summation Up to Here	317
23.	What is the Abstract World?	331
24.	Money, Part One	345
25.	Money, Part Two	359
	Carl Payne Tobey	375

Introduction

This book is an edited version of Carl Payne Tobey's private astrology lessons given to his students starting in 1955. It has never been publically printed and therefore was inaccessible to the majority of today's astrologers. It is my great hope that this book will reawaken its readers to the profound discoveries and insights that this man left us. The original work was created on a typewriter so Tobey used all caps to emphasize his points. Comments regarding the student forum have been deleted along with homework assignments and some mathematics, but the bulk of it is preserved. The all caps have been preserved so think of them as **bold** statements. Tobey is not 'yelling' at the reader, this was written before the internet. The **bold text** within the book has been added by me the editor along with *italics in the text*. One chapter on chart calculations has been deleted since all astrologers use programs or apps to calculate charts now. Also deleted are some comments in the text I no longer considered relevant. New illustrations have been added where I deemed them necessary enhancements.

Tobey was a major force in the American astrology community that was been all but forgotten since most of his work is out of print. It is time for his discoveries to be remembered and utilized in this new 21st century as astrology merges traditional with modern techniques in a global community of astrology.

Carl Payne Tobey had a long and extensive career in the publishing industry and astrology. He started a newspaper in Long Island, N.Y. in his early twenties and made a name for himself getting rid of corruption in city government. He later moved to Greenwich Village in New York City during the 1920's as astrology was taking hold in this major American city. He played the stock market during its great rise in the 1920's and managed to get out before the great crash of October 1929 by the use of astrology. He shared new ideas with the bright creative minds that were re-examining astrology's principles and practices such as Sydney K. Bennett (Wynn's Astrology), and Grant Lewi. He was American's first astrologer to use statistical research to verify its principles. His articles were published in Wynn's Astrology magazine, American Astrology magazine and the New York Astrology magazines from 1933-50. He later had a weekly syndicated column in U.S. newspapers in the 1970's.

Carl was an advocate of the equal house system and transits after long years of experimentation with many techniques. He was a great researcher and investigator of astrological techniques. He discovered why the planets were assigned to specific signs and he discovered the geometric pattern behind house rulership. In addition, he extended the use of arabic parts by calculating a new additional natal chart using traditional arabic parts that bring out hidden attributes of a personality.

He called astrology abstract design and a branch of geometry but since his death the mathematician, Benoit Mandlebrot, discovered fractal geometry with the use of IBM computers. It is highly recommended that readers goggle him and view a NOVA 2008 video of his discovery since it applies to astrology very directly. As Tobey's student I have used these principles since 1970 and I spent 20 years researching for evidence of these principles that are documented in my book, *Foundations of Astrology*, which available on Amazon.

It was Tobey's greatest wish for others to re-examine astrology's foundations and to build a modern version that is more functional and accurate than the model we inherited from prior generations. May his words put the reader on a path of discovery and personal authority based on experience, not tradition.

Naomi C Bennett

Carl Payne Tobey's Correspondence Course Created in 1955

Edited, Annotated, Illustrated and Digitized
by
©Naomi Bennett 2015

LESSON ONE

A MATHEMATICAL STUDY OF BIOLOGICAL AND PSYCHOLOGICAL DYNAMICS

Astrology is a mathematical study of biological and psychological dynamics. It is the oldest know science, and all other sciences appear to have been it's children. It comes to us out of prehistoric times, and suggests the existence of a prehistoric civilization enlightened far beyond our own in some respects. It was kept alive in the East, but it degenerated into much that was little more than superstition. It became associated with mysticism, fatalism and cultist, was taught only in secret schools, and was practically outlawed with the dawn of the Christian era._

Christianity taught a doctrine of free will. Fatalism was in conflict with this doctrine, and since it was believed that astrology was fatalism, it was outlawed. (See *'THE STAR CROSSED RENAISSANCE'* by Cameron Allen, Duke University). Although it's funeral was held, its own dynamics would not allow it to die.

A new word was coined. It was astronomy, a new science to replace astrology. Originally, all astronomers were astrologers. The new science was to ultimately deny any association between planets and man, but this did not come about immediately. In the beginning, it was merely the desire to deny astrology insofar as it might conflict with the freewill doctrine of the church. In the early late century, Paracelsus defined the difference between astrology and astronomy of that time. He stated that astronomy confined itself to character declinations, while astrology was used to predict the future. He claimed that astrology could not predict for the individual because he had a choice that he could make that would affect the future, but he held that astrology could predict the future of the masses. In affect, he was arguing that Man can live above his animal nature.

Modern textbooks carefully conceal the fact that the greatest minds they glorify are those of the astrologers of history. It is regarded as 'good taste' when textbook writers delete anything and everything that demonstrates the part astrology has played in history. Some of these astrologers have been Aristarchus, Pythagoras, Ptolemy, Copernicus, Kepler, Newton [ed. unproven], Paracelsus, Tycho Brahe, Benjamin Franklin and many others. Modern astronomers like to teach us that Copernicus discovered that the Earth was not the center of the solar system, but Copernicus was merely going back to a defense of Aristarchus, who taught a heliocentric astrology 200 years before the birth of Christ, and who learned it from the work of Pythagoras who lived 500 B.C. While glorifying all these names, the astronomers try to claim them as astronomers when they were actually astrologers.

To study astrology, one has had to be an individualist, rugged enough to brush off the criticism of orthodox education. One could not study astrology and be a conformist.

Perhaps the three men influenced the dawn of the 20th century astrology in a new direction were Allen Leo, Sepharial and Llewellyn George. They provided enough printed literature for new investigators to find a place to sink their teeth. Without them, it might have taken us another century to get started. The color and romanticism of Evangeline Adams probably drew more public attention. [ed. Aleister Crowley was Adams' ghost writer]

In this course, astrology will not be taught as a science of cause and effect, but as an abstract science, a branch of mathematics. To add 6 and 10, you do not need apples. It will not be taught that planets affect us. We do not know that they do. We do know that we have a complicated realm of coincidence. It would appear that cause and effect operate in accord with certain abstract, mathematical laws which condition their functioning, and that astrology explains these laws.

> Six apples and ten apples are sixteen apples.
> Six oranges and ten oranges are sixteen oranges.

The oranges have nothing to do with the apples. One does not cause the other, but the same arithmetical principles that apply to the apples apply also to the oranges. Mathematical principles are universal principles. They work anywhere, any time. Astrology deals with these same principles.

There have been many attempts to explain astrology in terms of physical science, vibrations, electricity or light waves, but they are too simple, while astrology is too complicated and too all-in-conclusive. Astrology seems to include everything. It involves the physical, the mental, the emotional, the vital, the concrete, the abstract. It even involves time and space, and strangely relates all of these things to each other. It is the mathematics of Life. (Paul G. Clancy called it the Algebra of Life.) [ed. Editor and owner of American Astrology Magazine] It is a study of the abstract principles of existence, and there can be existence only in accord with those principles. Astrology explains life in terms of geometry.

It draws strange parallels that can never be found without it. What connection might there be, for example, between executive ability and the sex organs, between interest in religion and the liver. We do not know, but astrology indicates that there is. There are many other strange parallels. What you will learn here is merely what the writer has been able to dig out in 30 years. The principal thing he has learned in that time is that he hasn't scratched the surface.

It is desirable that the student make no attempt to move too rapidly. There are certain basic factors that must be grasped. Speed may slow you down. Astrology is unlike anything else you may have studied. We want you to prove every point to your own satisfaction. In the end, we want you to take our work for absolutely nothing. Astrology works, but it has to work exactly the same for you as it does for us. If we claim that 6 apples and 10 apples equal fifteen apples, while you find that 6 oranges and 10 oranges equal 16 oranges, there is something wrong. We must find agreement all the way.

In the writer's approach to this subject, he had to deal with many erroneous claims. He had to discover which claims were true and which claims were false. He was told that you have to accept astrology on faith. This was the most fabulous claim of all. Accept absolutely nothing on faith. Astrology has to work in laboratory experiments. When you have finished this course, you will merely have reached a starting point. You will be like the salesman who was trained in the New York office, and then sent to Mexico City to start selling. Certain principles that worked in New York will also work in Mexico City, but down there folks speak Spanish.

Suppose we could say that there are twelve basic material elements and that all the elements are combinations of these elements. It would simplify things. Astrology deals with twelve basic principles, and everything grows out of intricate combinations and relationships involving these twelve basic principles. The number of combinations may not be infinite, but it might as well be. It is very great. An astrologer is only as good as his understanding of these twelve basic principles. Our greatest objective must be to learn as much as possible about these twelve principles. You will not know all there is to know from us, because we do not know that much.

There is evidence that the ancients may have known that civilization was going into an eclipse, and that they tried very hard to put certain information, hidden away in symbol form, where it could ultimately be found, interpreted and revived. There are some who believe that the construction of the Great Pyramid was for the purpose of preserving mathematical and astrological knowledge during the dark ages until new initiates with an ability to understand abstract principles could decipher the information that is hidden away in the dimensions and measurements of the pyramid. The Mexican Calendar Stone was carefully buried, only to be found may centuries later and to reveal a calendar more perfect that any then known to modern science. The first Spanish explorers, arriving in a new and unknown land, found the symbols of the signs of the zodiac carved on stone throughout Mexico, Central and South America. (See **'RED MAN'S CONTINENT' by** Ellsworth Huntington, Yale University Press.)

It would seem that all religious writers were attempting to get across the significance of two numbers – 12 and 7. Twelve tribes of Israel, twelve disciples of Christ, the Book with the Seven Seals, etc. The Sphinx is an astrological symbol. Ancient religious works are filled with terms which have an entirely different meanings in astrological terminology. This includes the *Bible*. If you possessed information, it was necessary to hide it in order to avoid persecution. These facts need not seem strange when you realize that there are towns in the United States today which have laws forbidding anyone to teach astrology. The Federal Communications Commission uses its pressure to keep it from being taught on the air, and radio and television stations live in fear of having their licenses revoked if they disobey the wishes of those non-elected persons who constitute a Washington Bureaucracy. As a result, astrological groups have sometimes incorporated as a religion, because under the constitution, you can't outlaw religion. This same procedure has been followed by advocates of Dianetics, who have changed their subject to Scientology and called it a religion to avoid persecution by the American Medical Association, an institution bent upon a monopoly of all things related to human health and even social relationships. The ultimate goal of socialized medicine would achieve such an aim, but it has been opposed by a great part of the medical profession because it might take control away from the A.M.A.

It is unlawful to ship astrological literature into Russia. It was a paradox to see an astrological convention open in Los Angeles, where astrology has been outlawed, but openly practiced, by the man who was the Lieutenant Governor and later Governor. You can practice astrology anywhere in the United States if you call it a religion. We practice it throughout the United States, and we do not call it a religion. The Post Office Department has no objection to astrology. You can practice astrology anywhere in the U.S., if you call it a study of cycles. While the FCC bars astrology by name, they

Lesson One

daily utilize data furnished by the Radio Corporation of America predicting magnetic storms from a study of the planets. Although we point out these facts and inconsistencies, they should not bother you. We have been in business for 20 years, and they have neither bothered nor hindered us. It will take time and a great deal of money to eradicate ignorance from high places.

Astrology bases everything on the numeral 12, while mathematicians long claimed that the most perfect system of mathematics would be based on twelve instead of ten, the duodecimal system, instead of the decimal system. This fact appears to have significance. To understand the significance of the seven throughout ancient literature, it is only necessary to realize that in ancient literature, there was no zero. That was later invented by the Hindus [and passed to the Arabs]. When a circle was cut in twelve parts, and the lines between the parts were numbered, there was no zero point. The first line was numbered as one instead of zero, and therefore, the halfway mark was seven, not six. Seven is not one-half of twelve, but you start counting the second half with seven, just as you start counting the first half with one. Astrology's seventh principle is a very dynamic one, as we will later see. It deals with time and change, for without change time ceases to exist. In the abstract world, there is no time. Time is merely an expression of matter and space. There is psychological time, but it is unlike clock time. (In recent years, many mathematicians have shifted their faith to the binary system of math, based on 2, but this is probably a fad, based on the fact that modern electronic calculators employ the binary system plus another system based on 16, because 16 is the 4th power of 2. The binary system was discovered by Leibnitz who lived 1646 to 1716 A.D. and who employed it to try to convert the Emperor of China to Christianity.)

Although the material parts of the solar system are the only material factors with which astrology deals, there are many other factors, but they are geometrical and in the realms of pure abstraction. It should be mentioned that there are schools of astrology attempting to deal with fixed stars, but we recommend that the student stay away from any such theories until he has finished Lesson Eleven of this course. After that, he is on his own. You will find that the astrologer speaks of things such as the signs of the zodiac as if they were as real as the Empire State Building. They are as real, but they are not material. They are mere geometrical angles and mathematical points. In his early days of investigation the writer tried to visualize the zodiac as a possible magnetic field, but this conception breaks down, unless a magnetic field is something quite different from what we suppose it to be. Also, the poles of the earth's magnetic field do not conform to the poles of the zodiac.

The average astrology student of today has no clear conception of what the zodiac is. He may view it as something extending far out in space, but it isn't. It is all right here. It doesn't necessarily extend beyond the surface of the earth. It has no connection with the fixed stars. It is an abstraction. It is a group of mathematical points which can be found from the relationship of the earth's equator to the earth's orbit. It would have no significance for a being born on Mars or any other planet. It is purely a product of motion – the earth's motion – two earth motions, the rotation of the earth on it's own axis and the revolution of the earth along it's own orbit. It is geometry, involving two planes of space, the plane of the earth's equator and the plane of its orbit. To determine the zodiac, it is necessary to consider no other factors in space except for the fact that there are two foci to the ellipse of the earth's orbit, and we must know which of these is occupied by the Sun.

It is important that you have a clear conception of what the zodiac is, and what it is not, for then you can be saved many arguments with yourself or others as to why certain systems of astrology being practiced are without valid foundation. Attempts to use a heliocentric (Sun as center) zodiac fall down, because there is nothing about the zodiac that is heliocentric. We cannot draw a heliocentric zodiac, because we know too little about the path the Sun is taking through space. Each planet would have its own zodiac, which would have to be calculated from the relationship of its equator to its orbit and it would be quite different from our zodiac. Its twelve points would not be in the same place. The zodiac, as we use it, constitutes a series of dynamics. If either motion of the earth were to suddenly cease, the zodiac would also cease to exist. Remember that! **The zodiac is a product of motion alone.** When you realize this you will not be harboring the illusions concerning it that are prevalent in many minds today. Everything in astrology concerns dynamics and kindred phenomena. Without motion, astrology would not exist.

Just as Euclid's geometry failed to meet the requirements of a mechanical and atomic age, some of the old conceptions of astrology must give way to the new geometry of dynamics. Euclid's geometry failed to consider dynamics. Einstein and Relativity have changed things. There is evidence that the Arctic may have, at one time, been tropical, meaning that the equator was across a different part of the earth's surface. At such a time, the zodiac may have been different from what it is today.

On the next page we have a diagram. It will require some explanation. It is intentionally drawn out of proportion in order to illustrate and emphasize certain factors. You will see four large circles and one small circle. The small circle represents the Sun, which is actually many, many times the size of the Sun. The four larger circles represent four positions of the earth in it's trip around the Sun, spring, summer, autumn, winter. Note the odd fact that the Earth is nearer to the Sun when we, in the Northern Hemisphere, have summer. The reverse would be true for people living south of the equator in the Southern Hemisphere. If heat is really something that travels through space from the Sun to the Earth, then the average temperature south of the equator should be warmer in the summer and colder in winter than summer and winters in the Northern Hemisphere. It is believed by some, however, that because there is far more ocean south of the equator that north of the equator, the ocean absorbs heat from the Sun in Summer and gives that heat off in the winter, modifying temperatures south of the equator from what they might be otherwise. It does seem odd that when we, north of the equator, have winter, the earth is 3 million miles closer to the Sun that in summer. There is the alternative possibility that heat as we know it may generated here at the Earth AFTER light from the Sun reaches the Earth, in which event, distance of a planet from the Sun might have no bearing on the temperature of that planet, a possibility that materialists, dogmatists and astronomers would hate to entertain.

This diagram will emphasize the fact that the Earth travels in an ellipse, not in a circle and that it is closest to the Sun when we have winter. Now, we run into the difficulty of trying to illustrate a 3-dimensional factor on a 2-dimensional piece of paper. Each circle representing the Earth has a solid straight line representing the axis of the Earth, with the north pole at the top, the south pole at the bottom. However, for the pole to be at this angle, you would have to be looking at the Earth with your eyes in the plane of the Earth's orbit. Suppose you hold the Earth in the position given, but drop the spring position of the Earth down so that it is behind the Sun, raising the autumn position so that it is in front of the Sun. You would no longer be able to see the Sun because it would be concealed by the autumn position of the Earth, which would also conceal the spring position of the Earth, which would be behind both the autumn position of the Earth and the Sun. The, you would find the poles of the Earth exactly as given. The north pole would always tilt toward the right. It would not turn around as the pole of a spinning top would do. It would not tilt to the left when in it's summer position. Note that in summer, the Northern Hemisphere tilts toward the Sun, while in winter it tilts away from the Sun. This angle at which the hemisphere tilts seems to be the most important factor in determining temperature.

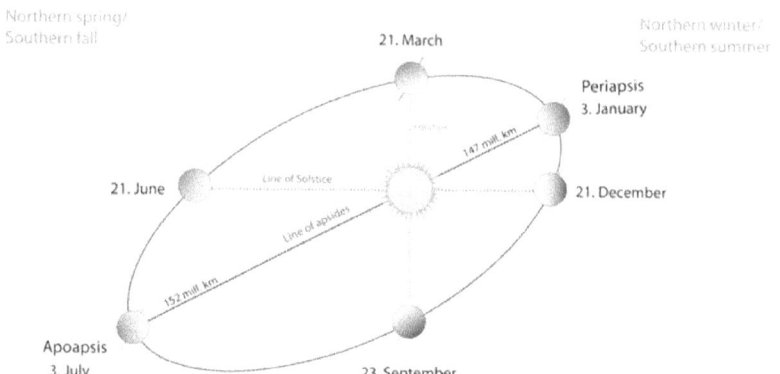

Earth's Orbit Around the Sun

However, there are only two moments out of a year when a straight line drawn from the Sun to the Earth will also pass though the plane of the Earth's equator. At those moments, and only during those two moments, can a straight line pass through both the plane of the Earth's orbit and the plane of the equator. These two moments are known as the spring and autumnal equinoxes, and they become the markers upon which we can base the whole zodiac. Draw a straight line from the Earth to the Focus occupied by the Sun at one of these moments, and allow it to point always in the same direction. The Earth moves on. This line no longer points to the Sun, until six months later, the other end of the line will point to the Sun. The line will point at no specific point on the Earth's surface, because the Earth itself is rotating within it's zodiac. Temporarily, and for a matter of years, the line will point at some fixed point in space, like a star, but even this is not permanent. The line points at absolutely nothing material permanently. It is purely an abstraction, and yet, upon this abstraction all else is based.

This could all be wild dreaming except for one fact. Conclusions based on this line function. They work. They can be depended upon. This brings up the great question. How did men of an unknown time in history figure this out? It seems impossible that it could have come to light through observation. It must have been calculated by some master mathematician who knew something about human dynamics and mathematical principles that we do not know today. His discovery eclipse's the discovery of the atom by modern scientists. Next, using this abstract line, he drew a circle around the Earth in the plane of the Earth's orbit, and divided it into twelve equal parts, and these became the signs of the zodiac. He knew something about twelve that we do not know. He may have been a student of the duodecimal system.

We have reached the point where we have a circle divided into twelve parts. Up till now, it is a mathematical figure – no more, no less. The astrologer finds it related to twelve principles in nature, quite extraordinary principles. We are going to devote a great deal of time to these principles. In fact, you can devote the rest of your life to them, and you will always be learning something new. They are the principles of human dynamics. It would be truthful to say they are the principles of biological dynamics, for they do not confine themselves to humans. They apply for a dog or a cat, but we cannot study astrology without considering two other factors, evolution and heredity. As the writer has stated elsewhere, a horse can never become an accomplished pianist because of his heredity. Heredity is definitely a limiting factor. There is more fatalism to heredity than to astrology.

Throughout your study of astrology, this mathematical figure is going to be your ruler. You are going to use it for purposes of measurement. The zodiac is not the only place where you will use it. It will be used elsewhere. In fact, it can be used in so many different places that it knocks any idea of a magnetic field into a cocked hat, unless there are millions and millions of magnetic fields all around us, and there may be, we do not know.

Mathematical rules work regardless of time or space. They are abstractions. They are, in no way, affected by circumstances. They do not change. Observations made by Euclid or Pythagoras 2500 years ago can be made today. Even the mountains and fixed stars have changed in certain respects during that time, but not the rules of mathematics. We need an illustration that will furnish us with a parallel, and we are going to utilize a well-known mathematical formula for that illustration. Please don't run away. We will make it simple.

We have stated that astrology is a study of biological dynamics. Perhaps we should purify this even more. Although we use astrology to grasp and understand biological dynamics, there is a part of astrology which can only be classified as a higher branch of mathematics. Now, let us strike our parallel. We are going to use the Pythagorean theorem.

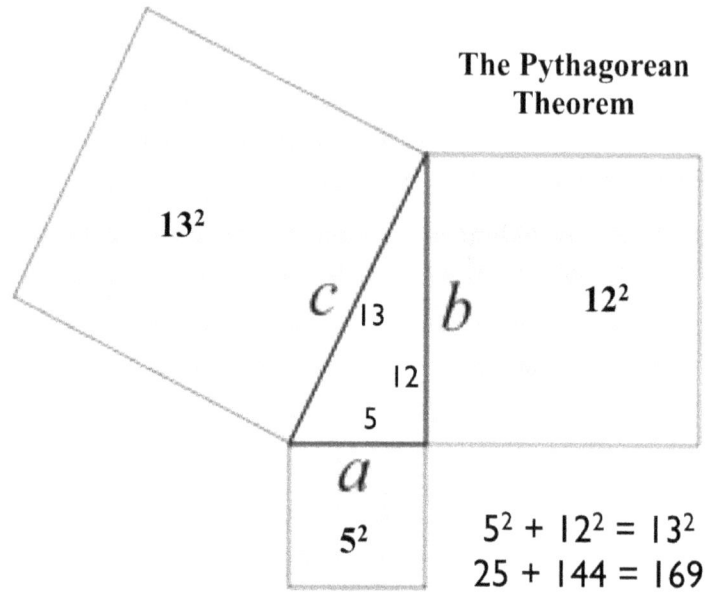

The Pythagorean Theorem

$5^2 + 12^2 = 13^2$
$25 + 144 = 169$

At the top is a right-angled triangle, meaning one where one of the angles is 90 degrees, like the corner of a square. Around this triangle, we have drawn three squares. Pythagoras discovered that in any such triangle, the area of the large square is exactly equal to the area of the two smaller squares. Ever since his time, this has been know as the Pythagorean theorem, (However, it was actually know by the ancient Chinese and Egyptians earlier.) The size of the triangle, or the relative length of the two legs (short sides) of the triangle will not alter the rule. The theorem is expressed: $a^2 + b^2$ equals c^2.

You can make up millions of such triangles of all sizes, and the law will always work. In some cases, you will deal with fractions, but you can use any odd number for the short side and work out a triangle where al sides can be expressed in positive integers (whole numbers). To get the other two sides, all you need do is square the first side, and cut the result in half. Since the result is an odd number, and not divisible by two, you have to have an answer that is a positive integer (whole number) plus 1/2. Now add 1/2 to get the longest of the two sides, and deduct 1/2 to get the other side. In other words, if the short side of the triangle is 7, the square of 7 is 49, and when we cut 49 in two, we get 24 1/2. Add 1/2. and we get 25. Deduct 1/2, and we get 24. Thus (7 X 7) + (24 X 24) equals (25 X 25).

Even using all the odd numbers to infinity in this way will not give you all the possible triangles that can be made out of positive integers (whole numbers). There is an infinite number of others. You will also note that in this particular series of triangle, the sum of the two longer sides is always the square of the shorter side.

Having given this illustration, we have a very important point that we want to get across. In fact, this is vital to any real understanding of astrology. When all right-angled triangles conform to this law, we have coincidence. This does not mean that there is any cause-and-effect phenomenon involved. One triangle is not the cause, nor is another triangle the effect.

Just as this rule will work for all possible right-angled triangles, the division of a circle into twelve equal parts will work in astrology under many different unrelated conditions. Later, you will see that the right-angled triangle itself is very important in the study of astrology.

In mathematics, there are undoubtedly infinite other rules similar to the Pythagorean theorem that can be applied to triangles in which no angle is 90 degrees. No mathematician has ever taken the time to work them out. Perhaps the idea has never entered anyone's head. Never gain the impression that mathematicians have ever scratched more than the surface of their subject. There is so much about which we have never thought to inquire.

Everything, absolutely everything in astrology is a study of angles and mathematical points. We will even find that certain angles have some mysterious connection with the distance of an object from the central point of a sphere. The inference is that an object cannot move without setting in motion some very complicated system of dynamics. Time and space may assume entirely new meanings to you. The solar system is one monstrous atom, and Heaven knows what might happen if one of its electrons (planets) was pulled away. This is new geometry, but it is a dynamic geometry, not the dead geometry of Euclid.

We will save ourselves much trouble and many sleepless nights, if we start out by considering astrology, not as a cause-and-effect phenomenon, but as a system of higher mathematics. Do not let this scare or drive you away. It is important to your understanding, but there are vast numbers of students, using astrology from a practical point of view, who have almost no education whatever in the field of mathematics. One such student, doing very well otherwise, told the writer, 'You know, I can't tell you how much is 9 x 9, without working it out in my own way.'

Many students catch and grasp the basic principles with

almost no knowledge whatever of the mathematical side of astrology. Yet, such people have helped to keep astrology alive down through the centuries. **It must be stated, however, that under these circumstances many errors, some of a mathematical nature, have crept into astrology as it has been taught over the last few hundred years. These must be brought to light and corrected.** Under these circumstances to think that the combined efforts of all its materialistic enemies have been unable to dent interest in the subject might almost be interpreted to mean that some guiding principles never intended to allow it to die out. This fact is as mysterious as the man who worked out these laws originally. It has been as difficult to wipe out astrology as to wipe out religion. There are some things that refuse to die. Astrology is one of them. It has outlived every enemy it ever had. It has outlived the civilizations of its enemies.

Thus, we have reached a point where we have a circle divided into twelve equal parts. Let us go on from there.

Because of the ancient's plan of hiding knowledge behind symbols, many weird interpretations have sprung from their writings. We are going to take four ancient terms and tell you what they mean. The terms are FIRE, EARTH, AIR and WATER. Because of the constant use of these terms, which were astrological, moderns have convinced themselves that these ancients were under the impression that there are only four elements. In 'Mathematics for the Million,' Hogben points out that Pythagorus associated these words with triangles, and Hogben thought it was quite silly but amusing. So, let us tell you what these words mean. They are psychological terms.

> FIRE means VITAL.
> EARTH means PHYSICAL.
> AIR means INTELLECTUAL.
> WATER means EMOTIONAL.

The twelve signs of the zodiac were divided into four groups. There were FIRE signs, EARTH signs, AIR signs and WATER signs. The three signs of a group were always spaced 120 degrees apart, so that each group formed a perfect equilateral triangle, and the four groups, when fitted together formed the circle divided into twelve equal parts.

Do not lose sight of the fact that we are still in the realms of the abstract, because all this grows from that mathematical point in time, when it is possible to draw a straight line through both the plane of the Earth's orbit and the plane of the Earth's equator. We measure from there.

Biological dynamics have to do with a circle divided into twelve equal parts, representing the vital, the physical, the intellectual and the emotional – four equilateral triangles, with three corners each, adding up to twelve, the base of the duodecimal system of mathematics. AS we go along, you will find that the pieces all fit together perfectly, and everything always comes out even.

There were more words – CARDINAL, FIXED and MUTABLE.

The zodiacal signs were also divided into four CARDINAL signs, four FIXED signs, and Four MUTABLE signs, making up the twelve. This gave one Cardinal sign of each element, one Fixed sign of each element and one Mutable sign of each element.

Just as the zodiac can be divided into four equilateral triangles, it is also divided into three squares, one representing four Cardinal signs, one representing four Fixed signs, and one representing four Mutable signs.

We have expressed this in our diagrams with geometrical figures. Throughout astrology, you will always be dealing with geometrical figures. You will always be dealing with 12-sided figures or divisions thereof. This appears to be a basic principle of nature known to the ancients, but let us point out that you can find this division of a circle into twelve parts elsewhere in nature. It is common to say that a snowflake has six sides, a pattern repeated six times. Actually, however, each one-sixth is the same pattern repeated twice, one mirrored. Therefore, like the zodiac every snowflake has TWELVE sides. Here again, we see the base of the duodecimal system.

To think of the zodiac and its implications as ridiculous is to think of a snowflake as ridiculous. What is more ridiculous than that all snowflakes should have the same number of sides. Because we find that all snowflakes do have the same number of sides. We recognize that a principle of nature is at work, and we accept the result. Crystals also form with six sides, and various types of rock formations do the same thing. Nature functions mathematically. In the zodiac also we find a principle of nature at work, and we have to accept the result.

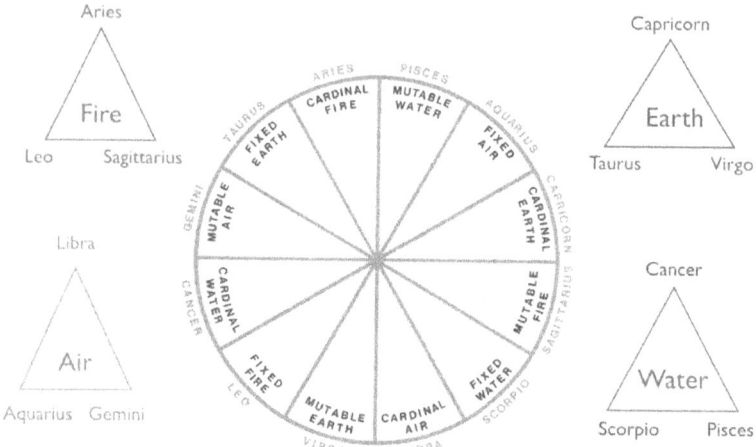

The Four Elements of Fire, Air, Earth and Water

Some writers have drawn attention to the symbol of the Christian religion – the cross – and they maintain it to be the astrological square. The Bible is filled with astrological terms and symbology. The symbol of the Jewish Religion is the six-pointed star, two equilateral triangles. Actually, there should be no conflict between astrology and religion. There is no conflict between astrology and any legitimate branch of science. There may be conflict between astrology and unproved theories and dogma but unlike astrology, scientific theories are often in the realm of fashions. They have no permanence. We need think only of the billiard ball conception of the atom that was prevalent not so long ago. The modern theory of the atom conforms more to the ancient's saying, 'As above, so below.' Because RCA set up their own investigative and research department, their Propagation Department, and dropped' accepted' and fashionable theories, they found that geometrical figures formed by the planets can be used to predict the condition of terrestrial magnetism at any and all times. The geometrical figures established by their research were the same established by the astrologers long before the dawn of any written history.

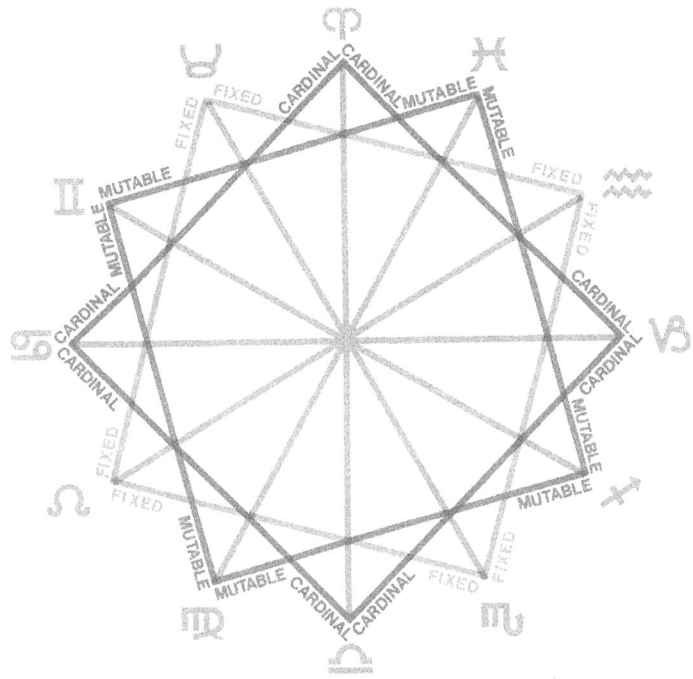

The Three Crosses of Cardinal, Fixed and Mutual

LESSON TWO

THE UNCONSCIOUS INTERPRETIVE APPARATUS
AND THREE SURVIVAL DYNAMICS

In Dianetics, L. Ron Hubbard gives an important clue when he tells that the purpose of the life dynamics is TO SURVIVE. We will show that while it is the purpose of some life dynamics TO SURVIVE, it is the purpose of other dynamics NOT TO SURVIVE in the present form. The dynamics function mathematically and geometrically, and this functioning can be calculated and predicted.

SURVIVAL IS THE PRIMITIVE PURPOSE OF THE WATER SIGNS OF THE ZODIAC.

There are three Water Signs which form an equilateral triangle in the mathematical figure we have called the zodiac. These are the three emotional signs, **Cancer, Scorpio and Pisces**, and they represent three different types of emotion which continually involve compulsions. These three signs, their purpose, and the part of the body with which the ancients associated them may be noted as follows:

Zodiacal Sign	Purpose	Part of Body
Cancer	Individual Survival	Stomach and Breasts
Scorpio	Family Survival	Sex Organs
Pisces	Social Survival	The Feet

To understand this lesson, we will ask you to consider the statement that LIFE IS 100% INTERPRETATION, and that most interpretation is unconscious. A great part of it is misinterpretation.

Sight is the interpretation of light waves. A hazy moving object in the dusk may become a bear for the small boy, and he will actually see a bear. His interpretive apparatus will fill in any missing details.

Hearing is the interpretation of sound waves, and so on with the other of the five orthodox senses. We refer to sight, hearing, smell, taste and touch, because for a time it was fashionable to deny all other senses. We do not know how many senses there are. There are more than five, and there might be twelve.

Everything coming through the senses has to be interpreted. If you speak no language but English and you receive a telegram in Spanish, your problem of interpretation will become more complex.

Interpretation is largely an unconscious process, and therefore, we must introduce THE UNCONSCIOUS INTERPRETIVE APPARATUS.

When this apparatus functions in a healthy fashion, we have instinct, intuition and good health, but it is a complex mechanism, involving may factors such as heredity and past experience, and its misinterpretations may be followed by abnormal reactions such as pain, illness, compulsions and even insanity.

Emotion is reaction to interpretation or misinterpretation on the part of the unconscious interpretive apparatus.

Dreams are other reactions, and are largely misinterpretations of what is constantly coming in over the extrasensory apparatus.

The conception that emotion is a reaction to unconscious interpretation of incoming extrasensory data is the result of a series of experiments over many years. The experiments began as the result of a single incident that we will mention. It happened many years ago.

A strange feeling came over the writer as he was about to leave for another city on a business trip. He didn't want to go. Reason told him to go, but this strange feeling said not to go. There was conflict, and an experiment was decided upon. He would follow his feelings and check the result.

Within an hour the telephone rang. It was an attorney calling. He had traveled 250 miles to see the writer and would arrive in a few minutes. His visit proved financially profitable to both parties. Upon his departure, the business for which the writer's journey had been planned was completed by long distance telephone.

Had reason been followed, the writer would have left before the attorney arrived.

Continued experimentation reveled that emotions often result from extrasensory information not obtainable through the five orthodox senses. This is not often observed because people are not on the alert for it.

Sigmund Freud was far from the first person attempting to interpret dreams. In ancient times, they were used in an attempt to predict the future, and such illustrations are contained in the Bible. Although there are rare cases where people dream true, and an interesting such case will follow, we will find more evidence if we

Lesson Two

consider the average dream as a misinterpretation of what is coming in over the extrasensory system.

The writer's son tells of an upsetting dream, in which a young lady neighbor takes sick and dies. The above theory is explained to him, and it is agreed that results shall be observed carefully.

Within an hour, the young lady asks to use the telephone to call a veterinarian because her horse is ill. Twenty minutes later, she returns and announces that the horse is dead. The horse had been ill at the time of the dream, which appeared to be a misinterpretation of the existing facts.

We have a similarity in a television set which picks up video waves and interprets them. When the set is not tuned in correctly, we receive all kinds of designs closely resembling some artists' conception of modernistic art.

Incidents buried deep in the memory can be re-stimulated in a dream. In such a dream, the names of two men met thirty years before are mentioned and thus recalled. The dream is then related to a neighbor, because of the unusual factor of recall, for the men had met very casually at the time, and the meeting was of no significance. The neighbor is impressed because he knows both men personally. They now reside in a town 2500 miles away, from which the neighbor has just moved. The neighbor and the writer have something in common. Would the dream have occurred otherwise?

If the student wishes an example of dreaming true, and there are many such cases, he will find an interesting case in the volume NEW FRONTIERS OF THE MIND by Dr. J. B. Rhine, head of the Para-Psychology Department of Duke University.

Dr. Rhine could never forget or brush aside an incident that occurred when he was a boy on a farm. His father awakened from a dream in which he had seen a neighbor, miles away, trapped in his burning barn. So vivid and upsetting was the dream that Dr. Rhine's father dressed in the middle of the night, hitched up a horse, drove several miles to the neighbor's farm, only to find the barn on fire with the neighbor trapped inside. He rescued him, but the rescue was possible only because of the dream.

Consider that the individual is subject to a constant bombardment of 'messages' coming through other than the five orthodox senses, as well as the orthodox senses, and the unconscious interpretive apparatus is constantly at work in an attempt to decode these 'messages', with no help or operation from the conscious, because modern education has dogmatically taught us that there are no such 'messages'. It works on its own, automatically, and the result, in most cases is MISINTERPRETATION, which has many effects, including pain, dangerous compulsions, psychosomatic illness, aberrations, emotional upsets, mental crackups, abnormal behavior, etc. In the few cases where the unconscious interpretive apparatus, with sympathetic conscious help, interprets correctly, the individual is said to have good intuition.

Nervousness often appears to be the result of activity in the unconscious interpretive apparatus. The writer has satisfied himself, by careful observation and recording of data, that when an important event affecting him is taking place at a distance, he experiences a nervous reaction. He has also noted illness connected with such events.

A sudden, unexplainable feeling or emotion may be a 'message' that has been picked up, unconsciously interpreted or misinterpreted, and there has been a reaction in the form of an emotion, a compulsion, nervousness, and in some cases, illness. If the interpretation is correct, the emotion might serve a good purpose, but if in error, it may be dangerous.

Much valuable data about the functioning of the unconscious interpretive apparatus can be obtained through a careful study of laboratory experiments with hypnosis. Under such circumstances, interpretation can be directed by an operator. The interpretive apparatus will obey orders and accept commands. The hypnotized subject may be told that he will feel no pain while a tooth is pulled. The tooth is pulled and no pain is experienced, because pain is a reaction to interpretation. The subject may be told that when he awakens he will have a headache upon a certain signal, and the subject will experience the headache. There can still be conflict, and a directive may be obeyed only partially.

An experiment at Harvard University will display some interesting data concerning compulsions. (See *THE PSYCHOLOGY OF SUGGESTION* by Boris Sidis, once head of the N.Y. State Pathological Hospitals.)

When an intelligent man is placed under hypnosis, the operator tells him that after he awakens, upon a certain signal, he is to rise, secure an umbrella from a corner of the room, raise it, and walk up and down the room six times.

After awakening and when the subject is engaged in animated social conversation, the signal is given. He continues his conversation, but rises, secures the umbrella, and walks up and down the room six times. HE DOES NOT RAISE THE UMBRELLA.

When enlightened as to the planted suggestion, he explains, 'I had a terrific desire to raise the umbrella, but it seemed so silly that I fought it down.'

These principles have long been exploited by advertising agencies, and they rely on bypassing the conscious and getting their suggestions into the unconscious, where the interpretive apparatus can be directed. They rely on repetition. A newspaper editor once remarked to the writer, "The people will believe anything if you tell it often enough and long enough." That is the principle behind all modern advertising. Reach the interpretive apparatus and you can cause a compulsion. Someone is forced to reach for a cigarette.

These are artificially created compulsions. There are also naturally created compulsions, and all compulsions have a dangerous potential. Compulsions are created by thousands of years of history, by your heredity, and by some very primitive things, but the primitive functions mathematically, according to geometrical patterns. It is possible to understand these functions, and when we understand them, like the man with the umbrella, we don't have to do as the compulsion tells us. To thoroughly understand a compulsion is a move to exclude its existence.

A COMPULSION IS FREQUENTLY THE RESULT OF A SURVIVAL DYNAMIC BEING BROUGHT INTO PLAY UNNECESSARILY AS THE RESULT OF A FAULTY INTERPRETATION OR MISINTERPRETATION ON THE PART OF THE UNCONSCIOUS INTERPRETIVE APPARATUS. THERE, IT BECOMES IMPORTANT THAT WE KNOW AS MUCH AS POSSIBLE ABOUT THE CHARACTER OF THE SURVIVAL DYNAMICS AND THE MANNER IN WHICH THEY FUNCTION.

Let us pause to remind you that we earlier stated that it is our purpose to give you as complete an understanding of the twelve basic principles of astrology, as represented by twelve signs of the zodiac, as possible, because the more thoroughly you understand these principles, the easier everything else will become. When you grasp these principles thoroughly, you'll almost go the rest of the way on you own. You will ultimately reach a point where you will grasp things more rapidly than we can tell them to you. You will get ahead of us. Now, let us deal with the very first of these principles.

THE INDIVIDUAL SURVIVAL DYNAMIC

The primitive purpose of **Cancer is Individual Survival**.

This is the most primitive of all life purposes. Are you going to get enough to eat, or are you going to starve to death? Only one thing counts. Are you going to get enough to eat? Unknown to themselves, in many people, there is a record about this, and it plays over and over. It constantly repeats this question. There is no rest, for this record plays, on, day and night. It never stops. There is a buried fear of a food shortage, of possible starvation.

In a civilization where there is an excess of food, this dynamic loses its utility, but it continues to function, and it constantly influences the interpretive apparatus, resulting in misinterpretations. It employs the same methods adopted by modern advertising agencies, for they copied it.

Later, you will have the opportunity of studying those people whose lives are dominated by this dynamic. Their behavior will have a new meaning to you. You will understand them better than they understand themselves.

One person may become a thief or a sharp businessman. His methods may ultimately destroy him, but if they do not, they may do ample damage to others. He may be very selfish, and he may overeat, thus ruining his health. There may be balancing factors, so that he gets along without too serious consequences. After all, he is friendly. He is not violent. He is nice to you, and you will have to like him, because he seems harmless. You may feel sorry for him. He is such an inoffensive person. He wants company, for he is insecure. He never likes to be alone. He might marry for money. He has a close affinity for a dining room or a kitchen. He is usually looked upon as domestic, because he unconsciously clings to the home, where the food is kept.

He saves things. In fact, his wife complains about the way he keeps the home and the back yard cluttered up with junk. He is a conservative. (Calvin Coolidge and John D. Rockefeller were of this sign.) He may hide money away in strange places. The women may be babyish (and so are the men), welcoming protection, and usually drawing it to themselves. Such people are always interested in shortages, and will buy up a short supply, in order to resell it at a profit. These people are great traders, and are constantly testing you to see how ripe you may be for a trade that would be profitable to them. The men have a favorite expression, and no matter how much they accumulate, they will keep repeating it. It goes, 'I'm just a poor boy trying to get along.' This expression always seems to be a dead giveaway. It will peg them every time. The factor of arrogant pride is completely lacking. They are humble and not above begging. They make excellent salesmen, because they sense what the client needs, or they will study carefully until they learn, and they will tolerate any kind of abuse in order to clinch a sale.

There is never complete relaxation, for something might go wrong, and there is ever a fear of poverty in old age. Such fears are ever being fed into the interpretive apparatus. Yet, these people are kind. When John D. Rockefeller became the wealthiest man in America, he became noted for giving away newly coined dimes. They cost no more than old worn out dimes. The primitive still operates.

A study of the birth dates of 500 men listed in *WHO'S WHO IN COMMERCE AND INDUSTRY* by the writer (Later published in *SEASON OF BIRTH* by Dr. Ellsworth Huntington of Yale University.), revealed that Cancer men are the most successful in the accumulation of money.

The disease cancer was originally named after this sign of the zodiac. The disease is an accumulation of extra cells. There is no statistical data at the moment to show whether there is any connection. It should ultimately be investigated to determine whether the disease may be the result of unconscious misinterpretation relating to fear of non-survival due to a food shortage.

It should be noted that the ancients associated this sign with the stomach and the breasts.

Various zodiacs found in different parts of the world had different symbols for Cancer, but there appears to be no place where the sign was not symbolized by a shellfish. The most common symbol was the crab to portray the characteristic of tenacity. The crab grips and hangs on, and the Cancer native is likely to grip and hang on to money or possessions in the same primitive manner. Evangeline Adams published the statement that she had found more prostitutes born under Cancer, than under any other sign. They had to eat. In dream symbology, kitchens or dining rooms appear to have some association with the individual survival dynamic. Such dreams may portray an unconscious fear of insecurity. We suggest, as an unproven fact, that this dynamic may have some association with the sense of smell. We know that the sense of smell is over emphasized, and these people are very outspoken as to whether an odor is pleasant or unpleasant. We wish to emphatically state however, that our evidence on this point is not sufficient for a conclusion. [ed. I found this to be true also.]

THE FAMILY SURVIVAL DYNAMIC

The primitive purpose of **Scorpio** is family survival.

This is the next most primitive of all life purposes. The life of the family began before that of the individual and extends beyond the life of the individual. Are you going to continue the family? Will someone steal your mate? By making sex a desired act, nature endeavors to perpetuate the family. The ancients associated Scorpio with the sex organs, but because of the quick temper that is also associated with Scorpio, there may be an additional connection with the adrenal glands.

At birth, this dynamic is always conditioned. There is almost an infinite variety of possible patterns a sex life can follow, and some of them can be very destructive. There are stimulants, curbs and shock absorbers. The sex dynamic is powerful and not something that can be handled successfully by invoking one set of rules for all persons, which can be a dangerous procedure on the part of society. When insanity involves violence, it also involves the sex dynamic. All other violence involves the sex dynamic directly or indirectly.

Pains and fevers also have an association with this dynamic, but this will not include all types of pain. It will not include a toothache. We discuss this elsewhere. As we have stated, pain rises as the result of unconscious interpretation. It can be closely identified with sex. The sadist has to inflict pain to become sexually aroused, while the masochist has to endure pain to become so aroused.

It is an odd circumstance worthy of investigation by the medical profession that the astrological and mathematical factors that create excessive sex desires under some circumstances will be accompanied by biological conditions necessitating surgery under other circumstances. This suggests the possibility that many physical ailments are unhealthy functioning of the sexual system, resulting from misinterpretations by the unconscious interpretive apparatus.

Conflicts involving this dynamic are perhaps the most vital studied in astrology. They involve pain, violence, murder, rape, and matters that occupy much space in sensational magazines and newspapers, furnishing the background for best-selling fiction. Accidents are usually caused by faulty functioning of this dynamic. One's attention is usually placed elsewhere, often in another moment of time.

This dynamic can express itself in temper and violence, when the unconscious interpretive apparatus interprets an incident as a threat to family survival, but the force can be poorly directed. It misses its mark.

The writer once had a Boston terrier as friendly as they come, but she objected to anyone pulling her tail. If you pulled her tail, she would bite, but she would not bite you. You would be behind her, and she would bite whoever was in front of her, without investigating. If the boss gives Mr. Smith a bad day, Mr. Smith may go home and beat up his wife or children. He does not beat up the boss. The force follows the course of least resistance. Children are often the objective because they can't defend themselves. The release of emotion follows that course of least resistance. If the boss himself has this dynamic stimulated, everyone at the office may have a bad day. If the teacher has her family survival dynamic touched off the night before, the children must be punished. The husband may love his wife and hate a man who admires her, so he beats up his wife. Children are probably the chief victims of the misdirection of this dynamic.

Although vindictiveness is associated with Scorpio, there is an unconscious primitive cunning for this dynamic fails to function before superior power. It seldom directs its force against a more powerful opponent, but will submit to and endure pain on such occasions, and this is where masochist tendencies appear to begin. In sadism, the desire to inflict pain is aimed toward the loved one instead of a possible competitor. Jealousy arouses the sex passion.

We have stated there are conditioning factors, and there are circumstances where general tendencies can be reversed. The old buffalo bull will fight to the death rather than allow a young bull to share his cows. The cows will become sexually stimulated and will also attack the old bull as soon as his defeat is apparent, and for future reference, note that the bull was the symbol of another sign of the zodiac, Taurus, the sign exactly opposite Scorpio.

This dynamic can express itself in love or hatred. Love brings family continuation. Hatred is intended to protect the family. If the mate is indiscreet in sexual relations, love may be translated into hatred. The dynamic causes compulsions. When dominated by it, individuals do not understand nor control their own behavior. They are automatons. A harmless incident may be followed by rage due to faulty functioning on the part of the unconscious interpretive apparatus. It may be much as if a demon has taken over. The individual may be conscious of what he is doing without having control. Possible consequences are hidden from him. He is blind to them. When the rage is over, there may be sorrow, remorse and the most apologetic reaction.

There were three different symbols employed by the ancients to represent Scorpio and the family survival dynamic, the scorpion, the serpent and the eagle. It has been said that the eagle was supposed to portray the higher manifestations of Scorpio, while the scorpion was supposedly expressing the lower manifestations.

The story is told (and denied by modern biologists) that when ringed by fire, the scorpion will plunge its poisonous stinger into its own body and commit suicide, and this is supposed to portray the destructive potential of the force when misdirected. The serpent was often used to portray wisdom—nature's wisdom.

We understand why the eagle was sometimes employed as a symbol when we realize that in its harmonious application this dynamic produces executive ability. It enables one to direct the activities of others, which is helpful to family survival, for the good executive is able to support his family. Scorpio can be very human and emphatic rather than sympathetic. The sympathetic or compassionate person may suffer pain upon seeing someone wounded, but the empathic person will act. Instead of feeling pain, her will rise to the occasion. This has to be characteristic of the surgeon, for all surgery seems linked with dynamic. He cannot do his work efficiently if he faints at the sight of blood.

Scorpio supplies ability to direct others and obey commands of superiors, often producing good military men. Theodore Roosevelt and General George Patton are to be included. There is the ability to arouse emotion in others, as demonstrated by the two outstanding evangelists of this century, Billy Sunday and Billy Graham. These men are driven by the sex dynamic.

THE SOCIAL SURVIVAL DYNAMIC

The primitive purpose of **Pisces is Social Survival**.

The second survival dynamic places greater value on the family to survive. The third dynamic places greater value on social survival and may sacrifice the individual and the family in the general interest of society.

The third is the strangest, most mysterious and perhaps most interesting, of all survival dynamics. It is a principle overlooked by Darwin, for it involves survival of the weak.

The interests of the individual and the family may be ignored. Socialism is merely an expression of this dynamic. We also see its better manifestation in such organizations as The Society for the Prevention of Cruelty to Animals, the Society for the Prevention of Cruelty to Children, The Salvation Army, The Red Cross. We see it in the erection of hospitals and other similar institutions. We see it in social legislation. The fight for equal rights for the Negro came with Neptune, ruler of Pisces, in Scorpio.

Unfortunately, the negative manifestations are more often in evidence, because Man is having difficulty in discovering his relationship with society and his family's relations with society. Maladjustment in the functioning of this dynamic leads to insanity and illnesses of other forms. There is utter confusion. 'Primitive' astrological interpretations linked Pisces with prisons, hospitals, institutions, the underworld, scandal, fraud, deception, crime, secretiveness, alcohol, drugs, and anesthetics. When we see how the pieces fit together, they look less primitive.

Sympathy and compassion are qualities of Pisces. They are greater than any respect for law, order or convention. These become secondary. The law is circumvented. The objective must be achieved, secretly if necessary, but very often an illegal course is followed. The effort to pack the US Supreme Court was a manifestation of this dynamic. Socialism need not be considered as a product of Man. It is the functioning of the social survival dynamic. There is compassion for the underdog, the downtrodden, the abnormal, the sick, the weak, the beggar, the criminal, the servants, the employees, the lower classes, lower beings, pets, animals, the alcoholic, the dope addict, etc.

Just as the first two survival dynamics are often misdirected, the third survival dynamic is more often misdirected. When the unconscious interpretive apparatus begins pushing up emotions founded upon misinterpretations, there are many weird results. A sympathetic newspaper editor and his family once tried to convince the writer that Al Capone was one of America's greatest humanitarians. You will find an ample number of persons to defend most gangsters and criminals. The answer lies in the fact that there is some good in the worst of us and some bad in the best of us. This was a fact that Warden Lawes tried to recognize. This dynamic was strong in his birth chart, and he was the country's greatest prison system reformer.

The ancients associated Pisces with the feet. It is also to be associated with rhythm. This dynamic predominates in the birth charts of musicians. Savages dance to rhythm. Peasants dance to rhythm. Primitive people always dance to rhythm. More advanced people dance to rhythm. We dance with our feet. A love of poetry is an expression of this dynamic. Poetry is rhythm. Rhythm seems to be some form of expression of the social survival dynamic. L. Ron Hubbard lists the sense of rhythm among the unknown number of senses.

This dynamic became extremely strong in 1933, and the country was swept by new social legislation in an effort to protect 'the forgotten man'. Much of it survived and became a part of society, but other parts, such as the National Recovery Act, fell by the wayside. In our own country, waves of people turned to Russian Communism, evidence of poor functioning on the part of the unconscious interpretive apparatus. The motive may have been worthy but resulted from unconscious misinterpretation.

The pathological liar is not a willful liar. He is not conscious that he is not telling the truth. He is having trouble with this dynamic.

We have many pathological liars. They prove quite successful in selling and in advertising. Businessmen seek them out.

When this dynamic functions healthily, the psychic faculty results. There is the ability to read the minds of others, while dreams may be accurate video of what is occurring elsewhere. One may tune into Jung's collective unconscious.

When the dynamic is functioning improperly, one's social relations present problems, and a hunger develops, a hunger for cigarettes, alcohol or drugs.

In an effort to overcome the enemies of society, or those persons momentarily interpreted to be enemies of society, the method is not a frontal attack, but one to trick, ensnare, deceive trap, persuade, suggest, hypnotize and overcome with propaganda. We see this dynamic functioning daily in international relations. We fill our state department with people in whom this dynamic is powerful, at times with abnormal results. This dynamic was strong in the birth chart of Luther Burbank, who reformed botany and treated flowers like children. He talked to them, and maintained that they responded to his love and affection.

Too often, lofty motives are without means of achievement, and they are said to be impractical. They are impractical when they ignore the existence of the first and second survival dynamics. This third dynamic is often considered impractical by organized society. Any share-the-wealth policy is usually frowned upon by those who momentarily possess the wealth. Such a policy is interpreted as being in conflict with the individual survival dynamic and the family survival dynamic, and both may react and function against the social survival dynamic. Someone may go to jail. Every Robin Hood has conflict between the first and third survival dynamics. Some very weird results follow conflict between the second and third survival dynamics.

A woman client who had inherited a good deal of money and had no cause for any fear of insecurity was considerably mixed up. Surgery had been employed to remove her gall bladder and appendix, which had grown faulty, but she continued confused. Her birth chart showed a terrific conflict between the second and third survival dynamics, a conflict between social survival and family survival.

She confessed that throughout her marital life she had committed continuous adultery with numerous men, and that her four children were of different fathers. She covered her indiscretions well. She was suspected by neither her husband nor society, for she was a leader in various philanthropic organizations and highly regarded in her community. Her indiscretions always involved men

Lesson Two

from a lower social strata, often men she employed.

We begin to see the light when she tells us that her behavior was not so much the result of any sex passion as the result of a deep feeling within her own emotions than men needed her. It gave her satisfaction to believe that she was filling a social need. Unconsciously, she was helping men continue the existence of families. It was sort of a communist family institution. She had the money to support the children.

The symbol for Pisces was two fish attempting to swim in opposite directions but tied together by reeds. You can draw your own conclusions about what this symbol was intended to portray. It might illustrate the inability of individuals to function as such, since they are tied together within the emotions (Water) by the social survival dynamic. The individual finds it impossible to function alone because he is part of society whether he wishes to be or not.

In the accompanying diagram, we have emphasized the Water signs. The triangle in the zodiac referred to as the Water Triplicity represents the life survival dynamics. Opposite each Water sign is an Earth sign. Water is always opposed by Earth in the zodiac. The Water and Earth signs together can be represented by the six-pointed star, made by overlapping two triangles. We find it atop every Jewish synagogue.

As you study these three basic life dynamics, you will realize that we are dealing with something very deep in nature, something that has been functioning for thousands of years, without folks knowing much about it, although the ancients appear to have known about it. You will ultimately watch these dynamics function mathematically and geometrically, and you will realize how crude is a society that attempts to control itself and its destiny without mathematical or other knowledge of these dynamics. Left to fight it out among themselves, these dynamics might result in annihilation rather than survival, but nature has provided a system of shock absorbers to condition the functioning and prevent it from getting completely out of hand. These shock absorbers are the Earth Signs. An Earth Sign is always there, opposite a Water Sign. In our next lesson, we will deal with these Earth Signs.

****

We have been asked to explain the duodecimal system. This will come for those interested, although it's understanding is not essential to this course. Someone asks about the meaning of the word DYNAMICS. One definition given by the dictionary, which covers our use of the word is as follows: THE MOVING MORAL, AS WELL AS

PHYSICAL, FORCES OF ANY KIND, OR THE LAWS RELATING TO THEM. The word also means: THAT BRANCH OF MECHANICS TREATING OF THE MOTION OF BODIES (KINEMATICS) AND THE ACTION OF FORCES IN PRODUCING OR CHANGING THEIR MOTION (KINETICS). The first definition can represent our dynamics expressing themselves through man, while the second definition can represent our dynamics expressing themselves in the solar system. We have been asked for a definition of the word FOCI. It has been used in its mathematical sense: EITHER OF TWO FIXED POINTS ON THE PRINCIPAL AXIS OF AN ELLIPSE.

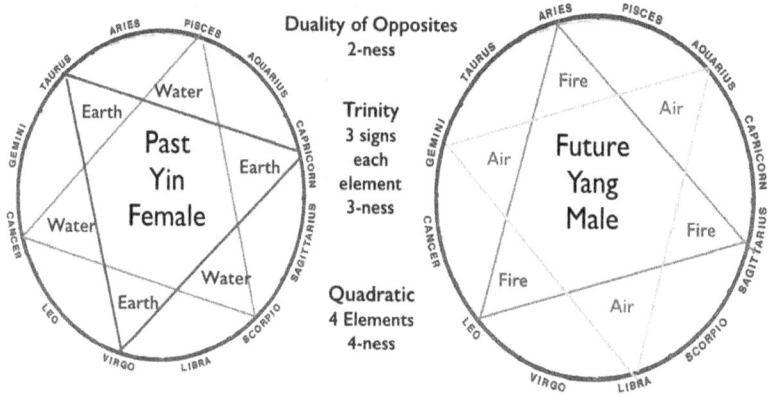

Water is opposed to Earth   Fire is opposed by Air

LESSON THREE

THE SURVIVAL DYNAMIC REACTORS

IF YOU SEE A SIGN WHICH READS 'SPEED LIMIT 25 MILES,' it can be an omen of what might happen if you drive at seventy. The word SIGN means OMEN, and thus the term SIGNS OF THE ZODIAC.

We have introduced you to the three survival dynamics as represented by the WATER OR EMOTIONAL signs of the zodiac. The ancients were ahead of us in their recognition of these dynamics, but they didn't call them dynamics. They called them gods.

Across the circle from, or opposite to, each WATER sign is an EARTH sign. IT IS THE PURPOSE OF THE EARTH SIGNS TO CONTAIN THE SURVIVAL DYNAMICS.

In Physics, we are told that the survival dynamics often lack intelligent direction and can get out of hand, as in the case of the man who had a bad day at work and went home and beat up his wife or one of the children.

Nature has set up an interesting set of REACTORS, one opposite each survival dynamic, to contain these dynamics and keep them within safe limitations (an Earth Sign opposite each Water Sign).

Water has no form, and it will run off in any and all directions when it has no container. The ancients saw a parallel. Emotion was without form, and it might run anywhere when not contained. Thus, emotion resembled water, and we have the WATER signs.

Earth has form. You could put earth around water and contain it. You could build dams out of earth. The restrictive, oppressive signs of the zodiac became the EARTH signs.

It is the function of the EARTH signs to organize and give form. They relate to one's ability to fit into one's environment, which is that which is already organized and has form. They provide the means for self-control, and in excess, they represent frustration. While the EARTH Signs have a very valuable function, when their influence is excessive, the tendency is not to survive, but to succumb, to give up all hope.

The EARTH signs develop a sense of duty, a sense of responsibility, and when this is carried to excess, the results can be negative. It can result in ill health. There is need for the EARTH signs. It is necessary that we regulate our behavior, but we cannot bottle up the survival dynamics. In regulating force, it is essential that we give it a useful outlet.

The EARTH signs can be identified with a phenomenon bearing a close resemblance to memory, but much broader in scope than memory. Things are recorded somewhere. Modern biologists might say in the cells, but we won't say. Ultimately, we will present a piece of evidence that will indicate that this factor akin to memory may extend back over thousands of years. It may have something to do with heredity. Emotion causes action, but eventually, there is reaction, and between this cause and effect, there has to be a record that is continually maintained. [ed. DNA?]

THE REACTORS (Earth Signs) operate or do not operate, depending upon what is going on in the solar system. They all operate eventually, but they are often delayed, which is expressed in the saying, 'The Mills of Gods Grind Slowly but Exceedingly Fine.' We can think of emotional cause and reactive effect, but the time difference between cause and effect is not a constant but as a variable that is conditioned in accord with various relationships in the solar system. Cause and effect can sometimes be separated by wide spans of time. A cause in the life of the father may have its effect in the life of his son or in the life of his grandson.

When dealing with the six WATER and EARTH Signs, we are dealing with the effect of the past on the present or future. We come into an established environment at birth. We face heredity, rules, regulations, habits, conventions, traditions, laws and legal circumstances. It is the inclination of the EARTH Signs to accept what has been developed in the past without protest, to adjust self in order to conform, to cling to and follow in the footsteps of the parents, to worship the forefathers and consider their views as wisdom, to take an interest and pride in history, and to be oppressed.

This half of the zodiac must be identified with the past, while the other half must be identified with the future. In the zodiac, nature divides the past from the future, and this is going to give us reason to re-evaluate our conception of TIME. The unconscious of some people functions with data from the past, while the unconscious of other people functions with data from the future. A man may alter his whole life when he re-evaluates his conception of TIME.

In her own way, working through the EARTH signs, nature attempts to establish order and justice, but the functioning can often be crude and primitive, possibly because, despite her good intentions, nature does not obtain too much help from conscious Man.

Just as we have an equilateral triangle in the zodiac, made

up of the three WATER Signs, we have a second equilateral triangle in the zodiac, made up of the three EARTH Signs, as we have shown (Lesson Two). These triangles form the six-pointed star that is found frequently in ancient symbology. The three EARTH Signs are as follows:

CAPRICORN	Opposite	CANCER
TAURUS	Opposite	SCORPIO
VIRGO	Opposite	PISCES

THE INDIVIDUAL SURVIVAL DYNAMIC REACTOR

CAPRICORN (Opposite Cancer, the Individual Survival Dynamic) represents the Individual Survival Dynamic REACTOR. IT IS THE PURPOSE OF THIS REACTOR TO CONTAIN THE INDIVIDUAL SURVIVAL DYNAMIC.

Before you arrived, the struggle for food had been going on for thousands of years. A civilization had been building up, and when you came along you faced an environment. Certain things were expected of you, and if you conformed, you were allowed to eat. There were times when you may not have wanted to conform. What did you do? Did you conform anyway? If you did, there was a certain amount of frustration in your life. Perhaps you took care of an old uncle till he died, and perhaps he left you some stocks and bonds or some real estate in his will. You may have been rewarded, but you paid a very high price, because you frustrated yourself. You didn't allow other parts of your nature to grow and manifest. You are now dependent on those stocks and bonds, but it is too late to do much about it, unless you re-educated yourself, and unless you completely re-evaluate the past and become conscious of what you did to yourself. If you can do this, there is still a chance for freedom.

But, perhaps you did not frustrate yourself, and perhaps the outcome was different.

When a person is born strongly under Capricorn, it is the tendency to give in to one's oppressors, to conform, to adjust one's self to the environment, to be a good boy, to save and be thrifty, to accept authority, to curb one's appetites and keep them under control, to do the unpleasant things in life because they have to be done, to place great value on material quantities, to do things the hard way, to assume great responsibility, to be the goat, possibly to rise to high places only to wear one's self out and succumb, to turn away from anything that promises quick and easy profits on the grounds that any such promises are unsound and the profits highly improbable, to be pessimistic and depressive, to always see the negative possibilities and try to insure against them without being able to see more favorable possibilities, to take a dark view of the future, to be sound and practical and to judge the future by the past.

In a great many cases, we find the person, in whose birth chart this Capricorn REACTOR is strong, very successful in early life. He meets with approval of older people whenever he goes. His reliability is valued. His responsibility is something that is noted. He is pushed forward by older men, because they can depend on him. He develops good contacts, but there comes a day when these older men begin to die off. More and more of them die off. Ultimately, Capricorn is surrounded by younger men. He continues to live according to the rules of the old masters. The younger men are without respect for these old masters and are unimpressed. His views are considered as obsolete and reactionary. He is no longer appreciated, but instead, is regarded as an obstacle. Others feel that his

usefulness has been served. He doesn't fit into the new order of things. He can't understand it. 'After all, the world got along for a long time without these new-fangled ideas. These young men are apt to wreck the world. They are unsound.' He feels that they lack experience. If old Mr. Goat were still alive, he would see them, but Mr. Goat died some time back and can't influence things now.

CAPRICORN no longer fits into the picture. The world's evaluation of him has been deflated. He is a sad man. He is very depressed. There is no longer a place in the world for him. Statistics have shown that the manic depressive is born strongly under this Capricorn REACTOR.

CAPRICORN is the goat of the zodiac, and the ancients symbolized this sign with the goat, the scapegoat. The CAPRI means 'of the goat family.' The word scape means escape, the word scapegoat is of antique Jewish origin. The sins of the people were symbolically placed on the head of the goat, after which he was suffered to escape into the wilderness. A scapegoat is a person or a thing bearing blame for others, and this is typical of the Capricorn personality. Capricorn is identified with the planet Saturn, from which grows the word Saturnian, which usually implies seriousness and lack of frivolity, but the dictionary gives the word as meaning a golden age, marked by peace, happiness and contentment. This is what Capricorn seeks by conforming to things as they are.

It is interesting to note the professions with which astrologers have associated CAPRICORN. They include: Undertakers, lawyers, printers, coal miners, farmers. This dynamic is very strong in the charts of professional people, doctors, ministers, lawyers, teachers, etc., but this need not be true indefinitely. It is true only to the extent that they are conformists and seekers after security. This REACTOR is strong in the minister who tries to interpret the Bible literally, the doctor who worships the American Medical Association as a god, the lawyer who sees only the letter and not the spirit of the law, and the teacher who never sees a truth unless it may have found its way into an established and approved textbook.

CAPRICORN has long forgotten why he is as he is. He has forgotten his original discovery that you can eat more readily when you conform. Life is now merely a matter of HABIT. His thinking is a matter of habit. He has no new records. The same old ones are played over and over and over, down in his unconscious. He is dominated by what Ron Hubbard called THE REACTIVE MIND. He is filled with prejudice and conditioned reflexes. He is suspicious. In each new situation, he sees a parallel. If he was once swindled by a man named Thompson, no other man named Thompson is going to swindle him. In his unconscious, Thompson equals a swindler, and although he is not conscious of his reasons for doing so, he 'instinctively' dislikes any man named Thompson. It seems to be that same Thompson in disguise. If he were swindled by a Spaniard, then he may develop a prejudice against all Spaniards.

Most courts of justice are Capricornian. Cases often drag on and on. Justice may operate, but it may take years. Cases are postponed and postponed. Meanwhile witnesses die. Principals die. When the case is finally won, if it is won, perhaps only the descendants gain any benefit, but first, a large part of the winnings must go to pay the lawyers.

The danger of Capricorn lies in the possibility that the ego may die. The life force fails to flow. Yet, if we are to have law and order, we must have Capricorn. We must have people to assume responsibility. Yet, if we are to have law and order, we must have Capricorn. We must have people to assume responsibility, but nothing should be overdone. Capricorn is inclined to overdo it. New ideas are no longer explored. There is no spirit, except that which comes in bursts, and which must be followed by equalizing depression. Anything that would disturb the status quo is viewed as evil.

'Why change things? We have always done it this way. This textbook has been selling for twenty years. It taught me everything I know. Why do you want a new one now? Can't you leave well enough alone? Why disturb the People.'

CAPRICORN may ultimately reach a point where he is

unable to visualize the future. He lives and re-lives the past. He dreams of the good old days. (Like Ashley in 'Gone With the Wind'). There is nothing to which to look forward. The mind can look in one direction, backward, into the past.

Keep in mind that the first survival dynamic is in the back of all this. Nature is still trying to overcome the possibility of a food shortage. There is no conscious. The old records are being played. In place of conscious thinking we have habit. There is obsession. There is unhappiness and depression. The life force is subdued. 'How can you get along without the past? If people are not going to do things as they were done in the good old horse and buggy days, how can they survive? What is the use of trying to survive? There is no father and no mother. How can one survive without a father or mother, or without the old boss who was so wise?'

The past has been identified with individual survival. In the 'reactive mind,' PAST equals SURVIVAL and FUTURE equals NON-SURVIVAL. This leaves the individual without hope. There is nothing left but to succumb. One can get sick more easily. Dominated by the above unconscious reasoning, the life force is no longer plugged in. The mind doesn't fight back. The body doesn't fight back. Deterioration and disintegration have set in. It is an obsession when you don't believe you can get along without the past, and such an obsession is destructive. Unconsciously, people get locked in the past. They display an interest in the future. They may talk about all their accomplishments of the past. They are constantly re-lived, but the future is no longer visualized. Instead, it is merely anticipated with fear.

The ancients associated Capricorn with the knees, the bones, the teeth, the skin and the hair. The skin and the hair are parts of the body that are being discarded. Decay of the teeth seems to be cyclic and to be associated with the functioning of this reactor. The young person strongly under the influence of this reactor appears to have skin disorders. The person born when Capricorn is at the eastern horizon or ascendant often seems to have an off walk due to some factor concerning the knees.

The philosophy that is conditioned by this reactor often causes a person to buy at the top. He is cautious. He will not buy stock until its value has been proved. When earnings have reached their high point, he has finally become convinced. The stock is valuable, so he finally buys it, for he sees it as established. Just about that time, a new invention changes everything. The stock has reached its apex and decline sets in.

Let us not lose sight of the original, basic function of this reactor, the sign Capricorn. It has purpose, and the purpose is good. To some extent, it is necessary to conform to our environment. To some extent, it is necessary to benefit from past errors and keep life well organized, but if we are to continue to survive, we must also be interested in changing our environment to conform to the future. We must not allow ourselves to become locked in the past. We must live a good part of our mental lives in the future. The man who is constantly working to complete what he visualizes to exist in the future is a much happier man. He is also a healthier man. We must have good balance between our consciousness of the past and our consciousness of the future. We must have hope and faith in the future, because these allow the life force to manifest. 'Where there is life, there is hope.' When we have faith and hope, we have the energy to do something about the future. On the other hand, when we assume that FUTURE equals FAILURE, the life force no longer flows through us. There is no energy with which to approach the future. There is only despair. We are afraid to ask for help from others, because we assume they will turn us down. 'Why try?' Why do anything if we are going to fail anyway? Why have any more failures? The only alternative is to succumb.'

THE FAMILY SURVIVAL DYNAMIC REACTOR

TAURUS (opposite Scorpio, the Family Survival Dynamic) represents the Family Survival Dynamic Reactor. IT IS THE PURPOSE OF THIS REACTOR TO CONTAIN THE FAMILY SURVIVAL DYNAMIC.

Before you arrived, the family had been perpetuated for a long time. You arrived with some heredity. You resembled your parents. A being whose parents were dogs will look like a dog. Regardless of any planetary setup existing at the time, he will not look like a kangaroo. There is no conflict between heredity and astrology. The two work together.

A boy may look like his father, but not look exactly like his father. Time changes things. In his characteristics, the boy may be quite different from his father. Again, there are two forces at work. One resembles habit. One force is attempting to reproduce a new product from the old mold, but another influence is altering the pattern. There is evolution. The planetary setup at the moment of birth represents the difference between father and son, rather than the resemblance. Yet, it would seem that there is some tendency for children to be born at those times when planetary conditions, prevalent at the time of the parent's birth, repeat themselves. Since planetary patterns never repeat themselves exactly within millions of years, it becomes impossible for a child to be exactly like his father or mother. We might mention that we have quite a number of cases where two people, born on the same month, day and year, married, and the first child was born on the parent's birthday. In one instance, there were three children. The first and third had the same birthday as the parents, while the second was born exactly six months from that birth date.

In order for the family to survive, there must be reproduction. The Family Survival Dynamic is often without direction. It will function anywhere, any time. It wants an outlet regardless. It may carry a man to houses of prostitution. The Family Survival Dynamic is also working through the girls in the houses of prostitution, but it is not accomplishing its purpose.

Nature recognized the need for a curb, and she provided TAURUS, The Family Survival Dynamic REACTOR.

When you came along, you probably faced a family environment. There may have been a mother and father, grandparents, uncles, aunts, etc. To a greater or less extent, all of these people had an interest in you. They were protective. There was also a home. To that home, you may have become very much attached. It was safety. It protected you from weather. It was a fort. If something chased you, you ran home. Nothing could get you when you were home. None of those imaginary things could get you there. You were safe when you were home, particularly when you were in bed. Children often associate a warm bed with safety. The greatest place of safety is home in bed, where there is nothing to fear. One can rest and go to sleep in complete safety.

Out of all this grows love of family and love of home. This can be extended to love of real estate, love of land. All of this is associated with Taurus. Sex is without form. The family must have form. It must have a home, a fort, a place of safety. The family environment is a limitation to sex. The home environment becomes established, a part of you. It influences habits. When you try to select a mate, there is an unconscious urge to select one who will fit into the family environment. This is the operation of the Family Survival Dynamic REACTOR-Taurus.

If this REACTOR is not strong, things do not work out this way. One may not love the home and the parents. Any attachment may be very weak.

Out of this REACTOR, grow the characteristics we have associated with Taurus. Certain characteristics are the reverse of what we find in Scorpio. Instead of impulsiveness, we have sluggishness. Sex reactions are delayed. The force is stored up, but is more powerful when finally released. Anger is aroused with difficulty, but when finally released is far more intense.

The ancients symbolized the sign with the bull. Remember the story of the old buffalo bull, who fights to the death, sacrificing individual survival, in endeavoring to preserve the family. When Taurus finally agrees to fight, it is a fight with complete annihilation as its objective. Unless interrupted, such may be the result. This seldom happens, because it is rare that there is sufficient cause to arouse this kind of a Taurus reaction.

Taurus likes big homes, lots of land. It is all part of an unconscious building of a fort to protect the family. Taurus likes to do everything in a big way. Whether he is prosperous or not, he is apt to look prosperous. He is a builder. His original inclination to build a fort may take other forms. He might be a contractor. He makes a good engineer. He understands weight, volume and density. He likes to be big himself. He thinks in terms of quantity. He likes things when they are big. This all stems from the original purpose of building a big fort to protect the family. Taurus is FIXED EARTH. The bigger the fort, the greater the family security and the greater the opportunity for family survival.

Although TAURUS may take on the family virtues, it is just as easy to take on the family faults. There is an unconscious urge to imitate the parents or grandparents, to acquire their habits, to continue their traditions. There may be too much consideration for what the family may think. There may be a lack of initiative, because it is more comfortable at home with the family, where one can sleep. There seems to be a voice that constantly says, 'Don't do what the family would not want you to do.' When asked why he never married, an elderly bachelor told us, 'I thought a great deal of my family. I never felt that I could marry any girl who would meet the approval of the family, and I knew well that my family could never approve of the kind of a girl I would want to marry.'

There can be inability to get away form the old part of the family, and go forth to produce the new family in a new home. Such ties are not easily broken. They can be carried to extremes. It may be difficult to accept new ideas. The old family ideas have long, deep roots. Taurus wants to be proud of his heredity. He is likely to know as much as possible about his genealogy. Stubbornness is a characteristic. Taurus may be sluggish and slow to grasp things. It may take much education before he can grasp the abstract side of things. He is coming out of a fog. He becomes a prisoner of dogma. Yet, he can be the worst enemy of dogma, because he will fight dogma with dogma.

It is difficult for Taurus to change purpose in life, and the original purpose was limited by the family environment, but once a purpose has developed there is blindness to all else. It is interesting to note how many big, scientific or philosophical books have ultimately come from the pens of Taureans like Spencer, Freud, Marx, Lester Ward, Emmanuel Kant, Spinoza, and even Hitler with his 'Mein Kampf.'

William Randolph Hearst was a Taurean, and the empire he built was characteristic of the sign. His Mexican ranch was the equivalent of an empire itself. It was so strongly fortified, with its own army of cowhands, that it was one point within Mexico where Pancho Villa did not attack. It was a perfect dream of the Taurean. The family would be safe in a place like that.

The characteristics of Taurus people, will be more easily understood when you realize what is causing them on the unconscious plane, what nature is trying to do. This is the Family Survival Dynamic REACTOR at work. It is trying to keep the Family Survival Dynamic contained and under control. It is trying to keep the family as it **was**. It is attempting to perpetuate the family according to the same old pattern that has existed in the past. As with the First Survival Dynamic Reactor, this can ultimately lead to frustration.

THE SOCIAL SURVIVAL DYNAMIC REACTOR

Virgo (opposite Pisces, the Social Survival Dynamic) represents the Social Survival Dynamic REACTOR. IT IS THE PURPOSE OF THIS REACTOR TO CONTAIN THE SOCIAL SURVIVAL DYNAMIC.

In Lesson Two, we saw that sympathy, compassion, and a charitable attitude toward the weak and afflicted are characteristics of the Social Survival Dynamic.

Nature appears to have understood that if you give everything to the weak, the result is disintegration. Sympathizing with the weak and suffering with them is not a cure, and so nature provided a REACTOR to containing these emotional qualities. A man is too weak to survive. First, we try to cure him. We give him medical or other attention, and then we try to find a job for him and make him a slave.

Astrology has associated VIRGO with the working classes, the laborers, labor unions, also with diets, medicine and attempts to heal.

As in the case of all EARTH signs, VIRGO strives to be

practical. If you have a sick man, make him well. Make him useful. Find him a job. Get him functioning. make use of his physical anatomy. Turn him into a productive factor. Make him some kind of a slave. That is being practical.

VIRGO people as a whole are workers, often to the point of frustration. They are efficient. Being close observers, they don't miss any details. They do a good job. They make the most valuable employee. There is a great power of concentration, which is the opposite characteristic found in connection with the Social Survival Dynamic itself (Pisces). Pisces is a dreamer, misses the details, but observes the broader pattern of the whole.

Somebody has to do the work, and VIRGO is there, waiting to carry on. 'All work and no play makes Jack a dull boy.'

It is the inclination of Virgo to over-work, to exclude all else. The work to be done assumes too great a significance. Work becomes habit. It becomes automatic. A way of doing a job is learned, and from then on, each day is the same old grind. There may be new and better ways of doing the job. Mass production methods make it possible to do the same job better with half the labor, but this idea is resisted, on the grounds that it will put people out of work. Old methods must be retained so that everybody will have a job. Everybody must work. The purpose of life becomes work. We are told that people are happier when they are working. This is partly true, but it can be carried to extremes. It produces a world of Technician–Slaves. They are slaves to society. We see the same principle in the ant and bee civilizations. Our educational world is largely designed to mass produce slaves.

It is a VIRGO characteristic to tolerate work routine and drudgery. This means failure to advance to better things. Perhaps VIRGO does not like the employer and talks about him continually, but VIRGO continues to work for that employer.

VIRGO IS PROPER.

There is always a 'right' way of doing things. Customs must be maintained. Words must be spelled in the accepted way. There is always an accepted way of doing things, and that is the only way. There must be modesty. One must wear the right clothes. Social customs are law to VIRGO, who always know what is 'expected.' Emotion is usually subdued when possible. It is conditioned before it is expresses. One must say the right thing at the right time. Styles are a Virgo creation. 'THIS is what is being worn this year.' The Virgo secretary will be most pleasant, but you must answer all the necessary questions before you can get your name sent in to Mr. Jones.

In astrology, relations with those outside the family circle, excluding those which might hold possibilities along lines of becoming members of the family circle, are involved with the Social Survival Dynamic, and the purpose of the Social Survival Dynamic REACTOR is to see that these relations are PROPER, that standards of good behavior are observed at all times.

When VIRGO becomes stronger then the Family Survival Dynamic, there is often sexual frustration, and the Family Survival Dynamic may never get an opportunity of functioning. A woman must not show passion, because that wouldn't be good taste. She mustn't do anything that would arouse the partner, because this might mean loss of respect. Sex can be covered with such a veneer that the ancients symbolized this sign with THE VIRGIN, and writers have sometimes associated the sign with the old maid. The VIRGIN is always shown with a sheaf of wheat, indicating that the WORK has been accomplished.

When you conduct a meeting strictly in accord with parliamentary procedure, you are allowing the Social Survival Dynamic to function. If there is a politician in the room, in whom the Social Survival Dynamic itself is powerful, he will find a way of twisting the procedure so that his group will survive best. Meanwhile, the remainder of those in the room will be so intent on trying to understand and interpret the parliamentary procedure, that their objective will probably be forgotten or lost.

The VIRGO-REACTOR has a very useful purpose, but it is always subject to much in the way of exploitation. Everybody exploits the working man. His own representatives grow rich on his dues. Honest toil is rewarded, but a way is always found to be certain that the reward is not sufficient to allow him to stop working. Labor representatives are ever intent on getting him larger wages. His wages go up and up. This is intended to make him happy, and it often does, until he discovers that he has gained little, because the cost of living goes up just as rapidly as his salary. His employer gets his labor. His union leader gets his dues. The government collects taxes. The banks collect interest on the money advanced on his salary, and business men have a line of salesmen at his door to see that anything left over is disposed of with as great dispatch as possible.

Thus, in the EARTH Signs, we have a goat, a bull and a virgin.

Now, that we have discussed six of the zodiacal signs and have covered half of the zodiac, study again the diagram in Lesson Two. Get these six signs firmly implanted in your mind. The WATER Signs represent the emotions, the Survival Dynamics. The EARTH Signs represent the emotions the Survival Dynamics. The EARTH Signs represent natural efforts at self-control. This self-control is not something you will upon yourself. It is a part of nature. The person with extreme self-control is born that way. These REACTORS were placed there by nature. Self-control is an automatic procedure of nature. The key to most of what we call abnormal behavior in people is found in the functioning of the Survival Dynamics.

These six signs were called the female signs by the ancients. They relate to the effect of the past on the present. The Survival Dynamics go way back. The REACTORS function in accord with EXPERIENCE, individual experience, hereditary experience and the social experience of the species.

In a way, we might relate these six signs to what is sometimes called the lower Man. The functioning of these signs is largely in the unconscious or subconscious. They relate to what we call Man's lower nature. They relate to the past, to what Man inherited. When we study their functioning, we see Man as a prisoner of the past. Let us hope that by understanding his connection with the past, he can free himself from the past. He can then go on to better efforts.

We promised earlier an odd piece of evidence indicating that a factor akin to memory can go back thousands of years. The writer's mother, having been ill most of her life, did not read much. She was not a well-read person, but she appeared to have keen intuition. She could sense danger. When she was nearly 80, and in better health than in all of her life, she lived alone in a house in Florida, while the writer's brother lived in another house on the same property. She had very beautiful handwriting. One day, a letter was received from her. In the middle of the letter, the handwriting changed, and appeared to be that of a very old person. One paragraph appeared in this odd handwriting, and then the letter continued in the normal handwriting from where it had been interrupted.

The one paragraph read, 'On Sunday, we visited the temple of the Aramaeans for the fifth time in the family.'

That this paragraph had been in the middle of her letter was never revealed to the writer's mother. Instead, at an opportune moment, a subtle effort was made to learn whether she had ever heard of the Arameans. She had not. She did not know who they were. The Aramaeans date back 2000 years, and few people aside from biblical students ever heard of them. Although religious in her own way, she had never been a church-goer. She belonged to no church. She was not a social mixer. She preferred seclusion.

We will not attempt to explain this incident. We merely record it for what it may be worth. It suggests that we are influenced by records of some kind which may go back much farther than we suppose, and we usually find such incidents identified with the Social

Survival Dynamic.

It is important to realize that although intelligence shown everywhere in nature's operations, its functions are automatic, and like a piece of machinery, biology and psychology can get out of kilter. It is up to us, through proper understanding to correct matters.

The Astrological Alphabet

Planets	Keywords	Zodiacal Signs
☽ Moon	emotional, self survival	♋ Cancer
☉ Sun	energetic self expression	♌ Leo
☿ Mercury	practical work/service	♍ Virgo
♀ Venus	attraction between people	♎ Libra
♂ Mars	sexuality, loyalty, drive	♏ Scorpio
♃ Jupiter	energy, opportunity	♐ Sagittarius
♄ Saturn	limits, duty, responsibility	♑ Capricorn
♅ Uranus	original, explosive, abrupt	♒ Aquarius
♆ Neptune	imagination, fantasy	♓ Pisces
♇ Pluto	energy, drive, obsession	♈ Aries
♀ Venus	stability, stubborn, luxury	♉ Taurus
☿ Mercury	quick, humorous, ideas	♊ Gemini
☊☋ Lunar Node	impulsive, unexpected	

Lesson Three

Aspects (angles) between planets

☌	0°	Conjunction	neutral, depends on the planets and sign
✶	60°	Sextile	compatible, gets along easily, communicating, social
☐	90°	Square	tension, conflict, frustration, demands, stress
△	120°	Trine	energetic, creative, vibrant, exciting
⚻	150°	Quincunx	weak, lack of energy, off balance
☍	180°	Opposition	tension, stress, change
⚺	30°	Semi-Sextile	fearful, lack energy, passive

LESSON FOUR

THE GEOMETRY OF TIME

Euclid's geometry made no allowance for TIME. It would be appropriate for a dead world without motion, if there were such a world. We do not live in that type of a world, but in a world of dynamics, where Euclid's geometry is inadequate.

In astrology, geometry involves TIME and MOTION.

Astrology is a study of TIME and MOTION. It shows that the present is merely the battleground of the past and the future, both of which are contained within the present moment; a startling statement perhaps, but let us look into this matter of TIME and MOTION. These two words are inseparable.

Without TIME, there is no MOTION. Without MOTION, there is no TIME.

There are different kinds of TIME, and one kind of TIME is just as valid as another. Our kind of TIME is merely Solar-System TIME, but our education has so locked us into this kind of time that we are unconscious of any other kind, and we submit to its limitations. Our accepted and conventional kind of time is merely an expression of the relationship of the Earth to the Sun. Actually, the whole Solar System operates in accord with this same kind of TIME, but the rest of the universe may not. Perhaps, our time decelerates when compared to other TIME, or other TIME accelerates as compared to our TIME. Although it is assumed that the speed of light is a constant, this is but an assumption, as yet unproved.

We have succeeded in manufacturing clocks and watches that operate on Solar-System TIME, but they have no value in another part of the universe.

Visualize space as containing but one solid and non-composite object, a ball. There could be no motion but imaginary motion, and that could be any kind of motion that you wish to imagine. THERE COULD BE NO TIME.

Not until you have two objects in space, can there be either time or motion. Then, there can be only two motions. All other motions or imaginary motions will be duplication of these same motions.

Either object can move along a straight line drawn through the two objects, but it is impossible to say which one is moving, or whether both are moving.

One object revolving around the axis of the first object, unless the axis of the first object is the same line that passes through the two objects, in which event, it will be impossible to say which object is rotating. It may be stated that either object is moving in relation to the other or either object may be considered as stationary.

If the axis of rotation is not the same line that passes through both objects, one will then appear to revolve in a circle. If during rotation, the two objects pull apart, one will appear to revolve in a spiral. If there is a backward-forward motion along the line connecting the two objects, one object will appear to travel around the other in an ellipse.

With only two objects in space, when they pull apart, we do not have to consider them as moving away from each other. It would be just as correct to say that both are contracting. When they approach each other again, it would be just as correct to say they are expanding.

These confusing factors are known as RELATIVITY, wherein TIME is questionably described as a fourth dimension. Although such views are usually attributed to Einstein, they were earlier advanced by H.G. Wells in 1895 and by C.H. Hinton in 1884, and by others even earlier.

Space containing one object could have no time. These facts can furnish us with the reason to question TIME as a fourth dimension. There can be no TIME until we have two objects plus motion.

When we have three objects, things become complicated.

With three objects in space, two stationary in relation to each other while the third moves, we can say that the third is moving, or that the first two are moving together.

SOLAR SYSTEM TIME

Consider the Earth as traveling around the Sun in an ellipse. In approximately 365 1/4 days, the Earth is back where it started. Or is it? It is only if you consider the relationship of the Earth's equator to the Earth's orbit. It depends upon what you use as a frame of reference. If you use the so-called fixed stars as a reference IT IS NOT. It is close but it is not exact and in time it will be altogether different.

We can only describe something in relation to something else. The Earth rotates on its axis in 24 hours of our time, if we are describing the Earth in relation to the Sun, but if we are describing it

Lesson Four

in relation to the stars, it completes the rotation in 23 hours and 56 minutes. We can talk all we want about Constants. Actually, insofar as we know, there are none. Any constant is dependent upon an ASSUMED frame of reference. One assumed frame of reference is as good and as authentic as some other frame of reference. If you accept one frame of reference and I accept another, we obtain different results, and one set of results is as authentic as some other frame of reference. If you accept one frame of reference and I accept another, we obtain different results, and one set of results is as authentic as another. This is where science repeatedly falls down. It accepts some frame of reference that is no better than some other frame of reference. The politicians of science get together and agree on a frame of reference, which means that they blind themselves to any other frame of reference. Ptolemy's frame of reference, when he used the Earth as a center, was every bit as legitimate as the Copernican frame of reference, using the Sun as the center, but Ptolemy's frame of reference was more complicated. Insofar as we know, space has no center. If it does have, we have no reason to believe that our Sun is that center. If we deal only with the Solar System, it is convenient to use the Sun as the center. If we deal with an Earth astrology, it is more convenient to use the Earth as a center.

Einstein maintained the speed of light to be a constant, because of the baffling fact that light always arrives at, or departs from, an object at the speed of 186,284 miles per second, regardless of the motion of the body in space. If an object is going toward light, light strikes that object at the same speed as it would were the object going away from light. This suggests the possibility, which science has not considered, that light only strikes stationary objects. This might be explained by considering the hypothesis that there is no continuous motion, that both matter and light travel in jumps, that when matter moves light stands still and when light moves matter stands still. Such jumps would have to be in very tiny intervals of time, infinitesimal fractions of seconds, atoms of time. Under those circumstances, these atoms of time might possibly furnish a constant, but as things stand we have no known constant in the universe to work from. We have only relative constants.

We measure TIME in seconds, minutes, hours, days, weeks, months, years, decades, centuries, eons, etc., but this is one particular kind of time. A day is one rotation of the Earth on it's axis IN RELATION TO THE SUN. All smaller employed in intervals of time are fractions of this kind of a day.

Insofar as we know, all known factors which can be employed to measure time are mathematically incommensurable. By that we mean that time cycles do not fit evenly into each other. A day is one rotation of the Earth on it's axis WHEN we use the Sun as a frame of reference. A year is one revolution of the Earth around the Sun WHEN we employ the Earth's equator as a frame of reference. A year is NOT a definite number of days. We say it is 365 1/4 days but even that is an approximation and is dependent upon what we use as a frame of reference.

SUPPOSE WE WERE TO USE THE PERIOD OF GESTATION AS A UNIT FOR MEASURING TIME?

Instead of measuring time by how long it takes the Earth to rotate in relation to the Sun, what if we were to measure TIME by the period of gestation? This would be objected to on the grounds that the period of gestation is not a CONSTANT. Neither is any other know period of time. If we are to believe the astronomers, each day is longer than the same day in the previous year. The astronomers tell us that the solar system is slowing down, but the solar system can only slow down in relation to something else, and it is just as true to say that the 'something else' is speeding up in relation to the solar system. It is all RELATIVITY. Astronomers tell us that the universe is expanding. It might be just as correct to say that all its parts are shrinking in size.

ANOTHER CONCEPTION OF TIME

We divide TIME in another way, into three parts, the PAST, the PRESENT and the FUTURE.

By the present, we mean NOW, but WHAT do we mean by NOW? WHAT do YOU mean by NOW?

We often think of TIME as represented by a straight line, running to infinity at either end. A line has no height or width, only length, and so this would be the visualization of a one-dimensional kind of time. WHERE ON THIS LINE IS NOW?

We might represent NOW as a moving mathematical point, progressing along this line in one direction. Although this is a commonly accepted notion of NOW, we will soon find that it is unsatisfactory.

A mathematical point has no dimensions, while NOW HAS LENGTH.

We cannot conceive of a NOW that does not have length, for NOW is relative. Supposedly, the Earth travels over 17 miles per second. If you were in space, try to conceive of NOW as that small particle of time when the center of the Earth passes you. It is too small a particle of time for you to conceive, so NOW has to be longer

Lesson Four

than that.

You might consider your life as NOW, this year as NOW, today as NOW. When you awaken in the morning, now may mean until you have to get up. Think it over and you will realize that NOW MEANS UNTIL SOMETHING CHANGES.

There is no TIME until something changes in its relation to something else. Euclid's geometry did not involve MOTION, and so it did not involve TIME.

TIME means CHANGE, and it cannot mean anything else. Our conventional kind of time means change in the solar system. Before there were astronomers, physicists or watchmakers, this kind of time was employed. By whom was it employed? By whom was it originated? It was first employed by the ancient astrologers. It was their time. It is astrology time. If we are to know more about it, let us learn what astrology can tell us about this kind of time, but first, let us consider another important factor.

PHYSICAL SENSES DETECT ONLY THE PAST

You look at a star. You do not see the star as it is NOW. You see it only as it was. If you look at a star 200 light years away, you see it as it was when George Washington might have been looking in that direction. Astronomers claim to look at objects as they were 500 to 1,000 million years ago.

If we theoretically consider NOW as a mathematical point on the TIME LINE, it becomes impossible to contact NOW with any of the five physical senses, which are fitted only for contacting the past.

Speed is relative. It takes time for light of travel to the eye, and for the mind to interpret light rays. The time interval may seem infinitesimal to you, but for all we know there may be infinitesimal beings that live and die in less time. To them it would be a long time. Sound travels even more slowly. You touch and taste something and it takes time for a message to go over the nervous system, and for the mind to interpret, a very small interval of time, but time is relative. It is always short when compared to a longer time, long when compared to a shorter time. A day is short when compared to a year, long when compared to a minute. To us, the existence of a time interval is dependent upon our ability to conceive it.

Since the five physical senses can contact only the past, we must look to the mind for any contact with NOW. Perhaps you can begin to see that NOW cannot be considered as a mathematical point along the imaginary time line, because NOW includes various parts of the past. Insofar as the five physical senses are concerned, NOW would have to be completely a product of the past.

DOES NOW INCLUDE ANY PART OF THE FUTURE?

If you see an object falling from the sky, you may consider NOW as BEFORE it hits the Earth. 'Before sunrise' is placing NOW in a frame of reference that involves the future. When you say that it is 100 days till Christmas, you are measuring NOW from a 'point' in the future. Any such references involve CALCULATION, a mental process, and in all such references, NOW includes a part of the future. We can better understand the ancients when they told us that the past and the future are contained within the present moment. The Hindu Yogi, who contemplates eternity, finds himself in a now that includes both past and future.

It is possible to calculate both the past and the future. We can calculate where a planet was, or where it will be, but all such calculations are dependent upon an ASSUMED constant. There is no real or basic constant that we know about. This is merely a Solar-System constant, an astrology constant. Nothing can be described except in relation to something else. We say a woman has blue eyes, but this merely compares them with all other not-blue eyes. They are not brown. Two girls can have blue eyes, and they are not the same color.

Calculation of the future may be more accurate than memory of the past. All records of the past are subject to error.

Heredity is a record of the past. From his appearance, we can estimate that a dog is not the offspring of a kangaroo, and we can predict that future kangaroos will not be the offspring of this dog. We know the past within limitations. We know the future within limitations. It is our objective to narrow these limitations. We have arrived at a NOW THAT INCLUDED PART OF THE PAST AND PART OF THE FUTURE. It cannot be a mathematical point on the time line, because it has length.

Solar-System Time may be better understood if we consider a watch filled with cog wheels, where one cog is pushing another cog of another size. Perhaps the small cog revolves five times to one revolution of the big cog. This is because the cogs are geared together. Solar-System Time is like that. Although there are no visible gears, the planets move as though there were such a connection. You can predict the motion of one planet in terms of another planet. There is no factor of acceleration or deceleration involved. They all operate according to the same time system. You can fill in the gaps with theories like gravitation etc. Kepler discovered that motion of any planet is determined by abstract law involving the other planets. Life on the earth is also geared to Solar-System Time. No one has yet claimed that the revolutions of one planet are responsible for the revolutions of another planet, and it is not necessary to claim that planets affect people, electrically or otherwise, to explain the phenomenon of astrology. Because the earth spins on its axis 687 times every time Mars goes around the Sun, it is not necessary to say that the revolutions of Mars are causing the earth to spin on its axis, and as far as we know, no one has ever so asserted. Because life on the earth operates according to the same kind of time as that to which the planets operate, is insufficient reason to maintain that one causes the other. The fact is that we find life 'generated' to Solar-System Time, and that is how astrology appears to have come about. It is not necessarily cause-and-effect. It is pure mathematics. There is a design of the whole—cosmic design. Mathematics is cosmic design.

We have no evidence that one planet is slowing down in relation to another. This is quite remarkable when you stop to think about it, but no one seems to stop and think about it. If one single planet were operating in conformance with a different kind of time, it could appear to slow down or speed up in relation to the other planets. When the astronomers tell us that the solar system is slowing down, or that the universe is expanding, they may merely be pointing to the possibility that all objects do not operate in accord with the same kind of time. There can be an infinite number of different kinds of time. Let us consider another kind of time, one that is very real to you and me.

PSYCHOLOGICAL TIME

Psychological time is INDIVIDUAL TIME. It is different for different people. Time is different for a nervous person than for a relaxed person. Time moves much more rapidly for some people than for some other people. You may say, 'Well, that is merely the way it seems'. This is quite true, but it is true about all time. Time is merely what it seems. The rotations of the Earth would be different for a person on the Sun than for a person on the Earth, it does not. We always see the same side of the Moon.

When compared with Solar-System Time, Psychological Time decelerates or Solar-System Time accelerated. In psychological Time, one year to a one-year-old child is said to be equal to sixty years to a sixty-year-old man. With age, time speeds up. The older you are, the faster the years speed by. Psychological Time is just as valid as Solar-System Time, but it is more convenient to use Solar-

System Time, because Psychological Time is different for different people, and Solar-System Time gives a common standard for all beings on the earth. Nevertheless, when we use Solar-System Time, we should be conscious of the fact that it is but one of many different kinds of time.

FRAME OF REFERENCE

Keep in mind that if there were but two objects in space, one moving away from the other, there would be no way of determining whether the speed of the moving object was accelerating or decelerating, because there would be nothing with which to compare the speed.

When asleep, you dream a long experience in a tiny particle of time. Thus, the mind is not necessarily limited to the use of Solar-System Time. It can employee other standards of time.

One hour of pleasure is much shorter than one hour of pain. When you are in pain, psychological time slows down. When you enjoy yourself it speeds up. Also, pleasure is remembered more readily than pain. A pleasurable event anticipated in the future seems farther away than a painful event anticipated in the future.

The important thing to realize is what happens when we accept a frame of reference. Any motion is dependent upon your frame of reference. According to one frame of reference (FOR), an object may be traveling in a straight line, while according to another FOR, it is traveling in a circle. If we have to consider a straight line as relative, then all trigonometric measurements establishing distances become relative. We must realize that it is impossible to establish motion or time without first accepting a frame of reference. It is all right to do this if we know we are doing it and if we are conscious of the fact that there are other FOR. You whole life is like this, and you can become a complete prisoner of FOR unless you are cautious and on your guard. Can you return to the past? Frankly, you often do in a partial way. You do so particularly when you go to see your grandmother, but you do not return to it exactly because your grandmother has changed.

With only two objects in space, allow them to move apart and return to their original positions, and they have moved backwards into the past. The more objects you have in space, the more difficult it is to return to the past, because they are all changing in relation to each other. The number of possible combinations increases at such a pace that it becomes virtually impossible to return to the past, and that is the way it is with our lives. As you think these things out, insofar as our present knowledge is concerned, you will realize that time has no substance or reality at all. It is dependent on a FOR.

It is common to speak of the dimensions of space. We try to give it the same kind of reality that we give a material object. Insofar as we know, space can be the zero factor of the universe. We can measure space only in terms of objects. Objects have length, breadth and width, but visualize empty space continuing no objects. How would you measure it? Where would the dimensions be? You may speak of the amount of space in a room, but in reality you are not measuring space. You are measuring an enclosure. When you attempt to measure space of itself, are you not asking, how big is nothing? How can you measure what does not exist? Future discoveries might change things, but up till now, no one has been able to prove that space has either substance or dimensions. Physicists debate as to whether space is finite or infinite, as to whether it has limitations. Is zero or nothing infinite? Does it have limitations? If something does not exist, how can it have limitations.? How can other than material things have dimensions except abstract dimensions?

MUST CAUSE PRECEDE EFFECT?

We think of effect as always following and never preceding cause. You can push an object. You can also pull it. Instead of being pushed into the future, can we be pulled into the future? Can something that is going to happen tomorrow be affecting us today? Let us consider the possibility that it can. This is contrary to conventional conceptions of scientist, but scientists are baffled and confused in the face of psychological and emotional problems. Even scientists have nervous breakdowns. Sir Isaac Newton had one.

The five orthodox senses deal only with the past. There are other senses that deal with the future. The statistical investigations of Duke and other universities and institutions establish precognition, and the fact that we have senses that penetrate the future. We discover ourselves dealing with a NOW which combines past and future, tending toward the ancient conception that past and future are contained within the present moment, a thought that is not easily grasped because we have a mental block when we limit our FOR to standardized time.

In Lessons II and III, we have seen that the WATER and EARTH signs of the zodiac relate to the past. WE will later see that the FIRE and AIR signs relate to the future. We are endeavoring to help you to grasp the zodiac and the twelve basic principles of astrology, and before continuing along these lines, it becomes important that you reconsider and evaluate your conception of time—that you consider that EFFECT can precede as well as follow CAUSE. Within your mind and otherwise, it is not necessary that you be limited and conditioned by Solar-System Time. You can alter the past and its grip upon you by reevaluating it, and you can alter the future by recalculating it.

A planet travels around the circle we call the zodiac in a counterclockwise direction. While it is passing through one zodiacal sign, we are conditioned by the pattern of the past (or our conception of that pattern). and while it passes through the next sign, we are conditioned by the pattern (or our conception of that pattern) of the future.

HOW CAN SOMETHING BE INFLUENCED BY THE FUTURE?

Remember the day when a B-25 crashed into the side of the Empire State Building in New York City? [ed. July 28, 1945, 9:40am] George Miles worked in the Empire State Building. His desk was exactly at that point where the plane was going to enter the building, and he would always be at his desk at the time when the plane was going to strike. You can see that George's outlook would be very dark.

George was a very religious man who lived 18 miles away in Westchester County. On the morning of the day when the plane was to hit the building, George was waiting for the bus that was to take him to the train that was to take him to New York and his desk that was to be wiped away by the plane. Just before the bus arrived, he was seized with dysentery. As army men know, dysentery can be caused by fear, perhaps by fear in the unconscious realms. George had not read the following day's newspapers, and he had no conscious knowledge that the plane was going to hit the building, but his biological reaction was the same as though his extrasensory system had picked up a message which had been interpreted by the UNCONSCIOUS INTERPRETIVE APPARATUS we talked about in Lesson II. He returned home and missed the bus that was there on time to take him to his rendezvous with destiny. Because he missed a bus, he missed a train, the last train that would make it possible to keep his appointment with destiny. The next train was just too late. The unconscious timing proved perfect.

George did finally arrive in the lobby of the Empire State Building in time to be waiting for an elevator when the plane struck and one of its motors passed George on its way down the elevator shaft. Unhurt, he spent the rest of the day in the gruesome task of identifying his deceased associates.

Modern scientist might make every attempt to pass this off as coincidence in order to uphold and defend the mental blocks of the accepted conclusion that cause always precedes effect. As Charles Fort asked. 'What if it shouldn't be coincidence?' Scientists will have a difficult time attempting to convince George that it was a coincidence, because George is a very religious man. The above facts were obtained from George personally.

When in the newspaper business, the writer had an odd faculty of getting exclusive stories or news-beats by 'accidentally' arriving at the scene of an event just in time to see it happen.

Twenty years ago, there was a social event that kept the writer up till 4:00 A.M. and caused him to imbibe extensively. He knew, or thought he knew, that his biological reaction on the following day would be akin to that commonly known as a hangover. Living at Nutley, N.J., he decided that he would sleep late the following day, gain ample rest and make no attempt to go to New York, but something happened or something was about to happen.

At 7:00 A.M., the writer awakened as fresh as a lily, which didn't seem to make sense. It was a beautiful morning. Birds were singing. The outdoors was inviting, and although he tried to go back to sleep, there was no sleep. He felt too good, so he arose and boarded a train to New York.

Had his extrasensory perception picked up a set of plans that had already been formulated? This was to be the day of the great train robbery, not in the Wild West, but within 20 miles of New York.

The train stopped at a lonely station. A car with a running motor stood at the curb. At the end of the train, someone released the air brakes. Armed men were suddenly on the train. A package containing $50,000 was taken from the mail car. The train could not proceed until a police investigation was completed, during which time the news sources would be cut off from this event.

Before the arrival of the police, and as soon as it was possible to do so without risk of getting shot, the writer stood in the one railroad station phone booth, dictating the story to International News Service. When the train finally reached its destination, the passengers were greeted by an 'extra' of the New York Journal containing the story of the great train robbery. Hours later, other news channels obtained the story from regular sources–the police.

Reaching New York, his work finished, his story on the streets, there were no birds singing, the day had dulled, the writer was overcome by the missing hangover. He went to a hotel and continued his sleep, while throughout the US, a newsbeat had been scored.

We should take a broader view of biological reactions. They may be caused by something in the past or something in the future. It would be possible to tell an endless story of similar occurrences. Those who are alert can find similar cases. There is design to the past, present and future. We must become conscious of design.

CAN THE MIND TELL TIME?

Psychologically, it is not necessary that you function in accord with Solar-System Time, but can the human mind tell time by Solar-System Time? It would appear that when we reach what Hubbard has called the Necessity level or some higher state of consciousness, the human mind can calculate Solar-System Time.

A great many years ago, when the writer's daughter was a baby, she contracted pneumonia at a time when survival from the illness was quite low. The writer was alarmed, frightened, and the child's survival became his only point of interest or frame of reference. In those days, windows were thrown open in the dead of winter to give the patient air. It was necessary to keep the room warm. Coal had to be placed on a furnace fire hourly, day and night. Fearing a possible slip-up, the writer took this task unto himself. Sleeping on a living-room couch, with an alarm clock at his side, he found the alarm clock quite unnecessary. Again and again, exactly one minute before the alarm was to sound, he would awaken. In one case, the awakening was preceded by a dream in which the writer was hiking when he was seized with a terrific pain in the foot. Examining the foot, he discovered a large nail going into his shoe and his foot. As he yanked it out, a stream of sand flowed from the hole, as from the upper part of an hourglass. The unconscious was employing a symbol to convey a message—the time. The unconscious mind can tell Solar-System Time to the minute.

THE ASTROLOGY CONCEPTION OF TIME

There can be no conception of time without a frame of reference, and astrology opens the door to an entirely new conception of time. It represents time geometrically and in connection with distance, just as it represents life geometrically in a horoscope. At the top of the next page, we have a geometrical figure representing time. We see the zodiac divided into twelve equal parts, half of the parts representing the past and half representing the future. The present moment becomes a combination of the whole. Parts representing the

Lesson Four

past alternate with those representing the future.

If we consider this diagram as spinning in relation to ourselves, we see the past and future blended together. If we paint the future segments blue and the past segments red, when we spin the wheel, we will see but one color, purple. Under these circumstances, allow purple to represent NOW. It becomes a blend of blue and red, a blend of past and future. it will make your understanding of astrology easier if you keep this diagram in mind.

With reference to the functions of the mind, psychologists have dealt with the terms SUBCONSCIOUS AND unconscious, but occultists have sometimes made use of another term which we are going to adopt. It is the term SUPERCONSCIOUS. We will refer to the unconscious as having two parts, the SUBCONSCIOUS and the SUPERCONSCIOUS. We will relate the subconscious to the past, as well as to the WATER and EARTH signs, while we will relate the superconscious to the future, as well as to the FIRE and AIR signs.

In all probability, this lesson and the above diagram will give you much to think about. It is important to gain a new conception of time and space. Time is relative and it means change. Of itself, time is non-existent. On the basis of present knowledge, it is merely a means of expressing relative motion. Time can be considered only insofar as nothingness can be considered as something of itself. Space has no dimensions. Only objects have dimensions. Astronomers have been unable to measure space because they have found nothing to measure. They build bigger telescopes and discover more and more nothingness, completely overlooking the substance of what is immediately at hand, the abstract mathematical zodiac.

In Lesson II, we asserted that everything in life is a matter of interpretation. Not only do we change things when we reinterpret and reevaluate, but we alter everything when we change our frame of reference. We suggest that you study this lesson very carefully to grasp some of the conceptions that have been offered. If things are not clear to you, ask questions. We have covered a lot of ground. You may have difficulty in grasping the idea that a straight line and a curved can be one and the same thing when you change your FOR (frame of reference). Later, we will have much to say about your FOR. Even in mathematics, you will get what appears to be a different answer to the same problem when you change your FOR in the decimal system 6 + 7 = 13, but in the duodecimal system 6 + 7 = 11. The FOR has been changed.

We might say that your INTEREST is your FOR. When a man falls in love he changes his FOR, and when he does this everything changes for him. The world looks and feels different. In our civilization, we often find ourselves fighting time. We try to pack so much into Solar-System Time that we never relax. Think of the covered wagons with their oxen, fighting the months to get across the country, while now we cross the same land in hours by plane. Senses other than the five orthodox senses appear to function better during relaxation. When you press too hard or tie yourself to the past, you appear to cut off your contact with the future. Part of your mechanism isn't functioning. The religious man has faith in God, which is to say that he has faith in the future and the cosmic design. He relaxes. The materialist places all his faith in the past. He can't escape its effects. He is off balance, unable to relax, unable to change his FOR, and he has no contact with the future. He has neither intuition nor extrasensory perception. He has no precognition. When religious persons pray, they pray about the past only to the extent of asking that their sins be forgiven (re-evaluating the past). Otherwise, they pray about the future. In requesting a design of the future, they unconsciously help to design the future, because the unconscious tends to obey the command. Biological, mental and emotional reactions begin to conform to the design of the prayer. A prayer is similar to a command to the unconscious mechanism. In this case, the 'I' makes the demand, while in hypnotism, the operator commands the unconscious of the hypnotized subject, and the unconscious obeys the command.

This discussion has been necessary before we can continue with our discussion of the remaining six basic principles, the remaining six signs of the zodiac, the FIRE and AIR signs. We have studied the survival dynamics, and now we must consider the non-survival dynamics. While the survival dynamics function to continue existence in its form of the past, the non-survival dynamics function in an effort to destroy the form of the past that the desired form of the future may come into being.

Some modern mathematicians are returning to conceptions of Pythagoras, because they sense cosmic design in the universe, as it was sensed by Copernicus, Kepler and Newton. Pythagoras stated that the universe is built on number, and atomic scientists are beginning to make similar statements. The ATOM goes back to the ancient Greeks. Some writers today tell us that Einstein disproved Newton's claim that gravity is a force, but Newton did not claim gravity a force. He clearly stated that he regarded it neither as a force nor as a property of matter. His conception of gravity was purely mathematical, a matter of abstract mathematical points. He asked other scientists not to attribute to him any idea that gravity is a force or a property of matter. Yet matter behaves in accord with the

Lesson Four

abstract laws of gravitation. Newton was a student of the work of Hermes and had a library on the subject of alchemy. He wrote over 500,000 words on the subject that no one has ever read up until now. These writings have never been published. He also wrote 1,300,000 words on theology that have been ignored.

We want to leave the student with the idea that both mathematics and astrology are a study of abstract cosmic design. Nature functions only in accord with abstract cosmic design. Our purpose is to ever learn more about that design. A plane flies through the air and across oceans only because it is conforming to that cosmic design. Making your own life successful in a broad sense (not using money as a frame of reference), is a matter of living in accord with the abstract cosmic design. To understand the design, we must have a new conception of time and space. So long as it ignores astrology and what it has to offer, it is doubtful whether science can ever reach a true conception of time and space. The prior diagram may be a shock to some people. It should be considered very carefully, because it has a lot to offer. The student must remember that our present moment is very much involved with both the past and the future and cannot be considered as something in itself.

LESSON FIVE

THE NON-SURVIVAL DYNAMICS

We have considered the Survival Dynamics and the Survival Dynamic Reactors, and we must now approach the Non-Survival Dynamics. We have already pointed out that while the Survival Dynamics are related to the past, the Non-Survival Dynamics are related to the future. The present moment is merely the battleground of the past and the future. Man is confused, because he does not understand this constant battle that exists deep in his unconscious.

We could have selected other titles for the Non-Survival Dynamics, but this term explains qualities and relationships which could not be reached by other terms. To match each Survival Dynamic, there is a Non-Survival Dynamic, and the three Non-Survival Dynamics present us with another perfect equilateral triangle within the geometrical frame of reference we call the zodiac. As in all geometry and elsewhere throughout the study of mathematics, in astrology we always find perfect symmetry, design and balance.

When we speak of non-survival, people are apt to think immediately of death and suicide, but such identification should be avoided at the outset, for when we speak of non-survival, we refer to form rather than substance. In all probability, actual death is merely non-survival of form, but we are not in a position to prove this. It is, however, the most ancient conception and the one to which the religious world has clung. The further we go in astrology, the more indication we find that physical death is merely non-survival of form, because death in astrology takes on a much broader meaning. Divorce, for example, is death to a marriage. The child's house is built of blocks, and when he destroys it, the blocks remain. He merely destroys form. The abstract pattern of the house existed before he built it, and continues to exist after he destroys it. Any change is death to something.

There are three Non-Survival Dynamics to match the three Survival Dynamics. Each is associated with a sign of the zodiac, and the three carry the same names as the Survival Dynamics. They are:

Dynamic	Zodiacal Sign
Individual Non-Survival	LEO
Family Non-Survival	ARIES
Social Non-Survival	SAGITTARIUS

These are the Fire Signs. The Water Signs represent the Survival Dynamics, and the Fire Signs represent the Non-Survival Dynamics. The Water and Earth Signs relate to the subconscious, while the Fire and Air Signs relate to the superconscious. The next diagram shows the manner in which the Fire Signs fall into the abstract figure we call the zodiac. We have elsewhere referred to the Fire Signs as the Vital Signs, and the ancients sometimes called them the Spiritual Signs. We have avoided such a term because of its many different meanings in different minds.

Man is the center of a terrific struggle. One half of the inner dynamics is endeavoring to perpetuate the past in its old form, while the other dynamics are endeavoring to destroy the old form to allow the existence of a new form. When we see these forces functioning in politics, we refer to them as the conservative and progressive or radial elements. The same struggle goes on within family circles and within the individual himself. In extreme cases the Social Survival Dynamics result in throwbacks and recession, but even a throwback may have as its purpose the correction of an error, like the man who forgets some important papers and returns for them. The Social Survival Dynamic often functions to drag down any individual who gets too far ahead of the crowd, or too far ahead of his 'time'. It accomplishes its objective in many ways. It may cause him to co-habitat with an inferior person, giving the laws of heredity an opportunity to produce an in-between being. In its negative phases, we often see the Social Survival Dynamic dragging people down through illness, by making them alcoholics, drug addicts, thieves, criminals, and sometimes by causing insanity. We often see the Family Survival Dynamic dragging people down through hatred, cruelty, discipline, etc. We also sometimes see the Individual Survival Dynamic dragging people down through selfishness and self-indulgence.

It should be noted that the Survival Dynamics go around the zodiac in a clockwise direction. The beauty of mathematics lies in the fact that everything is perfect symmetry. In the study of the

Lesson Five

zodiac and astrology, we encounter this same beautiful symmetry. Everything is perfect design. Although, as we shall later see, there are two missing planets, we can describe the astrological nature of those planets before they are ever discovered. Could we spend as much money as the government spent on the development of the atom bomb, we could determine the positions of these planets without ever seeing them.

[Eris was discovered in 2005, is about the same size as Pluto and outside of Pluto's orbit. This planetoid is a possible candidate as ruler of Taurus.]

Suppose you have a jigsaw puzzle with one missing piece. What is the shape of that missing piece? You put the remainder of the puzzle together, and there a hole is left. The shape of the hole shows you the exact shape of the missing piece. Although you do not have the piece to inspect, you know its exact shape. Everything in mathematics is similar. Everything in astrology is similar. When a mathematician discovers a formula, he has discovered a design. When Kepler discovered the three basic laws of motion, he had merely become conscious of mathematical design. When Newton discovered the laws of gravitation, he had merely become conscious of mathematical design. When Einstein discovered Relativity, he had become conscious of mathematical design. The scientists have never seen an atom. They are merely conscious of mathematical design. They predict what an atom will do from their understanding of its design. The zodiac is a mathematical design. When you discover a quality in one sign of the zodiac, you can discover the opposite quality in another zodiacal sign. That is mathematics. All mathematics is design, the design of nature, the design of the abstract world, because a design is abstract. Higher mathematics is merely a study of design, and that is why the mathematician sees his subject as beautiful, while the layman sees it as confusion. The layman fails to become conscious of design. Finding a series of numbers in nature, the mathematician seeks the design of the series, and when he has discovered this design, he can compute the numbers as far as he wants to go toward infinity. Astrology is merely the mathematics of the life dynamics. It functions exactly the same as any other branch of mathematics. Mathematics is an abstract science, but everything material functions only in accord with abstract law. The zodiac is a perfect mathematical pattern, and we will later see that the planetary system itself fits into this same mathematical pattern. There is nothing haphazard about the astrological pattern of the solar system. It is important to grasp the significance of astrology's symmetry, because again and again, you will be able to gain the answer to your questions by observing the shape of the nothingness that remains in the jigsaw puzzle.

THE INDIVIDUAL NON-SURVIVAL DYNAMIC

The purpose of the Individual Non-Survival Dynamic (Leo) is not to exist in your present form, but to re-form. A five-year-old boy wants to be a six-year-old. While Cancer may cling to the parents, Leo wants to become independent of them. Leo is the exact opposite of Cancer. While Cancer is the introvert, Leo is the extrovert. While Cancer is insecure, Leo is secure within himself. While we find Cancer on the defensive, we find Leo on the offensive. Cancer is subjective and Leo is objective. Cancer represents 'ME,' while Leo represents 'I'. Some would call Leo the spiritual ego, the god within man, the life force. Cancer fears change, while Leo desires it. Cancer seeks money and possessions, while Leo seeks prestige, and abstraction. If you have prestige, you can borrow money. Cancer is modest and Leo is proud. Cancer wants to stay where he is. Leo wants to move on. Cancer thinks in terms of the effect of the world on 'ME', while Leo thinks in terms of how 'I' affect the world. The Cancer salesman is careful to deal in a product the people need and want, like groceries, while the Leo salesman is a high-pressure man. He intends to condition the people to his product. Leo will see possibilities in a new invention, but Cancer will depend on the already established habits of society. People have been eating for a long time. They will always buy food. Cancer will try to heed the buyer's thinking. Leo will try to think for him. Leo leads; Cancer follows. Cancer can represent fear, while Leo represents courage.

The Non-Survival Dynamics always display a dissatisfaction with the past, while the Survival Dynamics always associate security with the past. Leo is never satisfied with himself as he is today. He wants to change and expand. He is constantly endeavoring to expand his sphere of influence. He changes himself when he expands his sphere of influence. When he fights, he does not need a fort, because he fights on the other fellow's territory. He is aggressive. He doesn't like to wait for opportunities. He prefers to go forth and create them. Without educational conditioning, it would be his tendency to go forth and take what he wants. Might makes right.

Which of these principles is the more successful? Insofar as material success and the accumulation of money is concerned, statistics indicate that Cancer rides at the top of all signs of the zodiac, but if statistics bearing on prestige were available, it is possible that this condition might be reversed. Of course, a man with money may have prestige in many circles.

Leo can be kind and generous, but there is always the necessity of curbing any tendency toward arrogance. Leo may suffer because he ignores people who do not intend to be ignored. When change comes, it may not be the kind of a change he expected.

Ancient astrologers portrayed Leo as the Lion, the king of all the beasts, and the symbols of the zodiac were sometimes referred to as the beasts. Leo was associated and identified with the heart, and when we have serious afflictions to the Individual Non-Survival Dynamic, we often find them accompanied by heart attacks. We might say that a heart attack is the result of an unconscious or superconscious desire not to survive in the present form. The writer has often noted that, prior to a heart attack, the individual was irritable, fed up with the status quo, and desirous of some kind of change that seemed out of the question to him. Life in its then-present form was intolerable to him. It has been noted that, while some people make broad changes under some astrological circumstances, others die of heart attacks under the same circumstances. In one such case, a man was all set to make a very broad change and move his family to another part of the country, without knowing how either he or the family were to survive in the new land. Close associates prevailed upon him to change his mind. Two days later, he died of a heart attack.

In endeavoring to change his form, Leo may or may not achieve his objective but he will achieve some objective. In trying to get the boss's job, he may get fired. Quite often the achieved objective is foreign to the desired objective. When a person gets married, change has been achieved, but the results are seldom those that were expected. It is the purpose of Leo to change, but change always involves other circumstances.

When humbleness has been acquired, it would seem as though Leo and the other Fire signs possess what is called divine guidance, and divine guidance might be termed correct calculation. If we can calculate the future correctly, we know what to do, and most of our calculating is, as we shall later see, a matter of unconscious or super conscious origin. Man possesses an unconscious calculating device that is superior to any electronic calculating machine that Man has ever built. Quite often, Leo underestimates his opponent. Quite often, Leo underestimates negative possibilities, and is taken by surprise when they occur. Cancer was afraid of negative possibilities in the first place. The key to Leo achievements must be correct calculation.

Multiple events fit themselves into the pattern of the future. A series of what appear to be accidental events occur in such a way that the pattern of the future is allowed to develop. Material events can happen only in accord with abstract design. The orbit of a planet is an abstraction, but a planet can travel only along that orbit. Its course can be calculated, even to its deviations from an ellipse. Other events can be calculated because they fall into the pattern of design. Dr. Carl Jung reveals his consciousness of this fact when he employs the term SYNCHRONICITY. It would appear that humbleness plus faith in the future play an important role relative to an individual's ability to harmoniously tune into what appears to be, but isn't, an accidental pattern. Materialism defeats its own purpose, for it places all its faith in the past. It is successful only until there is change. Materialism is unable to deal with change. The man who devotes his whole life to the accumulation of wealth has to leave it behind when death overtakes him. At least one such man had a good sense of humor about it. Shortly before he died of a heart attack, he said to the writer, 'Where I'm going, those nighties they give you don't have any pockets in them.' This statement came simultaneously with a complete loss of interest in his business, which was national in scope. He began ignoring the business, and nothing his associates could do would change him.

When we find a humble Leo, we find a person with a terrific potential. It is the nature of Cancer to be cautious of a stranger or of the unknown. Leo is the reverse. He is the we-met type. He is ready to shake the stranger's hand with a tight grip. He expects to absorb the stranger into his own sphere of influence. He likes to meet strangers. He likes to go beyond the limitations of those who make up his environment, into the territory of strangers. This is part of his reformation and expansion, and while he is usually capable of mingling with strangers, bestowing kindness and receiving kindness, it is necessary for him to be careful that he does not miscalculate the reaction of strangers. He may go forth, conquer and expand, but when he unconsciously forces his will on strangers, it seems a part of nature that forces unite and combine against him. Strangely, when this happens, Leo is bewildered. It is something he doesn't understand. Two such Leo's were Napoleon and Mussolini. When Cancer makes a proposal, he does it humbly, fearing that it may not be accepted, but when Leo makes a proposal he assumes that it will be accepted.

Promises have a different meaning to Leo than to others. A promise is a means to an end. Its purpose is to bring about change. Once the change has been effected, the promise may be forgotten, but it can be revived. It is something that belongs to the past, while Leo's concern is with the future. Also, changing circumstances often make it impossible for a promise to be fulfilled. At the time the promise was made, it was an intention, but changing circumstances alter things.

When European nations borrow money, it is probably their intention to repay the money, but circumstances change, and they are unable to do so. Fulfilled promises are not the characteristic of Cancer, the Individual Survival Dynamic, however, but of Capricorn, the Individual Survival Dynamic REACTOR. The EARTH Signs will struggle the hardest to fulfill promises, the Earth Signs representing REACTION. In fact, fulfilling of promises can often bring the downfall of the Earth Signs. When circumstances change, it is logical that promises should be re-evaluated by all concerned. The value of money shrinks or expands, and this is seldom taken into consideration where our courts of law are concerned. We may find cases where Leo makes a promise in his old form, but does not consider the promise as binding on the new form.

It will be of great help to your future astrological interpretation, if you will always remember that the purpose of Leo and the Individual Non-Survival Dynamic is NOT to exist in the present form, but to take on a new form and a new design.

THE FAMILY NON-SURVIVAL DYNAMIC

The Family Non-Survival Dynamic is represent by ARIES. It is always the purpose of Aries to change and alter the form and design of the family relationship. The symbol of the sign was the Ram, to denote the characteristic of being headstrong, and afflictions involving the Family Non-Survival Dynamic often result in injuries to the head or headaches.

Study the difference between Aries and Scorpio. The latter sign impulsively fights for the interests of the family. You hurt a Scorpio if you attack any part of his family, but Aries is more apt to think of the family as part of him, and if the family is not part of him, something happens. There may be a break. When a large number of Aries people are studied, it is remarkable how many cases we find where there is an unexplainable break with some member of the family. It may be a parent, a brother, a sister or a child, but Aries has a definite conception of what the future of the family is to be, and if any member of the family proves to be an obstruction to that plan, there is a break. It may be subtle. It may not show too strongly on the surface. The Aries child may slip away from the family, take up with others, pioneer, and go his way.

The Aries individual may move to a distant place. There is no apparent discord. He may keep in touch with the family and be on distant good terms with its members. He will do anything to help them, send them money, but he has his own life to live. Unconsciously, he is out to change the hereditary strain. He may marry one of foreign birth or someone quite far removed from his own heredity. There is the superconscious urge to create a new strain. He may accept, into the family, persons of different blood. An adopted child may be just as dear to him as his own. He is out to create his own empire. In this new empire, his word is law. So long as everyone conforms, it will be a peaceful existence, but if you have different ideas, they are not acceptable. They will be kindly vetoed.

The soul of the dictator is found in Aries, but only within his own domain. His children are supposed to obey. He lives their lives. He knows what is best for them, and he will map their careers. They are supposed to follow his course. If they do not, they are considered the prodigal children. In extreme cases, they might be disinherited, but more often, they might be pushed away but supported. Both Scorpio and Aries can be jealous, but the jealousy manifests differently. While Scorpio clings, Aries pulls away. Like Leo, Aries is proud, and a sucker for flattery. The sign can live on flattery. It is like food. It is quite essential for Aries to feel appreciated. He will then give away what he has and go out and accumulate more. It will give him vitality and strength.

Aries does not want to occupy an inferior position. He wants freedom. He would rather be the head of a small organization than second-in-command in a large organization. His business is his child, and he will put everything into it. He will protect it. He doesn't want to conform to a pattern originated by others. He doesn't usually do too well in politics, except in a small community which he can control. We will state exceptions to this rule.

You will always understand any odd behavior on the part of Aries better if you realize that it is the superconscious Family Non-Survival Dynamic at work within the unconscious. The individual is not likely to know just why he does what he does. He follows his urges. We will call them urges rather than compulsions. Some of the greatest pioneers in history have had Aries strong in their horoscopes in some way. Although, John D. Rockefeller had Sun in Cancer, he had Aries as his ascendant. John Hays Hammond, Sr., had Sun in Aries. He built his mining empire. John Hays Hammond, Jr., is also Aries. With his father's fortune, he built his own electronic empire. Wyatt Earp had Sun in Aries. He was the most famous sheriff of the old west. He left a name for himself in Abilene, Kansas, Dodge City, and Tombstone, Arizona. He was forever pioneering, carrying his brothers with him, but he was their recognized leader. He finally left Arizona and retired to California to escape what he claimed to be a trumped-up murder charge. Old Doc Holliday was as much a part of his family as his brothers, and he was always risking his life for any of them.

Aries ascendants include Clara Barton, founder of the Red Cross; Alexander Graham Bell; Alexis Carrel, pioneer in biology; Edmon de Valera; Douglas MacArthur; D.W. Douglas, aircraft pioneer; and Sidney K. Bennett, probably the greatest pioneer in astrology during the first half of this century. Aries Suns include John Burroughs, the naturalist; Walter Chrysler; Clarence Darrow, Anthony Fokker, aircraft pioneer; Nikolai Lenin; Robert Andrews Millikan, the physicist; the senior John Pierpont Morgan, another great empire builder; and three men who tried to reach the presidency– Charles Evans Hughes, Thomas E. Dewey, and Herbert Lehman. They all succeeded in becoming governor of New York State but couldn't make the presidency.

We find many empire builders under this sign. When this sign is powerful, people are less fitted to work for others. There is strong will, dynamic power vitality and spirit, but you will notice that none of these men could be accused of perpetuating the past. One Aries man did reach the presidency, and we still hear a lot about him – Thomas Jefferson. A second Aries man reached the presidency, but he was never elected to that office – John Tyler.

Despite the number of Aries men who have been great pioneers and empire builders, if we check the Who's Who type of directory, we usually find Aries running low. You furnish your own data to get into these directories, and Aries is more concerned with his own achievements than with having his name in these directories. He has his own realm (family) and he is content to rule within that realm and mind his own business insofar as the rest of the world is concerned. Also he is quite likely to be misunderstood elsewhere. He is patriot within his own sphere.

The ancients associated Aries with the head, and when you find someone who is often having head injuries, this sign is likely to be prominent. Aries can endure a great deal of pain without flinching. Very often these people are quite lucky at gambling. They like to play with Lady Luck. They seem to have a precognition that pays off when they make a bet. They don't win all of the time, but their successes seem far above average. The same applies in business. They are often successful because they guess right. If this goes to their heads, they guess wrong. They do have the courage to gamble and take a chance. They don't base their bets on past experiences, but on hunches or urges. They often have a superconscious ability to contact or calculate the future. They live more in the future than in the past. Where sex is concerned, they are more conscious of results. Unconsciously, they want to improve the family strain. It is not a matter of blind emotion. Scorpio is driven by emotions that have their roots far in the past. This is not true of Aries. Neither does Aries need company. He is choosy. Unless he can have his chosen companionship, he would rather be alone. There is self-sufficiency. If there is insecurity, it involves only the factor of recognition. Aries would like to be recognized for what he considers himself to be. If he is the best carpenter in town, he will feel hurt to hear some other person mentioned as the best carpenter in town. Perhaps anybody would, but it will mean more to Aries.

It must be realized that when we mention Aries as the Family Non-Survival Dynamic, the word family can have a broader meaning than when we mention Scorpio as the Family Survival Dynamic, because Aries does not draw the bloodline. If you happen to live in the household of Aries, you have been approved, and you are just as much a part of the family as a blood relative, perhaps more so. You must also realize that the motivating power is in the unconscious. The purpose of Aries concerns the design of the family of the future. It is to give the family better design. It is opposed to, and not bound by, the continuance of hereditary design of the past. There is the desire to eliminate the flaws of the past from the form of the future. The pioneering urges are an effort to build a new day of life for the family of the future.

We have some cases where Aries has shown violence in his efforts to control his family, his wife or his children. 'It was for their good.' Yet, he will demonstrate great violence to protect them from outside dangers. Whatever the weaknesses of his ancestors may have been, Aries is conscious of them, and he is out to improve the family of the future. This is the manner in which the Family Non-Survival Dynamic functions.

THE SOCIAL NON-SURVIVAL DYNAMIC

The Social Non-Survival Dynamic is represented by SAGITTARIUS. It is ever the purpose of Sagittarius to change and alter the form and ideas of society, and the chief way in which this dynamic manifests is through education, science, travel, religion and reform. Its symbol was the Centaur, half man and half beast – a man's head and torso, with the body of a horse. With bow and arrow, he was also the archer, symbolic of the fact that Sagittarians are noted for their outspokenness and ability to shoot straight to the mark. It is hard for them to hold something back. What they think is so, they have to state. This is a natural tendency to teach what they consider their own wisdom.

We can understand SAGITTARIUS better if we study it in contrast to Pisces, the Social Survival Dynamic. The two signs are exact opposites. They may both seek truth, but the wisdom of Pisces always stems from the past, while the wisdom of Sagittarius stems from the future. Pisces attempts to preserve the wisdom of the past, and is more representative of mysticism, cults, churches, the occult, esotericism, theosophy, reincarnation, Karma, spiritualism, etc. Pure science, if there existed such a thing, would be more representative of Sagittarius. Statistical tests have shown a greater degree of extrasensory perception in Sagittarius than elsewhere in the zodiac. The psychic is more common to Pisces. Tests at Duke University have shown that the person with the so-called psychic ability, strangely, makes the lowest scores in laboratory guessing experiments. Occult knowledge contains value, but it has to reviewed critically. The same may also be said of all scientific heroes. The Sagittarius proves to guess right more often, but that does not mean that his guesses are always right.

Sagittarius represents more what we would call the creative scientist. He has 'flashes'. With a million possibilities to choose form, he occasionally picks out the right one. He has a hunch. He tests it, and it works. The inventor, at least to himself, recognizes these hunches. Most scientific discoveries had their inception when somebody followed a hunch. This never happens to the average educator nor to the average academic scientist, because he is always limited by a frame of reference. We read of an astronomer who denies that Pluto is a planet, because such a planet does not accord with the nebular hypothesis. Other scientists have abandoned the nebular hypothesis as an impossibility, where the solar system is concerned. One science writer refers to 'those amazing and unexpected leaps of the imagination in which the chief charm of science will always reside.' (See *Limitations of Science* by J.W.N. Sullivan) The astronomer who tells us that Pluto is not a planet is a prisoner of a frame of reference, the nebular hypothesis. He falls in the same category as the individual who cannot consider certain possibilities because they would be in conflict with this particular religion or cult. One of the greatest characteristics of Sagittarius is that now and then, it breaks out of a frame of reference. To break out of a frame of reference is often to make a discovery.

A particular type of astrology may be considered as a frame of reference, and this would apply to any astrology which was designated as a cause-and effect phenomenon, but when we go beyond such a frame of reference and designate astrology as pure mathematics, we have broken out of a frame of reference. Because one 'system' of astrology works, this in no way invalidates some entirely different system of astrology. It must be investigated on its own merits. There can be an infinite number of ways of solving a mathematical problem. It is not necessary to stick to a textbook method.

However, scientific and philosophical progress, as represented by Sagittarius, comes in jumps. A new truth is realized, and a new frame of reference is set up. Although it is a broader frame of reference, it still has its limitations, and these limitations prevent further progress beyond a certain point until such a time as there is another realization and another jump into a new frame of reference. Such frames of reference would appear to be infinite.

The important difference to remember as existing between Pisces and Sagittarius lies in the fact that Pisces is always trying to preserve or re-establish what has existed in the past. The spiritualist is endeavoring to contact people who existed in the past. The believer in Karma is endeavoring to establish causes that lie in the past.

Astrology and many occult truths have been preserved by the Pisces type of Mind. Truths and untruths have both been preserved, but let us look at the approach of another man. This man is a Sagittarius, an engineer in the employ of a corporation. This firm had spent great sums of money paying astronomers to investigate possible causes of magnetic storms. The astronomers would not turn to the planets as having an association with magnetic storms, because that would be astrology, and the frame of reference of astronomy is supposed to exclude any possibilities of astrological truth. Any facts that would upset the theories of astronomy are carefully avoided at all times. Such facts are forbidden territory, and an astronomer can lose his job for impartially investigating such facts.

However, a privately owned corporation is outside the academic frame of reference of astronomy. The Sagittarius engineer reasoned that the cause of magnetic storms could not be terrestrial. It came from space. Therefore, the most likely place to look for the source was the planets. The corporation financed several years of research, and ultimately announced that because magnetic storms coincide with planetary movement, they are predictable. Since that time, all important magnetic storms have been predicted.

It happened that the findings set up the same set of principles that had been advocated by Ptolemy in his astrological writings. The planetary aspects were the same. However, this did not cause the Sagittarius to turn to ancient teachings of astrology. His statement to the writer is interesting. He said, "We have no opinion relative to astrology. We know nothing about it. If our researches prove basic principles of astrology, all well and good. We are neutral. We are only interested in the facts. The facts appear in our statistics and our statistical graphs. We don't want to know the astrological theories, or any other theories, in advance, because we do not want to be influenced or prejudiced by them." These words may not be exact for they are quoted from memory, but they are approximate.

It is important to realize that the purpose of Sagittarius is to destroy accepted frames of reference and overcome their influence or limitations to thought. The Sagittarian seeks a religion or a philosophy, but whatever the religion or philosophy according which he was brought up, he ultimately breaks out of it. In matters philosophical, he thinks for himself. He is a reformer, but too often, when he doesn't accomplish his first reform within his lifetime, he stays caught in his first new frame of reference. It is difficult for him to go on when his first reform has not been accepted by society. When his views are not accepted, he develops an anxiety complex. It is difficult for him to be an individual and go on, because his purpose is not just to reform himself. Leo reforms himself. Aries reforms the family, but Sagittarius wants to reform society. It is not enough of him to accept a truth. He wants to teach it. He could go on alone, but this doesn't appear to give satisfaction. There wouldn't be any one to talk to. He is dead serious about the matter. He wants to get his ideas across.

He may not know it, but his superconscious purpose is to destroy the present form of society, it represents ideas and conceptions, and when this purpose is thwarted he is frustrated. The anxiety complex is quite likely to result. If his ideas are accepted, he can go on. There will be another jump, another disclosure. Most Sagittarians are anxious, without knowing why. They are constantly sensing something from the future, but they may not understand it. Orthodox training may have caused them to smother their most essential assets. Because they were taught that there is no precognition, they may smother their most valuable talent. They are ahead of society. As a rule, the Sagittarian will do well to teach less and learn more. He has the ability to learn, but he wants to teach. Although Sagittarius gets caught in his temporary frame of reference, and often meets disappointments as a result thereof, his disappointments themselves are often what spring him into a new frame of reference. We will have more to say about frames of reference when we reach the opposite sign, Gemini.

Astrologers of the past have associated Sagittarius with the thighs and with the liver. Could the liver have any connection as an organ of extrasensory perception? We don't know, but people's minds do not appear to function well when the liver functions poorly.

We often find the Sagittarius persecuted for his views when he is very right, or at least partially right. This is partly because of his tendency to voice his views from the housetops. A reformer can be very unpopular. When you question what is now established, you cause an automatic reaction of the Survival Dynamics. There is fear connected with the Survival Dynamics, and when you frighten someone, he may attack you. This writer read the original of a letter written by one of the most outstanding astronomers in the country to the head of an educational institution, seeking dismissal of a younger astronomer because he had written articles on astronomy for an astrology magazine. A personal discussion between the writer and the mentioned head of the institution prevented the older astronomer's plea from being acted upon. When various facts were brought to the attention of the man who had to make the decision, he ruled against the astronomer. The younger astronomer was a Sagittarian.

An inspection of the birth dates of German spies caught in this country during World War II showed that more than half of them were born with the Sun in Sagittarius. They were caught merely because they were too free in expressing their views. Pisces would have been more secretive. The Sagittarius is basically honest. Whatever he says or teaches, whether it is right or wrong, he believes it.

A few people who were born with Sagittarius rising were Bernard Baruch, Elbert Benjamine (Church of Light), Mary Baker Eddy, Ernest A. Grant (Guiding light behind the America Federation of Astrologers), Manley Hall, J. Edgar Hoover, Charles Lindbergh, Robert Millikan, Eleanor Roosevelt, Theodore Roosevelt, Margaret Sanger, Herbert Spencer, George Westinghouse, and Frances Elizabeth Willard, reformer.

A few persons with Sun in Sagittarius include Winston Churchill, Charles de Gaulle, Tom Mooney and Mark Twain. There are less people born with the Sun in Sagittarius than in any other sign. The birth ratio hits a low spot in the year when the Sun passes through Sagittarius.

Sagittarius is not noted for diplomacy. While Pisces avoids persecution by being subtle and secretive, Sagittarius asks for it by shouting his views from the housetops. It would seem that the Pisces 'soul' knows about the persecutions of history. He instinctively knows that you can be persecuted for telling the truth. This is the sign of crusaders. There is no compromise with principles. We find many authors, statesmen and many men and women who fought for a cause, born under this sign. We often find them sponsoring an unpopular cause, a cause that is won in the end, but not during their lifetime. In this sense, they are seeking the future. They are living ahead of their time. They are forever battling the evils of society, willing to make great personal sacrifice that the future world may be a better one. Perfection is not reached at one stroke. The Sagittarian plan may be along right lines but filled with defects. In studying Sagittarians of history, we often note that although they were headed in the right direction, their ideas were still wide of the mark.

It should be noted that there is nothing akin to habit in the Fire Signs. Habits are qualities of the Water and Earth Signs. Habit is a quality of the Survival Dynamics. The Fire Signs furnish the energy to create the future. They feel and sense the future, but there may be a lack of accuracy due to faulty calculation. There has to be guidance, and we have more to say about that in our next lesson.

LESSON SIX

THE NON-SURVIVAL DYNAMIC GUIDES
PART ONE

In Lesson Two, we dealt with the Survival Dynamics. In Lesson Three, we dealt with the Survival Dynamic REACTORS. We illustrated that the Survival Dynamic REACTORS are always opposite the Survival Dynamics in the zodiac.

In Lesson Five, we dealt with the Non-Survival Dynamics. Opposite each Non-Survival Dynamic, we find a Non-Survival Dynamic GUIDE.

Hidden with the unconscious, within the super-conscious of each and every one of us are three GUIDES. A study of these three Non-Survival Dynamic Guides is a study of the DESIGN of the intellect.

A natural ability to predict or calculate the future is inherent in Man, but it does not function in the majority of people. This is partly due to education, which has placed this talent beyond society's frame of reference. It is also partly due to mental and emotional indigestion on the part of society and its individuals.

We have been taught to be 'practical' rather than intellectual. The Greeks were well on their way in the culture of Alexandria. They produced the greatest of mathematicians. They had made remarkable progress with their mechanical inventions, but in 48 B.C. their great library was destroyed by the Romans, and the second library of Alexandria was destroyed by the Christians to abolish 'pagan' science. That which is 'practical' is often a matter of perpetuating the past on the theme that it is safe to do things as they were done yesterday. The Greek philosophers and mathematicians were true intellectuals. They saw DESIGN in nature and throughout the abstract world. The materialist never see DESIGN. They have no contact with the world of the abstract.

We must all understand what is meant when we use the words INTELLECT and ABSTRACT, because modern usage of these words is very loose. We have passed through an era when people have been taught to think objectively in terms of things and their size, rather than in terms of abstractions and overall principles which never change. The materialists do not see the abstract as something of itself, and are unable to visualize it except in material terms. Psychology's Watson, and the whole behaviorist school of thought demonstrated an inability to visualize abstract principles. They were completely unable to distinguish the observed from the observer. The tiniest particles have been picked apart in an effort to discover life itself as a piece of matter hidden behind a piece of matter. Even the Spiritualist finds it necessary to explain the departed as functioning in an astral body, which is merely a body of more rarefied material, like that of a giant star. Almost nowhere do we find any effort to discover life as an abstraction. Most modern religious conceptions are materialistic conceptions. Materialistic interpretations have grown up around conceptions that were originally abstractions.

Mathematics is a science of ABSTRACT DESIGN, although it is often taught merely as a science of measurement. Size and measurement are elastic and relative. You can measure something only as it relates to something else. The laws of mathematics are, in no way, dependent on matter for their existence, but matter is completely dependent upon the laws of mathematics for its existence. They are abstract laws. In the abstract world, nothing ever changes, and where there is no change, there is no time. Although some materialist have claimed that a mathematical formula is non-existent until man thinks of it, this is the same as saying that Neptune was non-existent until we thought of it. This is a way of making Man the creator of what only he discovers.

In our use of the word INTELLECT, we will mean that part of the MIND (not brain) that is capable of seeing or visualizing the ABSTRACT as something separate and apart from the material. ABSTRACT will mean existing independently of the material.

To all great mathematicians of all times, mathematics has been a science of DESIGN, and they have all described it as something beautiful. The average student may see nothing beautiful about his mathematical textbook. Instead, it may represent drudgery and confusion. This is merely what textbooks writers have made of mathematics. To Pythagoras, Aristarchus, Euclid, Khayyam, Copernicus, Kepler, Fermat, Einstein, and others, mathematics was a thing of beauty. They saw SYMMETRY AND DESIGN. Some were seeking a divine plan, for nothing exists or functions except in accord with mathematical design. The men who have revolutionized scientific thought have usually been those who could visualize COSMIC DESIGN. They are followed by materialist who explain their discovery in warped materialistic terms. The materialist is a non-intellectual who can judge the future only by the past. He can explain anything after it happens. He never discovers abstract

Lesson Six

principles because he is unaware of its existence. It is beyond his frame of reference.

We have earlier explained how astronomy broke away from astrology with the Christian era and became a materialistic science. As written, the modern history of astronomy is largely fiction. It would have us believe that the ancients were little above animals in their mental conceptions, and that their astronomy came about merely as the result of their wanting to know when to plant crops. All of this fiction has been a part of the effort to promote materialism. The astronomer would have you believe that until 1543 A.D. people believed the earth to be the center of the solar system. Nothing could be further from the truth. The idea that the Sun traveled around the earth was a product of Christianity. It was called the "realist" view of things. Materialists always have a "realistic" view of things.

Discovery of the Sun as the center of the solar system is attributed to Copernicus. Actually, when Copernicus published his DE REVOLUTIONIBUS in 1543, he did not present his views as original. He merely employed mathematics to prove that one obtained more perfect mathematical DESIGN when one went back to the pre-Christian, pre-astronomy, astrological point of view, and considered the Sun as the center. He was defending the ideas and conceptions of Aristarchus, who lived more than 200 years before Christ. He was upsetting the geocentric (earth-as-the-center) views of Ptolemy, who lived in 150 A.D. It was the mathematicians who came to the defense of Copernicus (not the astronomers), because they recognized that he had found more perfect abstract DESIGN. Mathematical history indicates that before Aristarchus, Pythagoras also taught a heliocentric (sun-as-the-center) system in 500 B.C. Thus, as usual, we find the astronomers were 2000 years behind in adopting a heliocentric system. This is probably an under estimation, because there were other civilizations thousands of years before the Greeks, and nowhere do we find evidence that they taught that the Earth was the center of the solar system. In another 2000 years, astronomers may teach that we believed the Earth to be square, because Rand McNally publish their maps within a square frame.

Because he believed in COSMIC SYMMETRY AND DESIGN, Copernicus sought more perfect mathematical design, and he found the design to be more perfect mathematically when he adopted the views of the pre-Christian Greeks and considered the Sun as the center.

Kepler lived 1571-1630. He was a German astrologer who wrote books on astrology. Modern astronomical textbooks claim him only as an astronomer. He believed in a divine plan, and as a result of his belief, he attempted to find more perfect mathematical DESIGN in the solar system. He discovered the three laws of planetary motion. He discovered that if you draw two lines from the center of the Sun to two points on the orbit of a planet, the motion of the planet from one point to the other will have a definite relationship to area enclosed.

Sir Isaac Newton was also an astrologer, who refused to argue astrology with Halley, because Halley never studied the subject. [ed. This is an unproven claim but Newton was an alchemist that require astrological knowledge] He was a mathematician who saw beauty, symmetry and design in the universe, as a result of which he discovered the mathematical laws of gravitation. To this day, neither astronomers nor physicists have been able to fit gravitation into their materialistic scheme of things. They have been unable to explain gravitation in terms of cause-and-effect, because there is a complete absence of a time factor.

Albert Einstein never studied astrology, but he was a mathematician and an abstractionist as well as an intellectual. Like others before him, he was seeking beauty, symmetry and design in the universe. He discovered relativity.

The atom is a blow to all cause-and-effect conceptions. We refer to the mathematical conception of the atom, because we know only about the mathematical conception of the atom. No one has ever seen an atom. According to this mathematical conception of the atom, an electron can leave one orbit and appear in another orbit simultaneously. There is no time factor for the electron to pass from one orbit to the other. It does not traverse the in-between space. For the electron, that 'space' is non-existent. To materialistic science, this is both a shock and a new principle, but it is an old principle to the world of psychic phenomena, where there has long been a word for it that does not appear in the writer's dictionary. The word is TELEPORTATION, and it is frequently found in literature dealing with psychic phenomena. Physical science is now up against the fact that it finds itself completely unable to explain matter except in abstract mathematical terms. The causal hypothesis and the whole materialistic conception of things is ripping at the seams.

We have described the zodiac as an abstraction rather than as something material. We have described astrology as something abstract rather than as something material, just as we have described mathematics as pure abstraction. It is vitally important that we get across to you what we mean when we speak of the abstract, because you are not going to understand what we are about to explain unless you grasp our meaning. So let us take another example of something that is completely abstract rather than material.

Lesson Six

A number is an abstraction. Each number has limitless characteristics, but no two numbers anywhere to infinity will have EXACTLY the same characteristics. 510,510 is the only number under a million that can be divided by the first seven primes. Thus, if we were to give you a problem, and you discovered that the answer would have to be under a million, and also that the answer was divisible by the first seven primes, you could know at a glance that this is the only possible answer to the problem. It would save you a lot of work. These facts are pure abstraction. Their truth is not dependent on anything material, but material things can be employed to illustrate the abstraction for those who cannot visualize the abstract. Materialists are those in whom the INTELLECT does not function.

Occasionally, we find an individual who appears born with a knack of computing mathematical problems in his head more quickly than can be accomplished with an electronic calculator. There have been children who beat the greatest chess players, until they were educated and learned to do things the hard way. These people never seem able to explain their methods, and 'science' has always found it more convenient to ignore such cases than try to explain them. There is an explanation, however, because if you determine the characteristics of an unknown answer to a problem, the answer can be obtained much more simply than any methods found in a mathematical textbook, and in much less time. The human mind is capable of solving problems than one man-made calculating device can approach.

In this presentation of astrology, we are presenting an abstract mathematical pattern of the zodiac. Life functions only in accord with this abstract mathematical design. It is the abstract design of life, life itself being considered as abstract. We find the INTELLECT represented by the AIR signs of the zodiac, which we have termed the Non-Survival Dynamic GUIDES. In the zodiac, the INTELLECT is represented by another perfect equilateral TRIANGLE. (It should be realized that the triangle is the simplest possible two-dimensional figure. You cannot have a two-dimensional figure of less than three figure sides, but you can have one with any number of sides if the number is greater than three.) There is a GUIDE opposite each Non-survival Dynamic in the zodiac.

The three GUIDES and their zodiacal counterparts are as follows:

GUIDE	ZODIACAL EQUIVALENT
Individual Non-Survival Dynamic Guide	Aquarius
Family Non-Survival Dynamic Guide	Libra
Social Non-Survival Dynamic Guide	Gemini

As we have pointed out previously, the Survival-Dynamics and the Survival Dynamic Reactors go around the zodiac counterclockwise, while the Non-Survival Dynamics and the Non-Survival Dynamic Guides go around the zodiac clockwise. Remember this, and it will give you a more graphic picture.

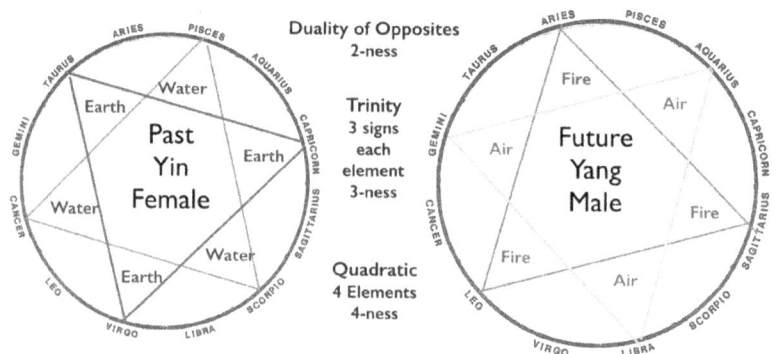

[ed. Water and Earth signs go counter-clockwise in the order of Individual, Family and Social Survival Dynamics and Reactors. The Fire and Air signs go clockwise in the order of Individual, Family and Social Non-Survival Dynamics and Guides.]

By visualizing the abstract it is possible to visualize the future, providing you do nothing now that would change the future, but this visualization may not be in the conscious but in the superconscious. It is necessary to calculate the future, but this process need not necessarily be a conscious one. Just as we find an unconscious interpretive apparatus associated with the subconscious, we find an unconscious calculating apparatus associated with the super-conscious.

The GUIDES do not function for a great many people, who

have been hypnotized into the belief that there are no such guides, for these guides are contrary to the doctrine of materialism in both the scientific and religious worlds. Although we have cut ourselves off from the guides in order to adapt ourselves to our prevalent social structure, they sometimes work in spite of us. Neither do the guides function in the face of mental and emotional indigestion. Neither do they work in the face of fear. Fear belongs to the Water and Earth Signs. It is never found in the Fire and Air Signs. Fear causes one to cling to material security. We can see why Christ placed such great emphasis on FAITH in God. The man who really has faith harbors no fear, and the GUIDES HAVE A BETTER opportunity to function. An over-emphasis of WATER and EARTH in a chart or horoscope may make faith extremely difficult unless mental and emotional digestion can be effected. Mental and emotional indigestion is the principal cause of many varieties of illness.

The subconscious of the average person is filled with experience that has never been digested mentally and emotionally. It has been our experience that when emotional indigestion is cleared up, the GUIDES begin to function normally. Suddenly, there is no indecision. The individual knows what he wants to do, knows what he should do, and does it without hesitation. Emotional indigestion is the cause of many hidden unconscious fears. With a healthy being, there are no hidden fears. His view is always of the future, and it becomes necessary for him to utilize every waking moment either altering that future or harmoniously fitting himself into it.

However, we will later see that there are astrological times when the GUIDES are clouded, other times when they work in spite of us, just as we might say that there is a time to be awake and a time to be asleep. If we are asleep when the GUIDES ARE clouded, we will be less inconvenienced. It is our view and experience that there is much that we can do to clear up emotional indigestion, and much that we can do to cooperate and allow the guides to function as they were intended to function. There may be little the individual can do until he overcomes his materialistic education, which has taught him to ignore and never investigate anything lying outside the frame of reference of modern religion, education and science. Through religious creeds, scientific hypotheses and education, the masses have been hypnotized to hold their attention within the frame of reference of modern educational limitations. One of the principal aims of our research, at the present moment, is to find the means of clearing up mental and emotional indigestion, and in some cases, we have had remarkable results.

It is interesting to note that just as it was the mathematicians who came to the rescue of the claims of Copernicus, 400 years later, it was the mathematicians who came to the rescue of the work of Dr. J.B. Rhine of Duke University, when it was being attacked almost universally by the psychologists, biologists and physicists of the United States and Canada. It is possible that after the mathematicians endorsed the methods of Rhine in open convention, the critics ran to their seclusion because as materialists, they were complete unprepared and incapable of dealing with the mathematical side of the picture due to their inability to deal with the abstract. Insofar as the materialists were concerned, extrasensory perception could not be, because a thought would have to be something material that would travel through the air and ultimately make a landing. The mathematicians took an abstract view of the evidence, and asserted that it was impossible to obtain the Rhine results by chance. The materialist ran for cover, because they did not have the mental equipment to deal with abstract mathematics.

THE INDIVIDUAL NON-SURVIVAL DYNAMIC GUIDE

The Individual Non-Survival Dynamic Guide is represented by AQUARIUS. Its symbol was a man pouring water from an urn, and it is possible that this symbol was intended to portray the separation of the abstract from the material. It could represent the 'soul' leaving the material body. Aquarius was associated with the ankles and with the blood. In it's negative phases, it is associated with paralysis. This can apply biologically or when a labor union goes on strike in an effort to force an issue.

The Aquarian is an abstractionist who sees things, not as they were, not as they are, but as they will be. He unconsciously senses the trend ahead. The process of unconscious calculation is ever going on. Instead of identifying security with the past, he sees only the imperfections of the past, taking the good for granted. The past and present stimulate only restlessness and irritability. He never figures that it can't happen here. Instead, he is sure that it will, and he is alert for it. He is inclined to view material things as responsibilities rather than as assets. If they hold him down or limit him, he wants to break away from them. He harbors the spirit of the hobo. He likes to keep on going on. Because he always sees how things could be done, he is inventive. Evangeline Adams wrote that these people tend to live a hundred years ahead of their times. They often accomplish the impossible. Let us see who some of these people have been.

Among persons who had Aquarius on the ascendant at birth, we might list Abdul Baha (mystic), Charles de Gaulle (and many other

Lesson Six

successful military leaders), Havelock Ellis (ahead of his time with sex), George Washington Goethals (who built the Panama Canal after others had failed), Osa Johnson (explorer), Dr. Carl Jung (pioneer in psychiatry and in questioning the causal hypothesis), Ana Nonus Kingsford (mystic), Krishnamurti (mystic), Andre Lamont (occultist), Abraham Lincoln (who started a job the world hasn't yet finished), David Lloyd George, William G. McAdoo (who build the first tunnel under the Hudson River), Karl Marx (about whose originations we are still fighting), Meher Bab (mystic), J.P. Morgan, Sr., (who gave us our Railroads,). Emmeline Pankhurst (one of the original suffragists), Wiley Post (first man to fly around the world solo), H.G. Wells (whose novels were an uncannily accurate portrayal of the future.) Paul Whiteman (pioneer in music), Sir George Wilkins (explorer). and the Duke of Windsor (who couldn't stand the old style limitations and confinements of being an old fashioned king).

Among persons having the Sun in Aquarius, we might name Evangeline Adams (astrologer), Roy Chapman Andrews (explorer), Sidney K. Bennett (astrologer). Jack Benny, Edgar Bergen, Eddie Cantor (and many other comedians whose role is surprise), Charles Dickens (and many other authors), 'Diviner' (German astrologer), Louis DeWohl (astrologer), Thomas Edison (and many other inventors), Havelock Ellis (again), Clark Gable (and many successful actors and actresses), John Barrymore, Rupert S. Gleadow (astrologer), Augusta Foss Heindel (occultist), Blanca Holmes (astrologer), L.E. Johndro (astrologer), John L. Lewis and Samuel Gompers (the strike was their weapon), Abraham Lincoln (again), Douglas MacArthur (who wouldn't conform to Harry Truman), S.R. Parchment (occultist), both Jean and Auguste Piccard (balloon pioneers), Sir Ernest Shackelton (explorer), Frederick Spenceley (occultist), Sir Henry Morton Stanley (explorer), Hugo Stinnes, Jules Verne (whose fiction predicted the submarine), Franklin D. Roosevelt (who revolutionized the US Government and almost revolutionized the US Supreme Court), Adlai Stevenson, Evarts C. Walton (astrologer), Charles Darwin (who made us evolution conscious and changed the course of biology), Charles Lindberg ((first to fly the Atlantic alone), and 'Wrong Way' Corrigan.

One does not have to study these names long to know that these people are different. The astrologers and occultists were not stopped by the blind conventionalism of the educational world. All of these people were ready to investigate or plunge into the unknown. They were not hampered by insecurity. They were not trying to perpetuate the past. They were non-conformists. They were never willing to leave well enough alone. They were not content to live and let live. Their purpose could hardly be called survival. They fear not what is ahead. They do not fear death, nor are they worried about starvation. Ties are easily broken. Time is changed, and they want change. They think in terms of motion, not in terms of stationary objects. They love action and excitement. There is a sadistic delight in seeing the old order of things destroyed. Ideas are more important than money. The two together can do extraordinary things. One man is tied to a certain place, because that locality is his home. His family and friends are there. He has a job which he cannot leave. This man is not likely to be an Aquarian. An abstractionist, Aquarius is not tied to material things. He sees more reality in abstract ideas.

The material world is in a state of constant flux, but not the abstract world. It is important not to mistake the world of imagination for the world of the abstract. The world of the imagination is merely a place where material things are shifted around visually and mentally. The world of the abstract, as found in the laws of physics and mathematics, never changes. It is without time. From one millennium to another, everything remains exactly the same. Although you may learn about the abstract world from others, you can have a direct contact with that world within yourself. Did anyone tell Pythagoras about the Pythagorean theorem? Did anyone tell Kepler about the laws of planetary motion? Did anyone tell Newton about the laws of gravitation? Most discoveries appear to be accidental, but actually, the individual is looking for something that he feels. Something within himself leads him to the point where the discovery is made. His conception of things may not have been exact before he made the discovery, but there was a general pattern or design. He may not have been conscious of what he was seeking, but in his super-conscious, this was known. To go on strike seems to be an Aquarian idea. It isn't just a means of forcing action on an employer. It is also an outlet for the worker, a break in the killing routine, a bit of excitement, an opportunity for a change of pace, a means of mental and emotional digestion.

Unlike Cancer or Capricorn, Aquarius is not conservative. He is radical. All men who turn up with a new and better idea are looked upon as radicals in their time. They are not considered as intelligent, but are looked upon as 'crackpots'. Fulton with his steamboat was a crackpot. The early motorists were crackpots. This writer can recall when, as you drove for a Sunday spin through the country in a motor car, the whole family of a farmer would run out yell, 'Get a horse'. We were told that an automobile would never be practical. There was nothing like a good, old reliable horse. If the teachings of Christ are studied, we find this Aquarian principle strong, but we often find the Christian church standing for the very opposite principles. The past is worshipped. If a couple make a mistake and get married only to discover incompatibility, they are denied the right to correct the mistake. They are told that marriages are made in heaven, which considerably detracts from the advisability of going to such a place. Christ was an intellectual, but many of his followers can interpret his teachings only in materialistic terms.

All of the astrologers and the mystics were seeking a better way of life. Most everything the Aquarian accomplishes is regarded as impossible until he does it. It is not so far back when the great majority of both sexes did not regard women as sufficiently intelligent or well informed to be qualified to vote for public officers. Why did men like the Wright Brothers, Wiley Post, Linberg, Corrigan, and so many others, want to fly when it was safer to stay on the ground? Men like H.G. Wells and Jules Verne had only their intellect to guide them in accurately portraying the future. To them, it was probably the only way that things could happen. They had to go that way.

We see a different principle working in connection with British royalty, where tradition is far more important than human happiness. Surprisingly, however, they do not insist that their navy fight with the same old wooden ships.

The success of Aquarian comedians seems to be based on the fact that they can follow the functioning of the average human mind. They know it will follow a pattern of habit, and they inject an element of surprise, which is mental and emotional relief to the audience. The conventional routine of thinking is broken, with the result that there is exhilaration which expresses it self in the form of laughter. The humor of a joke disappears after it has been told a number of times.

To the Aquarian, evolution is too slow, and he finds he can do much to speed it up. We fight against taxes and government payrolls, but these things take people out of circulation and leave more business and more ways of making money for the taxpayers. They can sell things to those on the government payroll. What if all those on the government payroll suddenly became farmers?

Leo likes change and excitement just as much as Aquarius, but he does not have the same ability to see where it is leading. There is need of the guide, but a long time might elapse before change makes this need apparent. Leo may have calculated the change differently. He may often get opposite results to those he expected. A good example of such opposite results would be when a Leo, Herbert Hoover met up with the 1929 stock market crash. He was unprepared for it. On the other hand, when an Aquarian Franklin Roosevelt, met up with the bank holiday four years later, he rose to the occasion.

He solved the problem by altering the laws and principles of the government, of the banks, and of the stock market. Twenty-three years later, we have had no recurrence of a panic, while prior to 1933, panics arrived cyclically. We have had the same cycles since, but we have had no panics.

If the Individual Non-survival Dynamic Guide is harmonious in a horoscope, there is the tendency to harmoniously design the life in accord with what is about to happen. This is not necessarily done consciously. It is done superconsciously. The individual merely follows his urges. He needs no guide other than the one that is hidden in his own unconscious.

When the Individual Non-survival Dynamic Guide, is inharmonious, there may be just as much genius, just as much ability to see ahead, but the individual sees too far ahead for all practical purposes. We might say that he is several cycles ahead of himself, and this is as disastrous as being several cycles behind. Before the stock market crash in 1929, there were many in Wall Street who 'knew' that the crash had to come. Some sold the market short too soon and lost their shirts. Others sold their stocks too late and lost their shirts. A song or a book is often written and ignored, because the world isn't ready for it. The same song or book becomes very popular after the writer is dead.

Lancelot Hogben, the mathematician, writes, 'The most brilliant intellect is a prisoner within its own social inheritance.' The intellectual is seldom appreciated in his own day. After he dies, a materialistic conception of him is prepared, and we worship that materialistic conception.

When the ISD Guide is afflicted, the result is terrific impatience and irritability with the present form, and the individual is called destructive. A boy may have a yen for throwing rocks through plate glass windows. There can be sarcasm and a critical attitude toward everything anyone else may do. To destroy is a thrill. We often see a person destroy himself by means of an 'accident'. Unconsciously, he wants to get on with things, which he cannot do in his present form. When studying accidents or illness astrologically, it is always well to look carefully to see what purpose has been served by the accident or illness. You will find that a very definite unconscious purpose has been served.

It is quite apparent that the list of names we have given might be considered as a group of non-conformists, people who were unwilling to accept things as they found them. Many of these people were way ahead of their time. They were conscious of the future rather than of the past. We could also have included many

Lesson Six

statesmen whose views were condemned as too radical. While it is the nature of Aquarius to touch off dynamite to see what will happen, in these people, we find selfishness at a low ebb. An Aquarian may destroy himself for a cause. His security is not in material things but in abstract things. The most revolutionary labor leaders have been born under this sign. They destroyed old conceptions of servitude. Aquarius is unorthodox. The Aquarian, within himself, is not sensitive to what society thinks of him, because he looks upon society as dull and stupid.

Both marriage and divorce are associated with this guide. Each is a means of changing one's individual life. There is a take-a-chance attitude, because one thing will always lead to another. The hobo attitude prevents one from definite attachment to environment. This principle would not apply to a marriage that is based solely on a desire for security.

Just as the Water and Earth Signs are locked in the past, Aquarius and the other Air and Fire Signs are locked in the future. If you know what is coming next, it is difficult to wait for it. The Aquarian is not susceptible to mob psychology. He thinks for himself and often has a hypnotic effect upon others. We often find an excellent sense of humor when he can point out the obvious that others never see, with the result that it lends surprise and strikes people funny.

The three Guides exist in each and every one of us, but they are often subdued. When the unconscious is too clogged with the past, with mental and emotional indigestion, the GUIDES become dormant and will not function.

To predict the future is to understand the functioning of nature. A good chess player calculates his own moves far ahead, and is able to predict what a poor chess player will do next. The bullfighter knows in advance that the bull will go for red. It is the nature of the beast. In predicting the future by astrology, we must not be misled by the so-called favorable and unfavorable aspects. The next man to be elected President need not be the one who has the more favorable aspect, but the one whose chart best fits or blends with the interval ahead. Too many people consider a day as favorable if they can do what they want to do, unfavorable if they can't. Many an individual has been murdered because he was able to do what he wanted to do. You might have considered the victories of Hitler as favorable for him, but see where they led. Neither must we lose sight of the fact that we can make the future. Too many people are dissatisfied with the kind of a future they made for themselves. In a revolution, the wealthy are often the first to be murdered. The poor man is never murdered for his riches. Thieves are not attracted to the pauper.

You change yourself when you change your environment, because you react differently. You also react differently when in the presence of different people. You may be at ease in the presence of one person, nervous and restless in the presence of another. You select associates in whose presence you have the kind of reaction that suits you. You are a different person in the wilderness than in the city. Change of environment is a means of not surviving as you are. Change is a means of Individual Non-Survival. When you change your environment radically, you change you inner-self. For this reason, we usually find that Aquarius likes to meet new people. He is happy in public office or in public work, because he is always contacting new faces and personalities. He is changing himself. Large corporations have caught on to this principle, and they keep shifting their men from one part of the country to another.

Cancer and Capricorn do not force change, because, to them, it suggests insecurity. It is not the true nature of either Leo or Aquarius to resist change. There is a lack of fear of the result. If the Aquarian is discharged from his job, he is likely to react with a feeling of relief and a sense of freedom. Change is always an opportunity. Cancer or Capricorn might immediately explore the possibilities of getting the job back again.

We often find the Aquarian unconsciously training himself for a job that doesn't exist. A few years later, that kind of a job comes into existence, and he is ready for it. In some cases, we find him training himself for a job that will not exist during his lifetime.

Just as any mathematical problem has to have an answer containing certain characteristics, there is often but one way in which the future can happen, for the future also has to have certain characteristics, and astrology will ALWAYS tell us the characteristics of the future. Although the astrologer may err in his details of the future, there is never a reason why he should err in his calculations of the characteristics of the future. These are always plainly written.

In Lesson Four, we discussed TIME. To understand Aquarius and the Individual Non-Survival Dynamic GUIDE, it is necessary to grasp a new conception of TIME. Time is elastic and relative. Dr. Carl Jung has asserted that time has quality and that whatever is born at a particular moment has the characteristics of that moment. Of itself, TIME is non-existent. It is but a way of describing a relationship among things. As conventionally used, time is merely a planetary relationship, the relationship of the Earth to the Sun. An instant of time is a planetary relationship. A planetary relationship is a mathematical DESIGN, and that design is what we call the horoscope.

I might refer to the moment of time when a certain plane

Lesson Six

will land at an airport in New York. The plane finally lands, but due to a storm, the time does not coincide with the anticipated planetary time. The time is nevertheless just as real as any planetary moment. It is still the time when that plane lands in New York. If suddenly, the Earth were to stop turning on its axis, and remain with one side facing the Sun, tomorrow's noon would never arrive. On the Moon, noon's are about 28 of our days apart. Time is adjustable. Our inventors have changed the time it takes to cross the continent in relation to planetary time.

Verne and Wells had the ability to grasp the DESIGN of the future. There are people completely unable to visualize the future. As an example, during the 1890's the astronomical department of Harvard College published a 'scientific' paper, 'proving conclusively' that it is physically impossible for a gasoline driven mechanical device to fly thorough the air and carry the weight of a motor, fuel and one man.

The Survival Dynamic Reactors often outweigh the Non-Survival Dynamic Guides. At such times, progress is difficult. We are living in an era when the Non-Survival factors outweigh the Survival factors, insofar as the horoscopes of people of the age where they can affect our destiny are concerned. When the reverse is the case, time tends to stand still.

People attempt to maintain order, but this is never more than partially and temporarily possible. Yet, in the design of the abstract world, there is perfect order, and there is neither time nor change. The number 2311 is prime. It always was and always well be. It can never change into a composite number. It is the inherent nature of matter and life that it changes. The only true security lies in the abstract, where there will be no change. The Christian world visualizes a 'time' when there will be no 'time', when the struggle will end. This is their heaven. It is eternal. Only in the abstract world, where everything is eternal is this possible, but there are always materialists to interpret such things in a material frame of reference.

In the material world there is constant change that is not constant. It speeds up and slows down if we use the rotations of the Earth (days) as a constant. Even the speed of a planet is not constant. It is more rapid in one part of its orbit than in another part. If we were to employ the speed of the Earth or another planet as a constant, days would not be equal, but would vary in length. So-called 'time' is always dependent upon a frame of reference, while the Sun itself is moving at the rate of 150 miles per second.

LESSON SEVEN

THE NON-SURVIVAL DYNAMIC GUIDES
PART TWO

In dealing with the twelve basic principles found in astrology, we must always view them from two points of view, how they function in the unconscious, and what we can do with them when we know about their existence. The engineer can do things with his knowledge of mathematics that another person cannot do. The astrologer can do things with his knowledge of astrology that another person cannot do. It is vitally important to understand how the astrological principles function on the unconscious level, and these lessons have been presented in such a way as to uncover what is happening on this unconscious level. To accomplish his own conscious purpose, it is convenient for Man to know more about the hidden purposes of nature, that he may be in a position to become a good diplomat and do a little trading with nature. In considering the Family Non-Survival Dynamic GUIDE, we encounter a vast amount of unemployed ability. Long ago, the writer witnessed that he could accomplish far better work in exploratory mathematics when this Guide was stimulated. He discovered that these were the 'times' when he could best visualize factual abstract data.

THE FAMILY NON-SURVIVIAL DYNAMIC GUIDE

The Family Non-Survival Dynamic GUIDE is represented by LIBRA. It's symbol was the balance or scales of balance. The sign was associated with the kidneys. It is quite possible that the scales represented the principle of balance in nature. The beautiful requires balance. We find beauty and balance in nature. We find beauty and balance throughout the study of mathematics and physics. We find this GUIDE prominent in the horoscopes of the best mathematicians and physicists, and the greatest mathematicians have always been men who saw beauty in mathematics. The beautiful woman is one whose features and form are perfectly balanced. She is regarded as more beautiful if both eyes point in approximately the same direction. If one eye were considerably larger than the other, it would detract from her beauty. Not all people are attracted to beauty. Some are attracted to the gross. Mathematics loses its beauty when we look at the type of problem found in a youngster's arithmetical text book. If a boy has $1.69 and can buy material at 13 cents a yard and sell it at 17 cents a yard, how much money can he make on his first transaction? Survival Dynamics seem to dominate the textbooks.

Only because of the principle of balance can we compute things mathematically as far toward infinity as we wish to go. We can leave the material world behind and enjoy ourselves in the abstract world, but when we return we can apply what we have learned to the material world if we wish to. Kepler discovered the three laws of planetary motion, Newton the laws of gravitation, because both realized there had to be balance, symmetry and design. We find Libra associated with balance, symmetry and design.

The unconscious purpose of the Family Non-Survival Dynamic is to change the form of the family. Without a guide, this dynamic might proceed in almost any direction. The purpose of the Family Non-Survival Dynamic GUIDE is to make the family more beautiful, to give it better balance, symmetry and design in its form. This Guide attracts to beauty. It endeavors to improve the family-to-be by attracting to a mate who is more perfectly designed mathematically, a beautiful girl or a handsome man. The most beautiful woman is often born when Libra is on the eastern horizon. We find the sign rising in the charts of Constance Bennett, Joan Fontaine, Jean Harlow, Miriam Hopkins, Irene Rich and Norma Shearer as well as in the charts of Warner Baxter, Humphrey Davis, Bing Crosby, Regis Toomey, Gary Grant, Adolphe Menjou and Tyrone Power.

When a man or woman is drawn to a beautiful or handsome mate, there is unconscious improvement in the form and appearance of children-to-be. It is a form of BALANCE when the male and female seek each other. The magnet attracts the needle. The Earth attracts the Moon and the Moon attracts the Earth. Let us not believe that such attractions were unknown until Benjamin Franklin took to flying kites, for Thales, who lived more than 200 years before Christ, experimented with amber and electrical attractions as well with the lodestone of natural magnet.

The type of people we seek as friends is determined by the Family Non-survival Dynamic GUIDE. When a young person begins to seek mixed company in a social way, this GUIDE is directing things. The young person becomes less tied to his parents. The breaking away process is beginning to develop. This is not a sex factor which is separate (Family Survival Dynamic). He begins to prefer the associations of the pretty girl to that of his family. This is new and refreshing, but two families want to survive, and half a loaf is better than none. Each family can survive on a 50% ratio. Ultimately, the Family Survival Dynamic operates, and there is sex. A child is born. It is 50% of each family. Two families have survived to a lesser ratio. The Family Non-Survival Dynamic and its GUIDE continually operate to prevent the possibility of incest. A brother-sister relationship would give 100% survival to the heredity strain. There would be but two parents and two grandparents. Nothing new would have been added.

The Family Non-Survival Dynamic and its GUIDE are ever weakening the Family influence upon hereditary factors mathematically: 1/2, 1/4, 1/8, 1/16, 1/32, 1/64, 1/128, 1/256, 1/512, 1/1024, etc. In ten new generations there is less than 1 part in 1,000 of the old family strain left, unless there has occurred some intermarriage of families, as when someone married a distant cousin. The mathematical proportions of heredity are similar to those of gravitation, involving the inverse arithmetical square. The more miles a planet is away from us, the less its gravitational pull. The more generations an ancestor is away from us, the less his hereditary influence upon us.

This example may help you to understand how two different things can function according to the same mathematical formula, and thus produce a coincidence that has the appearances of a causal factor. This is what we mean when we say that the solar system and human dynamics function to the same mathematical formula.

With all the Non-Survival factors we find a tendency to plunge into the unknown and 'take a chance', but actually direction is determined by the GUIDES. If enough people should become familiar with these GUIDES, knowledge about them could revolutionize science and civilization. It is two different things to plunge into the unknown when the guides are functioning and when they are not and it must be remembered that emotional indigestion tends to prevent the guides from functioning.

The mathematical theory of probability is employed for testing invisible abstract laws and gaining information about things that are invisible. If you toss a coin millions of times, the theory will tell you how many runs of a given number of consecutive heads should occur. It will predict with surprising accuracy, but the laws of probability will furnish approximations and not actual figures.

If you toss a coin 25 times and a head turns up each time, the odds are 33, 554, 431 to one that there is a head on each side, but we never are certain unless we check the coin, because the laws of probability tell us that if we toss a coin long enough, ultimately we are bound to get a run of 25 heads and it is just as likely to come at the start as at any other place. This, under the laws of probability, there is never absolute proof. We can gain no proof of the theory of probability itself that its absolute. Our proof of the theory is relative. After we look and we find that there is actually a tail on the other side of the coin, then we say that the run of 25 heads was due to CHANCE.

CHANCE is an ambiguous term like SPACE. It is merely a word to fill a gap and give a name to something we can neither explain nor understand. We are merely saying that as far as we know there was no reason for the 25 heads to appear at the start. That does not prove that there was no reason.

A man may tell you that he went to a party, and by chance he met the girl he later married, but if we find that the Family Non-Survival Dynamic Guide was pronounced at that time, and that such an 'accident' could have been predicted, it was no accident and it was not chance. However, not every marriage is the result of the operation of this Guide. People marry for many reasons. One girl married because she is seeking financial security. When the Family Non-Survival Dynamic is stimulated, new people come into our lives, and this can be predicted. Therefore, it is not chance.

After marrying, a girl may have the Family Non-Survival Dynamic and its Guide highly stimulated, and a new man may come into her life. The first time she left her parents, and now she may leave her husband. It is easy to find cases where she leaves her husband and children, or it may be the husband to whom all this happens. Unless the Family Survival Dynamic REACTOR gets in its work quickly much can happen, because the Family Survival DYNAMIC can achieve its purpose either way. Children produced, regardless of the number of mates, the greater the survival of the hereditary factor. If a man can have 20 children by five wives, he has 20 different mediums to carry on the hereditary factor, and on the subconscious level, this serves the purpose.

Theoretically, the hereditary factor diminishes at a rate that never extinguishes itself or gives out. If you continue the fractions 1/2, 1/4, 1/8, 1/16, 1/32, etc., to infinity, you can never reach zero. Some infinitesimal part is always left.

When we can bring this Family Non-Survival Dynamic GUIDE to the surface, we have unusual powers of visualization, the ability to visualize the abstract, and this is why it produces some of the greatest mathematicians and physicists. Roger Babson was born with Libra on the ascendant. He saw patterns and design in stock market behavior and economic cycles. We find many artists and musicians born with Libra prominent, but quite often these people do not commercialize their talents. Consequently, they do not show up in the 'Who's Who' type of directory. They are likely to be seeking art, design, symmetry, etc., for its own sake, for their own personal happiness. By itself, Libra is not much on pushing itself forward. Like the other Air signs, it is not a selfish sign. Its natives are not likely to turn to anything gross. Stephen Foster had Libra rising, but his fame came after his death. Sir Isaac Pitman had Libra rising, and he produced a speed system of writing–shorthand. Among astrologers who have had sun or ascendant in Libra, we might name Charles E.O. Carter, Dal Lee, Bessie Leo, Charles Hayne, Marc Edmund, and Myra Kingsley.

We must always remember that when we are dealing with the Non-Survival factors, the Fire and Air Signs, the unconscious purpose is change of form or RE-FORM.

Most Libra people underestimate their own potentials. They are not keenly interested in achieving fame. Sometimes they find it embarrassing and as a rule they would prefer the society of smaller groups of their own choosing.

Although the purpose of Libra is change, where its ability to visualize the abstract is concerned, there is no change in the abstract world which is therefore without time as we think of or conceive of time. When Einstein looked into the abstract world he saw everything that Euclid saw nearly 2,500 years earlier. Nothing had changed but he looked further and saw more. Of course, you can say that there is a factor of speed in the abstract world, and speed involves time or something akin thereto. You can say that one series of numbers reaches a given point more rapidly than another. Thus:

Integer	Square
1	1^2
2	2^2
3	3^2
4	4^2
5	5^2

In the second column, you will reach 10,000 in 100 steps, while in the first column it will take 10,000 steps. A mathematical formula speeds things up. Understanding the symmetry of mathematics enables us to reach an answer more swiftly. Understanding mathematics or anything in the factual abstract world helps us to change things more rapidly. A system of trial and error takes much longer.

Folks used to believe in long courtships for young couples. There is less of that now. We are doing almost everything in less time. The more we know about the abstract world, the more we can accomplish in less time. The long courtship was to make sure that everything would be all right. We can tell more about the compatibility of the young couple in a few minutes by astrology than the long courtship would ever determine. Although laws of the abstract world do not change themselves, we are ever discovering new laws we did not know about before. Thus, in a sense, we travel within the abstract world, and again in a sense, this sort of travel involves 'time'.

Where abstract law is concerned, absolute proof is possible. To illustrate what we mean by this, almost 2,500 years ago, Euclid and other Greek mathematicians were interested in whether there was any limit to prime numbers or whether they continued to infinity. A prime number is one that is not divisible by any other number other than itself and one. A few examples are 2, 3, 5, 7, 11, 13, 101, 103, 2,311, 30,031, 510, 511, 9,699,691, etc. Euclid proved that prime numbers infinite, because if you multiplied all know primes together and added one, the result would not be divisible by any know prime, and therefore either that number would have to be prime or divisible by a prime larger than any know prime. Thus, there would have to be another prime in any event. We know for a certainty that if we go on counting we will always come to more prime numbers. We can gain absolute proof of abstract truth, and after we gain such proof, we can apply it in the material world. That is why men are flying great ships around the world.

Although the unconscious purpose of the Family Non-Survival Dynamic Guide is to constantly inject new factors into heredity and lessen the influence of a particular family of the past, it is not necessary that all the calculating be done on the unconscious level. By becoming conscious of the abstract laws involved, we can conduct our own speedup process and apply it in many departments of life. Whatever Man can do in a year, there is always a way of doing it in less time if we find out about it.

It would be the exception to the rule to find the Guides functioning freely. The survival factors are always getting in their work, too, but when the non-survival factors outweigh the survival factors, change is allowed to occur. The last hundred years have brought great progress, but it is not necessarily true that this progress will keep on at the same pace or at a more rapid pace. Whenever the survival dynamics grow too strong and outweigh the non-survival factors., we are apt to go back to ancestor worship and some more dark ages. For children to progress, it is necessary of them to break away from some of the fixed ideas of their parents and ancestors, and a great many parents regard this as a bad sign. They don't know where it might lead. 'What's the matter with things as they are? Why not leave well-enough alone?'

A divorce may or may not be a good thing, but what we call morals are often merely the operation of the survival dynamics. 'Do everything as it was done yesterday. Believe that those who came before you were wise. Don't ever question what they said. Take Moses' word for it. Don't ever have a real thought of your own. Just imitate.' Monkeys imitate too.

Summing up, the Family Non-Survival Dynamic Guide represents attraction or gravitation between people, and thus it produces what we call our social life. Of itself, it is not a sex factor, which has to be injected by the Family Survival Dynamic. Therefore, it can attract people of the same sex as well as people of opposite sex. Your 'best friend' can be of the same sex as yourself. Even your best friend may have much to do with breaking the hold that your family may have upon you. As you break away from the old family environment, you begin to manifest more as a new and different being. Whenever you break away from old factors, you give the GUIDES a better opportunity of functioning. This is not telling you that there is nothing good about the old. Far from that, but you will learn to swim better if you try going into the water.

THE SOCIAL NON-SURVIVAL DYNAMIC GUIDE

The Social Non-Survival Dynamic Guide is represented by GEMINI. It's symbol was the twins. It is interesting to note that although zodiacs found in different parts of the world differed to some extent, GEMINI was always represented by twins. In Europe, it was twin children. In ancient America, one zodiac represented the sign by a man and a woman, another by two generals. There was always a factor of duality. Biologically, Gemini was associated with the lungs, the arms, and the hands. There are two lungs, two arms and two hands. It is also interesting to note that in the practice of Yoga where efforts are made to achieve high philosophical understanding, the exercises begin with the control of one's breath. Three independent non-astrological investigators in the United States and England have delved into the statistics of twins, and all have found that multiple births run to a maximum in the month of June, which happens to be the time of year when the Sun is in Gemini. The Dionne Quintuplets were born with the Sun in Gemini as were Mary and Margaret Gibbs, Siamese Twins. Oddly, a secondary peak of twin births occurs in December, when the Sun is in Sagittarius. These two signs represent the Social Non-Survival Dynamic and its Guide. These are also the periods when live births run to a minimum. There appears to be a compensating factor in nature. When the birth ratio reaches a minimum, multiple births reach a maximum. This is not completely true, for the low point of live births in Gemini is not as low as that in Sagittarius, but Gemini provides for more twins than Sagittarius.

We have dealt with Sagittarius as the Social Non-Survival Dynamic and we have shown that its progress is often hindered by a tendency to tie to a frame of reference, a particular 'scientific' theory or a specific religion. Thus, a GUIDE is required, Gemini is that GUIDE. Gemini is always shifting around from one thing to another. It is a truly intellectual sign, but an army is needed to complete all the things that Gemini starts. As you will see later in these lessons, we are living in a time when we cannot find the truly pure type of Gemini, and our presentation of the sign will be slightly different from some of the qualities that you will find in most Gemini people of today. To understand the sign, however, we will have to have a more permanent conception of its basic fundamentals, and we obtain those fundamentals by merely putting all the pieces of the jigsaw puzzle together and examining the shape of the hole that is left by the missing piece.

Gemini is often accused of having a dual personality, of being two people in the same anatomy. This is because the frame of reference can be so quickly shifted. It is often difficult for Sagittarius to break out of a frame of reference, but Gemini must give equal attention to every new frame of reference that happens to come along. Tying one's self to a particular frame of reference is too often identified with something akin to loyalty. A man must vote Republican because he is a Republican, or Democratic because he is a Democrat. An astronomer never investigates astrology because he is an astronomer. He feels that it would be disloyal to his colleagues to go beyond the frame of reference of astronomy. We find this tendency everywhere in society. The frame of reference often becomes more real to someone than reality itself. An automatic process sets in, and all facts which do not conform to the frame of reference employed are excluded. This is an everyday occurrence. It is heresy to note or observe facts that do not conform to the frame of reference. People go to war to defend frames of reference they know nothing about, but not Gemini.

Gemini has produced many good writers, engineers,

electricians and mechanics. Among writers having Gemini rising at birth, we might mention Sir Arthur Conan Doyle, George Bernard Shaw, Alfred Tennyson, Paul Ambrose Valery, Jules Verne (also mentioned as having Sun in Aquarius), Ben Ames Williams, Walter Winchell, Kenneth Grahame, T.E. Lawrence, Jack London and Christian Morgenstern, while among those having Sun in Gemini have been Charles Francis Adams, Arnold Bennett, E.M. Delafield, Sir Arthur Conan Doyle (again), Ralph Waldo Emerson, William Butler Yeats, Thomas Hardy, Hedda Hopper, Elbert Hubbard, Grant Lewi, Edward Bulwer Lytton, and Thomas Mann.

Mechanical ability is quite common to this sign, because these people grasp and understand abstract mechanical principles. A Gemini woman can probably change a tire or fix her own car if she has to. Note that in the case of Jules Verne, mentioned above, we list him as a writer and he has Gemini rising, while we listed him for his prophetic skill and he has Sun in Aquarius.

It is not the nature of Gemini to hang to some particular frame of reference. Grant Lewi always told people, 'I'm not a joiner,'. He didn't want to be drawn into groups for fear that they might have some frame of reference to which they wanted to tie him. Gemini usually has many frames of reference and is always busy acquiring more. These people make good editors. They never bore people because they always have some new angle on something. Their interest of tomorrow is different from that of yesterday. To some people, they may seem inconsistent. The sign represents mental change and that goes on forever. Gemini people like to travel mentally and physically. A constant change of environment usually suits them fine. There can be a good deal of nervousness, restlessness and impatience. They want to get on to tomorrow. They are refreshing.

We seldom find these people in a mental rut, although we often find anxiety in both Gemini and Sagittarius. Gemini natives are usually free from the limitations of any particular frame of reference. They are free to go anywhere mentally and often physically. They can seldom be accused of dogma. We have never had a Sun-in Gemini man as President of the United States. He wouldn't have the patience to stick to one thing long enough to get there. James Farley came closer than any other Gemini man, but he was selling cement and running the Post Office Department at the same time. He did both very well.

As an intellectual sign, Gemini finds the easy way of doing things. Unlike Virgo, Taurus or Capricorn, these people see no reason to do things the hard way. When we see a long ten-page single-spaced letter in our mail, we can be quite sure of two things. It is from a

Gemini lady, and it is interesting and worth reading. Such letters are usually typed. They have so many interesting points of view on so many different projects simultaneously.

There is nothing wrong with a frame of reference if it is properly employed. One man may limit himself to medicine and devote his life to it. If we want the population of Chicago, we don't have to go and count people in New York, but when we have the figures on Chicago, we might like to compare them with figures form New York. In the academic world we find too many limiting frames of reference. A teacher often judges everything in every other field by conditions he finds in his own field. Because of lack of actual experience, he may tie himself to dogmas and they become his kind of reality.

Thus, we find that the principal purpose of the Social Non-Survival Dynamic is to RE-FORM society, but a GUIDE is needed. Because he is always changing his frame of reference, Gemini will be more likely to see the defects in the plan of re-form. He can often change his whole slant on life in an instant by changing his frame of reference. To you, the world is whatever your conception of it may be. If your conception isn't good, you can be very unhappy. If you have a few Gemini people around, listen to them, and they can probably alter your conceptions. It is seldom that Gemini ever lets anything become too important to him and you can save yourself a lot of grief when you are like that.

Most any religion excludes data. The majority of 'scientific' theories exclude data. In these pages, we are excluding any data we do not know about. Whenever facts can be presented that cause us to question some of the statements we have made, they should be carefully examined. The whole astronomical fraternity systematically excludes data, often deliberately. Let us back this statement up with some actual facts.

A decade and a half ago, Dr. Bart J. Bok, astronomer of Harvard University was scheduled to deliver a talk at the American Museum of Natural History in New York. Word was passed out that he was going to take the hide off astrology. By the time Dr. Bok faced his audience that audience consisted mainly of astrologers from up and down the east coast of the US. Unknown to Dr. Bok they had brought with them a court stenographer. In his talk, Dr. Bok paid tribute to the work of this writer, with which he stated that he was familiar. The tone of his talk was 'Let's get together and see what we can find out.'

After the meeting, the writer 'chanced' to mention to a young astronomer that a court stenographer was present. Soon a courier was sent to every astrology magazine. They were told that since no admission had been charged, the meeting was private; that they had no right to publish the talk and that should they do so they would be sued. It is not likely that their claims would have held up in court, but the magazines respected his wishes in the matter. The American Federation of Astrologers did publish the speech, and copies are probably available.

Next, *Sky Magazine*, an astronomical publication connected with Harvard University, published a speech supposedly delivered by Bok on that evening at the American Museum of Natural History. It was a talk condemning astrology, and there was no remote connection between what Bok said and what *Sky Magazine* stated he said. The whole story by *Sky Magazine* was a deliberate hoax, a falsehood and as outright a bit of intellectual dishonesty as has ever been perpetrated anywhere at any time.

Later, an astronomer connected with the group called on the writer and asked the writer not to hold any of this against Dr. Bok, offering assurance that Bok was not responsible and stating that the matter was out of his hands.

The head of the astronomical department was Harlow Shapley who probably can boast more degrees, honorary and otherwise, than any man in the United States. Therefore, one question was put to the astronomer.

'I'll only ask you one question. Is this the work of Harlow Shapley?'

The astronomer replied, 'It would be embarrassing for me to answer that question, and I would prefer not to.'

On another occasion, when an astronomer prepared a paper purporting to show statistics to disprove an astrological claim, the writer was able to prove that the results were obtained only by excluding data, which of course was dishonest. When these facts were presented to a certain astronomer who was making use of the paper, his reply was as follows: 'Well, after all, his intentions were good. He was against astrology.'

A principle has been placed in nature to protect us against this sort of thing. That principle is GEMINI, the Social Non-Survival Dynamic GUIDE. The Stalin Communists did not invent propaganda. Our own astronomers are unequaled experts in this field. Throughout the world today, the systematic exclusion of data, in order that we may believe the world to be something that it is not, is common practice. It is very important that we allow our children to know this for their own protection. Many teachers are forced to exclude data in order to hold down their jobs. The exclusion of data is not always conscious. It is often subconscious. What our eyes may see is censured in the subconscious. Things are deleted and are never allowed to reach the conscious. Dogma works in this fashion. In the majority of cases, the exclusion of data is not dishonest. It is an automatic functioning of the subconscious. To vast numbers of people, their frame of reference is identified with security. They fear having a frame of reference upset. Charles Fort devoted much of his life to accumulating data that had been excluded by the academic and 'scientific' worlds. You must never fear having your frame of reference upset. There can be no intellectual freedom until many accepted frames of reference are upset. Man is today a complete prisoner of standardized accepted frames of reference. They are a block to the functioning of the Non-Survival GUIDES. It is unwise to 'believe' in anything. This statement does not conflict with Faith. You can have faith in the future and in God. You can have faith in the abstract. You can have faith in your ability to meet tomorrow, and if the GUIDES are functioning, tomorrow will never give you any trouble. Therefore, it is vitally important to allow nothing to interfere with the functioning of the GUIDES. Progress and the improvement of society (non-survival of form or RE-FORM) can be brought about only through altering our frames of reference. When a mathematician as great (and he is great) as Hogben teaches us that mathematics is a science of measurement, he is cutting us off from the greatest part of truth. He is giving us a limitation in the form of a frame of reference. The student is unlikely to go beyond that frame of reference, and until he does, he will never understand what mathematics is.

Fermat was a different kind of a mathematician. He was the father of a relatively new science known as Number Theory. Fermat wrote out many new mathematical theorems, but he was always too busy and did not have time to write out or publish the proof of his theorems. Yet, with one exception, the proofs of all of his theorems were re-discovered after his death. The one exception is classically known as Fermat's Last Theorem [1637]. In Lesson One, we mentioned the Pythagorean Theorem represented by the expression that in any right-angled triangle, a^2 plus b^2 equals c^2. Fermet wrote another theorem which stated that when 'n' is greater than 2, a^n plus b^n cannot equal c^n. Fermat made a note to the effect that he had found a simple, 'beautiful' proof of this theorem, but that he did not have time to write it down. Because proof has been found of all other theorems of Fermat, no doubt is expressed as to his finding it, but no other mathematician has ever been able to find proof of the theorem. [ed. This theorem was finally proved in 1994 by Andrew Wiles] They have found proof for many values of 'n', but no overall proof for all values of 'n' has ever been found. Prior to World War I, a German institution offered a very large financial reward for proof, but it was never collected. Since the reward was in old German Marks, it had no value when the war was over.

In tracing the history of the development of the modern calculus of probability, Hogben, the person who has done more than any other to clarify mathematics for the common man, despite his limited frame of reference, tells us, 'Today it may seem a far cry from the card table to the insurance corporation. It is still more surprising to see the astrologer in the background of the picture.'

Both modern astronomy and mathematics are offspring of the original astrology, but each has adopted a limiting frame of reference. In each case, progress has been limited and retarded by an adopted frame of reference, but in the field of mathematics we have no evidence that any dishonesty has been involved. The limiting frames of reference originated in the church, probably with the best of intentions, in an effort to subdue any ideas of fatalism and try and uphold the doctrine of free will. Yet, this was a matter of truth being excluded by a frame of reference. From a heredity point of view, there is a factor of fatalism in the sense that a horse cannot become an accomplished pianist because he has hoofs instead of hands. You can't play a piano with hoofs—as far as we know.

A frame of reference can be, at one and the same time, useful and a curse. Obeying orders to stick to his frame of reference helps the astronomer to keep his job, get paid, and support his family. His conduct serves the same limited purpose as that of the bank robber who also supports his family. Barring the possibility of a revolution, the astronomer enjoys the additional factor of security. He isn't likely to be picked up by the cops, but in a revolution, which usually means a complete change in the frame of reference, these people are usually the first ones who are stood against a wall and shot. They may go on through generations, but they are never certain that the revolution may not come tomorrow and when it does, their numbers are up. When the non-survival factors sufficiently outweigh the survival factors, the revolution always comes. When the revolution comes they will be unprepared for it, because people with a fixed frame of reference have no functioning of the GUIDES. They are always caught off guard. They are completely dependent upon a continued functioning of the survival dynamics and the reactors.

We live in a world where right and wrong are determined by loyalty to a particular frame of reference. Religious frames of reference differ in different places and in different churches. In a remote part of Mexico is a tribe where our customs would be frowned upon. They have a religious wedding service. When the marriage service is completed, the bride is required to go away for one week with the best man. It is his duty to train her so that at the end of the week she will be left fit to serve as a wife to her husband. It would be considered as highly immoral for a bride to live with her husband without this training interval.

To us, these people are 'ignorant'; but to those people, we are 'ignorant'. It can depend on one's frame of reference.

People in whom the GUIDES function never have anything to worry about. Whatever the future may be, they can meet it. If they understand the functioning of the survival and non-survival dynamics as well as the reactors and the guides, they can better understand tomorrow.

The astrology that has been passed down to us also associated Gemini with one's relations with brothers and sisters and relatives. Brothers and sisters are those in whom the hereditary factors are exactly the same. Two brothers (excluding half brothers) have exactly the same ancestors. Yet, while they are similar in many ways, they are completely dissimilar in other ways, a fact that astrology alone explains. **Heredity explains similarities**, like all the members of a centipede family having a lot of legs, **while astrology explains dissimilarities**, as in the case of one man who is ambitious while his full-blooded brother is not.

Brothers and sisters in a family may have quite different frames of reference aside from those that are forced upon them by their families. They may all be brought up in the same church, but one may change his religion and the others do not. The more brothers and sisters we have, the more possibility there is in early life of being subjected to different points of view. We are forced to put up with the frames of reference of our brothers and sisters while we are still young.

We can be more free of dogma if we consider all possible frames of reference. The astrologer who rules out the possibilities of other sciences that have been called occult, such as palmistry, divination, telling fortunes by cards, etc., has limited his frame of reference just as an astronomer is limited.

We are continually influenced by our feelings and it is important to KNOW whether those feelings are stimulated by survival or non-survival factors.

This completes our preliminary study of the twelve basic principles of astrology. We will live with these twelve principles throughout the rest of this course, for we will find them in other places than the signs of the zodiac. We will find them in the astrological 'houses' in the planets themselves, and in the planetary aspects. These twelve principles are mathematical abstractions. They operate everywhere.

LESSON EIGHT

DESIGN IN THE SOLAR SYSTEM

It has already been emphasized that the greatest mathematical and astronomical discoveries were made by men who were seeking cosmic design. They were often very religious men who were seeking a divine plan. It is quite apparent that the ancients knew about, or were seeking, a design in the solar system. If they were seeking it, we do not know whether they found it. We do know that the design was there. It is possible that they may have know about it and concealed the truth in the same manner that we tried to conceal the truth about atoms. We fear that information about atoms in the wrong hands may destroy the Earth. It would appear that the ancients may have had some similar fears. There was some belief that knowledge was for the chosen few. Although there is no indication that Pythagoras had such views, his followers did, and the Pythagorean schools were secret schools. Those taught were sworn to secrecy. The Pythagoreans were mighty serious about this, and violations were subject to the death penalty. In the fourth century B.C., Hippasus, a member of one of the Pythagorean societies made a public announcement that he had discovered a solid with 12 faces [ed. dodecahedron inside a sphere along with the irrational number $\sqrt{2}$] (12 again). Because he offered this information to the public, the death penalty was immediately imposed. He was drowned in his bath for giving away mathematical truths. (In our own day, the Rosenbergs were executed for a similar offense.) Insofar as can be determined, such a 12-face solid (with 5-sided surfaces) were unknown to Pythagoras himself, unless he too was holding out.

Since we must consider all possibilities, we must also consider that more ancient ancients than those we know anything about may have known far more than the particular ancients we do know something about. Knowledge may have become lost, just as a lot of people today are wishing the secrets of the atom could get lost.

However, we do have the fact that the ancients saw a significance in numbers or integers that modern mathematicians have ignored as mystic. The numbers 7 and 12 were very important to them. Later in these lessons, we will show how, in astrological geometry, 7 become the 12. Let us quote a paragraph from Hogben's popular *Mathematics for the Millions:*

When we amuse ourselves at the expense of these early societies struggling to grasp the language of number in the childhood of civilization, it behoves us to ask whether we ourselves have completely grown out of magic. Caution is all the more pertinent when we recall the queer theosophical preoccupations of men like Pascal and Newton, who contributed so much to the sort of mathematics which is most useful in solving problems of measurement in the age of machinery. For European civilizations the numbers in which magical properties reside are more particularly seven and three. Theology bequeathed to us the seven golden candlesticks, the seven evil spirits cast out of Magdalen, the seven sorrows, the seven deadly sins, the seven (deadlier) virtues and the seven fold amen. The number seven has not been neglected by the unofficial theologians more usually referred to as philosophers. In the year that Piazzi discovered Ceres (as asteroid), seven planets were known: namely, Mercury, Venus, Earth, Mars, Jupiter, Saturn, Uranus. In the same year the Prussian philosopher Hegel wrote upbraiding scientists for the neglect of philosophy. He illustrated his disapproval of the amount of time astronomers wasted in looking for a new planet when philosophy clearly established the only possible number as seven. Since then other planets have been discovered. Neptune followed shortly after (1846). Pluto was discovered in 1930, because astronomers are materialist so long as they remain in their observatories.

Actually, in seeking more planets, astronomers were keeping an open mind, which is very helpful to scientists but very rare for astronomers. Hogben himself discloses that he is locked within a frame of reference brought about by the mental limitation he imposes on himself when he defies mathematics as a mere science of measurement. What we wish to emphasize is the religious and philosophical determination to keep alive the significance of the integers 7 and 12. Without this determination, astrology would have died out completely, because the division of the circle into twelve equal parts is our most basic key. Had it been divided into 11 or 13 equal parts, everything would have been lost. We agree with Hogben that astronomers are usually materialists, but mathematics is not materialism. It is completely a study of abstractions, and because Hogben limited himself to a conception of mathematics as it might be applied to material things, his frame of reference did not permit him to view more than a very small part of the whole. Some of the greatest facts of all had to be excluded. Modern science works within a relatively narrow frame of reference which makes it necessary to constantly exclude a very large ratio of the facts. If the scientist loves his wife, and her affections are stolen by another man, he encounters what was left out of his textbook. He encounters emotion. He will find it hard to convince himself that his emotion is less real than the materials he has been measuring, but none of his formulae will help him when it comes to measuring his emotions, much less controlling them. Theologians, philosophers and astrologers have made errors, but that would appear to identify them with so-called 'scientists'.

We will show later in these lessons, there was definite reason for keeping alive the significance of 7 and 12, and we will show how these two numbers relate to each other.

First, let us get a picture of the solar system. We have the Sun as the center, surrounded by circles of various sizes called orbits. Although these are not really circles but ellipses, they are not too eccentric and they are almost circles. These imaginary ellipses are the paths over which the planets travel. It should be realized that they do not lie in the same plane of space. The orbit of Pluto is inclined to that of the Earth by 17 degrees, that of Mercury by 7 degrees. The others are closer. The orbit of Pluto has the greatest eccentricity, that of Venus the least. In the following diagram, our relative distance between orbits is highly inaccurate, because we are only concerned with the order of the orbits.

We want to call your attention to the order of these planetary orbits. This is one thing you will want to learn, if you do not already know it. Starting at the center and going out into space, it runs: Sun, Mercury, Venus, Earth, Mars, Jupiter, Saturn, Uranus, Neptune, Pluto, and whatever may exist beyond Pluto. **Between the orbits of Mars and Jupiter, there are hundreds of little objects called asteroids or planetoids which also revolve around the Sun, but we know of no astrological significance they may have.** The biggest would make only a good sized mountain on the Earth. We will ignore them because we know nothing of any consequence about them. You don't have to ignore them, but we will for now.

The ancients made an association between the planets and the signs of the zodiac. They called the planets the 'rulers' of the zodiacal signs. We do not know for certain how that work 'ruler' crept in here, but let us point out that the word has a double meaning. A ruler may be a king who rules over a land, or it may be something with which you measure. If we employ the second meaning of the word it takes on an interesting significance in astrology.

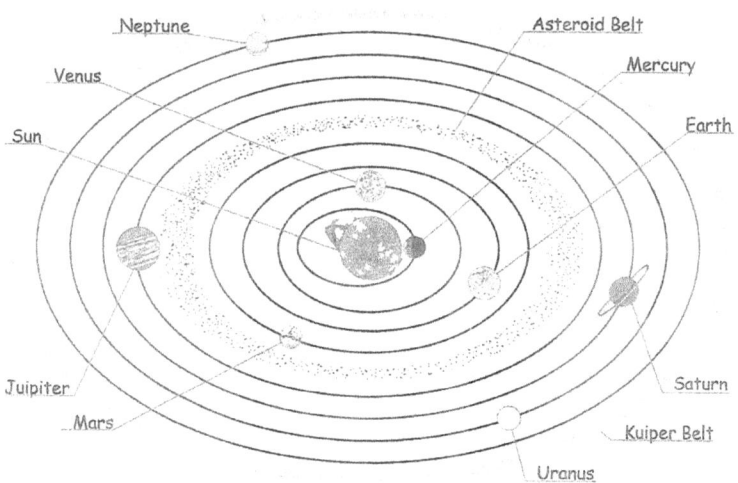

[ed. **Classic Solar System** with Pluto and Eris as new sign rulers, is there one more to complete 12 rulers?]

Each zodiacal sign had a ruling planet. There is another object nearby that we did not mention. It is the Moon. The ancients employed the Moon as one of these rulers. Insofar as we know, the ancients knew nothing about planets beyond Saturn. Any planet beyond Saturn is invisible to the naked eye. If you are on the Earth that leaves SEVEN visible bodies: Moon, Sun Mercury Venus, Mars, Jupiter and Saturn. If you were on the Moon, there would still be seven visible bodies, because you would view the Earth instead of the Moon. The ancients had a definite way of assigning these seven bodies to 12 zodiacal signs. This is shown in the next diagram.

Lesson Eight

Hellenistic Planetary Order with Sign Rulership

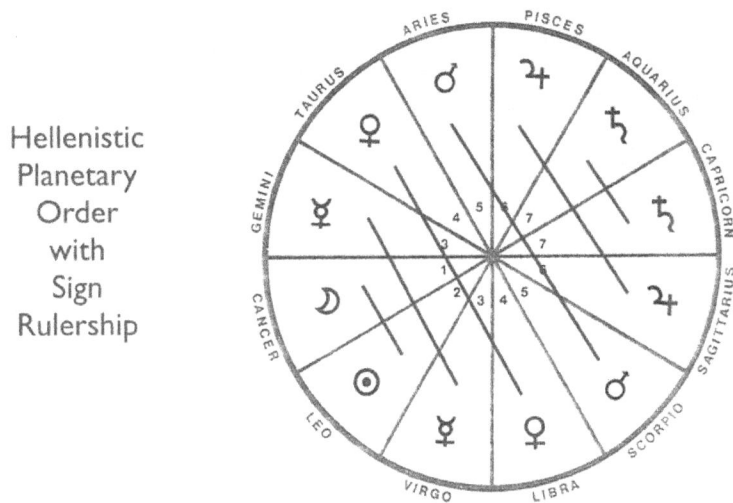

Ancient Rulership to Zodiac Signs

This is the incomplete design left to us by the ancients, and for thousands of years nobody noticed that the rest of the design could be filled in, could be completed, when the key was realized. **The key is mean distance from the Earth.** The numbers indicate the order in which each planet appears when mean distance of the various bodies form the Earth is considered. It is known that the ancient mathematicians prepared magic squares where several numbers were purposely omitted. The person who was seeking design would immediately understand and could detect the missing factors. The above diagram carries the subtle suggestion that ancients far back may have known more about the solar system than astronomers know today. Thwore diagram suggests the existence of two undiscovered planets beyond the orbit of Pluto. Because people did not think in terms of cosmic design, the significance of the above diagram remained secret for thousands of years.

The Moon was assigned to Cancer, the Sun to Leo, Mercury to both Virgo and Gemini, Venus to both Libra and Taurus, Mars to both Scorpio and Aries, Jupiter to both Sagittarius and Pisces, Saturn to both Capricorn and Aquarius. [ed. Hellenistic Planetary Order] In this way, they had seven bodies ruling twelve signs. There is an off factor here which, to our knowledge, had never been noted by modern astrologers at this time when the writer began investigating astrology. Although he spotted it in 1933, he originally called attention to it in

1938 in a book entitled, *A New Experiment in Astrology*. The book was more or less ignored by the majority of astrologers, and reviews pictured it as claiming almost everything on Earth except what it did claim. To this day, the content of the book has not been grasped. If it had been, much of astrology as it exists would be difference. Elbert Benjamine, founder of a theological school of astrology [ed. aka C. C. Zain, Church of Light, born 12 Dec 1882, 5:55am Abel, Iowa] made alleged quotations from the book, and when he was asked to explain where he had found the various statements quoted, he admitted that he couldn't find them anywhere in the book. At the time when he made the quotations, he had never read the book.

If you will look at the diagram above, you will note that beginning in Cancer and running counterclockwise to Capricorn, the ancients assigned the planets **IN EXACT ACCORDANCE with the bodies' mean distance from the Earth**. Because the Moon is nearest, we have assigned it the number 1, the Sun-2, Mercury-3, Venus-4, Mars-5, etc. Mercury Venus and Mars can be nearer to the Earth than the Sun, but when considering average distance, the Sun is closer.

If we start in Gemini, and go around the circle clockwise to Aquarius, we find the same kind of sequence. The order coincides with mean distance from the Earth. This gives us an interesting problem in mathematical probability. We have part of an arithmetical pattern here. What is the probability that these planets were arranged in this fashion by chance?

There are 5040 (12 squared x 7 x 5) ways in which the planets could have been arranged in those signs from Cancer to Capricorn, but only two of those ways would have coincided with the factor of mean distance. (The other way would be to start in Capricorn and finish in Cancer, going clockwise.) Cutting 5040 in half, this makes the odds 1219 to 1 against this arrangement being due to chance.

Considering the five remaining spaces, what are the odds against those also being assigned in accord with mean distance? There are 120 ways in which 5 planets could have been arranged in 5 spaces, only 2 of which would have conformed to the pattern, making the odds 50 to 1. When we consider the odds against the second arrangement applying after the first arrangement had already applied, the odds are (2520 x 60) - 1 to 1, or 151,199 to 1.

Here is one of the most extraordinary facts of astrology that has been overlooked and ignored for the last 2500 years. An astronomer can ignore a fact of this kind, but a mathematician cannot. However, this is but a tiny part of the coincidence. Even greater odds are involved. The symmetry, the mathematical design, does not stop here. It continues.

You will note that by putting Mars in Both Scorpio and Aries, the ancients were associating what we have described as the FAMILY SURVIVAL DYNAMIC with the FAMILY NON-SURVIVIAL DYNAMIC.

By associating Jupiter with both Pisces and Sagittarius, they were associating the SOCIAL SURVIVAL DYNAMIC with the SOCIAL NON-SURVIVAL DYNAMIC.

By placing Venus in both Taurus and Libra, they associated the FAMILY SURVIVAL DYNAMIC REACTOR with the FAMILY NON-SURVIVAL DYNAMIC GUIDE.

By placing Mercury in both Virgo and Gemini, they associated the SOCIAL SURVIVAL DYNAMIC REACTOR with the SOCIAL NON-SURVIVAL DYNAMIC GUIDE.

They neglected to put the Sun or Moon in both Cancer and Leo, which was the only necessary step left to complete this particular symmetry. Then they would have associated the INDIVIDUAL SURVIVIAL DYNAMIC with the INDIVIDUAL NON-SURVIVAL DYNAMIC.

We have not reached the end of the design.

When Uranus was discovered, the materialists accepted the event with great glee. This, the astronomers told us, disproved astrology. Instead of seven solar bodies, there were eight. The magic qualities of 7 were disproved, or so they thought.

There was a bit of confusion in the world of astrology also. This did appear to upset things, but unlike the astronomers who are supposed to make so many millions of observations but yet fail to observe, the astrologers began making observations, and in time, they came up with a conclusion. It had been a mistake to put Saturn in Aquarius. It belonged to Capricorn. Uranus was the ruler of Aquarius. Strange as it may seem, all astrologers so agreed on this. In studying Uranus, they found the same qualities that they found in studying Aquarius. Still unconscious of the fact of mean distance, they had placed an 8 in Aquarius and thus continued the sequence. This increased the odds against the first part of the pattern being due to chance to 20,159 to 1. Neptune was discovered, and after some years of observations, the astrologers agreed that Neptune and not Jupiter belonged in Pisces. Still unconscious of the factor of mean distance, they had again continued the sequence and had placed 9 in Pisces, and this time they increased the odds to 181,339 to 1.

In 1930, Pluto was discovered. This time, there was some disagreement. Some astrologers placed Pluto in Scorpio, others in Aries. Placing it is Aries conformed to the pattern again, and drove the odds to 1,814,399 to 1. Oddly, placing it in Scorpio also conformed from the other point of view. When you count around the other way, 10 falls in Scorpio.

Even more strange is the fact that the astrologers who identified Pluto with Scorpio were an occult group and their conclusions came out of study of Greek mythology. Even these methods brought about an unconscious conformance with the arithmetical pattern that was piecing itself together.

The writer first observed that this connection between planets and zodiacal signs conformed to mean distances in late September 1933, and from that time on assigned Pluto to Aries. *The student may later find it of interest to note that Jupiter, Mercury and Sun were in Libra at that time, the sign that we identify with an understanding of mathematics.* More interesting might be the fact that the whole idea just popped into the writer's head while in bed, dozing off to sleep. He suddenly saw the pattern of the whole, and forced himself out of bed to write it down, in fear that he might not remember it on the following morning.

The pattern is not yet complete, but only two pieces are missing from the jigsaw puzzle. And we know what they are like and where they belong. To complete the pattern, there must be two more planets outside the orbit of Pluto, and the first must be assigned to Taurus, the last to Gemini.

The zodiac is an abstract mathematical pattern. It is divided into 12 equal parts. The association of planets with abstract signs of the zodiac implies there are 12 objects other than the Earth in the solar system when the Moon is counted. On another planet, our Moon would have no significance, and the number of signs of the zodiac for another planet like Jupiter which has its own 12 (at least) moons, could vary, just as the number of electrons in atoms of difference metals vary. Thus, life on another planet could be expected to be quite different from life on Earth.

For the benefit of the mathematically minded, we would like to explain the computation of odds referred to above. The astrologers have unconsciously fitted ten planets into ten spaces in one of only two ways that would conform to mean distance of the bodies from the Earth. The number of ways that ten numbers can be arranged in ten spaces will be factorial 10, which means (10 x 9 x 8 x 7 x 6 x 5 x 4 x 3 x 2 x 1). You can multiply these out if you choose. The answer is 3,628,800. Since two of these ways would conform to the pattern, one counting clockwise, the other counterclockwise, the chances are 2 in 3,628,800 or 1 chance in 1,814,400. This gives odds of 1,814,399 to 1 against this pattern having been an accident. With the discovery

Lesson Eight

of two more planets the pattern will be complete. However, we are already close enough to visualize the complete design. And that means close enough to give the astrological characteristics of the missing planets. The first planet beyond Pluto must have the same characteristics as Taurus, while the last planet out must have the same characteristics as Gemini.

Just as there are seven visible bodies in the solar system, as viewed by Man on the Earth, there are seven white keys in an octave on a piano. Just as there are five black keys in the octave, there would appear to be five planets invisible to Man's naked eye. This does not mean that the planets cause the keys on the piano nor that the keys on the piano cause the planets. It merely illustrates an acausal relationship in the coincidence, the same mathematical design.

On the next page, we offer another diagram showing the planets and their numbers going around the circle both ways, starting from Leo and going clockwise, starting from Cancer and going counterclockwise. This is a perfectly symmetrical pattern. It is a mathematical design. In all of their associations of planets with zodiacal signs, the astrologer al all known times have unconsciously conformed to this design. We have added two theoretical planets and have called them 'Y' and 'Z'.

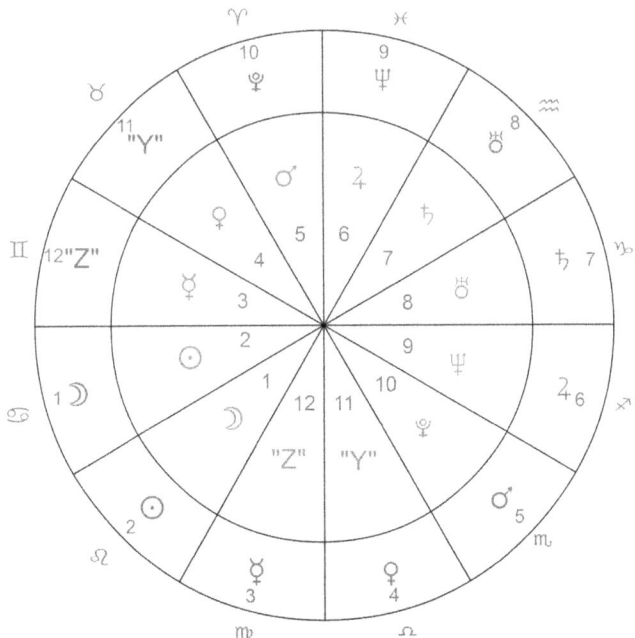

Dual Rulership of Signs and Houses

Rulerships of Duality
Sign and House

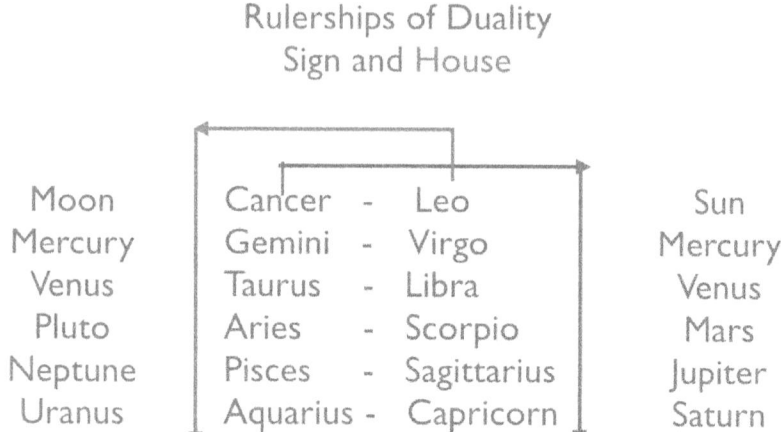

Clockwise and Counterclockwise Rulership Count

Sign Count	House Count
Cancer	Leo
Leo	Cancer
Virgo	Gemini
Libra	Taurus
Scorpio	Aries
Sagittarius	Pisces
Capricorn	Capricorn
Pisces	Sagittarius
Aries	Scorpio
Taurus	Libra
Gemini	Virgo

Complete Zodiac Rulership Pattern

     The mathematical pattern is complete. You can now compare this with the earlier diagram. Nothing that appeared in the other diagram has been changed or altered, but the other half of the picture has been added. We have completely symmetrical pattern when the missing pieces are filled in. Astrology shows a mathematical relationship between distance from the center of a circle and twelve divisions of space around the circle, just as the mathematical **Pi** shows a relationship between the diameter and circumference of a

Lesson Eight

circle. No matter how large the circle, **Pi** always shows the exact relationship of diameter to circumference. Did the ancients actually know and understand this whole pattern, and did they hide it in the same manner that they hid the corners of their mathematical magic squares?

Now let us look at another diagram on the following page. Here we have merely drawn lines to connect the numbers in the clockwise count with the numbers in the counterclockwise count. We get an interesting design. It is a design that closely resembles that of a magnetic field.

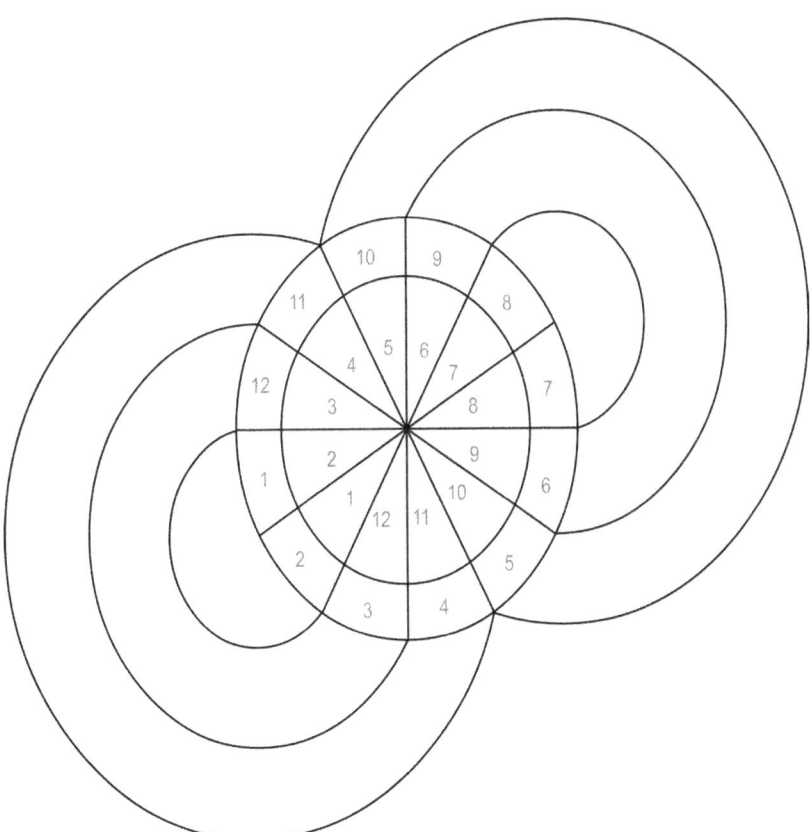

Zodiac imagined as a Magnetic Field

This is the same diagram shown above with additional lines drawn around the outside of the circle, connecting the numbers in the clockwise count with the same numbers in the counterclockwise count around the circle. **This does not imply that we dealing**

with a magnetic field, but it is suggests that some similar mathematical law may apply. The Earth will be the center of the above circle, as it has been the center of other diagrams.

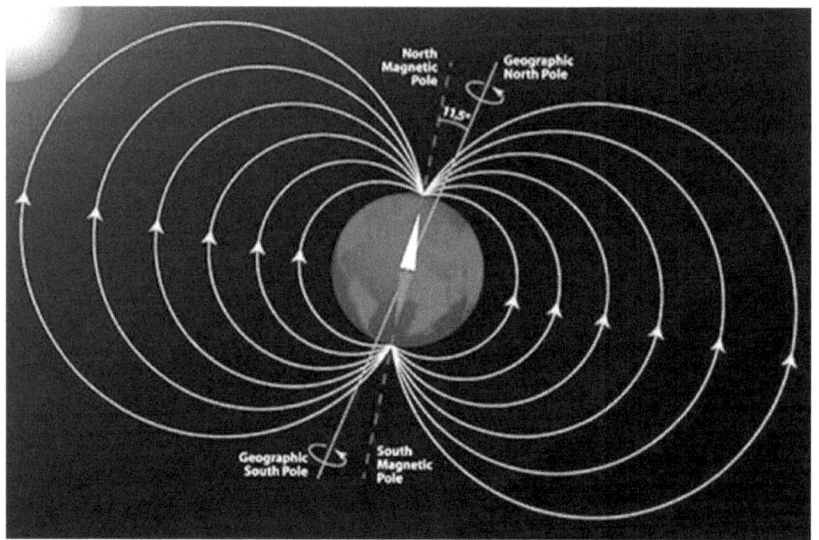

Earth's Magnetic Field

That does not mean that it IS a magnetic field any more than the solar system is a piano. If you study this design, you will find that a SURVIVAL DYNAMIC is always connected with a corresponding NON-SURVIVAL DYNAMIC, and a SURVIVAL REACTOR is always connected with a corresponding NON-SURVIVAL GUIDE. An INDIVIDUAL factor is connected with an INDIVIDUAL factor. A FAMILY factor is connected with a FAMILY factor. A SOCIAL factor is connected with a SOCIAL factor. There are no exceptions to the rule. **The pattern is complete symmetry. There are no missing pieces. The jigsaw puzzle has been put together.** The mystery lies in the fact that for at least 2500 years nobody ever put the pieces together. As you grow more familiar with the pattern, it will become simplicity itself. It is nothing but an abstract mathematical figure, but the only such figure that has ever caused us to find a connection between distance from a center and divisions of a circle into twelve equal parts. These two factors appear to involve a factor of coincidence, but it may be only the acausal coincidence that we find connecting a piano and the solar system. We can employ the white keys to represent visible planets, the black keys to represent invisible planets. As you will later see, both counts, the clockwise

Lesson Eight

and the counterclockwise, have a very definite significance, and each is to be employed under different circumstances.

We will not need to devote much space to an explanation of what the planets mean, for the simple reason that they mean the same thing that is meant by the signs of the zodiac. The same twelve basic principles expressed in the zodiacal signs are expressed in the planets. Just as you have linked a basic principle with a particular zodiacal sign, you will now link the same principle with a planet. The following table will show the manner in which this applies.

	Zodiacal Sign	Planet	Sign #	House #
Water Survival				
Individual	Cancer	Moon	First	Second
Family	Scorpio	Mars	Fifth	Tenth
Social	Pisces	Neptune	Ninth	Sixth
Earth Reactors				
Individual	Capricorn	Saturn	Seventh	Eighth
Family	Taurus	'Y'	Eleventh	Fourth
Social	Virgo	Mercury	Third	Twelfth
Fire Non-Survival Dynamics				
Individual	Leo	Sun	Second	First
Family	Aries	Pluto	Tenth	Fifth
Social	Sagittarius	Jupiter	Sixth	Ninth
Air Guides				
Individual	Aquarius	Uranus	Eighth	Seventh
Family	Libra	Venus	Fourth	Eleventh
Social	Gemini	'Z'	Twelfth	Third

The numbers at the right side of the page are the same numbers that appear in our diagrams. The **Sign#** column represents mean distance from the Earth insofar as the named planet is concerned. The figures in the **House#** column represent the count the other way around the zodiacal circle. In this way, 1 is joined with 2, 3–12, 4–11, 5–10, 6–9, and 7–8. It will be necessary to retain both of these counts as we will later see. Each has a significance.

If you omit one and substitute 12 (for the 1 would become 13 if you continue counting), the two integers joined each time will always total 15.

We have shown that there is **only 1 chance in 1,814,400** of the counterclockwise count of the planets in the zodiacal signs being due to chance. We have also shown that there was 1 chance in 60 of the astrologers hitting the target five consecutive times relative to the clockwise count, but the target was hit again when the occult group associated Pluto with Scorpio. There are 720 ways in which 6 planets can be arranged in 6 spaces (6 x 5 x 4 x 3 x 2 x 1), only 2 of which would conform to mean distance, meaning that there is 1 chance in 360 that these selections were due to chance alone. Now, to determine the probability that the entire mathematical pattern was a matter of chance, we can say there is one chance in 360 x 1,814,400 or one change in 653,184,000. **The mathematical odds against the possibility that the astrologers were deceiving themselves are 653,183,999 to 1.**

In Lesson 4, we presented a diagram identifying time with the signs of the zodiac. This was a pattern. Patterns are not due to chance. They involve abstract laws. They are called natural laws because we find them in nature, but what we find in nature is not the mold. The mold is the abstract law itself. In nature, we find only what has been formed by the mold. However, by making the identification of planets with signs of the zodiac as we have done in this lesson, we encounter a new association, **because we can now associate time with the planets in the same manner as we have done with the zodiacal signs.** Certain solar bodies are related to the perpetuation of forms of the past, while other bodies are to be identified with destroying the form of the past that the pattern of the future may come into being.

So, if we arrange the solar bodies in the order of their mean distance from the Earth and relate them to past and future, we will come up with the following table:

Avg. Mean Distance

One	Moon	Past
Two	Sun	Future
Three	Mercury	Past
Four	Venus	Future
Five	Mars	Past
Six	Jupiter	Future

Lesson Eight

Seven	Saturn	Past
Eight	Uranus	Future
Nine	Neptune	Past
Ten	Pluto	Future
Eleven	'Y' Eris	Past
Twelve	'Z'	Future

The symbols, 'Y' and 'Z' represent two hypothetical planets out beyond the orbits of Pluto. We have never seen these planets. Their existence is merely a matter of calculation. Neither have we seen an atom. Its existence is merely a matter of calculation. However, we have demonstrated that the probability of those planets being there is 653,183,999 to 1. The astrological pattern is not complete until these two missing pieces of the jigsaw puzzle are added.

It is extremely difficult of the writer to visualize how the whole superstructure of astrology could have been discovered by Man except in the same manner that the atom was discovered, by calculation. If the original knowledge came from the calculations of super-mathematicians, who were they? Surely, no one that history can tell us anything about. If these super-mathematicians knew from their own astrology that civilization was to go into a decline for thousands of years, it might account for much that was done. Why do we dig up the twelve symbols of the signs of the zodiac carved on stone throughout the world? The conception that the great pyramid was a tomb motivated by a king's vanity is childish when we consider that it is a mathematical figure involving facts of astronomy. When we pat ourselves on the back while observing the great structures, buildings and dams we have constructed, we ignore the fact that no modern structure compares in cubic yards of material with the wall that surrounded the ancient city of Babylon. The ancients left behind them messages in the form of design and symbols which have remained un-interpreted for thousands of years. After the tremendous amount of labor that was employed in carving the Aztec Calendar Stone, what was done with it? It was hidden. It was buried in the ground, where it was not discovered until more than a century after Cortez entered Mexico City. The diameter of the large circle is 12 feet. (Do not place significance on 12 here because the foot is an arbitrary measurement.) The stone is three feet thick, and its weight is over 20 tons. In the center of the circle is the symbol of the Sun (not the Earth). Around it was the symbols of FIRE, AIR, EARTH AND WATER. Other markings represent such cycles as days, weeks and months in the Aztec Calendar system. At the time it was found, it was a more perfect calendar than any that had been designed by astronomers of the time. Interesting is the fact that after the stone was found by the Spaniards, it was hidden again by the church, in the fear that knowledge of the symbols and the story told by the stone might cause people to abandon the church. It was buried by the theologists for another 150 years.

What Hogben describes as the cradle of civilization may actually have been the tomb of a former civilization. Of course there are legends about Atlantis and Lemuria, sunken continents which supposedly held more advanced civilizations than ours. We are not authorities on Atlantis and Lemuria, but speculations on the possible existence of such civilizations are interesting, and even if these speculations contain a vast amount of false information, they should be combed for any few threads of fact which may possibly exist.

One such speculation included the claim that the Lemurians colonized the east coast of Asia and the west coast of South America before the continent sank into the Pacific, and that after the disaster, those on the coast of Asia thereafter bowed to the east to the former motherland in their religious cults. This conforms to the curious fact that the religious cults of South American bowed, not to the east, but to the west, in their religious ceremonies.

The ancients have been described as being superstitious by some of the moderns, but they could have described our moderns as being superstitious. The nebular hypothesis and many so-called scientific theories are actually superstitions. The astronomers are busy making observations. They are busy counting the number of stars in the heavens., and they might as well count the grains of sand on the Earth.

We associate the survival factors with stability, the non-survival factors with instability. Oddly, the stability of an atom is said to have a relationship with whether the number of electrons is odd or even.

It will help your astrology if you begin early to think of astrology as a science of design in the same way that mathematics is a science of design. Your personality and your character is a design. It is actually different in some respect from the design of any other person. The design of the solar system at this particular moment is also the design of whatever is born at this particular moment. In astrology, you are always comparing the design of one moment with the design of another moment. Two moments of time can be harmonious or discordant to each other. In that respect some days may appear harmonious or discordant for you. That which may appear discordant may be more harmonious when you understand it. It is necessary for you to become familiar with your own design.

Much of your own character is invisible to you. There are parts of your nature that may never have had an opportunity of expressing themselves. Some hidden part of nature may suddenly be stirred tomorrow, because the design of tomorrow atunes to the design of your birth in a way that has not previously occurred. All astrological designs resemble dials, and you can think of the dials on your radio or television sets. A slight twist of the dial may tune out Kansas City and tune in Chicago. The astrological dial is more complicated. It is constantly turning. It is ever tuning things in and tuning other things out. That is why your interests shift from year to year, from day to day, from minute to minute. We are always comparing design, one with another. The man who experiences a sudden sweep of popularity has merely run into a design that allows his own personal design to express itself

LESSON NINE

THE ASTROLOGICAL HOUSES AND PLANETARY ASPECTS

In a rather primitive fashion, astrology has passed down to us what have long been known as the 'houses' of a horoscope. Like a 'sign' of the zodiac, a house is merely one-twelfth of a circle, so there are twelve astrological houses to a horoscope just as there are twelve astrological signs to the zodiac. The twelve houses represent the very same basic astrological principles outlined in lessons 2 to 7.

When a surveyor is measuring land, he has to have one 'point' from which to begin his measurements, and so it is with astrology. If we can be sure of one point on the circumference of a circle, we can measure off the other points. Some other starting point would do just as well, but we have to have some point from which to begin. In lesson one, we began measuring the zodiac from that mathematical point where a straight line can be drawn through both the plane of the Earth's orbit and the pane of the Earth's equator. Some other point would have done just as well, so long as we were sure of it.

If we could see the plane of the Earth's orbit, it would cut across the sky from that point on the eastern horizon where the Sun rises, to that point on the western horizon where the Sun sets. Follow the course of the Sun from sunrise to sunset, across the sky, and that is the plane of the Earth's orbit. It is the ecliptic, the plane of the zodiac. In winter, this circle will be lower in the southern sky than in summer, for in winter the Earth tilts northward away from this great circle, and in summer it tilts back southward again, so that the great circle comes farther north to our observation.

We will use that mathematical point where the rising Sun crosses the circle of the horizon as a point from which to measure. In other words, the point where you see the sun rise on the eastern horizon is what we call the Ascendant. We will measure the astrological houses from this point.

Different schools of astrology measure the 'houses' in three different planes of space. Although we will explain all three planes later, for the present we will confine ourselves to one of these planes, the one which our experience has indicated as most reliable. You can investigate the other two planes at your leisure. We will keep everything in the same plane of space, the plane of the Earth's orbit.

We will measure the 'houses' along this lane in the same manner that we measure the zodiacal signs along this plane, but there will be one important difference. **The houses will remain fixed with the Earth. They will move only as the Earth moves, while the zodiacal signs move only in accord with that straight line that passes through both the plane of the Earth's orbit and the plane of the Earth's equator.** (lesson one) The zodiac is almost, but not quite, stationary with the fixed stars. There is actually a slippage, and in something like 26,000 years, the zodiac slips all the way around the circle of the fixed stars.

Starting at the Ascendant, or the point where the Sun crosses the eastern horizon as it rises, we will divide the circle into twelve equal parts, going counterclockwise, each space occupying 30 degrees of space, and these twelve spaces will be the twelve astrological houses of the horoscope.

A more primitive astrology has identified these twelve houses with twelve departments of life. Let us see what these departments of life are. In describing them, to avoid confusing the student, we will omit some claims which our experience has caused us to consider false. We will list the houses together with the things in life to which they are supposedly related, and in making this listing we will adhere to the same somewhat primitive conception that has been passed down to us. In this way, the student will have a better grasp of the entire situation when we are through. We urge you to realize that there is a certain primitiveness in this historic presentation, and yet, regardless of its primitive aspects, it is actually ingenious. It is ingenious in that it is basically sound. It is primitive only in that it jumps all the way from the mathematical to the material world, with too little consideration for the psychological and emotional factors that lie between. However, this is only an attempt to practicalize and make astrology useful, and if that is a fault, we possess the fault to a greater degree today than did our ancestors. The important thing to realize is that there are many points where a psychological or emotional cause can be interrupted before it manifests in material consequences. That is the difference between fatalism and free will. The latter is dependent upon knowledge and education, and to an ignorant person or one who does not care to improve himself, life can actually be more or less a matter of fatalism.

First, we will present a table showing the various factors with which the houses of the horoscope have become identified in the astrology that has been passed down to us. Then we show a diagram illustrating the twelve houses of the horoscope and also listing the factors with which each house has become associated or identified.

Lesson Nine

The astrologers of at least the last 2000 years have watched the planets travel around the circle, passing from one house to another. They have called some planets favorable, others unfavorable, and they have forecast good fortune for the department of life described by a particular house when a 'favorable' planet passed that way, misfortune when a 'malefic' planet crossed a house. Astrology is not as simple as that, and although this conception is on the primitive side, it is, nevertheless, basically correct. In many instances, it has been ignored or looked upon as superstition merely because of its simplicity, but the basic principles are true, despite the fact that they have been mixed up with much that is untrue.

House	Identification
First	Self, personality, personal expression and physical appearance
Second	Money, liquid assets, trade or barter
Third	The mind, relatives, brothers and sisters, short journeys
Fourth	Home, parent of opposite sex, land, mines and real property
Fifth	Children, personal projects, speculation and gambling*
Sixth	Help, pets, inferiors, employees, servants
Seventh	Marriage, partnership affairs, competitors
Eighth	Death, debts, money of other people, partners, estates
Ninth	Religion, philosophy, education, long distance travel, Life in foreign countries
Tenth	Business, the factor of authority, parent of same sex, discipline
Eleventh	Friends and social matters, fraternities, social groups
Twelfth	Work, service*

* Fifth House, the words romance and love affairs are omitted Twelfth House, the words prisons, hospitals, mental institutions, confinement are transferred to the Sixth House, this will be explained later.

When we think of the dark ages we have passed through since the days when master minds must have known a great deal more about astrology, it is less difficult to understand that errors have crept into the subject. It is more difficult to understand how knowledge survived at all through those centuries of ignorance, bias, bigotry, prejudice and intolerance. Even the church did all in its power to destroy this knowledge.

On the next diagram, we present the astrological houses as they appear in a horoscope. Compare this with the similar diagram in lesson 8, and you will see that our numbering matches the counterclockwise count in that diagram. The counterclockwise count illustrates the manner in which the twelve astrological principles described in lessons 2 to 7 fit into the twelve astrological houses, while the clockwise count shows how they fit into the zodiac. In other words, the houses run in one direction, while the signs of the zodiac run in the opposite direction. The planets go through the zodiac in a counterclockwise direction, while they go through the houses in a clockwise direction. The planets move from west to east, but because the Earth turns from west to east, and the houses turn with the Earth, the planets move across the sky and through the houses from east to west, just as the sun and moon rise in the east and set in the west. Once in every 23 hours and 56 minutes the zodiac will appear to move westward, and it will go all around the circle of the houses. This constant change of zodiac to houses ever continues. Human emotion and psychology are also ever in a state of flux.

Employing the same designations for the twelve astrological principles as those explained in lesson 2 to 7, we can now identify the astrological houses with these principles in the same manner in which we have identified them with the zodiacal signs. We illustrate this identification in the table below. It will be noted that this is contrary to a system that has been taught by many astrologers who have attempted to identify Aries with the First House, Taurus with the Second House, etc., with both houses and zodiacal signs running to a counterclockwise count. [ed. Aleister Crowley promoted this concept as ghost writer for Evangeline Adams.] We abandoned this system as an error in 1936 and have never had reason to return to it.

Lesson Nine

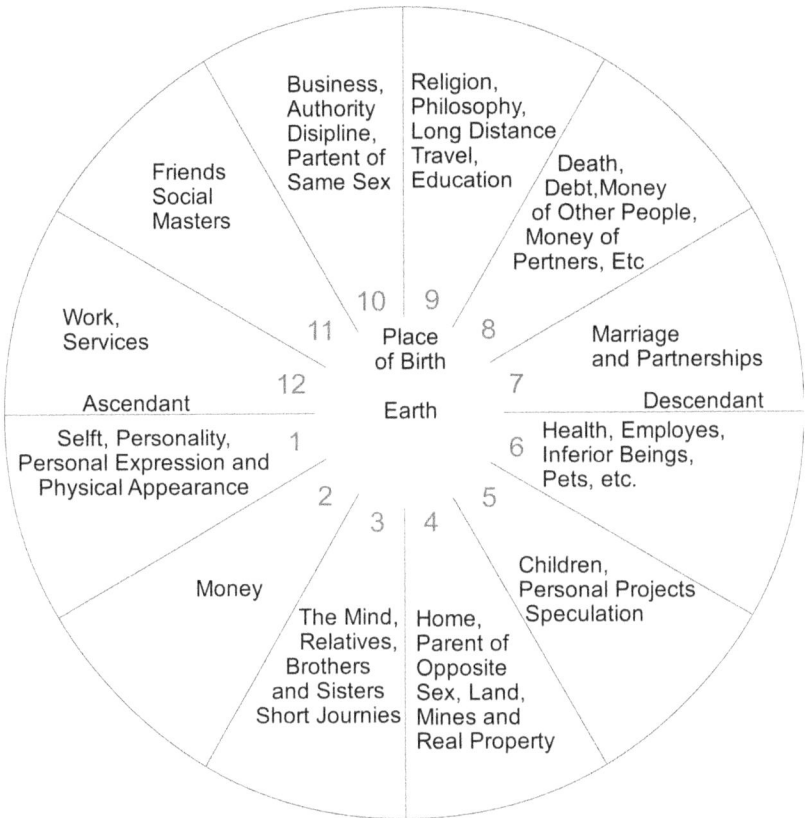

Leo House Count Meanings

House	Identification	Ruler
First	Individual Non-Survival Dynamic	Leo
Second	Individual Survival Dynamic	Cancer
Third	Social Non-Survival Dynamic Guide	Gemini
Fourth	Family Survival Dynamic Reactor	Taurus
Fifth	Family Non-Survival Dynamic	Aries
Sixth	Social Survival Dynamic	Pisces
Seventh	Individual Non-Survival Dynamic Guide	Aquarius
Eighth	Individual Survival Dynamic Reactor	Capricorn
Ninth	Social Non-Survival Dynamic	Sagittarius
Tenth	Family Survival Dynamic	Scorpio
Eleventh	Family Non-Survival Dynamic Guide	Libra

Twelfth   Social Survival Dynamic Reactor   Virgo

It will be noted that this double count as presented in a diagram in the prior chapter, identified the 2nd House with Cancer, the Individual Survival Dynamic, and money. Money is man-made, but it is an outgrowth of the struggle for individual survival. If a man has money he can buy food when he needs it. It is known that the ancients associated Saturn with death, and they called the 8th House the House of Death. Here, we associate Capricorn and Saturn with the 8th House, while the system we abandoned attempted to associate death with Scorpio. In actual practice, we are sure that the student will find that this system works, while the Aries-First-House system does not appear to function. That is the important thing. To those of you who have never studied the Aries-First-House system, you may be better off. There is much that you will not have to unlearn.

The two counts agree insofar as Gemini is related to the Third House and Sagittarius is related to the Ninth. These are the points where the two counts cross. Leo is related to the First House principle, Cancer to the Second House, Taurus to the Fourth House, Aries to the Fifth House, Pisces to the Sixth House.

Our experience cause us to shift the association of prison, hospitals, secret enemies, asylums, etc. from the Twelfth to the Sixth, which was designated as the House of Health. Obviously, people who are confined to prisons hospitals, asylums, etc. are sick people. It is all a health factor. People who have secret enemies are usually mentally sick people. A mental condition usually has to exist before the secret enemies are created. Other people do not have secret enemies. Some people go forth and make friends of their enemies.

Aquarius is related to the Seventh House, Capricorn to the Eight House, Scorpio to the Tenth House, Libra and Venus, the planet that was always associated with social matters, are related to the eleventh House, known as the House of Friends, and Virgo is associated with the Twelfth House.

Now or ultimately, the student may find it advantageous to go over the principles explained in lessons 2 to 7, carefully identifying these principles with the astrological houses and the planets in the manner herein set forth. **It is our opinion that no one thing has held back the progress of astrology more than the association of the signs of the zodiac with the astrological house principles beginning in Aries and The First House and running counterclockwise through the zodiac. It has left astrology very much mixed up and confused. In our opinion, a major operation is necessary to divorce Aries**

Lesson Nine

from the First House. Our years of experience with the system herein outlined suggests the complete abandonment of that system which has been passed down to us by astrologers of the dark ages. We do not believe that it formed a part of the ancient astrology. It appears to have come about through some accident or error. You now have the identification of the twelve astrological principles with zodiacal signs, planets and houses.

The writer is often asked, "Where did you learn astrology?" The answer is mainly through the laboratory type of experiment, but after learning the basic principles as presented by such astrologers as Alan Leo, Llewellyn George, Carter, Evangeline Adams, and others, we met the one astrologer whose association was of the greatest benefit to us. His name was Sidney K. Bennett, and he wrote under the pen name of Wynn. He wrote an astrological column for the Chicago Tribune, the N.Y. Daily News and other papers of the syndicate. He was regarded as a radical by the older astrologers. He was despised by some of the publishers who published astrological textbooks because he questioned their systems. Bennett is the one astrologer of the last century whose work should not be overlooked. Although we have come a long way since our first contact with Bennett, who is now living in New Zealand, it is only fair that we state that had it not been for our association with Bennett, we would have taken much longer to accomplish much less.

Bennett was another of those persons who was consciously or unconsciously seeking cosmic design in the universe, like the mathematicians. Although he never claimed to be a mathematician, he had the mind of a mathematician. Like Kepler and Copernicus, he was seeking an overall pattern. He captured a very important first part of that pattern, and in the early 30's he published a mimeographed booklet entitled *The Aspect Houses*. It wasn't many pages, but it contained the key from which all of our own discoveries later grew. Years later, when Bennett was studying our data on the connection between 'rulership' and distance of planets from the Earth, he asked us how we ever hit upon the idea in the first place, and looked stunned when he was told that it was merely an extension of his own ideas.

We come to the planetary aspects. Planets are said to be in aspect when they are a certain geocentric distance apart in the plane of the Earth's orbit. Some aspects were said to be favorable, others unfavorable. The principle aspects were as follows:

Degrees	Name	Nature
0	Conjunction	Good or bad, depending on the nature of the planets
30	Semisextile	Favorable or unfavorable, depending on The nature of the planets (more later)
60	Sextile	Favorable
90	Square	Unfavorable
120	Trine	Favorable
150	Quincunx	Unfavorable
180	Opposition	Unfavorable depending on planets

More and more astrologers have been reaching the conclusion that **planetary aspects are neither favorable nor unfavorable, because it is chiefly a matter of understanding them**, and some of the aspects that were formerly regarded as the most unfavorable have begun to be viewed as opportune when understood. The person who finds the opposition aspect unfavorable is merely that person who fears change in the status quo. He is in the same position as the man who never learns to swim because he is afraid to jump into the water. His fear of the water, not the water itself, is responsible for the fact that he never learns to swim. So, in this course, let us go forth with the idea that nothing is good nor bad but thinking makes it so. There are no planetary factors that you cannot overcome, and the aspects that appear to cause disaster for one man cause the success of the man who understands them. In studying astrology, realize one thing: there is nothing to fear except ignorance.

Sidney K. Bennett studied Sanskrit and did a great deal of studying of ancient manuscripts. He was an exceptional student, and in studying some Hindu works in Sanskrit, he hit upon something. He discovered that the Hindus had associated the planetary aspects with the house principles. The idea was not clearly expressed, but Bennett figured it out, and he realized that the same twelve basic

Lesson Nine

astrological principles applied to the planetary aspects as well as to the zodiacal signs, the planets and the houses.

Two planets can be 0, 30, 60, 90, 120, 150, 180, 210, 240, 270, 300, or 330 degrees apart. This would give us twelve planetary aspects. However, when two planets are 30 degrees apart, measured in one direction around the circle, they are 330 degrees apart, measured around the circle in the opposite direction. When they are 60 degrees apart in one direction, they are 300 degrees apart in the other direction. When they are 90 degrees apart in one direction, they are 270 degrees in the other direction. When they are 120 degrees in one direction, they are 240 degrees in the other direction. When they are 150 degrees in one direction, they are 210 in the other direction. The opposition is 180 degrees regardless of which direction it is measured, because it is the half way mark.

Thus, while we have twelve planetary aspects, five are duplicates of five others, so that actually, the **twelve** is reduced to a basic **seven** planetary \ aspects, and this is how the **TWELVE** becomes **SEVEN** or the **SEVEN** becomes **TWELVE.** Here we find a geometric significance in the association of Seven and Twelve. Seven visible solar bodies, five theoretical invisible bodies. Seven white keys on the piano, five black keys. In all kinds of ancient literature, in fables and in religion, the significance of seven and twelve has been pressed upon us. 7 + 5 = 12.

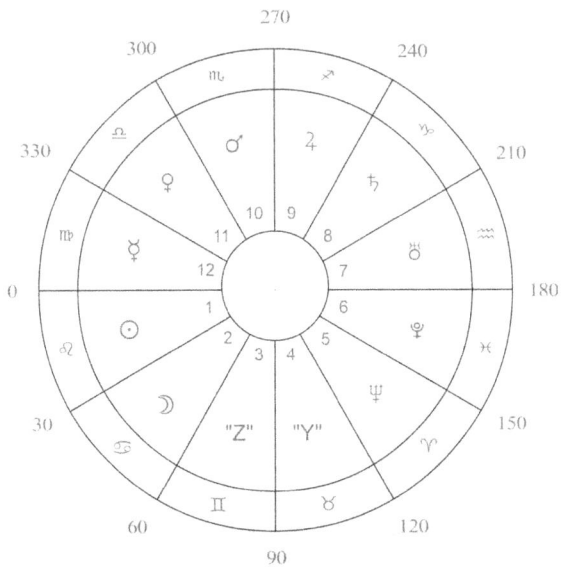

30 Degree Aspects

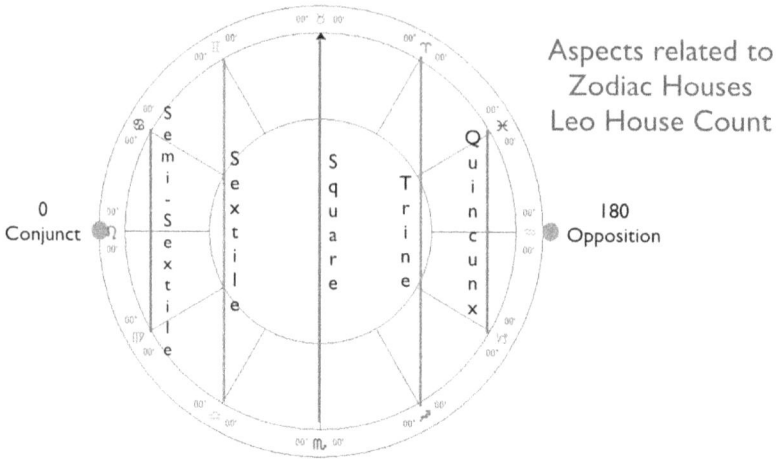

The conjunction or zero aspect becomes a Leo (Fire) or First House aspect.

The semisextile or 30-degree aspect becomes a combination of the principles of Cancer and Virgo (Water and Earth), the second and twelfth house principles.

The sextile or 60-degree aspect becomes a combination of the principles of Gemini and Libra (Air), the 3rd and 11th House principles.

The square or 90-degree aspect becomes a combination of the principles of Taurus and Scorpio (Earth and Water), the 4th and 10th House principles.

The trine or 120-degree aspect becomes a combination of the principles of Aries and Sagittarius (Fire), and the 5th and 9th House principles.

The quincunx or 150-degree aspects becomes a combination of Pisces and Capricorn (Water and Earth), the 6th and 8th House principles. It is interesting to note that this links the house of health with the house of death.

The opposition or 180-degree aspect becomes associated with the Aquarius principle (Air) and the 7th House.

We continue to deal with the factor of design. The same basic principles are designed into the whole network of astrological data. Bennett was the first modern astrologer to begin searching for this design. He published the first important key when he brought forth his long-out-of-print booklet, *The Aspect Houses.* He published another work called *The Equilibrium Houses,* showing that houses could be measured from the sun or from a planet in

Lesson Nine   **139**

the same manner as they are measured from the ascendant. It was probably his use of the work 'equilibrium' that set the writer off seeking the complete symmetry or design, and which led to his discovery that 'rulership' was to be identified with mean distance of planets from the Earth. It was only necessary to continue the train of thought which began in Bennett's mind, to reach the conclusion that for the system and design to be perfect, there must be two undiscovered planets beyond the orbit of Pluto. The equinoxes, the ascendant and the planets themselves are all 'points' from which we can begin measuring.

It has taken nine lessons to explain these fundamentals. We are about ready to start drawing up horoscopes. One of the great problems with astrology today is that we have thousands of students who can draw up horoscopes, but who can never learn to read one. This is because they have never actually learned the basic principles of astrology. They have learned its mechanics, and they stop there. They have systems that are all mixed up and confused, with the result that they are unable to interpret. They do a very accurate mathematical job of setting up a horoscope, and they find themselves at a complete loss to understand what it means.

We have reversed the usual procedure. Instead of teaching you to set up charts first, we have tried to get across the basic principles of astrology. Nothing is so important as getting a clear understanding of these twelve basic principles. Your ability to interpret will always be dependent upon your understanding of those principles. In the end, experience will teach you the most, and you will never stop learning more about these twelve principles. Undoubtedly, you will discover things we have overlooked. Every new mind that approaches astrology does so with new and different powers of observation. If you walk into a room with us, you will observe things that we miss, and we will observe things that you miss. You are now approaching a rich gold mine. You are bound to make all kinds of new discoveries yourself as you go along. Different students will have different interests. One will be interested in health, another in finances, and still another in psychological or emotional problems. There can be hundred of different points of view from which astrology can be approached. In all probability, you will become a specialist. Some things will interest you more than others. Different students will seek out different kinds of cases, but we will all be interested in what makes people tick. We want to know why people behave like human beings, and you are fast approaching the answers.

We have dealt with four main classifications of astrological factors. These are:

> The twelve Zodiacal Signs
> The twelve theoretical Solar Bodies
> The twelve Astrological Houses
> The seven or twelve Planetary Aspects

There are other factors such as the planetary nodes, but we will discuss these further along. There are eclipses and occultations, but these are all a matter of planetary aspects and planetary nodes, which involve the relationships of certain planes in space to other planes in space. In the four groups of astrological factors listed above, we always deal with the same twelve basic astrological principles. Realization of this will simplify astrology for you over other systems that have been taught in modern times. It will not be necessary to think of planetary aspects as favorable or unfavorable, because you can think of them in terms of their actual characteristics. You will be able to see nature is merely trying to destroy the old pattern that the new pattern may come into being, and you can step aside, allow nature to do the work for you, and accept the new pattern as it manifests.

You can realize that **the 30, 90 and 150 degree aspects involve fear**. With the 30 degree aspect, the Individual Survival Dynamic and the Social Survival Dynamic Reactor are trying to function. When the Second House is called the House of Money, that is merely because money is the medium through which the individual survives in his relationship with society. In explaining Cancer, we have identified it with Man's need for food, but in describing Virgo, we have pointed out the Virgo person's interest in diet (food again). The 30-degree aspect connects the nature of Cancer with the nature of Virgo.

The 90-degree (square) aspect connects the Scorpio and Taurus principles (two fixed signs), the 10th and 4th Houses, The Family Survival Dynamic with the Family Survival Dynamic Reactor. It is an aspect of discipline. It is a double force. It has all the impulsiveness of Mars and Scorpio and all the reactionary qualities of Taurus. That is why it is so difficult to experience. It is easier when you realize that its whole purpose is family survival in its present form.

The 150-degree aspect (quincunx) connects Pisces and Capricorn, Neptune and Saturn, the 6th and 8th Houses. This is the health hazard aspect. It strongly suggest that a very large ratio of health problems are caused by our inability to break away from the past, heredity, etc., and live in our own times, or our inability to fit ourselves into the social pattern. This will not include all health problems, because some, like polio and paralysis, appear to be caused more by our getting ahead of our times. However, this aspect illustrates why the majority of health problems are connected with the planets Neptune and Saturn. Good health is dependent upon our living in the present NOW rather than in the past or future, but the great majority of health problems appear to be caused by people's inability to escape from the past. Trying to fit the past into the present is not healthy.

The three aspects just mentioned (30, 90, 150) involve Water and Earth principles. They are effects of the past on the present, and any of them can be accompanied by some health problems.

The 0, 60, 120 and 180 degree aspects, the conjunction, sextile, trine and opposition involve only Fire and Air principles. The conjunction and trine are all Fire, while the opposition and sextile are all Air.

The conjunction aspect represents a new beginning, the Individual Non-Survival Dynamic. The individual is conscious of what he wants to become. The opposition aspect represents the Individual Non-Survival Dynamic Guide. It involved what the other fellow does. Two people with common interests (like husband and wife) may have different ideas, desires and plans about how an objective is to be accomplished. There may have to be a compromise, and if a compromise cannot be reached, there may have to be a break, an important CHANGE. The opposition aspect is an aspect of CHANGE. It might be a marriage, or it might be a divorce. There are many kinds of change. The wife may merely join some clubs and get new outside interests. When her husband is trying to tell about his day at the office, she may be trying to tell him about her day at the club. Whatever conditions may be when the opposition aspect comes along, you can rest assured that it will change things. Often, it brings around just the desired changes, but most people worry, get impatient, and force a change prematurely, with negative consequences. It is well to always allow an opposition aspect to pass before taking action, and then you don't have to take it. Action comes about without your help.

The 60-degree or sextile aspect connects Libra with Gemini, the 3rd and 11th Houses. The sextile and the opposition aspects are purely intellectual. The 60-degree sextile connects the Family Non-Survival Dynamic Guide with the Social Non-Survival Dynamic Guide, and both guides function simultaneously. It is easy to understand why the astrologers have looked upon this aspect as favorable.

The 120-degree trine aspect connects Aries and Sagittarius, the 5th and 9th Houses, Jupiter and Pluto, the Family Non-Survival Dynamic with the Social Non-Survival Dynamic. It is a powerful aspect, the only one that connects two non-survival dynamics. It is not surprising that the astrologer have called it a creative aspect.

As we did with the zodiacal signs, and the planets, when we identified them with past and future, we can do the same with the astrological houses and the planetary aspects. We can identify the aspects as follows:

Degree	Name	Time
0	Conjunction	Future
30	Semisextile	Past
60	Sextile	Future
90	Square	Past
120	Trine	Future
150	Quincunx	Past
180	Opposition	Future

It is interesting to note that the Future aspects outweigh the Past aspects. We have four
Future aspects to three Past aspects. Now, we can classify the houses in the same way:

House	Time
First	Future
Second	Past
Third	Future
Fourth	Past
Fifth	Future
Sixth	Past
Seventh	Future
Eighth	Past
Ninth	Future
Tenth	Past
Eleventh	Future
Twelfth	Past

Lesson Nine

Other aspects than the above have been employed experimentally, but they have never come into general usage. A 45-degree aspect has been used as unfavorable, because it is one-half of the 90-degree square, but our statistical experiments have never shown such an aspect on a graph. Some astrologers have also experimented with 72-degree aspect, but we have not yet found any basis for such as aspect.

Bennett's limitation of the number of aspects to 7 or 12 appears to have a more sound foundation. It eliminates much that was haphazard and guesswork. It shows us the true nature of the aspects. We think of aspects and houses differently when we realize they are one and the same thing. Many students are confused when they see one astrologer measuring aspects from the ascendant, another measuring from the Sun. You can measure from many points. We do not maintain that this is the whole story, for we are convinced that the twelve parts each can again be broken into twelve parts, but that is a matter to which we will return later in these lessons. We have covered the basic groundwork that we were anxious to get across to you. Now, we must interrupt our course and get down to the practical side of things so that you can study and analyze specific cases on your own. We have dealt in basic principles. **From here on, it is vitally important that you watch astrology work**. You must see it function. In the end, you must learn astrology seeing it work. You are left without doubts when you see it work. However, it is not sufficient to see it work without understanding how and why it works. When you understand the twelve basic principles we have portrayed, when you understand the dynamics, the reactors and the guides, then, in addition to witnessing things on the objective plane, you will also grasp what is taking place beneath the surface. You will understand what nature is trying to do. It is important to realize that there is always a double purpose. You have a partner in nature who can get mightily troublesome when ignored. She strenuously objects to taxation without representation. Always remember that.

LESSON TEN

ERECTING THE BIRTH CHART

When we examined some of the methods used by astrologers in erecting and judging birth horoscopes, they would appear to be quite confusing. Several different frames of references are often employed at one and the same time, and this is a matter that we must clear up. You will recall our statement that houses and planetary aspects are one and the same thing. For this statement to be true, much is wrong with conventional astrology as it has been employed over the last few centuries, and it is to be doubted whether these are the methods that were originally exercised by the very ancient astrologers.

In recent times we find the astrologer erecting a birth chart in one frame of reference, in this case a plane of space. Then he computes planetary aspects in another frame of reference— another plane of space—after which he computes parallels in a third frame of reference or plane of space.

He draws his birth chart in a plane of space established by the longitude and latitude of birth. Then, he computes his planetary aspects in the plane of the Earth's orbit (ecliptic), and finally, computes parallels in the plane of the Earth's equator.

This is much like a sleepy man who, preparing for bed, takes off his shoes in the living room, his shirt in the kitchen and his trousers in the front hall. We know of no justification for such a procedure.

If he is using the Placidian House System, he computes the houses, using time instead of space as his frame of reference, but elsewhere he sticks to space. The whole thing is all confused and mixed up. As a result of reasoning and experience, we abandoned such methods some time ago, but we were not the first to do so. It would seem that the move was started by William J. Tucker in England, Carl Jung in Germany and Dal Lee in the United States.

The strange part of all this is that when we abandon these unnecessary complications, we simplify astrology and we do away with a lot of complicated procedures. The erection of a chart becomes very simple, and it is our experience that it then works, where heretofore it did not. It does not mean that all other 'systems' are wrong, and it should stop no one from investigating other systems. It is entirely possible that the conventional system of erecting a natal chart may embody three or four different 'systems' of astrology and when broken down into those different systems, it is possible that all might work individually. However, at the present time, the 'systems' would appear to be all mixed up with each other. From what we know of some of the occult followers of astrology of the past, it is also possible that these various systems were mixed up and confused intentionally and with the purpose of confusing. It could possibly have been a method of hiding the truth in the same fashion as was done by the Greeks with their magic number squares. Mathematically, if we are dealing with plane geometry, we must deal with one plane at a time. Solid geometry or spherical geometry is something else again. Astrology, as employed, is plane geometry. An astrological chart is plane geometry, because it is a two-dimensional figure. The natal chart, as conveniently used today, is an attempt to deal with three planes of space simultaneously, which might not be wrong if it were correctly accomplished.

It has always been the writer's experience that few things we might set out to investigate are 100% right or 100% wrong. If alert, we usually find a certain amount of truth and a certain amount of error in everything we investigate. Unfortunately, this method is not adopted in many universities nor in academic circles. Textbooks are constantly doctored to make them appear to conform with some dogma. The writer recently examined a college textbook on Plato. Throughout the volume, whenever the word astrology appeared, it had been changed to astronomy. It is doubtful whether the equivalent of the word astronomy existed in the days of Plato. As far as we have been able to determine, the word astronomy did not come into being until the Renaissance. Even then, Paracelsus defined astrology as dealing with prediction and astronomy as dealing with character declinations. Plato lived 400 years before Christ. The word astronomy can be found nowhere in the New Testament. And even during the Renaissance, it did not mean to Paracelsus what it means today.

Thus, when we discard a conventional 'system' of astrology, let us not do so with the conception that it is 100 % wrong. It may have contained some truth that we have overlooked. Let us not condemn one system because another system works. If astrology is pure mathematics, as we hold that it is, then there can be many systems of astrology, and when perfected, they will all work. A better understanding of this can be grasped if we consider that there is more than one way of multiplying two numbers, and each way will give the same answer. One method does

Lesson Ten

not nullify another method. Let us prove this, or let us give you a way of proving it to yourself. To multiply by the old system know as peasant arithmetic, two numbers are placed side by side on a piece of paper.

Next, you divide the first number by two, writing the answer below the first number, but disregarding a possible one that may be left over. You divide the lower first number by two writing the answer below the first number, but disregarding a possible one that may be left over. You divide the lower number by two, and you continue with this process until you have reduced the original first number to one.

Thus: 49   64
              24
              12
              6
              3
              1

Now, you go to the number in the second column and you multiply it by two. You multiply the answer by two, and so on, until you have multiplied in the second column the same number of times that you have divided in the first column.

Thus: 49   64
              24   128
              12   256
              6   512
              3   1024
              1   2049

Whenever the number in the left-hand column is even, cross out the corresponding number in the right-hand column. That would mean that since 24, 12, and 6 are even, we cross out the opposite numbers, 128, 256 and 512, leaving 64, 1024 and 2048. When we add these three figures together we get 3136, the answer. If you multiply 49 X 64 in the conventional manner, the answer will be 3136. The completed problem will appear as follows:

              49   64
              24   128
              12   256
              6   512
              3   1024

$$\frac{1 \quad 2048}{3136}$$

Turn the numbers around, placing 64 in the first column, 49 in the second column, and it will still work. Supply your own numbers and prove this system of multiplying to yourself. It is based on what is known as the binary system. It was long discarded by academicians until the manufacturers of electronic calculating machines discovered that for their purposes it is better, and this is employed in modern electronic calculators today.

We give this demonstration to show you that in mathematics, there may be an infinite number of ways of doing a problem and one way is just as authentic as another, except in the minds of people who have been writing textbooks. One engineer, who went to Moscow to try and find out why Russia can turn out engineers faster than we can, discovered that Russia has abandoned our moronic methods of teaching mathematics. New methods are already in the making in the USA now.

So, let us avoid dogma. Let us not accuse the advocate of some other system of being 100% wrong. He may be 20% wrong or 90% wrong, but he may be partially right. The battles of the advocates of various 'systems' of astrology should now be reviewed with these facts in mind. The natal horoscope, as drawn by either the Placidian, Regiomontanus Horizontal or the Campanus Systems, is based on a plane determined by the place of birth, which might be all right as far as it goes, but the planets are then placed in this horoscope, not in that plane of space, but in the plane of the Earth's orbit. This mixes everything all up. If a planet and a house cusp correspond with the same zodiacal degree, it is assumed that the planet is on the house cusp, which may not be true at all. Two mathematical points which are conjunct in one plane of space need not be conjunct in another plane of space.

Let us illustrate this factor:

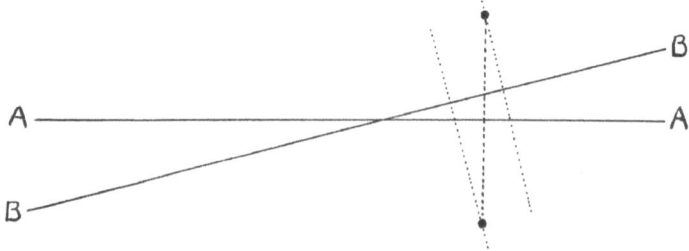

Planet Difference Between Two Planes of Space

Lesson Ten

In the above diagram, we have two planes of space illustrated by the solid line marked 'A' and the solid line marked 'B'. The two heavy dots are planets. A dotted line is drawn at right angles to the 'A; line and passes through both planets. Therefore, in the plane of the space determined by the 'A' line, the two planets are in conjunction. To be conjunct, two planets are merely in the same longitude, but not necessarily in the same latitude. In the plane of the solid 'B' line, we have to draw two dotted lines at right angles to the solid 'B' line. In that plane of space, the planets are as far apart as the two dotted lines. The planets are NOT in conjunction in that plane of space.

This will demonstrate why we cannot declare two planets in aspect until we have agreed on a plane of space in which they are to be measured. A measurement in one plane of space is different from a measurement in another plane of space. For this reason, all heliocentric astrology, including the work being done by RCA Communications Inc., contains an error, because modern astronomy is computing planetary conjunctions in a way they consider to be heliocentric, but their computations are actually made in the plane of the Earth's orbit, and consequently they are mathematically incorrect. In the work of RCA, they are conscious of this error, and they are making allowance for it. In the case of the astronomers adopted the Copernican (heliocentric) in place of the Ptolemaic (geocentric) system of astronomy, they changed over in but two dimensions of space and forgot about the third dimension. They continue to make their computations in the plane of the Earth's orbit. It would be equally as correct. For heliocentric astronomy to be valid, the positions would have to be computed in the plane in which the Sun travels. Before the birth of Christianity, heliocentric astrology was in use, but we are unable to determine in what plane computations were made. There remains the possibility that the old astrology may have been more valid and more accurate in its calculations than modern astronomy, but we do not know. A heliocentric conjunction (or other aspect) in the plane of the Earth's orbit, it is not an aspect in the plane of Pluto's orbit.

Empirical data would seem to indicate that when the astrologer computes his aspects in the plane of the Earth's orbit, he is on the right track, but when the frame of reference is changed, this plane is no longer valid, and a new plane must be established.

As we find them today, both astrology and astronomy contain basic mathematical errors, and we must clear these up.

In the Placidian House System, the house cusps are found, not by a space measurement but by a time measurement. We will not claim that there is no basis for such a procedure but if there is, then it opens up an entirely new realm of astrology that has never been explored. If the houses are to be determined in this manner, then planetary aspects would have to be determined in the same manner. To compute a sextile (60 degree aspect) you would not compute the planets in space. Instead, you would compute the time that it takes two planets to move from the conjunction to the square, and you would say that they are sextile when 2/3 of that time has elapsed.

In these Lessons, we are teaching a system that is based on empirical evidence, and therefore, we will not attempt to explore such possibilities as those outlined above, but we beg the student not to be dogmatic and not to close his mind to systems other than we teach. For all practical purposes, the student will find out methods much more simple than those conventionally employed today.

However, we declare the natal chart as employed to be invalid because it creates an illusion. It makes planets appear to be, in the chart, where they positively are not. We will abandon that system.

Let us set up a hypothesis that may or may not be true. It is only for consideration. We suspect that the ancients, either these who built the Great Pyramid or more ancient ancients, may have known more about astrology, astronomy and mathematics than we know today. We know that the ancient Greeks regarded knowledge as dangerous in the wrong hands. We know that in the magic squares filled out only part of the pattern, leaving the remainder to be deciphered by the 'initiated', those with the ability to visualize the abstract. In that case, it is possible that the present system of erecting a natal chart may embody four distinctly different systems of astrology instead of one, and it is possible that each holds truth when separated from the others. All four may supply the same answer in different ways, just as both of our illustrated systems of multiplication supply the same answer in the end. One system, and the one which we employ, keeps all the factors in the plane of the Earth's orbit. A second system, would keep all the factors in a plane determined by the place of birth. A third system would keep everything in the plane of the Earth's equator. This plane is actually employed in navigation. A fourth system would abandon space measurements for time measurements.

In our system, we take note of other planes than the one we employ, but we are concerned only with those mathematical points where the various planes of space cross the plane of the Earth's orbit. We work with mathematical points and find them just as significant as planets.

During June 1956, the writer drove a car 4,500 miles in two weeks, and although it was not his intended purpose, he collected crystal formations for study from various states. The same mathematical Laws that work in astrology work in rocks. Like snowflakes, some rocks form with six sides in a particular plane of reference. (We have in Lesson One noted that the six-sided snowflake is actually a twelve-part object.) Other six-sided objects grow out of the first at various other angles. This is mathematical expression. We might expect the same in astrology. We might suspect that there are many horoscopes at many angles, but we cannot employ these other horoscopes until the whole planetary system has been re-computed in the frame of reference that is to be adopted. That makes the conventional chart almost impossible if planetary tables now in existence are to be employed. Planets are computed in only two frames of reference, the plane of the Earth's orbit and the plane of the Earth's equator. Re-computation would have to be made for every horoscope and for every transit. A new set of ephemerides would have to be published, a much more complicated set, and publishers are trying to find a means of publishing ordinary ephemerides without losing money while doing so. The American Astrology Magazine Ephemeris and Wynn's Ephemeris had to be abandoned, because the cost of production was always greater than the selling price.

Some astrologers, notably Cyril Fagan of Ireland, are working with a Sidereal Zodiac based on the fixed stars. We cannot even consider this zodiac until certain mathematical factors have been determined, and we have been unable to get satisfactory answers to questions that arise. *Where is the center of this zodiac and why? In what plane of space is this zodiac to be determined? At the present time, the same plane of the Earth's orbit is used, but why should the plane of the Earth's orbit have any significance in anything so vast as a zodiac based on fixed stars?* Why should the insignificant planets of our solar system be used as 'rulers' of something that is cosmic? Why should the 12 signs of the zodiac be equal 30-degree divisions of space when measured from the Earth as a center? This is geocentric. These divisions would be otherwise if measured from some other point in space, and the position of the Earth varies by over 50,000 light years. If the Earth is the center at one time, it would be more than 50,000 or 200 quadrillion miles away from the center at another time. Another significant factor that one of our students points out is that during the last few thousands of years, great changes have taken place in the positions of the fixed stars. They are not fixed. Up until now, we have had no reason to consider astrology as in any way associated with anything beyond the solar system. Instead, we appear to find that the solar system and human dynamics merely function in accord with the same mathematical formula. For our immediate purpose, we can forget the fixed stars. Again, however, always keep an open mind for any further information that may turn up in the future.

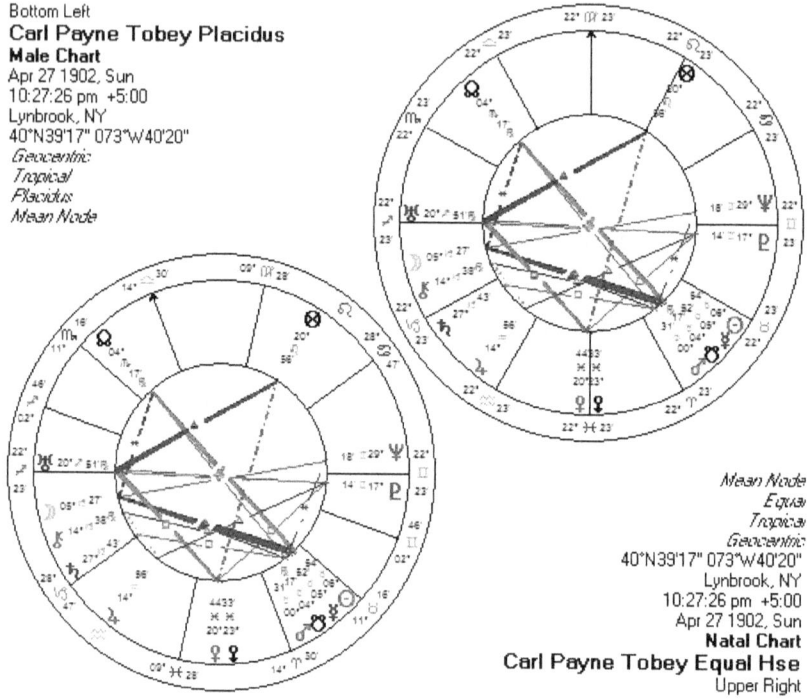

Bottom Left
Carl Payne Tobey Placidus
Male Chart
Apr 27 1902, Sun
10:27:26 pm +5:00
Lynbrook, NY
40°N39'17" 073°W40'20"
Geocentric
Tropical
Placidus
Mean Node

Mean Node
Equal
Tropical
Geocentric
40°N39'17" 073°W40'20"
Lynbrook, NY
10:27:26 pm +5:00
Apr 27 1902, Sun
Natal Chart
Carl Payne Tobey Equal Hse
Upper Right

For our purposes, we are interested in determining a mathematical point. We want to know that mathematical point where a plane of space determined by your location of birth crosses the horizon and plane of the Earth's orbit–the zodiac. A line drawn from your birth position to the place where the Sun is going to rise will supply what we want, and fortunately, your Table of Houses will give us that information. We call that mathematical point the Ascendant.

As soon as we determine this mathematical point, we will be able to draw up the natural horoscope.

In Lesson Ten, we showed you how to determine the Sidereal Time of birth. Study your Table of Houses. You will see that the tables are made up for various latitudes. Three different latitudes are carried on one page and run through 12 pages. House Cusps are given for each approximate four minutes of time. You are supplied with the degree of the zodiac on the 10th, 11th, and 12th, 1st or Ascendant,

Lesson Ten

2nd and 3rd Houses. The House Cusps given in the Table of Houses are those known as the Placidian House Cusp. We are not going to employ them, but you may as well see what they are all about and how they differ from the system we are going to employ, which is a much simpler system. When you erect horoscopes in the plane of the Earth's orbit, you can abandon all the house cusps given in the Table of Houses, with the exception of the ascendant or First House Cusp. That will remain the same, insofar as erecting horoscopic charts is concerned, after you have taken the degree of the zodiac shown on the ascendant, you can close the book. We can go on from there by ourselves.

Our description of a Table of Houses refers to the particular one that we have supplied. If you are using some other Table of Houses, the material may be arranged differently. If it gives you any trouble, let us know. If you have some other Table of Houses, you probably already know how to use it. The particular Table of Houses that we furnish covers all latitudes up to 66 degrees. Keeping the entire horoscope in the one plane of the Earth's orbit will do away with all complications for persons born in extreme northern or southern latitudes, except when one is so far north or south that the Sun doesn't actually rise or set during 24 hours. Under those circumstances, we have a problem which we do not yet know how to approach.

We are now ready to erect a chart, and this time the writer is going to use his own chart because it is one where maintaining everything in one plane is going to make a drastic difference and because he can't question its authenticity. There are other cases where the difference will be slight. The writer was born just outside of New York City at 10:32 P.M. on April 27th, 1902. This is a corrected birth time, because the recorded time was merely given as something prior to 11:00 P.M.

If you look up the longitude and latitude for New York City, you will find that it is 41 degrees north latitude and 74 degrees west longitude.

If you will look at your Ephemeris for April 27th, 1902, you will find the Sidereal Time given as 2:18. This is the Sidereal Time at noon at Greenwich, but the Sidereal Time for noon at New York will vary by less than one minute, so we will overlook the difference. Since the birth was after noon, we will add the birth time to the Sidereal Time, and we will add an additional four minutes because New York is at 74 degrees west longitude while the center of the time zone is 75 degrees west longitude, so New York is one degree east of the time zone center.

Thus: Sidereal Time at Birth.................2:18
          Birth Time after non..................10:32
          One Degree east of TZ center, :04

          Sidereal Time at Birth...............12:54

These figures supply the zodiacal degree on each of six cusps of the Houses according to the Placidian House Cusp System, and although we are not going to use this system, it would be well for you to know about it, because it is the most generally used system of the majority of astrologers of today. On the next page, we have erected two charts, the upper one showing the house cusps as drawn from the data supplied in the Table of Houses, the second or lower chart showing the house cusps as we will employ them in our own work. In the upper chart, you will note that both Sagittarius and Gemini each appear on two house cusps. Sagittarius appears on the 12th and 1st cusps, while Gemini appears on the 5th and 7th Cusps. On the other hand, Aquarius and Leo do not appear on house cusps at all, but between house cusps, in the 2nd and 8th Houses. These are known as intercepted signs. Our system will do away with all of this.

THE HOROSCOPE DRAWN IN
THE PLANE OF THE EARTH'S ORBIT

Now, look at the lower chart, which is the one we will employ. We have the same 22-Sagittarius on the Ascendant or 1st-House Cusp. We have taken that figure out of the Table of Houses, but we have not taken the other cusps from the Table of Houses. Instead, we have merely placed the zodiacal signs around this chart in their natural order, as you should have learned them by now. Each house is 30 degrees, and each sign is 30 degrees, and the two come out even. Because 22 degrees of a sign is on the ascendant, 22 degrees of a sign is on every house cusp. If 4 degrees of a sign was on the Ascendant, 4 degrees of a sign would be on every house cusp. The number of degrees on a house cusp is always the same as the number of degrees on the Ascendant.

Capricorn comes after Sagittarius, and so we put it on the 2nd House Cusp. Aquarius comes next, and we put it on the 3rd Cusps, etc., until we have gone all the way around the circle.

This is the chart we will use. It is a chart drawn in the plane of the Earth's orbit, the same as the plane of the zodiac and the plane of the ecliptic. Now the chart is a 2-dimensional figure. Everything is computed in one plane of space. We are interested in other planes,

Lesson Ten

but only in knowing where those planes cut or cross this plane. The Sun is always in the plane of the Earth's orbit since it is its center. In this chart, 22-Sagittarius is on the eastern horizon at the time of birth.

You will now note an interesting mathematical fact. Sagittarius is the 9th-House zodiacal sign, or the 9th House of the zodiac. It is on the 1st House Cusp. On the other hand, Leo, the 1st House sign of the zodiac is in the 9th Cusp of this chart. This interchange always occurs. It is simple arithmetic, but it does not necessarily occur in any of the conventionally used systems of astrology. If you have Scorpio on the 1st House Cusp, Scorpio being the 10th House Sign on the 10th House Cusp.

This means that when planets transit Leo, a 1st House ascendant has a transit to the 1st House, a 2nd House ascendant has a transit to the 2nd House, etc. This will become more important to you later when you are interpreting transits.

From now on, we will forget the chart showing the Placidian House Cusps, and we will confine ourselves to the lower or Earth's Orbit Chart. Our next step will be to put the planets in the lower chart, but we would like to discuss these two charts a little more. When the writer first began studying astrology he had the advantage of having kept a diary for some years. One of his first moves was to check the day-to-day transits to his chart during the interval covered by this diary. This proved a great asset, because a written record is always so far superior to the memory, which can be very faulty. From here on, he followed the daily movement of the planets. He found that planets going over the natal planetary positions were accompanied by interesting developments, some merely mental and emotional, but here they were, written up in advance. However, aside from the ascendant and 7th Cusps, he never found effects from transits to the house cusps. This confusion went on for a number of years, until the days when he worked as an associate editor for Sidney K. Bennett (Wynn, who we have mentioned earlier.)

One day, Bennett came out of his inner office and asked, 'Tell me, have you ever found that transits to house cusps work?' The writer answered with a loud and emphatic, 'NO', where upon, Bennett remarked, 'Neither have I,' and returned to his inner office. That's all the conversation that took place, but we had agreed on something.

It was after that, the writer took up mathematics as a hobby. It took many more years before he reached the conclusion that astrology was nothing more than mere mathematical expression, but after this conclusion, his astrological thinking was different, and he had to begin think about the mathematical imperfections that existed in the astrological charts. Unconscious of the work that had already been accomplished by Tucker, Jung and Lee, he began to realize that mathematically, you must treat one frame of reference at a time. You can employ many frames of reference, but the rules that work for one frame of reference do not apply for another. For example, in the duodecimal system of arithmetic, when you square any prime number greater than 3, the answer will always end in one, but this would not apply for the decimal system. In the binary system, the square of an odd number will always end in 1, and the square of an even number will always end in zero.

After considerable thinking on this matter, the writer sat down and wrote out the dates of the most important events he could remember insofar as his own personal life was concerned. Then, he drew charts for these dates and tabulated the planetary positions statistically. He discovered that the majority of events in his life occurred when planets were at 22 degrees of signs, when they were crossing the house cusps of the Earth's orbit chart. The events also coincided with the nature of the houses involved. This was particularly obvious where the slow-moving planets were involved.

For years, he had found no 10th House developments when planets crossed 15-Libra. The new 10th House Cusp was 22 degrees earlier in the zodiac, and when he studied events that coincided with transits over the 10th Cusp of the second chart at 22-Virgo, results came fast and furiously. In the case of Neptunian transits, this altered the timing factor by 11 years. He had found no accompanying events when Neptune crossed 15-Libra, but when he went back and studied the period at which time Neptune crossed 22-Virgo, sparks flew.

Those were the days when Elbert Benjamine began a campaign to 'standardize' astrology. It was his purpose to rule out as 'quacks' any astrologer who suggested that astrology, in the form in which his publications had advocated it, was anything less than the work of God Himself. Benjamine had already appointed himself a representative of God, because Los Angeles had ruled astrology illegal, and to escape the law and its possible penalties, Benjamine changed his organization from a Brotherhood to a Church. Under the Constitution, you can't pass laws that put a church out of business. Under these circumstances, as a representative of God, he could continue to operate unmolested. As his first three victims who were to be ruled out, he selected Sidney Bennett, Dal Lee and Carl Payne Tobey. However, his campaign ended abruptly following a letter from the writer announcing the beginning of legal action unless the attacks ended. This letter resulted in an apology from Benjamine and a request for a pact. He asked for an agreement that we would not attack each other's writings. We did not reply to this request. There was a numerous angle that never came out. In adopting the term 'Standard Astrology', Benjamine was employing a copyrighted term owned by the writer, whom he was attacking.

However, the whole period when Neptune was crossing 22-Virgo was filled with the Neptunian type of event. The writer had his home and his business in a building on 13th Street in New York. The most spectacular event of all during this period is worth mentioning. One day, a friend arrived accompanied by two gentlemen whom he introduced. They were US Secret Service Agents. They asked a favor. They wished to secretly hide themselves in the writer's home for a spell, from where they could watch an adjoining apartment. This developed some humorous situations, because it was necessary to explain these 'friends' who were staying with us to intimately known guests who must have thought the whole thing very strange. This situation continued for two weeks until Mars reached the ascendant of the chart, from where it squared Neptune. (Remember that we have associated Mars with authority, Neptune with Inferiors, and astrologers have long associated the Secret Service with Neptune because it deals with the inferiors from the underworld.) Right on the square of these two planets at the 1st and 10th Cusps of this chart, these two men, accompanied by about 20 others who suddenly appeared from nowhere, made what was, at that time, the greatest counterfeiting raid in history. The Ring's headquarters was immediately across the street. Public telephones in the neighborhood had been tapped for months. At the very same moment that this raid occurred, other raids were taking place all over the city, picking up less important individuals who were associated with the ring. Ultimately, there were over 300 arrests.

During the days when we were waiting for this raid to take place, and when we could discuss nothing with anybody except ourselves, we did discuss a good deal of astrology, and it was interesting to note that the Secret Service Agent who led the raid had Jupiter at the ascendant of the writer's own chart, at 22-Sagittarius. Gunplay had been expected, but the raid had been so well planned that the leader of the ring was in handcuffs before he had recovered from the paralyzing effect of surprise.

It would take a good-sized book to enumerate the manner in which developments have coincided with transits of planets over cusps to this one chart, but it should be mentioned that for many years, the writer had assumed the ascendant of his chart to be 21-Sagittarius, until a statistical analysis of the past showed that the sensitive zodiacal point was 22 degrees and not 21. This meant changing the birth time by four minutes, making it four minutes later.

You will see that correction of a birth time in most cases can be a statistical procedure. The birth time can be established, once the ascending sign has been determined, by a statistical tabulation to learn what degree from 1 - 30 is accompanied by planets at the time of the most events in the individual's life.

It should also be mentioned that realization that these were the house cusps which respond to transits was greatly delayed by the fact that the writer has two planets near house cusps at birth, Uranus 2 degrees from the ascendant at 20-Sagittarius and Venus at 20-Pisces near the fourth house cusp. For many years, he had erroneously assumed that events occurring with planets at 22 degrees were delayed reaction to transits involving Uranus and Venus in the chart. However, this contention did not stand up, because the charts of three other people born on the same month, day and year, but at different time of day, did not show similar developments. These other people had Venus and Uranus at the same points, but their house cusps were different. As a result, the writer was late in adopting this chart in the plane of the Earth's orbit, and Tucker, Lee and Jung were there first. Tucker had been advocating such a chart 20 years earlier.

As a concrete example of the distortions that actually occur in the conventional kind of a chart, on August 23rd, 1956, the writer was watching for the Moon to rise at Tucson, Arizona. He knew that Mars was at 22-Pisces, the Moon 8 degrees further along at 0-Aries. Thus, one might expect Mars to rise before the Moon, but it didn't. The moon rose first, Mars some minutes later.

Here is a case where the conventional chart would show Mars above the horizon in the 12th House, the Moon below the horizon in the 1st House, when the reverse is true. The Moon was considerably above the horizon in the 12th House, while Mars was below the horizon in the 1st House. If we look at the summer sky in the Northern Hemisphere, the zodiac slants from northeast to southwest in the morning and from southeast to northwest in the afternoon, while the reverse would be true in the winter.

LESSON ELEVEN

THE NATAL HOROSCOPE

The student's first glance at an ephemeris may make it appear complicated, but it is not nearly so much so as an ordinary railroad timetable. Planets run to the same schedule on Sundays and holidays. The solar system is more reliable than a railroad. Planets are always on time. They obey perfect mathematical laws. There are no strikes, although printers who print ephemerides occasionally make slight errors. If a planet is scheduled to be at a certain point in space at a given time, you can depend on it. It will be there at exactly that time. This is abstract natural law. If the student is sufficiently patient to give the ephemeris as much time as he gives a timetable before starting on vacation, he will have no difficulties.

An ephemeris tells you where the planets WERE, where they ARE and where they WILL BE. It deals with past, present and future. It also gives you the position of the Sun, the Moon and the Lunar Node. The last is merely a mathematical point about which we will have much to say later on. In order to locate something, we have to locate it in its relation to something else. That is the only way there is to locate anything.

The astrological ephemeris locates the planets in relation to the zodiac and in relation to the equator, although only partially in relation to the equator. Remember that the zodiac is a plane of space, and it is the plane of space of the Earth's orbit, which is the same as that of the ecliptic.

The use of the word ecliptic has confused a good many students of astrology who never appear to realize that the plane of the ecliptic is merely the plane of the Earth's orbit. This came about when Ptolemy and the early Christians discarded the work of the Greeks, Egyptians, Hindus and Babylonians, and insisted that the Earth is the center of the solar system. Thus, in thinking of this plane of space, it was considered as the path of the Sun around the Earth. It was called the ecliptic. When Copernicus proved that the ancient Greeks, Egyptians, Babylonians and Hindus were right after all, his work was banned by both the church and the astronomers of the day. The same happened when Kepler discovered the laws of planetary motion. His books were banned by the church in the same manner that the church now bans many books on sex. Dogma and prejudice are a matter of conditioned mental reflexes and demonstrate the dangers contained in the form that orthodox education has taken since the birth of Christ. Modern astronomers still stick to the term ecliptic. Up till now, we have seldom heard one refer to it as the plane of the Earth's orbit. Textbooks refer to the ecliptic, but describe it as the 'apparent' path of the Sun.

Letters from students have demonstrated an interesting fact. When the student has Sun or ascendant in Capricorn, there is greater difficulty in visualizing the abstract. Capricorn students need to see something concrete. On the other hand, once these students grasp something, they understand it and they remember it. Although learning may be more difficult, they are often better off once they do learn, because they retain. The picture has become more graphic.

Thus, the student with any Capricorn block may do better if he illustrates to himself by the use of material things. You can use a hoop to illustrate a plane in space, two hoops to illustrate two planes in space. Embroidery hoops would be perfect for this purpose, because one fits inside the other. Take two such hoops, one within the other, and then twist one so that looking at them edgewise, they form an 'X'. Now let one hoop represent the plane of the equator, the other the plane of the Earth's orbit. The two hoops cross in two places. One of these places is the beginning of Aries, while the other opposite thereto is the beginning of Libra. You can now take the hoop that represents the plane of the Earth's orbit and mark it off in twelve divisions around the circle, and these are the twelve signs of the Zodiac. A mathematical point that forms the center of both of these circles represents the Earth. You can also take a ball and mark off the circles with chalk.

It is an interesting fact that every student of this Course who has had trouble visualizing the abstract has had either Sun or Ascendant in Capricorn. The writer, with Moon in Capricorn, can appreciate this and sympathize with these students, because in his first year in High School, he flunked algebra. To prove that such difficulties can be overcome, he later developed a formula for prime numbers after all the mathematicians had failed in their efforts to find such a formula over a 2,500 year period. Let us prove to you that such problems as those of faulty visualization CAN be overcome. When you have difficulties of this sort, you must state them, tell us about them, and not be ashamed of them.

The lower diagram is a picture of that hoop that is to represent the plane of the Earth's orbit, looking right through the hoop, not edgewise or at any angle. The little circle in this center is the Earth. We have drawn lines from the outer circle to the inner circle. The

Lesson Eleven

vertical line running to the top marks off your longitudinal position on the Earth.

Coming back to the Ephemeris, in addition to giving you the Sidereal Time at Noon or Midnight at Greenwich, the ephemeris tells you THREE things.

It tells you where any planet (plus the Sun, Moon, or Lunar Node) was, is or will be, along that circle that we call the zodiac.

It tells you how far north or south of that circle any body may be. This is known as a planet's celestial latitude.

It tells you how far north or south of the other circle (the equator) a body may be. This is termed the planet's declination. We will have little use for it. Realize that a planet does not travel in the plane of the Earth's orbit but in the plane of its own orbit, and it is not necessarily on that circle, but north or south of it most of the time, although the orbit, of Uranus coincides very closely with that of the Earth, while the orbit of Pluto differs by 17 degrees. By the use of more embroidery hoops, you could illustrate the planes of the other planetary orbits. Each would have to cross the Earth's orbit twice, and these points where these various circles cross are called NODES.

In degrees and minutes, the Declination column tells you how far a body is north or south of the equator plane. The Latitude tells you how far a body may be north or south of the plane of the Earth's orbit. For the planets, this same information appears at the bottom of the page in additional columns, and at the extreme right of these columns is shown the zodiacal position of the Lunar Node.

We pointed out that the two points where the hoops cross are called the NODES. Now, if you let one hoop represent the Earth's orbital plane and another hoop the Moon's orbital plane, the two points where the hoops cross are the Lunar Nodes. The point where the Moon crosses coming north is called the North Node; the ephemeris gives only the position of the North Node, because the South Node is merely the opposite point in the zodiac. If the North Node is 11-degrees Sagittarius, then the South Node has to be 11-degrees Gemini, because Gemini is opposite Sagittarius in the Zodiac.

If you are going to represent all the planes of the planets plus the plane of the Moon and equator, you will need eleven embroidery hoops.

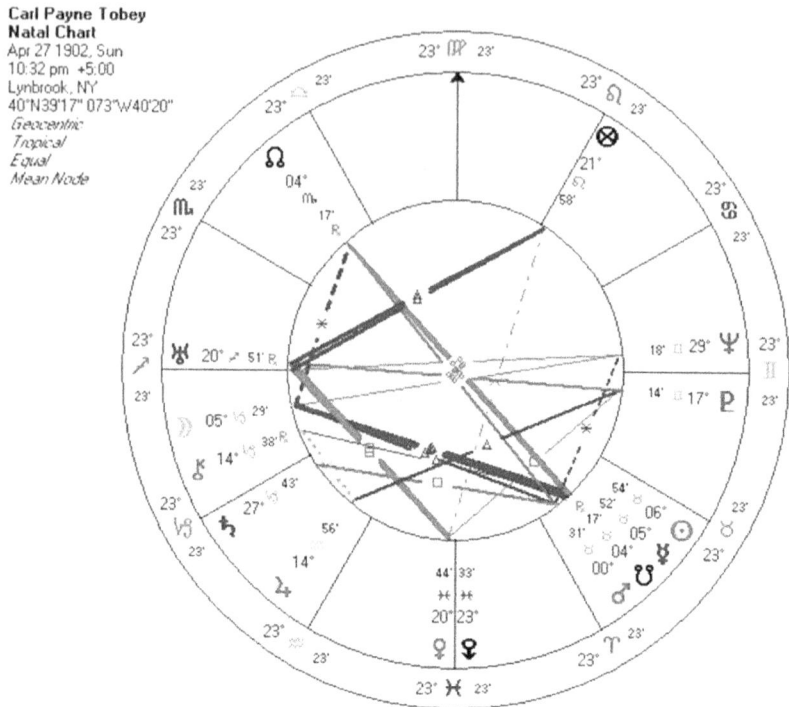

Tobey Birth Chart

You may never have tried to grasp a very difficult and complicated mathematical formula. You might give up after one look at the symbols. Therefore, we want to give you a little 'lecture' on grasping things of this kind. Everything that you need to understand and visualize is actually in your mind. That is where you are ultimately going to have to see it. It is all there, and all you have to do is contact it. Every bit of Truth that we know, and this includes all our mathematical formulas and all our natural laws, had to originally come from the mind of someone. We didn't find them out in a field somewhere.

Two mathematicians will reach the exact same conclusions, because they see exactly the same thing in the abstract, but they see it within themselves, subjectively. Yet, they both see the same thing. In teaching you astrology, we are merely trying to bring out knowledge that is within yourself. It does not always come out easily. Yet, it is there and it will come out. When you study a paragraph that is not clear to you, put it away and study it again at another time. Do this numerous times. Ultimately, you will understand, because the

Lesson Eleven 163

picture that we give you will suddenly match a picture that is within your own mind. Understanding is merely the matching of the exterior and the interior pictures. When they finally coincide, you have it. It becomes interesting to note that when understanding does finally come, it often occurs when the planet Venus is in strong aspect, either to planets in the heavens now or to planets in your natal chart.

Don't become discouraged when you do not grasp something immediately. Be patient and willing to keep coming back. Read a paragraph again and again if necessary, but with a time interval between readings. Give your mind an opportunity to 'turn over' as we say. The Truth is within yourself, and it is endeavoring to reach the surface, but all sorts of feelings and emotions get in the way, often distorting the true facts before they reach the surface. If it becomes necessary to read a paragraph several times, allow a day between readings. You will find that this makes a terrific difference. Relaxation is also important. You will understand much more quickly if you are relaxed. For this reason, it is almost impossible to grasp things when you are tense.

Once you have drawn a chart that matches exactly with the chart in this chapter, then you can have more fun, because the next step is to use different data and draw up your own chart from what you know of your time of birth. There will be cases where you do not know the time of a person's birth, but you do know the day, month and year of birth. Then you cannot draw the kind of a chart we show here. A certain amount of data is lost until the birth time can be determined by some method, but never let it be said that all is lost. Even when you do not know the time of birth, you still have a vast realm of knowledge that you can take out of a chart of the heavens for that day, because all of the people born within 24 hours will have certain characteristics in common, while other characteristics are different.

There are a few dogmatic old-timers in the field of astrology who will not consider a chart unless the actual moment of birth is known. These people have a lot to learn, and they won't live long enough to learn it. Even when the actual moment of birth is unknown, you can still know the zodiacal position of most of the planets, and this information in itself is of extreme value.

There is a group of astrologers who we might call precisionists. They insist upon a degree of accuracy that is beyond any practical value. If you wish to evaluate the work of these precisionists, follow their predictions as found in the astrology magazines, and you will usually find that they are consistently wrong. This should be sufficient evaluation of their work. Always remember that if you are going to measure the distance from New York to San Francisco, it is not necessary to employ a measurement unit of 1/10,000th of an inch. Miles will be good enough for almost any purpose. If you are going to string a telephone wire between the two cities, there will be the need for greater accuracy, but there will be a lot of other things you will have to consider also. You will have to allow for sag between poles.

Follow the procedure given above. If this seems a difficult point in the Course, relax. When you have finally completed that chart of your own birth, make a copy of it. Mail the copy to us. We will check it. if you are making any mistakes we will see them, and we can bring them to your attention.

When you draw up a chart, remember to take the Ascendant ONLY (or First House Cusp) out of the Table of Houses. Place the rest of the zodiac around that chart. Each cusp will have the same number of degrees of a sign as the number of degrees on the Ascendant. Don't try to use the type of chart shown in Lesson Eleven at the top of the page. Despite the fact that this is the Placidus chart that has been most often employed, it is filled with mathematical errors when the planets are placed therein in the customary fashion. Such a chart is mathematically incommensurable. Beware of the so-called 'standard' astrology, because it consists of standardized errors.

It is noticeable that the new student often makes his symbols of the planets in the chart very small in order to have them more correct proportionally, while the old student usually employs large symbols. The use of large symbols has its advantages because you see them better. Note the size of the symbols we use. Don't be afraid to use large symbols. You will come to it eventually anyway.

If you will study the chart in this lesson before trying to erect one of your own, you will see that it shows the degree of the zodiac on each of the twelve house cusps. Each planet appears in the chart, and beside each planet is the sign and degree occupied by that planet. Uranus is above the First House Cusp, because it is at 20-Satittarius and has not yet reached the First House Cusp which is at 22-Sagittarius. If Uranus were at 23-Sagittarius, we would place it on the other side of the line. Note that Pluto is in the Sixth House because it is at 17-Gemini and has not reached the cusp at 22- Gemini, while Neptune is in the 7th House, because it is at 29-Gemini, while Neptune is in the 7th House, because it is at 29-Gemini and has passed the 7th Cusp at 22- Gemini. The planets are traveling counterclockwise. Also note that we have placed both the North and the South Lunar Nodes in the chart, only one of which, the North Node, was in the ephemeris. The other is merely placed at the exact opposite point in the chart. This chart is a view of the heavens as they would appear if you were up in the air at a point at right angles to, or 90 degrees of **celestial longitude north of the ecliptic** or Earth's orbit.

The conventional charts, either the Campanus, Regiomontanus or the Placidian, are drawn with the observer of the chart 90 degrees of celestial longitude north of the place of birth (geographic, not ecliptic). Then, the planets are taken from the ephemeris and placed in this chart, a procedure that is mathematically incommensurable. The planets are not in the positions shown in the chart at all, and all such charts are in error. This applies to all charts used by those calling their work 'Standard Astrology'.

LESSON TWELVE

THE ART OF INTERPRETATION

The application of any science becomes an art. This is true of mathematics, and the mathematician can make mistakes. The mathematical machine or 'brain' may not be regarded as practicing an art, but the machine is a product of Man, and it can do only what Man has provided for it to do. It has no originality, and it is in no sense a brain. It can do nothing its inventor could not do if he wanted to make the effort and had enough time, but inventors are often lazy, and that is why they invent. There is an important difference between the electronic calculator and Man. The machine has no intuition. It is fairly common for modern teachers of science to praise the discoveries of such men as Pythagoras, Copernicus, Kepler and Newton and simultaneously condemn the methods by which those discoveries were made. Man can reach out and explore abstract realms, while the machine can do this only to the extent that Man has provided. For the machine, there is a god, and that god is Man. The machine is limited to the pattern that its creator provided.

Theological writers have often pictured Man as half god and half animal. From an astrological viewpoint, that part of Man that is represented by the Water and Earth signs is the animal, while that part represented by the Fire and Air signs is the god. The machine operates automatically. That part of Man that operates automatically is the animal. That part that does not operate automatically is the god. It would appear that the ancients saw more god in the Air signs than in the Fire signs, for you will note that in no instance is an Air sign represented by an animal. Man always represents God as similar to Man. He always creates God in his own image.

Before leaving Lessons Ten to Twelve, the student should make certain that he knows the technical factors of erecting charts of the heavens. Practice and checking is going to bring perfection. If you have other students around you, you should check each other. Whenever you have doubts, you should write to us and let us do the checking.

There is one simple rule that will help you. If you have a chart drawn for 6:00 A.M., the Sun must be on the east side of that chart. If you have a chart drawn for noon, the Sun must be in the upper part of that chart. If you have a chart drawn for 6:00 P.M., the Sun must be on the west side of the chart. If you have a chart drawn for midnight, the Sun must be in the lower part of the chart.

The most common error is to draw a chart that is exactly twelve hours out of the way. Students often get A.M. and P.M. mixed up, or they use the Sidereal Time for noon as the Sidereal Time at midnight, or vice versa. When you look at such a chart, this error is immediately apparent, because the Sun will be in the opposite place from where it should be. If you draw a chart for noon, do not expect the Sun to be exactly at the cusp of the 10th House, because in the kind of a chart we are employing, you are not looking at the chart from your birthplace, but from a point at right angles to the Earth's orbit (the ecliptic). You are looking south from a celestial point of view, and not from an Earthly point of view. You may be looking more to the southeast in the morning, more to the southwest in the afternoon, or vice versa, depending on the seasons from an Earthly viewpoint.

As we go into the second half of this Course, we are going to deal with interpretation, which, although it is an art, can be based on certain well defined and systematic principles. We receive a good many letters from students who tell us that they can erect charts, and they ask whether they can begin the second half of the Course and skip the first half. We turn down all of these requests. Some of you who have been through the first twelve lessons will know why. These students have usually learned too many things that are not so, and for us to grant their request would mean a continuation of errors and the mental confusion that would have to result.

There are some students to whom interpretation comes easily, others for whom there are obstacles, but the student who overcomes his obstacles my be the best astrologer in the end.

We do not like to interfere with a student's natural abilities of interpretation. When you reach correct conclusions by your own original methods, we are not going to interfere. If this seems logical and apparent, one should note that astronomical and mathematical writers constantly condemn such men as Pythagoras, Kepler and Newton because they made their discoveries by certain methods that proved successful, and the writers advocate methods that are often unsuccessful. If you develop original methods that prove successful, we will never quarrel with you about them. Instead we will try to learn from you.

It may be that these words should be directed more to the female of the species, because it is a fact of our own experience, that many women develop the art of interpretation more rapidly than do men. This becomes troublesome only when they cannot tell us by what method they reached their correct conclusions. Actually, this sort of thing is often due to the fact that women observe many things that men do not, a strange motion of the hand, an odd habit, etc. In our thirty years of experience with astrology, we have learned a great deal from women who were untrained observers, but who habitually and automatically observed many things that trained observers never see. The existence of this unorthodox power of observation often comes to the surface only after much in the way of painful questioning. A woman detects something the rest of us have missed. She can't explain how she detected it, because she never thought about the matter. To her, it seemed natural. Although it can be called intentional, it is unconsciously as systematic as any other kind of thinking. The world of science just hasn't taken the trouble to examine the system. An example may help to clarify the point.

Sitting in a restaurant and watching a stranger at another table, a lady suggested that he must be born on May 19th. Startled by this assertion, the science editor of a New York

paper rose, walked to the stranger, apologized for the intrusion and asked the man for his birth date. The man replied that it was May 19th.

The lady could not explain why she thought the stranger was born on May 19th, but this was unsatisfactory to a science editor and others present. She was questioned at great length. Finally, she named off a number of other people born on May 19th and pointed out that they all had a certain odd habit. She had noted that this stranger had the same odd habit. All this careful observation and the resultant conclusion appeared to have been something that went on in the girl's unconscious realm, and until pressed by painful questioning she appeared unconscious of her own methods.

We do not condemn such methods. We do strongly suggest determining what the methods are and how they work, and this can be accomplished. After discovering that he had an ability to solve mathematical problems in his sleep and awaken with the answers, the writer could not rest until he discovered how this was done. He would try to remember further and further back into dreams that preceded the solution, and he soon realized that in his sleep he had been looking at an abstract design. Everything in mathematics is design, cosmic design, and these designs can be seen in a waking state as well as in sleep. The difficulty lies in our inability to eliminate the objective from the subjective during the waking state.

The three mentioned mathematicians were so interested in the abstract world that they could blot out the objective world and see clearly into the abstract.

The school child is told that Sir Isaac Newton discovered the law of gravitation when he saw an apple fall from a tree. This is one of the tales of fairy-tale textbooks. Newton never claimed that gravitation was a property of matter. He described it as mathematical expression, and when other scientists of the day began describing it as an inherent characteristic of matter, he wrote to Bentley, 'You sometimes speak of gravity as essential and inherent to matter. Pray do not ascribe that notion to me; for the cause of gravity is what I do not pretend to know, and therefore would take some time to consider of it.'

There are hints that Newton discovered gravitation, not as a property of matter but as a property of an abstract ellipse. The apple may have demonstrated what he already knew. Newton did not perform experiments to get the answers. He first calculated the answers and then performed the experiments to verify his conclusions.

This discussion is brought forth because we want the student to be a free thinker and to learn how to use the best that his own mind has to offer. When the student begins thinking in terms of authorities, he blocks his own best mental abilities. We will teach you our own methods of interpretation, but we expect you to improve upon them wherever you can. Just as a single symbol may tell a mathematician a story that might require pages of the layman's figures, so a single planetary configuration can tell an astrologer a story which might fill a book. No student will live long enough to digest everything that his own individual horoscope can tell him. There will always be more, for it is one of those things that goes into infinity. You will, then, realize that no other astrologer could have the time to interpret everything that your own birth chart can tell you. You can be unfolding that for the rest of your life. It goes on and on, but the more charts of other people you study the more you will learn about yourself. This is the most important reason why we would prefer to teach you astrology instead of merely writing pages about what your own individual horoscope means. It is not our desire to make you dependent on us, but to make you independent and able to do your own thinking and your own interpreting.

Whatever natural abilities of interpretation you may have, use them to the full, but do not be content to use them without understanding them. Find out what you are doing and how you are doing it. If the work is being done down (or up) in the unconscious,

Lesson Twelve

find out how. Then you can call forth the ability at will without being dependent on its working on one day and not on another, although you will always have some days that are better than others.

Any planet in any sign of the zodiac has a specific meaning. Every person with a specified planet in a particular sign of the zodiac will have a certain basic characteristic. A hundred people born with that planet in that sign of the zodiac will have the same characteristic, but it will be altered, adjusted and sometimes disguised by other factors in the horoscope. The same will apply for a specific aspect between two planets, and it will apply for planets in the astrological houses. In introducing the art of interpretation, we will begin with three specific categories of information.

1–Planets in the signs of the zodiac
2–Aspects between the planets
3–Planets in the astrological houses

There are many other factors to be interpreted. This is the starting point. There are many other division and mathematical points to be considered. Let us simplify things by not trying to take in too much territory at one time. You can broaden your frame of reference as you go along.

It will be a great help if you become systematic, if you organize your knowledge as you go along, and in that connection we suggest some notebooks. Suppose you take one notebook and have a page for every planet in every zodiacal sign. For Moon, Sun, Mercury, Venus, Mars, Jupiter, Saturn and perhaps Uranus. You will need twelve pages for each planet. Depending on your age, you may not have known people born with Uranus in all of the zodiacal signs, but you will ultimately. This will mean that you will need 96 pages to cover the above planets. The writer has known people born with Neptune in all the zodiacal signs from Aquarius around counterclockwise to Scorpio. That is ten signs. He never knew anyone born with Neptune in Sagittarius or Capricorn. We can meet such people when we study history, however, and it would be well to have a page for Neptune in all twelve signs, and the same with Pluto.

Characteristics of these slow moving planets in a particular sign have to do with all of the people born during a certain period of years. One generation thinks differently from the next generation, and consequently these qualities are not as apparent because we see nothing unusual in a generation of people all of whom have certain characteristics that exactly match our own. This seems natural until you have given the matter a great deal of study. The empire builders born during the time when Neptune was in Aries saw nothing odd about themselves but they considered their children mighty peculiar. We never understand why our children think differently than we do. We are always wondering what is wrong with the new generation instead of wondering what is wrong with ourselves. You will probably reach a time when you will see it in a new light. It will become a hundred times more interesting to you.

As this is written, Neptune is just beginning its transit of Scorpio, and if we want to know what Neptune in Scorpio means, we may want to go back and study what was going on the last time it was there–165 years ago. Scorpio represents the Family Survival Dynamic. It is the sign of sex, while Neptune represents the Social Survival Dynamic. The Social Survival Dynamic comes under the domination of the Family Survival Dynamic or sex. What happened the last time it was there? Joseph Smith and Brigham Young were born. They gave birth to Mormonism and a plurality of wives. The Mormon Church was organized on April 6th, 1830, with Mars (ruler of Scorpio) conjunct Neptune (ruler of Pisces) in the sign of Capricorn (the legal sign). On June 27th, 1844, with Jupiter, Uranus and Pluto in the pioneering sign of Aries, the Mormons were driven from Illinois by mob violence. In 1847 they established themselves in Utah. Polygamous Mormonism is still practiced in some parts of the west where official sources close their eyes to it, and it will be interesting to observe what the re-entry of Neptune in Scorpio will bring about for Mormonism. What will it do for matters pertaining to desegregation, where the old white South fears that desegregation will lead to greater mixing of the sexes between the two races?

This is merely an example of the kind of things that will ultimately interest you about history. Very often, you will better understand history and the people of a particular era when you see the patterns as described by the planetary conditions of the time.

When you have a page entitled Venus in Aquarius, each time you come upon a birth date showing Venus-in-Aquarius, you will write the person's name on that page. After a while, you will have quite a number. This will enable you to see what characteristics these people have in common which are not common to other persons. You can test both theory and experience simultaneously.

You will need another notebook dealing with all the possible planetary aspects, such as Mars square Uranus, Mars opposite Neptune, etc. When you encounter a new person with Mars square Uranus, you can immediately compare that person with all the other persons you have met having Mars square Uranus. It would be well to have all the Mars-Uranus aspects on a group of pages together, because you will find certain qualities in Mars-Uranus aspects whether they are so-called favorable or unfavorable aspects. For example, you will find that all such aspects appear to be accompanied by mechanical ability but the so-called unfavorable aspects are more accident-prone.

You will need another notebook dealing with the planets in the various houses. A word of caution in this connection, however, for you will want to be very careful about placing information in this notebook unless you are positive that the birth time is correct. Otherwise you are apt to have a notebook containing much in the way of faulty information, and this would mislead you. It is better not to know than to think you know something that is wrong.

First, you should get to understand what the planets in the various signs of the zodiac mean, because in most cases this information will be definite and not dependent on an exact moment of birth, except in those few cases where a planet is changing from one sign to another during the actual date of birth.

Finally you will want to know what the transits mean. In astrology, the word transit has a different meaning than in astronomy. In astrology, the word transit means the relationship of the planets on a particular date after birth to the planetary pattern on the date of birth. In astronomy, a transit merely means the passage of a celestial object across the disk of another object, over the meridian of a place, or across the field of a telescope. Thus, in astrology, the word transit has much broader meaning.

From the moment of birth, all the planets as well as Sun and Moon are changing their relative positions, and as this happens, different parts of what is represented by the horoscope have an opportunity of manifesting in different ways. A powerful Family Survival Dynamic can manifest in many different ways during a lifetime. What is assumed to be love under one planetary setup at one time may be hatred or indifference under another planetary setup. That explains with one swoop why people do not stay in love. The planets change their positions, and the love that lasts longest is often one that is a subconscious expression of insecurity. The child may love the parents to the extent that the parents represent security. There are other binding factors, but most of them do not require monogamy. These include loyalty and platonic relationships. Platonic relationships do not involve insecurity, and therefore, for some persons are non-existent. On the other hand, not all insecurity is involved with monogamy. Neither is insecurity always binding. An insecure woman may leave her husband because she believes she can find greater security in another man.

Almost at a glance, to the experienced observer, the planets and their constantly changing relationships explain why our thoughts, feelings and emotions are constantly in a state of flux.

In basic principle, the notations of the astrologer are akin to those of the mathematician. The symbols are different, but when the mathematician writes 10 to the power 1001, he has a specific meaning that other mathematicians understand. He means the figure 1 followed by 1001 ciphers. When the astrologer writes ♀♓ he means Venus-in-Pisces, but he also means a long group of characteristics and possibilities as well as a certain potential. He means that the Family Non-Survival Dynamic Guide is under the domination of the Social Survival Dynamic.

A person born at such a time will have strange social urges. He is attracted to unusual types of people due to a deep sympathetic urge that carries him in a certain direction. The injustices of society are more apparent to him. He is likely to be attracted to those who are ostracized from orthodox society, those for who orthodox society has prepared no place, those who have been overlooked. He is compassionate. He does not take the rules of society seriously, for he sees injustice in them. He doesn't really care whether something is proper or not, because proper doesn't make it right. He may have a special interest in the criminal, the sick person, anyone who is operating outside the 'correct' limitations of organized society, the 'crackpot', the pauper or the beggar. He may show more respect for the prostitute than for the ladies who live on Snob Hill. There is something about her that interest him. What made her what she is? (A limited number of birth dates of prostitutes on hand shows them also having Venus in Pisces more often that in any other sign). He feels both sorry for her and sentimental about her. We may find him having many secret friends. In the presence of these 'unfortunate' people, he relaxes. He can say what he things with no fear of criticism. He knows he will be understood. There is no need for being a hypocrite. He is quite apt to regard drinking as a form of relaxation, and we are apt to find him in the association of people who drink a good deal. It is all an escape from the artificiality of organized society which is always a strain. He has a broader conception of things, because he is not limited in his thinking by any accepted frame of reference, for a frame of reference itself is a mental limitation, sometimes useful but often a means of justifying faulty conclusions.

Because Venus represents the Family Non-survival

Lesson Twelve

Dynamic Guide, all of this is designed to inject a new strain into the hereditary factors of the future. The thinking and the reasoning is on the unconscious level, but it comes to the surface in the form of sentiment, and it is the sentiment that is acted upon, although it is the unconscious purpose that is being served. The family must not survive in its old form. The form must be changed. There is the urge to marry a person from some other realm. This might mean a foreigner, one of another race, or one from some entirely different level of society. Nature is at work to produce the mongrel. The mongrel will be frowned upon by the old family strain, but experience has taught us that mongrels often have superior intellectuality, are more brilliant. Most Americans are mongrels. As in mathematics, when you put strange combinations together, it may be difficult to predict the result. We are dealing with the chemistry of characteristics.

This is merely an example of what one little symbol like ♀ ♀♓ can mean. Each planet in each sign of the zodiac has such a meaning of its own. You are going to learn them, and the more you learn them by yourself by experience, the better it will be. This is the type of knowledge you shouldn't memorize. Let the pieces fit together and crystallize in your mind as you go along. In explaining the principles represented by the planets and signs of the zodiac in earlier lessons, we have supplied you with the tools.

Always remember one thing.

THAT REPRESENTED BY THE PLANET IS DOMINATED BY THAT REPRESENTED BY THE ZODIACAL SIGN THAT IT OCCUPIES.

When you work with astrological symbols, you are approximating what the mathematician does when he works with algebraic symbols. The mathematician may say that X equals Y, while the astrologer practically says that Venus in Pisces equals Neptune in the 11th House. Here are two different astrological expressions that have the same meaning.

Ten people having Venus in Pisces will not all be alike.
One may have Mars in Taurus while the other has Mars in Scorpio.
This brings in a variation. Yet, certain basic characteristics are present in each case. The person having Mars in Scorpio will express them with less caution than the person having Mars in Taurus.

The teacher in mathematics may explain a principle to the

student, and he may supply and work out a specific problem while the student watches. He may show the student that a right-angled triangle with legs of 3 and 4 feet has to have a hypotenuse of 5 feet. Then he may ask the student to supply the hypotenuse of a right-angled triangle having sides of 5 and 12 feet.

We have shown you what it means when Venus is in Pisces. What does it mean when Venus is in Capricorn? We could write out an interpretation and ask you to memorize it. That would not make you a good astrologer. Instead, we are going to ask you what it means when Venus is in Capricorn. We want you to write out an interpretation of a person having Venus in Capricorn. Understand one thing. We do not care how wrong you may be. If you prove to be close to 100% correct, well and good, but it is the error of your interpretation that will tell us what we have failed to make clear to you. Start out by realizing that when Venus is in Capricorn, the Family Survival Dynamic Reactor. Search the birth dates of your friends. You will not have to erect any charts to determine whether they have Venus in Capricorn. The ephemeris will tell you that, except in cases where the ephemeris shows Venus to be in the first or last degree of a sign. In those cases, you would have to check the time of day the person was born to be certain.

Find as many persons having Venus in Capricorn as you can among people you know well. Check yourself, and see whether your interpretation fits these people. Take as many liberties as you wish in this respect. In other words, you will be writing up a theoretical interpretation, but you are privileged to check it against people you know to see whether it fits. This is a procedure you are going to be following from now on, so long as you deal with astrology. You are going to be working from a theoretical base that has not been previously supplied by any other teacher of astrology, but it must always check with experience. You will be combining theory and experience. For a time, we would like you to forget everything else in the horoscope and confine yourself to learning to interpret what each planet in each sign means.

This can keep you quite busy, because you can start some more notebooks. You can write out your own theoretical interpretation of every planet in every sign. This will be a starting point. From this point on, you will constantly be adjusting your original interpretations. Your purpose will be perfection of these interpretations. It is doubtful whether you will ever reach any absolute perfection, but you will always be getting closer and closer.

It will be much as if you were adding a series of fractions such as 1/2, 1/4, 1/8, 1/16, 1/32, 1/64, 1/128, etc. You will note that 1 always appears above the line in these fractions, while the numeral below the line is always double that below the line in the previous fraction. The more such fractions you add, the closer the sum will be to 1, but it will never actually reach 1, except at infinity. We say that the sum of such fractions approaches 1 as a limit. No matter how long you create and add more fractions, you can never reach or exceed 1.

In the same manner, although your goal is perfection, and although your goal is perfection, and although you constantly grow closer and closer to that perfection, it is never actually reached. We do not ask absolute perfection. Again, let us quote Paul G. Clancy when he said that astrology is the algebra of life. All the symbols in a horoscope are employed in a similar manner to that in which we employ algebra. That doesn't mean that you need know anything about algebra, but if you have studied algebra it will help you to understand why we do not have to set up any causal hypothesis to explain astrology. Any causal hypothesis involves that man-made conception we call time. When we express the Pythagorean theorem algebraically and say that $(a^2 + b^2) = c^2$ we do not mean that a and b, in any way, cause c, for all exist simultaneously. One does not come before or after the other.

When we consider a symbol such as ♂♒ we recognize a group of characteristics which in themselves may be considered as causing certain results, but the results are dependent upon how well the individual understands his own characteristics and what he does to channel them to gain the results that he desires. Thus, the results can be quite different in the case of the individual who has studied and understands astrology than in the case of the person who blindly follows sentiment with no conception of what the origin of that sentiment may be nor where it may lead. You can see that where we deal with horoscopes that contain factors of violence, the difference between the person who understands his own inner nature and the individual who does not is stupendous.

In many instances, the individual with no understanding of the nature the horoscope reveals actually does face what we might call fate. The machinist in a machine shop may lose a hand before he discovers that his periodic accidents are to be associated with his Mars-Uranus opposition but also with his own irritability. His accidents are preceded by irritability, and once he learns this he will think about it when he feels irritable, and it will remind him to be more careful. In his case, caution is required. In other cases, caution becomes an obstacle in the way of success. Thus, we ultimately begin to draw a close parallel between the words fate and ignorance. They go together. Where you have ignorance you have what has been meant by fate. The greater your true knowledge of abstract principles, the greater your freedom and the less your fate. The Christian church has tried to reverse this. It has been assumed that knowledge is dangerous. This conception was prevalent among the members of the Pythagorean school, although it does not appear to have been characteristic or Pythagoras himself insofar as we can determine. Yet, it was this very conception that led to the destruction of the Pythagorean school. There are some who suspect that Sir Isaac Newton may have detected the whole secret of the atom mathematically and that he detected his solution from the work of Hermes, after which he was afraid to reveal the information to the world of science for fear of what scientists might do with it. At any rate, he did not explode an atomic bomb in order to confirm some of his views on alchemy. The man whom some scientists describe as the greatest scientist of all believed in alchemy.

Mastery of astrology, like mastery of other subjects, helps you to overcome that man-made conception we call time. The writer lives on a ranch 19 miles from the heart of Tucson. Years back, the ranch was a stagecoach stop for traffic coming out of the mountains and headed west. It was an all day trip over rocky desert roads from the ranch to Tucson. One late afternoon, the writer was relaxing while awaiting the arrival of a relative on a plane from New York. The passenger was making the trip from New York to Tucson, 2,500 miles, in as little time as it formerly took the stagecoach to travel from the ranch to Tucson. Basically, what has made the difference is knowledge of mathematics and its working principles. We are left with the possibility that what can be accomplished in a millennium can be accomplished instantaneously when we know more about mathematics and nature.

The student of astrology begins to learn of natural abilities that he did not know existed. When he knows about them he can use them. The possibilities that can be opened are practically unlimited.

When you started in school, you were given a table of 26 symbols to memorize. They were the letters of the alphabet. Consider the number of words you can now form out of those 26 symbols. We furnished you with the letters of the astrological alphabet back in Lesson Three. Now, you have reached a point where you can join two of these letter like ♄♓ to abbreviate the statement: THE FAMILY NON-SURVIVAL DYNAMIC IS DOMINATE BY THE SOCIAL SURVIVAL DYNAMIC.

Ultimately, you have the whole natal horoscope to consider.

Lesson Twelve

It is filled with symbols. You will interpret them one by one, but you will be able to make an overall mathematical statement and say: THIS CHART IS JOHN. The accomplished and trained astrologer will often take one look at a horoscope, more or less take in everything at one glance, and give a mathematical expression to the whole which might be uttered in one word as WOW!

In time, you will meet some stranger, and in talking with him, you will recognize certain traits and characteristics that you will be able to place and define astrological. You will note a specific characteristic that belongs to Pisces or Neptune, and before you ever ask for a birth date, you will have pegged and classified that characteristic. You will know that a certain dynamic is over-expressed. You many know that something has to be in Pisces or that Neptune is strongly placed, but you will have more difficulty in determining what planet may be in Pisces or in what way Neptune may be emphasized. However, the moment you look at the chart, you will see what you are looking for with one glance, and when you do so, you will possess far more information than could possibly be obtained by observation. If you are a psychiatrist or a psychologist, you may, at one stroke, have more information than you could obtain by days of probing and analysis.

Observation of these characteristics is where the female of the species so often rates at the top. But we beg of her to learn and understand more about her own intentional powers of observation. We often call such unconscious powers of observation being psychic. It is our view that these powers merely involve a process of unconscious calculation. The more you learn about those unconscious functions, the more able you will become to control those functions at will.

You should be able to detect what we are attempting to do. We are trying to teach you our own established methods of interpretation without allowing them to block the functioning of your own natural powers of interpretation. We are trying to teach you an organized system of interpretation, but we do not want to risk allowing that factor of organization to become a mental block. We want you to think for yourself.

We want to supply you with the tools, but we want you to realize that you may ultimately develop better tools of your own. It is not our purpose to make you as good as we are. We want you to be better. We have often stated that mathematics is simple but Man has made it complicated. That is the case when people are afraid of mathematics. The complicated nature of the Man-made side of mathematics drives the layman away. We are more concerned in seeing you get the right answers than in seeing you get them in the right way. To us, the right way is the way that gets the right answers, just so long as you know how you are doing it. The psychic often gets the right answers without knowing how he does it. That is quite unsatisfactory. On his off days, he gets wrong answers. Although it is our aim to develop interpretation as a science, we do not want to lose sight of the fact that it is also an art. The good actress may have been trained, but she had to have natural ability to start with. Today, we are able to teach all children to read and write, despite the fact that some may have found it easier than others. If you are hungry to interpret, you will learn to interpret more rapidly, because you will allow no obstacles to stay in your way for long.

How quickly you learn to interpret will be partly dependent upon the amount of time you devote to it. Even if you find yourself being quite consistently wrong, this should not discourage you. Even then, you will learn by the process of elimination. Every time you learn that something is not right, you are that much closer to what is right.

If we want to know the temperature, we look at a thermometer. When we receive your written interpretation of Venus in Capricorn, we will observe it in the same manner that we would observe the thermometer. It will show us what you are doing. It will enable us to detect whatever you might be doing wrong. By observing one person having Venus in Capricorn, it is possible that you may pick up characteristics that do not belong to Venus in Capricorn but to some other feature of the individual's chart. That is something that we can immediately detect and call to your attention. So, just go ahead and write your own conception of what you think Venus in Capricorn means. Have no regard for how terrible you might think it to be. Send it right along. If it is really terrible, it will contain more clues. If it happens to be practically perfect insofar as we can see, there will be less that we can teach you. It is not the star scholar who needs our help. It is the one who has hit a snag.

There is one common error made by students of astrology. If the student dislikes some person who happens to have the Sun in Scorpio, he is too apt to attribute all of the bad characteristics of this person to all Scorpio people. It must be remembered that any planetary configuration can have a negative and positive side. Because you may have known a man who was killed by being hit over the head by a hammer, you are apt to develop a prejudice against all hammers. Yet, thousands of carpenters are making good use of hammers every day. They are building homes for millions of people.

Lesson Twelve

Let's not throw away the hammer. Instead, let us teach people the proper way to use a hammer. The same for astrology. Let us not assume that a person is bad because of his horoscope. Instead, let us teach people how to use their own horoscopes, or what abilities the horoscope signifies for some good purpose. We are dealing with principles of cosmic design. Those principles are perfection themselves. All evil must come from our failure to understand the cosmic design, from our failure to interpret it correctly.

LESSON THIRTEEN

ANALYTICAL INTERPRETATION

In opening a discussion of the interpretation of planetary aspects, it is necessary to introduce the planetary nodes. The majority of the astrologers of the early part of the twentieth century have ignored these nodes, although they were very important to the ancients, as is indicated by the terms 'Dragon's Head' and 'Dragon's Tail' applied to the north or ascending node and the south or descending node of the Moon. Today we call them the lunar nodes. [ed. Vedic Rahu is the north node and Ketu is the south node.]

It is quite easy to understand why they were ignored when we realize that these astrologers were trying to bridge the gap to what was fashionable in the world of so-called science. They were trying to adjust to the environment. They were trying to fit their subject into the error of 'scientific style'. Like so many other things, scientific theories and hypotheses come and go, live for a day and die. At that time, it was popular to think in terms of the ether of Sir Oliver Lodge, in terms of vibrations and waves. So, astrologers had to explain their subject in terms of ether, vibrations and waves. It was pointed out that when light reached the place or point of a planetary node, there was nothing there for light to bounce against, and so light went right on. How could a mathematical point have an effect? And so, the nodes were forgotten and ignored.

Grant Lewi placed great emphasis on the nodes. Statistics of RCA Communications Inc., in connection with their research dealing with the correspondence that exists between planetary motion and magnetic disturbances that interfere with short-wave radio reception, placed emphasis on the nodes. Letters from two astrologers unknown to each other asked of us the same question. Did we know why people born with the Sun near 13-Gemini or 13-Sagittarius seemed to have so much difficulty in making marriage a success? Of course, this meant success according to orthodox standards which are quite inadequate, but it was interesting to note that each astrologer had unconsciously called the exact position of the nodes of the planet Uranus (Individual Non-survival Dynamic Guide and Seventh House principle). Marriage is difficult where this principle is concerned because marriage is a Man-made institution that was molded in ignorance of this principle. When he wrote the

Ten Commandments, General Moses had his intellectual limitations.

Our own statistical investigations gradually lead to indications that mere mathematical points (We will supplement this term later.), **the planetary nodes, are more important than the planets themselves**, and this was the beginning of our realization that an entirely new conception of astrology was essential, an astrology unlimited and unhampered by the dogma of modern scientific hypotheses. When you deal with mathematical points, mathematical lines and mathematical planes which can have no material counterpart, you are in the realms of mathematics and abstraction. A mathematical point has no dimensions. A mathematical line has but one dimension. A mathematical plane has but two dimensions. There is no material counterpart until you reach three dimensions, and when you go onto a fourth dimension, you again have no material counterpart. You have again entered the world of abstraction.

You can use a pencil to illustrate a mathematical line, but it is inaccurate, because a pencil line has width and therefore two dimensions. You can use a sheet of paper to illustrate a plane, but it is inaccurate because the paper has thickness and is three-dimensional.

We were approaching our later view that astrology could not be a causal phenomenon, but must be considered as a matter of mathematical expression. We cannot explain why snowflakes and crystals follow the same pattern that bees follow when building the cells of their hives (the hexagon) except to say that the whole thing is a matter of abstract mathematical expression. Although the hexagon is the most economical means of building these cells, we can hardly visualize each hive of bees employing intellectual bees who labor over a drawing board computing the mathematics of what shaped room would require the least wall space to house the greatest content. Neither can we say that snowflakes cause bees to build six-sided cells. Nor can we say that snowflakes freeze in six-side fashion because they are copying the bees. Yet, a hexagon room enclosed by 60 feet of wall will contain over 259 square feet of floor area, while a square room enclosed by the same amount of wall will contain but 225 square feet of floor space. A room shaped as an equilateral triangle with 50 feet of wall will contain only 141 square feet of area. Of course, a circular room would contain a greater ratio of area to enclosure, but you can't fit circular rooms together. The more equal sides a room has, the greater the floor area, but if a room has more than six sides, you can't fit the rooms together. Among polygons of equal sides you can fit together only hexagons, squares and triangles.

Mathematically, the bee would appear further advanced than

Lesson Thirteen

Man. He builds warehouses out of hexagonal shaped rooms while Man builds warehouses out of square or rectangular rooms. We find a strange parallel in the fact that the ancient astrologers regarded planetary aspects based on parts of hexagons as harmonious and aspects based on parts of squares as discordant. The sextile aspect is merely one side of a hexagon, while a trine aspect is one side of a equilateral triangle or two sides of a hexagon. An opposition aspect can be considered as either two squares or three sides of a hexagon, and oddly, astrologer have disagreed as to whether the opposition aspect is harmonious or discordant. It has been our experience that the aspect brings tenseness, problems and worries while forming, but produces CHANGE that solves the problems and gives relief while separating. If there is any astrological symbolism behind the six-pointed star of the Jewish church and the four-point cross of the

THE ECONOMY OF DESIGN

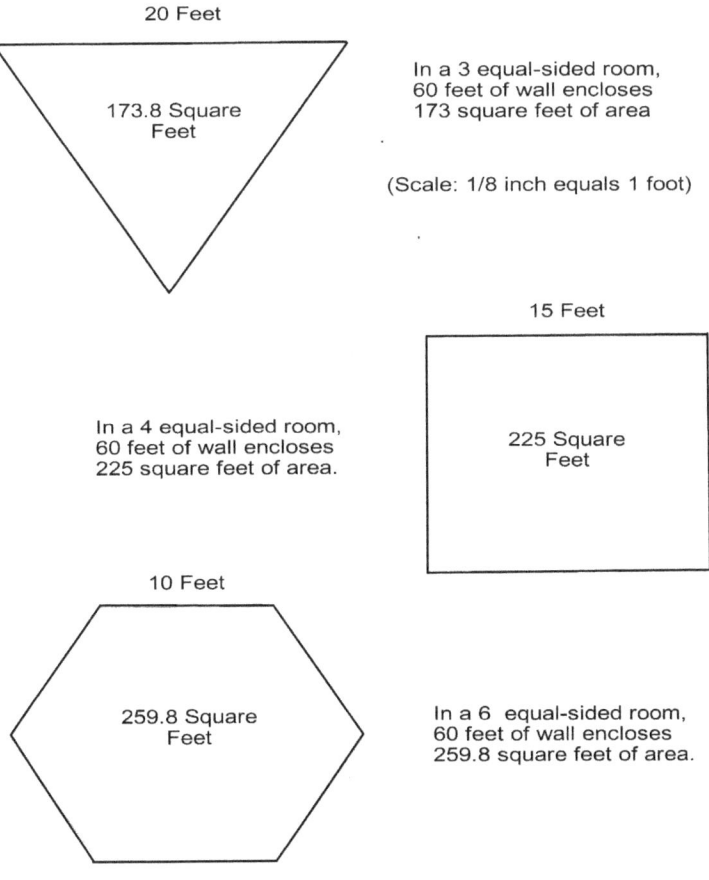

Christian church, then one would appear to indicate harmony and the other discord. Yet, the advanced astrologer realized that the 1-4-7-10 House Cross (Leo, Scorpio, Aquarius, Taurus) is something that can be transcended through understanding and higher knowledge or wisdom, while those astrologers who look upon the story of Christ as symbolism see Christ, not as a man but as an abstract principle. To them, it is the rise of the individual above materialism and into the abstract realms. Whether Christ ever lived as a man is beside the point. The principle is the same.

Just as astrology is concerned with geometrical and therefore mathematical figures, we find these figures throughout the mineral world. Different minerals are made up of crystals of different geometrical patterns. Not all minerals follow the hexagonal pattern. Salt crystals form on the square or 90-degree angle. This is true of other minerals, but the hexagonal pattern is quite common. The crystal mines of Arkansas seem to show everything in accord with the hexagonal principle. Where erosion had washed away a patch of a lava bed at the floor of the Grand Canyon, we found petrified wood covered by hexagonal crystals. At the Spring Creek Ranch in the Texas Panhandle are found strange objects composed of calcite an inch thick and two inches in diameter that are in the form of a perfect hexagon. They are said to be a hangover from the Triassic Age, which was the earliest period of the Mesozoic era. By careful selection, you could pave a bathroom floor with these strange objects, but most of them have other hexagons growing out of them at various angles. A geode is a strange object of nature that looks like an egg and is shaped like an egg. There is a location near Mammoth, Arizona where these eggs lay on top of the ground in quantity over an area of ten or more square miles. These are agate geodes. They are white on the outside like an egg. Originally, they appear to have been mere shells, but from the inner surface grow crystals until the object finally becomes a solid. A hollow ultimately becomes a solid. Where does the material come from? Or does material need to come from some place? When it is ready to appear it seems to appear. Astronomers are trying to learn how matter appears or forms in space. How does it appear as form in the hollow of these geodes?

An astrological aspect is merely an abstract geometrical measurement. True, it is sometimes a measurement between two material objects, but this need not be true. It can be a measurement between a planet and a mathematical point, or a measurement between two mathematical points where there is nothing whatsoever of a material nature. It can still have it counterpart in human affairs.

Because **the planetary nodes are even more**

important than the planets themselves, it is more important that you understand what a planetary node is. Remember that we used imaginary embroidery hoops to illustrate two planes of space. Put one hoop inside the other, twist one so that one hoop crosses the other at two points. Look at the hoops from above that point where they cross and you see an X. The point where the two hoops cross is the node. The other point where they cross is also a node. It is customary to call one point the north node, the other point the south node.

 What we call the north node of a planet is that point where the orbit of a planet crosses the plane of the Earth's orbit as the planet goes north. The south node is the other point, and when the planet crosses the south node, it is traveling southernly.

 Actually, no planet ever crosses the Earth's orbit. It crosses the plane of the Earth's orbit. Therefore it is not strictly true to consider these factors as mathematical points. When referring to a node, an astronomer means that the mathematical point where the plane of a planet cuts the Earth's orbit, but we could as well consider the node that mathematical point where the plane of the Earth's orbit cuts the planetary orbit. These two points would not be the same in space. One would be at the orbit of the Earth while the other would be at the orbit of the planet. However, if we draw a straight line from the Sun to the mathematical point that is furthest away from the Sun, it would of necessity have to pass through the other mathematical point. Thus, the important factor with which we deal becomes, not a mathematical point, but a mathematical line drawn from the Sun in opposite directions to infinity. The plane of the Earth's orbit and the plane of the planetary orbit join all the way along the line.

 As computed today, the planetary nodes are considered as heliocentric, those points where the above described line crosses the Earth's orbit. However, if we use these points as if they were geocentric, they appear to work. This is easy to understand if we consider that we are dealing with mathematical lines instead of mathematical points. Now, we can draw a new set of lines with the Earth as the center to those points where the line above described reaches in infinity, and their direction must be exactly the same as the direction from the Sun. Such a conception justifies us in using the heliocentric planetary nodes in our zodiac just as they are given in heliocentric longitude. This view might also completely justify Hugh MacCraig and others who are employing heliocentric positions in the Earth zodiac.

 We know from experience that when the nodes are employed in this fashion they function. We do not know whether they will also function when located by lines from the Earth as a center (geocentric nodes) to those points where the nodal line crosses the Earth's orbit, for these points have never been calculated and published (now available). A student well schooled in mathematics is now calculating these positions, however, and we hope it will ultimately be possible to publish them for experimental purposes.

It becomes vital to know the zodiacal position of the lunar nodes. The position of the north lunar node is given in the ephemeris. The south lunar node will be at the opposite zodiacal point. The Sun is not involved in this calculation, because the Moon goes around the Earth. The point where the two orbits cross is itself in motion, and it circumvents the entire circle of the zodiac in 18.6 years.

The planetary nodes have a similar motion, but it is too slow to be significant within a lifetime. The nodes of Mercury circle the zodiac once in something over 171,000 years, while the node of Uranus makes the trip in about 40,000 years. Oddly, the nodes of some of the outer planets appear to move more rapidly than those of the inner planets. In any event, however, no planetary node moves a degree within 100 years, so you can use the present nodal positions as close enough for any living being.

Present north nodal position are as follows:

Planet	North Node 2010	North Node 2000	North Node 1900	Annual Movement
Mercury	18TA 27'54"	18TA 20'48"	17TA10'48"	42.6"
Venus	16GE46'52"	16GE41'28"	15GE45'36"	32.4"
Mars	19TA48'59"	19TA44'22"	18TA57'22"	27.7"
Jupiter	10CN35'31"	10CN28'24"	9CN28'12"	36.7"
Saturn	23CN43'39"	23CN38'25"	22CN47'05"	31.4"
Uranus	14GE02'24"	13GE59'24"	13GE29'24"	18.0"
Neptune	11LE53'05"	11LE46'31"	10LE40'51"	39.4"
Pluto	20CN26'49"	20CN18'41"	18CN57'21"	48.8"
Eris	06TA12'	06TA07'	04TA21'	30.0"

Planets aspecting these points, or even the lunar nodes aspecting these points, have significance. **To have a body conjunct or square the node of a planet appears to be more important than to have it conjunct the planet itself.** The node of Mars will show up strongly where violence and surgery is involve. In fact, we have found but one case of a hysterectomy to date where

Lesson Thirteen

the woman did not have a planet (any planet) conjunct or square to Mars' nodes. That one case had Mars conjunct the node of Saturn. During a class, a protest against this statement was introduced by the wife of a physician. As a result, all the students were requested to accumulate all the cases of hysterectomies they could find, and to try and locate a case where this was not true. Many birth dates involving hysterectomies were produced. There was no case among them where some natal planet was not conjunct or square the nodes of Mars. That does not mean there are no such cases, and you might find one, but when you do, please send it to us. In fact, it will be very helpful to our research department if you will send in the birth dates of all the people you know who have found hysterectomies necessary. The data will be very welcome.

Planets conjunct or square the nodes of Saturn have a depressive correspondence, while planets conjunct or square the nodes of Uranus have a very restless and rebellious spirit. The functioning seems to be similar to aspects of the planets themselves but more pronounced.

The north node of a planet is also called the ascending node, while the south node is called the descending node. No one has yet prepared symbols for the planetary nodes, and if we invented symbols and placed them in each horoscope, the charts would become rather crowded, but you can compare them with each chart you draw. You don't have to worry or be concerned about their motion, except for the lunar nodes which are given in your ephemeris.

Another experience was important in our dropping any conception of astrology as a causal phenomenon. The ancients placed great emphasis on the occurrence of important events at the time of an eclipse of the Sun or Moon, and having observed many world-shaking events that occurred near the time of an eclipse, we set out to investigate this statistically. We found many events that occurred near the time of an eclipse,, but we also found many important events that occurred at other times. Eclipses can occur only when the Sun is conjunct or within about 15 degrees of a lunar node.

Our statistical investigations showed that most of the important world events which occurred when there was no eclipse, took place when the Sun was square the lunar nodes. Thus, it would appear to have nothing to do with the eclipses, because there can be no eclipse when the Sun is square the lunar nodes, but the results are the same.

Statistics also show that loss-of-life through fire increased when the Sun or Uranus is conjunct or square the lunar nodes. Yet, there is no increase in the number of fires during this period. Our investigation included all the fires in the US and Canada, where the material loss was over $100,000, over an eight year period. The data was furnished by the National Fire Protection Association which publishes all such data for insurance companies. Nearly all the 'famous' fires took place when the Sun or Uranus was conjunct or square the lunar nodes, but 'famous' fires are those where loss-of-life is heavy.

It is our considered view that what is involved here is human instability. The Sun-lunar node relationship gives us an average 86.5 day cycle of human instability. Human instability reaches its maximum when the Sun and lunar nodes are 0 and 90 degrees apart, its minimum when they are 45 or 135 degrees apart. At the maximum, people panic more easily. A very great ratio of loss-of-life through fire takes place during the night among people who are sleeping in strange surroundings as in a hotel. If they awaken in strange surroundings during a stable period to find the building on fire, they seem to know what to do. They think clearly. But if the same thing happens during an unstable period, they are confused and they panic, bringing about their own deaths. Hotel fires which during stable periods seldom involved loss-of-life, but hotel fires occurring during the unstable intervals have resulted in very heavy loss-of-life.

At other times, people seem able to relax and maintain calmness, not all people, the majority, but during these unstable periods, people feel something has to be done about something and right away. The result is that not only most wars have begun at such times, but most peace treaties have been signed at such times. Many men of great genius are born at these times.

Watch Congress! Its members can argue for months, but let one of these periods come along and they pass bills fast and furiously. If an election happens to be held at such a time, the result always seems to be the opposite of what people expect it to be. Any student who is interested in history will find it very interesting to see how world events have always coincided with these intervals of instability. Modern man knows nothing about such cycles, but the ancients were conscious of them. The ancient Chinese executed two astrologers because they were lax in their duty and failed to predict an eclipse. The ancients paid great attention to eclipses, but we have no evidence that they knew about the 90-degree angle of instability as well. [ed. CPT called this aspect Moon Wobble, the medieval term is lunar bendings]

We suggest the possibility that heart attacks are more frequent at those times when we are at the apex of human instability.

Lesson Thirteen

No statistical work has been accomplished in this direction, but newspapers often carry the news of the death or heart attacks of prominent persons at these times. Both of President Eisenhower's attacks came at such times.

From somewhere has come the tradition that for a planet to be conjunct the north node is favorable while a planet conjunct the south node is unfavorable. Over the years, we have been unable to find on iota of confirmation for this conception. We have been unable to find any evidence that the two nodes differ any way. The results appear to be exactly the same. The important turns during wartime seem to accompany these points of instability. An inspection of history will verify this.

We must not lose sign of the fact that the zodiacal signs themselves and the astrological houses are based on nothing but mathematical points. They are purely abstract. They are based on nodes, the crossing of planes. The zodiac is determined by the nodes where the plane of the Earth's orbit and that of the Earth's equator cross. *The astrological houses are based on the nodes where the plane of the Earth's orbit and that of the horizon cross.* These two nodes are the ascendant and descendent of the horoscope. In our procedure, we place the other house cusps at equal 30-degree intervals in the plane of the Earth's

In interpreting planetary aspects, it is well to first see how the planets are situated in their relation to the nodes. You should check each planet in its relation to each node. After that, you should check each planet in its relation to every other planet. Do not limit your inspection to the 0 and 90 degree aspects to the nodes. Pay attention to the 60 and 120 degree aspects (sextile and trine) also. These appear to be very helpful.

In Lesson 13, we advised you to first grasp the principle represented by each planet in each sign. You must do the same with the planetary aspects. You can take a dozen cases of people with Mars square Uranus at birth, and you will find certain common characteristics in each of these people, but you will not grasp what is going on, on the unconscious level unless you consider the principles involved.

Of itself, the square aspect is a 4th-10th House aspect. It involves the Family Survival Dynamic (10th) and the Family Survival Dynamic Reactor (4th) at one and the same time. Mars also represents the Family Survival Dynamic, while Uranus represents the Individual Non-Survival Dynamic Guide.

On the unconscious level, the family, the old family, the hereditary factors, are struggling to perpetuate. Also on the unconscious level, the Individual Non-survival Dynamic Guide is operating in an effort to point the way for change for the individual himself.

This is a very difficult aspect for marriage or intimate associations. The sex factor (Family Survival Dynamic) is very strong. However, the object of sex attraction is not a constant. Let us say that it is ever changing. Yet, the Family Survival Dynamic Reactor can hold things in check over varying periods of time, but sooner or later there will be an eruption.

The first effect is irritability, impatience and perhaps anger. The individual is happiest in motion or in the middle of constant change. The FSD (Family Survival Dynamic) is trying to bring children into the world. It is the aim of this dynamic to have as high a ratio of the old heredity as possible. Thus, in extreme cases, the aspect can lead to incest, for this would bring heredity survival above the 50% mark. It is quite common for the aspect to lead to adultery, because this will lead to a lower ratio of specific outside heredity in the overall family. If all children are by the same mate, some other family is influencing the family's heredity by an equal 50%. On the unconscious level, there is revolt against this.

With such mixed up motives on the unconscious level, you can understand why so many people fail to understand themselves. The poor conscious being knows nothing about all this, but from the unconscious level are pushed up complex feelings and emotions to motivate the individual in a direction that will satisfy these unconscious objectives. A very high ratio of people who consult astrologers by mail are those with Mars-Uranus aspects. There may or may not be such aspects in the natal chart, about every 21 years, on the average, Uranus by transit will form a 0, 90 or 180-degree aspect to natal Mars. Very stable people survive the aspect, but not without some indication of what is going on in the unconscious level. If there is adultery in a marriage, this is when it usually begins.

When people have problems they cannot understand, and Mars-Uranus aspects create such problems, they seem to want to tell the story to someone who is a complete stranger and who will listen sympathetically. In many cases, they do not want to face the person personally. It would be embarrassing. For them, to be able to do business with an astrologer by mail is an opportunity, and it is surprising how freely they will write. It is doubtful whether anywhere on Earth is as much evidence of the true nature of humanity as in our confidential files. Unfortunately, this data can never be published. However, the Mars-Uranus person is not likely to be reticent about blurting out the truth. If you want details, these people will give them to you, particularly if they can see that some scientific purpose can be achieved. In many cases, however, the person writing to the astrologer may not be the Mars-Uranus individual, but a member of the family, perhaps the mate.

If we take a purely objective view of this variety of aspect, we see that it creates restlessness, rebellion and irritability. It results in accidents, quarrels, estrangements, adultery, divorce and sometimes murder. It is something that refuses to be confined indefinitely. The nature is daring and bold. It is explosive. Where a cure of some situation is necessary, this sort of knowledge isn't going to be of much use. To know that a war is being fought is not sufficient knowledge to stop the war. If we are going to remedy the situation, we must look beneath the surface and see what is occurring on the unconscious level. We must examine the motives of nature, not those of the conscious personality. The conscious personality is merely the victim. He does not direct these unconscious processes, nor does he determine what feelings and emotions he is experiencing. We must help him to understand them, because these forces have a way of shutting themselves off when they are detected. Nature seems to crawl into her shell when you keep her under close surveillance. It is certainly a fact that planetary aspects never work the same way when you are watching them.

It is a peculiar fact that Mars-Uranus aspects are very common in the horoscopes of young widows and widowers. That is difficult to explain. Why do these people so often marry someone who is going to die? Is not the act of marriage conditioned by a future event? We often find the aspect in the chart of the mate of someone who is killed in an accident or who dies by violence. Why? It is seldom that we find the chart of a widow or a widower in which there is not some very strong Mars aspect, but quite frequently a Mars-Uranus aspect.

If you have followed our suggestions about notebooks, you will ultimately have the birthdates of many people born under Mars-Uranus aspects, but they will not all have planets in the same zodiacal signs. That will make a difference. If Uranus happens to be in Capricorn, its instability will be curbed in comparison to Uranus in Scorpio or Aquarius. Thus, you cannot completely interpret an aspect between Mars and Uranus without considering the zodiacal signs behind the planets. We dealt with this factor in Lesson Thirteen. Later, we will have to consider the effects upon the Houses also. Never lose sight of the fact that Mars represents the past while Uranus represents the future. Like many other combinations, the square of these two planets is a conflict between the past and the future. If they are square, the sign behind one battles for the past, while the sign behind the other battles for the future, because signs square to each other cannot both represent the past and cannot both represent the future.

The conjunction or opposition aspect will differ in this respect. Either both planets will be in a sign representing the past or both planets will be in a sign representing the future.

The marriage institution as we know it is an attempt toward stability. It is an attempt to keep human activity within certain limitations, and in that way keep it under control. The institution was designed by Man without taking into consideration all of the factors of nature. Man's own mental and intellectual limitations were concealed and covered up by inventing SIN. Thereafter, Man excused himself for his own imperfect plan by attributing the whole plan to God. In this way, leaders of the people were able to better control the people by presenting themselves as specially appointed representatives of God Himself. This was an authority they began to take unto themselves and to pass on to others. People were taught to FEAR God and in that way to fear the self-appointed representatives of God. If we are to improve the marital institution and if we are to improve our religion, these are facts that we must recognize and not hide away. A good religion should be based on FAITH and not on FEAR. Yet, we must not throw something away because it is not perfect. That is what the man who tries to become an atheist attempts. An imperfect plan still holds the possibility of perfection. Because it may be partly in error is no excuse for discarding the whole. We are far from perfection in any of our accomplishments. When Uranus is over-emphasized in a chart, it is the inclination to throw away the whole when an imperfection is discovered, instead of trying to see just what is right and what is wrong in order to correct what is wrong and preserve what is right.

Please understand that it is not our purpose to try and tell anyone what is right or wrong, but only to bring to light knowledge of nature's principles that we may have a better understanding of the factors with which we all must deal. We might shorten this statement by merely saying that we wish to exclude dogma. We want everyone to keep and open mind.

To come back to nodes, there is a sharp difference between an aspect between two planets and an aspect between a planet and a planetary node. Where an aspect between two planets is involved, each planet seems to retain its own importance, but where a node is concerned (except where the lunar node is involved, and we will touch on that presently), **the node seems to completely**

dominate the planet. You will note that when we discussed hysterectomies, we stated that person experiencing hysterectomies always seem to have some planet, ANY planet, conjunct or square the nodes of Mars. It didn't seem to make any difference whether the planet was Mercury, Venus, Mars or Saturn, the effect appeared to be the same. This is completely contrary to what we find where aspects between planets are concerned. **When planets are conjunct or square the nodes of a planet, the principles represented by the planetary nodes involved seem to completely dominate the situation.**

We are frankly puzzled in this respect where the nodes of the Moon are concerned. When the lunar nodes conjoin or square the Sun, it is the principle of the Sun that is emphasized, not the principle represented by the Moon. Such aspects bring CHANGE and instability, while if the lunar nodes were to predominate, we would expect the opposite effect. Yet, there seems to be no planetary condition that does more to express the principle of non-survival of form than lunar-node-Sun conjunctions and squares.

Never be disappointed when you find that an overall principle does not appear to work in a specific case, because in such instances, if you are alert, you are on the verge of a new discovery. It is the exception to the rule that always leads us to new discoveries. If we adopt a mathematical theorem and discover that it works only 99% of the time, by assembling the cases that do not work we will find the pattern of imperfection, and then we can adjust and correct the theorem. We will find that the exceptions to the rule themselves all fit together into a pattern.

For example, we stated earlier that we had found one single exception to the rule that women who have hysterectomies performed have some planet conjunct or square the nodes of Mars at birth. That one case had Mars conjunct the node of Saturn, but that may not be the explanation. With but one exception, we are in no position to determine the answer. We need many more exceptions to the rule. We have no doubts, however, that if we have enough exceptions we will have the answer to that one exception, and to all others at the same time.

If you are going to help yourself or help others through the use of astrology, you must constantly determine what is taking place on the unconscious level. People can handle problems on the conscious level themselves. If a man is being chased by a lion he has a problem, but this problem is on the conscious level, and he can recognize it for what it is. He may run, or he may shoot the lion or he might make a friend of the lion, like Daniel. He will not have time to draw up a horoscope. **The chief need of astrology is in handling problems on the unconscious level.** In order to remedy a situation constantly accompanying a certain type of planetary aspect, it is necessary to know and recognize what that aspect represents on the unconscious level. What is nature trying to do with the individual's life? If a man is robbing your home and you discover him in the act, he is quite likely to run away. Nature is often like that. When you discover what she is up to, she often retreats. When nature is up to something which you might consider as deviltry, catch her in the act and she is likely to discontinue the act. For this reason, many times the cure of an illness results from the mere discovery of its real cause. An illness always has some purpose it is trying to serve. If you can detect what's that purpose is, you have gone a long way in affecting a cure.

In interpreting astrological aspects, or in interpreting anything astrological, there are two ways of going about it, and you must apply both of these ways together, because one is a check against the other. Your interpretation can be based on experience, but this type of interpretation can never reach perfection, although it is very valuable. By studying 100 people who have Mars square Uranus, you can learn a great deal about the aspect.

The other method of interpretation is analytical. You employ astrological symbols exactly as you would employ mathematical symbols. They always represent the basic twelve principles of nature as we described them in earlier lessons. You employ them exactly as a chemist employs mathematical symbols. They become mathematical symbols to you. Equations will not be exact as they are in mathematics because we do not know enough to make them exact, although this is not entirely true, because we can say that ♀ ♓ = ♆ **11th Hse.** By this we mean that Venus in Pisces is equal to Neptune in the 11th House. In other words, when we know what it is like to have Venus in Pisces, we know what it means to have Neptune in the 11th House. Thus, when you have learned what every planet in every zodiacal sign means, you have also learned what every planet in every house means. All you have to do is adjust your knowledge by astrological equation. It should be noted that this analytical phase of astrology was impossible a few years back, and its introduction came first in the writer's, A NEW EXPERIMENT IN ASTROLOGY, published in 1938. It was impossible to employ analytical methods because the 'house value' had been employed, but we maintain that it was an erroneous 'house value'.

In an analytical system, with a knowledge of the nature of the survival dynamics, the survival dynamic reactors, the non-survival dynamics and the non-survival dynamic guides, you can analyze a complex planetary combination even when you have never seen that configuration before, but it will be experience that will help you to discover whatever errors of analysis may exist. A prospective surgeon may learn all he can in medical school, but when he performs his first operation, he is up against reality itself. The same with you. You must learn through analysis but also through experience. You must combine the two.

We have stated earlier in this lesson that planetary aspects never work the same when you are watching them. Experience would indicate that the person who knows the existence of negative aspects fails to experience the negative effects, but what about the favorable aspects? In this case, we might say that a person fails to get the favorable effects unless he does something about them. Let's put it this way. Suppose you have a very favorable set of planetary conditions at a given time. They might come and go unnoticed in many instances, but suppose you start a new business at such a time? In this case, you may get the favorable results for the rest of your life. The same would apply if you have a child at such a time. In other words, the same broad principle that we have expressed in our overall pattern is visible here. So-called negative aspects have to do with clearing up and re-evaluating the past, while so-called positive aspects involve your relationship with the future. Most aspects will have to involve both past and future, but an opposition or a trine of Venus to Uranus in Fire and/or Air signs from the 1st to 9th Houses would in no way involve the past, because all factors involve the future, while if you study the matter, it will become impossible to visualize any planetary combination that by aspect, zodiacal sign and house position will involve only the past. This in itself is a very interesting bit of mathematics and philosophy. Mars and Saturn both involve the past. If they are conjunct, the conjunction aspect involves the future. If they are 30 degrees apart, although the 30-degree aspect represents the past, one planet has to be in a sign that represents the future. The 60-degree sextile aspect represents the future. Although the 90 degree aspect represents the past, one planet has to be in a sign representing the future. The same principle applies for the other aspects.

LESSON FOURTEEN

SURVIVAL OR NON-SURVIVAL

To be a good astrologer, you must WANT to be a good astrologer. Some of our students with the least previous education are making the best progress, because they WANT to be good astrologers. They are determined to conquer this subject. Others are dragging behind merely because they have not yet decided that they WANT to be GOOD in this field. We have given the student every possible cooperation. We have never failed to answer questions nor explain the answers. Yet, some students are not cooperating with us. For example, some have not written that interpretation of Venus-in-Capricorn that we requested. Some of the interpretations that have been written, by students to whom astrology is completely new, are among the best we have read, but if you can't write a GOOD interpretation, write a bad one, and we will tell you. You are going to have to practice interpretation. If necessary, you are going to have to make mistakes, but mistakes are valuable, because they show us what is wrong. Mistakes themselves always form a pattern, and it is our job to detect that pattern and explain it to the student. When the student understands the pattern of his own mistakes, he never makes those mistakes again.

Although we still have LOTS more to tell you, from now on, you are going to have to work at astrology. You are going to have to WANT to collect charts and interpret them. You are going to have to WANT to be a good astrologer. You are going to have to practice. You are going to have to prove to yourself, by experience, that the principles work the way we say they do. You must not be satisfied to take our word for it.

How good an astrologer do you want to be? How far are you willing to go? We asked you to write an interpretation of Venus-in-Capricorn. Why not write an interpretation of Venus in each of the twelve signs, a theoretical, analytical interpretation? What do you THINK each of these configurations should mean? Write the interpretations and send them to us. If they are good, if you are on the right track, we'll tell you so. If you are not on the right track, just let us determine WHY you are not on the right track. Let us be responsible for finding the error in your work. That is our responsibility, and we are here to assume it. When you have succeeded in writing a good interpretation for Venus in each sign, you are going to be well on your way. After that, other interpretations are going to be easy for you. After a while, you will get so that you can look at a chart and see at a glance more information than you could put in a novel-length book. You will see the design of the whole.

Right now, however, you are at a crossroads. Are you going ahead or are you going to fall back? You have got to practice. You have got to work and let us criticize your work. We have let you go a long way by yourself, but no more of that. We have told you, but now you are going to have to start telling us. If there appear to be any obstacles in your path from your point of view, you better start telling us about them now. This is where we begin to get tough. After that little lecture, we will continue on our way.

In correspondence, students have been adopting a series of abbreviations, and without knowing each other, the students have all gone forward with the same abbreviations. Therefore, we are going to adopt the set of abbreviations that have been universally introduced by the students themselves independently of each other. In the future, we will save a lot of words by the use of these abbreviations, and we will introduce them here:

SD	Survival Dynamics
NSD	Non-survival Dynamics
SDR	Survival Dynamic Reactors
NSDG	Non-survival Dynamic Guides
ISD	Individual Survival Dynamic
FSD	Family Survival dynamic
SSD	Social Survival Dynamic
ISDR	Individual Non-survival Dynamic
FSDR	Family Survival Dynamic Reactor
SSDR	Social Survival Dynamic Reactor
INSD	Individual Non-survival Dynamic
FNSD	Family Non-survival Dynamic
SNSD	Social Non-survival Dynamic
INSDG	Individual Non-survival Dynamic Guide
FNSDG	Family Non-Survival Dynamic Guide
SNSDG	Social Non-survival Dynamic Guide
FOR	Frame of Reference

Lesson Fourteen

For the present, we will limit ourselves to these 17 abbreviations. Four represent groups of principles. Twelve represent astrology's twelve basic principles. The last one is added because of its almost universally used by our students. It just appeared to be the natural thing for nearly everyone to adopt these particular abbreviations.

To understand the functioning of the twelve astrological principles it is necessary to realize that EVERYTHING in astrology is a battle between the past and the future. Everything is a question of whether an old design is going to be continued or whether a new design is to be allowed to come into being. All designs are mathematical, for mathematics is nothing but a study of design. A mathematical formula is nothing but a design, a symmetrical design.

Everything in life involves this question as to whether the old design is to remain or whether a new design is to be adopted. When a child is born, a being starts functioning according to a new design. That design appears in the heavens at the moment of his birth. When a man dies, the old design is left behind. Without life to hold it together, the old design (the body) disintegrates and falls apart. This one design (a single life) is a composite made up of many smaller designs. From the date of birth onward, life is a battle to determine what designs are to be retained and what designs are to be left behind, so that other new designs may become an experience of the life. It is a battle between the survival dynamics and the non-survival dynamics.

When pondering an interpretation, it will become much easier for the student if he remains conscious of the fact that first he must judge whether an old pattern or design is going to be continued or whether a new design is going to come into being. At birth, a design comes into being. At death, an old design is discarded.

A revelation of astrology lies in the fact that death and divorce show up as synonymous. Divorce is the death of a relationship, a combination, a design. Death of an individual is the same thing. Under these circumstances, we are almost forced to the conclusion that a being existed in some form prior to birth and has to exist in some form after death. Prior to a marriage, both parties to the marriage existed. Alter a divorce, both parties to the marriage exist. The marriage does not exist. That had a birth and a death. It seems quite logical to assume that the 'soul', the consciousness, what religious people call the 'soul' had to exist before birth and has to continue to exist after death. This is not an argument for reincarnation, for we have no opinion on the subject. Reincarnation is a theory or a possibility, but there can be millions of other possibilities and explanations. It need not be necessary for the being to exist in the 3-dimensional material world. He might be in entirely different dimensions. You exist in some other kind of a world when you dream.

Something that has always fascinated the writer is the fact that the same kind of aspects that accompany divorce, in many cases, accompany death of the partner instead. This begs a very interesting question. If the couple had been divorced, would the partner have lived? Despite the various purposes it serves, marriage is often a strain. It is a severe strain to have to live with a person who has a discordant chart. It is a severe strain to live with a person whose chart badly afflicts your own. We see many cases where a person gets sick immediately following marriage, and gets well following a divorce.

We recall a case where a child had to be placed in a mental institution, but as soon as placed there, the child got well. There was a shifting back and forth, because as soon as the child came home she became ill again. After the problem became sufficiently complex, we were consulted. The mother had a badly afflicted Mars. The child was born at that time when Neptune in Virgo reached the mother's Mars by transit, so that Neptune in the chart of the child is always on mars in the chart of the mother. We were forced to advise that for the good of the child's health and future, mother and child must be separated. The child was allowed to live with relatives, and was soon back in school functioning normally.

About two-thirds of the people who consult astrologers are women. Therefore, we have that much more experience with women. When a woman of 40 or more shows up as a client, and we see a strong affliction between Mars and Uranus in her natal chart, we always feel like asking, "Are you a widow or divorced?" However, we are more diplomatic and we let her tell us voluntarily. This does not mean that you can't stay married if you were born under an affliction of Mars-Uranus, but it does mean that you have to have a lot more knowledge and understanding of human relationships than will suffice for other people. There are a great many people who can remain ignorant and still get along, but for some people, such an existence will become too uncomfortable to tolerate. The result is that a great many people with Mars-Uranus afflictions become very intelligent. Certainly, none of them are stupid people.

Bear in mind that if we collect the charts of widowers and widows, we find that the charts are of a certain type. Principally, they show an excess of Mars aspects. One woman told us that she was a fatalist. She had married four times, and all of her husbands died. She had Mars conjunct Uranus plus Venus conjunct Saturn. Did she marry men who were going to die, or would these men have lived if they did not marry her?

Remember that in a case cited above, the child got well when separated (divorced) from her mother. We think of a man who died of a heart attack. Shortly before the attack, he told us that this wife just wouldn't let him out of her sight. He was under a severe strain because of the manner in which his wife insisted on being a part of his life nearly all of the time. He obviously wanted to get away and would fly across the country to see us 'on business' when there was no business to discuss. His wife would fight against these trips. At birth, his Sun was conjunct Jupiter in Cancer. During most of his life, he had clung to her too, but now transiting Uranus had reached his Sun-Jupiter. He got away. He had been a very insecure man and he had always needed his wife. He would never make a business decision without asking her advice, but when Uranus, the lNSDG, came along, he no longer wanted to cling to the old pattern. He found a way out. He had a heart attack and died. We have not heard from him since. He eliminated us from his design also. What he is doing now, we do not know.

We have pointed out earlier that a person can get locked in a FOR. Physical death would appear to be a means of completely changing one's FOR but there are other, less drastic ways. Illness and many other problems can be the result of an association, but often it is improper to break the association and cure the illness. In many cases, such a break is considered to be immoral. In New York State, a woman cannot divorce her husband for any reason other than adultery, and even this is not sufficient grounds unless the woman can show that she tried to prevent the adultery. There may be no children to consider, but no matter, this woman cannot legally have a divorce. She may be very sick from the association but the law allows her but one legal way out–to die. All of this is the work of whatever dogma happens to be the most politically powerful in a particular area.

This discussion is for the purpose of getting one principle across to you, that everything in astrology is a question of whether a design is going to be continued, altered or completely changed. **Everything is a battle between survival and non-survival.**

We see one man marry poor and become wealthy. We see another of wealth marry and lose everything. Here is a man who married and then accumulated wealth and position. There was a divorce, after which he lost all of his money and he has never been able to make any money since.

Here is a man of very moderate means who takes a partner into the business. The partner never works. This goes on for years but from the moment he entered the business, the company began making money, and both men became quite wealthy. After ten years of griping about his lazy, good-for-nothing partner, the first man threw out the partner. Soon thereafter, the company began losing money and it finally failed. The original man never made much money thereafter. The second man became the lazy, good-for nothing partner in another firm and went on making money.

In other words, even money-making seems to be a matter of a design. Here is another man who was very poor until his fourth child was born. He began making money, and continued to accumulate wealth for the next 21 years, at which time, this fourth child broke away from him, refused to accept his domination, and went off on his own. The father never made any money after that. His fortune dwindled until at his death, there was little for the family to inherit. That fourth child did all right on his own, it would almost appear that the father was able to make money only so long as it was necessary for the protection of this one child.

During thirty years of astrological practice, we have served many very wealthy people of the country. We have always been alert to see what qualifications were responsible for their money-making. It doesn't seem to be a matter of qualifications because many of them have no qualifications. Money comes their way in spite of anything they can do. It is unfortunate that because most of these people are still alive, we cannot tell these true stories. The information is in the realms of the confidential. Nevertheless, although John Smith is making $100 a week, it may be possible for him, through sincere effort and hard labor, to increase this to $150 a week—or even $200, but John will go right on with his hard labor. If he invests his surplus in a wildcat oil scheme, he will probably lose it. John is following a pattern, a design, and until he understands that pattern, his hard-work environment is going to survive. He is going to cling to it, because to him, it represents security.

Some student is going to write in this question unless we answer it now. We have stated that when a child is born, a being starts functioning according to a new design, and that the design appears in the heavens at the moment of birth. If this is true, then does the design of the heavens at the moment of death indicate the pattern of the future existence of the being? This is something to think about and students of astrology have been thinking about it for thousands of years. It has probably been responsible for some of the versions of reincarnation.

However, to accept this idea, it is necessary to assume that the entity does not escape the solar system as an FOR. In fact, it means that he does not even escape the Earth as an FOR. This introduces a terrific limitation to thought. Of course, not all reincarnationists claim that ALL people are reincarnated here on Earth. We are not going to try to answer the question. We have never had enough evidence to justify an opinion, so we will remain open-minded. We do not know. If we ever find out, we will tell you.

All prime human characteristics are of two classifications, those that are intended to perpetuate the pattern for the past and those which are intended to produce new designs. All designs are mathematical abstractions. Sex is always trying to perpetuate the hereditary pattern.

The ISD is always trying to preserve the design of the individual, while the SSD is always trying to preserve a social pattern of nature that Man has outlawed. You can't outlaw nature. You merely make criminals that way. You also make sick people that way.

Nature is going to function regardless. If you want her to work with you, stop ignoring her. Stop ignoring what she considers to be her rights under a higher law. Man is very ignorant to think that he can pass laws and outlaw Nature. Nature is stronger than all civilization combined. Sometimes she is very patient. She can afford to be patient. She will live longer than you can in your present form. If you think you are thwarting her, all she has to do is wait for you to die. To oppose her is going to be a serious strain on you, and you may have to die more quickly. Civilizations are born. They make their laws and they die. Nature outlives all civilizations, all scientific hypotheses, all religious creeds. We find continents of old at the bottom of the sea.

It is a battle of survival of form, but the solution often lies in recognizing nature, cooperating with her, and being willing to accept survival or non-survival of form when nature, mathematics and astrology illustrate that survival or non-survival of form is the solution.

Get acquainted with all the human characteristics that people have but analyze them; always classify them; determine whether these characteristics have as their prime motive survival or non-survival. A young girl is thrilled because of a new date. The motive is non-survival of family forms. Lurking in the background, however, will be the FSD just waiting an opportunity to take advantage of this situation and perpetuate two hereditary patterns, each on a 50% ratio.

If you will follow our advice and always analyze things down to a survival and non-survival basis, you will gradually be discovering that life is basically much more simple than you ever thought it to be.

Yet, it's like numbers. To understand numbers you must

first understand ONE and then TWO. As you go on, numbers get more and more complicated, but everything grows out of ONE. You understand higher numbers by understanding lower numbers, but as you go higher and higher, you will find that no matter how high you go, there are always numbers that have some new characteristics that are not possessed by any lower numbers. For example, 3,628,800 is the lowest number that can be factored by the first ten integers or numerals. 435,891,456,000 is the lowest number that can be factored by the first 15 integers.

Whether you are interpreting a planet conjunct a node, a planet in a sign, a planetary aspect or a planet in a house, first determine whether survival or non-survival factors are prevalent. Will the individual meet a stranger, or will he go see his grandmother?

Naturally, you are going to have more complicated problems, but you will understand them better if, at the start, you start weighing everything in terms of survival or non-survival of form. Can a girl's attachment to her family prevent her from getting married? Will she have to marry a man who looks like her father?

Occasionally, you will meet a married couple who look so much alike as to be mistaken for brother and sister. Was the FSD trying to capture more than 50% hereditary factor? Was the FSD trying to accomplish incest?

In Lesson Fourteen, we had a good deal to say about negative Mars-Uranus aspects. We selected these aspects because they are the most important ones where the clients of an astrologer are concerned. Most problems crossing the desk of an astrologer concern this group of aspects, but unfortunately, the majority of astrologers have never happened to find this out. They are exclusively looking for women in the Moon and men in the Sun, while their clients are all wrapped up in the FSD. In other words, the clients want some answer to the problems that their own sex lives present. They go to church and are told to think about something else, but they go home and there are the problems. They don't understand them and they don't know what to do about them. What is more important, they find themselves unable to control them.

Let us look further into these Mars-Uranus aspects. What do the favorable Mars-Uranus aspects do? Kenneth Brown, New York astrologer, originally taught psychology at Columbia University. He studied astrology, and during the war, he became Personnel Director of a war plant. He began putting his astrology to work. All employees had to submit birth dates. He found that the employees with Mars-Uranus aspects were the best mechanics, regardless of whether the aspects were favorable or unfavorable, but the employees with the unfavorable aspects were accident prone.

We speak of favorable aspects. Actually, we should not call them favorable or unfavorable, because what we mean is that some aspects involve the past while others involve the future. The so-called favorable aspects involve the future.

Here is a good example. In collecting the charts of people who have been convicted of sexually molesting children, the most prominent aspect in their charts is a sextile or trine aspect of Mars to Uranus. At first this may be a difficult thing to understand until we consider that they were ahead of time. Had they waited a few years, the matter would not have been a crime. Had the sex act occurred later, it would not have been criminal. From this point of view, the whole thing becomes a matter of what we call time. It makes a big difference whether you are at a certain point in space just before a bullet crosses that point, when it crosses or just after it crosses. In the first and third cases, you are safe. In the second you are not. People with favorable aspects are in the habit of being ahead of time. People with unfavorable aspects (so called) are in the habit of being late. So called positive aspects are precognitive, while so-called negative aspects are retrospective. While some people are constantly seeing the future, others are seeing the past. In each case the view probably contains much that is inaccurate. Although the precognitive factor may be faulty, what is more faulty than memory? If we are to rule out precognition because it is faulty, we must also rule out memory, because it is just as faulty. It is well known that witnesses in a court room, testifying about the past, all who supposedly saw the same event, will tell many different versions of what occurred.

There is little doubt that some dreams are precognitive. There are many people who dream events before they occur. It has been our impression that all dreams may be precognitive, but there is an obstacle. The minds of a great many people can interpret the future only in terms of the past. In his book, <u>An Experiment With Time,</u> J.W. Dunne explains dreams as being a mixture of past and future. We would alter this and say that all dreams may be stimulated by the future, but they are usually presented in terms and symbols of the past.

Where you have a great excess of Water and Earth in a chart, it is the tendency of the native to always 'expect' things to follow the same old routine. He regards it as 'common sense' for tomorrow to be like yesterday. In fact, he wants tomorrow to be like yesterday. He never dares think about it being different for that would make him insecure. If tomorrow is not going to be like yesterday, he doesn't know what to do. On the other hand, where there is a great excess of

Fire and Air in a chart, the individual thinks of tomorrow as different, for here, the constant drive is toward change. It is the nature of Fire and Air to live in the future, while it is the nature of Earth and Water to live in the past. There is always the question: Do we like things as they are or should we change them? There are many people who do not like things as they are, but they are afraid to change them. Society and orthodoxy frown on change. Here is a personnel director who refuses to hire a man because he has worked in too many places. He wants people who will frustrate themselves and stick to a routine. One thing he does not want in an employee is intelligence. If the man who owns this multi-million dollar company, for which this personnel man works, should anonymously apply for a job, he would be turned down. He has none of the qualifications demanded by this personnel director. That could be dangerous, for the owner of this company did apply for a job in one of his own companies under another name and worked in a minor position for a year in order to learn what was going on. Nobody in the company knew of this presence. In fact, nobody in the company had ever met or seen him consciously.

At the time when we first began exploring the possibilities of astrology, most everything was based on tradition and religion, or to put it another way, almost everything was based on dogma. Unfortunately, the last thirty years have not changed the overall picture in the world of astrology at large very much. Astrological books are filled with claims which the sponsors have never tested to see whether they were true or false, or how much of them may be true or false. The astrological student should accept nothing until he has tested it out, not with one but many tests. He should approach the subject with a good deal of skepticism.

In this connection, we are going to bring up the subject of retrograde and stationary planets. A planet is said to be retrograde when, from an Earth-as-a-center viewpoint, its motion is clockwise instead of counterclockwise. First, let us see what makes a planet retrograde. In the case of Mercury and Venus, these bodies are nearer to the Sun than the Earth. Consequently, we see them moving counterclockwise when they are on the other side of the Sun. When, they come toward us and move (what is to us) clockwise, passing between the Sun and the Earth, going in the opposite direction. In your ephemeris, they will be going backwards or retrograde.

The other planets are further away from the Sun than the Earth. The Earth goes around the whole circle in a year, and as it does, it passes these other planets, making them appear to move backwards in the sky, or retrograde. Because it is going around the Earth, the Moon is never retrograde. The apparent motion of the Sun is never retrograde. All of the planets themselves are retrograde part of the time. The lunar and planetary nodes are always clockwise in their motion.

Years back, Evangeline Adams placed great emphasis on retrograde planets. She claimed that the stock market was always weak when planets, but particularly Mercury, were retrograde. Ever since that time, astrologers have been writing that the stock market is weak when planets are retrograde. This claim is entirely false.

In 1938, a Wall Street man came to call on the writer. He asked whether the writer believed that the stock market is weak when Mercury or any other planet is retrograde. The writer stated that he did not, and a test was agreed upon. It cost about $3000 to make this test. A record of market movement for every period when Mercury (and all the other planets) was retrograde was compared with every period when Mercury was direct. This record included the entire available history of the stock market. A figure was established for the average daily motion of the stock market when Mercury was retrograde and compared with figure for the average daily motion of the stock market when Mercury was direct. The two figures came out even. Results bearing on tests with the other planets were the same. All results were negative.

Tests were then continued to test all the astrological systems of forecasting the stock market that had been published. None of them stood up, with the exception of the lunar node cycle, but the cycle was too long for a legitimate test (19 years). This cycle appeared to stand up fairly well. But we had less than three complete cycles to test, and during the next fifteen years, this cycle broke down also. These tests continued, and we tested nearly all the possibilities we could think of ourselves. Although we found some statistically significant results, they were not too important.

A Boston banker spent in the neighborhood of half million dollars making similar tests. He told us he got good results and that they made far more money for him than his research costs, but he kept the results to himself. We would not advise you to try beating the stock market by astrology unless you have a half million dollars to spend on research.

Grant Lewi believed in retrograde planets, although Grant didn't very often fall for unreliable ideas. The two of us discussed this subject a great deal. He maintained that his business always slowed down when Mercury was retrograde. The writer went home and put a statistical yardstick to his own business records. He found that business was just as good when Mercury was retrograde as when it was direct. He went back to GL, showed him the statistical results and asked permission to submit GL's business records to the same statistical results. Permission was readily granted. The result was the same, business was just as strong when Mercury was retrograde as when it was direct.

This demonstrates that the best of us must realize how faulty our own memories and observations may be. We cannot trust memory. That is why it is important to keep records. Don't trust your memory. If you 'believe' something, it is easy to see it when it doesn't exist. On the other hand, it is human to be blind to anything that does not agree with an accepted hypothesis. This was once brought home to the writer with a great impact.

While interviewing one of the scientist's pet hypotheses and drew the very reluctant admission that there was no real proof. However, the admission did not come without annoyance and irritability on the part of the academician. We put this question to him.

'You admit that there is no statistical evidence for the claims you have publicly made. Suppose some outside party were to make a statistical test and found your claims to be wrong. What would you do?

He replied, 'I WOULDN'T BE INTERESTED.'

Please don't follow this man's example. Be willing to make statistical tests. Learn HOW to make statistical tests. We will discuss this subject later, but get in the habit of submitting ideas and claims to sever tests. **Remember that there are hundreds of unreliable books on astrology on the market, written by people with little or no experience in astrology. They merely picked up their ideas from someone else and passed them along.** One difficulty is that they do not even pass them along accurately. As with memory, statements are distorted.

We are anxious to have you realize that everything can be resolved down to the question of whether a pattern is to be perpetuated or discarded. In some cases, however, we must consider patterns of motions. The motion may be a constant. Is it going to remain as a constant? Will it accelerate or decelerate?

Aside from reckless or drunken drivers of automobiles, the fast driver may be a better and safer driver than the slow driver. He may be far-sighted. He sees further ahead and anticipates the future better. The slow driver may be near-sighted. He has never learned to gage the speed of other cars. He drives right into the path of an oncoming car that has the right of way. Either the car seems a long distance away to him, or he doesn't see it at all. Watch the slow driver, the fellow who honestly believes that he is a careful driver.

Lesson Fourteen

He often lacks understanding of speed and distance. He has no true conception of them. He drives right in front of an oncoming object and is oblivious to the danger. On the Los Angeles freeways, you can be arrested for driving too slowly. In the old days they used to tell the story of the Philadelphia lawyer who went to New York and was run over by a hearse.

Thus, patterns involve motion, and these too can be destroyed, as when the irresistible force meets the immovable object. Even so, the slow automobile driver needs concern himself only with two dimensions. The plane pilot must deal with three dimensions. His job is more complex.

We have divided all of the astrological factors, the zodiacal signs, the planets, the planetary aspects and the astrological houses into factors definitely representing either the past or the future. All problems resolve themselves down to this one basic factor. Will things remain as they are, or will they change? What pattern is to predominate, the same old pattern or the new one? Let us look at some of the common questions that repeatedly fly across an astrologer's desk:

Will I get married? Will my husband ever change? Will I get well? Will I be able to pay my bills? Should I buy a new car? Can I sell my house? Will my husband give me a divorce? Will I be happy if I marry this man? Should I hire this man? Should I buy this hotel? Would I be more successful if I moved out west? Can I ever have children?

Everybody is concerned with whether they should hold on to an old pattern or adopt a new one. Hitler wanted one pattern. The Communists wanted another. We had our own choice. Different creeds battle for different patterns in their own way. The architect is almost totally concerned with patterns of the future. He designs buildings but he may merely repeat old designs. Engineers design bridges. They all have to know enough about mathematics to build their edifices in accord with abstract laws. They must calculate how much weight the floors and the bridges will hold. Miscalculations may cause a building to fall down, or may cause an automobile driver to lose his car or his body. When the writer was a boy, the speed limit for automobiles in many towns was eight miles per hour. Today, he can drive down one of the main thoroughfares of town and the speed limit is 45 miles per hour. In some places, speeds that were illegal because they were too fast are now illegal because they are too slow.

We have dwelled at length on these factors, because it will make all interpretations easier, if you never lose sight of the fact that there is always the question as to whether things are to remain as they are or are to change. Some people want the pattern of the past to prevail because they feel insecure when facing any kind of change. Other people always want a new pattern, always want change, because unless things can exist in motion, these people get fed up, irritable and rebellious. Fortunately for these people, the solar system moves. Other people want change but they are afraid of it. They fear going after what they want. They talk about it all the time, but they never do anything about it. They may never do anything about it. They may never leave the town where they were born. Examine the horoscope of such people, and you will find out why. If you can question these people in such a way as to allow them to see why they cling to certain things of the past as security, when they are not security at all, you will kick a spring. You'll see them let go, and when they do, there will suddenly be a new flow of energy. They will be in action. They will be doing things. They'll know what they want, and they will move so fast that you will have a hard job giving them advice. They will no longer feel the need of it. Their health will be better too. However, when you want to travel at high speeds, you travel in the field of dynamics, and you have to know more about the mathematics of dynamics. Things have to be streamlined, and you may need swept back wings.

LESSON FIFTEEN

THE MYSTERIOUS SOCIAL SURVIVAL PROBLEMS

When we refer to Social Survival problems as being mysterious, we are telling you that there is a lot about them that we do not understand, but we are also telling you that here is the richest field for research that we can visualize. Solve these problems and you can do away with prisons, mental institutions, drug addicts, alcoholism and much illness, but we will not solve them turning our backs upon them. We will not solve them by burning witches. Science will not solve them by limiting itself to a frame of reference that excludes the unorthodox.

All of these problems have some correspondence with Neptune, Pisces, the Sixth House and the 150 degree aspect in astrology.

The road to the solution of these problems involves careful observation and the collection and organization of data pertaining to what happens to people and what folks do when they are under so-called negative SSD patterns.

One of the most powerful combinations is found in the so-called negative configurations involving the planets Mars and Neptune. For the moment let us consider the conjunction, square and opposition of these two bodies, and what we find relative to the people who are born under them. Other Neptunium patterns have similar effects, but there are differences.

In the first place, these people are sentimental, and they are very emotional. They have serious emotional problems within themselves. When emotion rises, it is overwhelming, and they are swept up by it. It is something that is too great to control. During one moment, they can be overcome by grief. During another moment, by joy, but even joy may express itself in tears. There is deep sympathy for the underdog or for animals and lower beings. In many cases relief is sought through alcohol, drugs, and what is usually described as wildness. There is deep compassion for the ill and for the so-called criminal. He is considered a victim. Prison reform has usually been carried out by this sort of person. If the individual shows any criminal tendencies himself, he is expert at planting the evidence on another person. He can be subtle and secretive.

There is a little of this in everybody, but we must study the extreme cases, the horrible cases, if we are to learn. We must study the insane, the alcoholics, the drug addicts and the inmates of penal institutions. You will find the milder cases all around you.

Much is concealed by the invention of the word illusion. Someone sees something. Most people do not see it, and so it is said to be an illusion, nonexistent except in the person's 'mind' or 'imagination.' On a number of different occasions some very brilliant man has come to us. He has had emotional problems. He has become somewhat of an alcoholic, and he has had delirium tremors, commonly referred to as the DT's. The DT's are merely a form of delirium associated with alcoholic indulgence. There are other forms of delirium, and the dictionary tells us that delirium is a more or less a temporary state of mental disturbance characterized by confusion, disordered speech and often hallucinations – also frenzied excitement or wild enthusiasm. When the above type of man gets on the other side of the writer's desk, the writer gets curious. After all, here is a brilliant man. He has achieved and accomplished many things, but he has had emotional problems. An attempt to escape them has led to excessive alcoholism, and it has led to the DT's.

'What happened? Just what did you see?'

We can't suppress this question. We want to know. The story is told. The man had 'illusions'. But, there is always another man. He had illusions also. We want to know all about his experience. We want all the details. Other people do not seem to be interested in these illusions. After all, why be interested in something that does not exist? However, after combing a number of these stories, we want to know why there is such a similarity in what these different men report as to what they saw. Why do most of them have to see animals, usually, but not always, little animals? This man specifies that they were all little animals. He never saw any big animals, but here is a man who was in a hospital at the time when the animals came. His hospital room just filled up with animals, and one of them was a big, lazy lion, who just lounged around the room and took it easy. In no case that has been related to the writer were any of the animals violent or unfriendly. The alcoholic merely seemed to find himself in an animal world. Oddly, the ancient religious writers quite often referred to the world of the emotions as the animal world. It is often said that the animal in a person comes out when he is emotional.

There are many heavy drinkers who never have the DT's and never have illusions. There are many people with the mentioned Mars-Neptune aspects who never drink, but when the Mars-Neptune people turn to alcohol or drugs, things can happen. These people are overly sensitive. They seem to contact something the rest of us cannot contact. What they see may be misinterpretation, but they certainly appear to see something. With his own eyes, the writer has never seen Tokyo, but many others who say they have seen Tokyo tell stories that are too similar for us to doubt that there is such a place as Tokyo. There may be discrepancies in their stories, but these discrepancies have never caused us to declare that Tokyo is an illusion just because the rest of us have not seen it.

A witness is testifying in a murder case. Under direct examination he tells what he saw. A lawyer cross-examines. The witness is making every effort to tell what he believes he saw, but the lawyer begins to show that the pieces do not fit together properly. There is something wrong somewhere. Part of the story is in conflict with another part of the story. Part of it could not be true if the other part is true. Did the witness have hallucinations, or did he misinterpret? Did the alcoholic see animals or did he misinterpret? We don't know.

An emotional person sees things differently. The facts are often colored by sentiment or other emotions. An emotional person has to see the world through the emotions, which is like seeing it through colored glasses. It looks different. It isn't the same. A prejudgment is sufficient to blind one. If you believe something exists, you see it more easily. If you believe it does not exist, it is difficult for you to see it. The person with a prejudice is partially blind. Prejudice and emotion are closely linked. Fear and prejudice are closely linked. The Russians have been invaded a number of times. They fear invasion. It is easy for them to see 'signs' of invasion. It was almost impossible for Americans to see any 'signs' of an attack on Pearl Harbor. It would be easier for them to see such signs today.

The alcoholic has never actually been invaded by these little animals in a physical sense. Yet he sees them. Is evolution involved? Is the mind contacting something in the past? Is there a group mind involved? Does it have to do with Jung's 'Collective Unconscious?' Psychologists, in an effort to portray a mystery, have sometimes spoken of the 'soul of the mob.'

Note that the ancients symbolized Pisces with a fish, Cancer with a crab and Scorpio with a scorpion, beings even beneath the animal world. These are the three Water signs, representing the survival dynamics. The Earth signs, representing the SDR were represented by a bull, a goat and a virgin. The NSD were represented by a ram, a lion and a centaur, but the NSDG were always represented by people, Justice holding the scales, the Water Pourer and his jug, and the twins. The ancients portrayed the emotions, the SD, with the lowest form of life, the intellect, the NSDG, with the highest available form of life. So when the emotional person seeks an escape in alcoholism, he meets up with the animals. If he could sink low enough, would he see fish? If the theories of evolution be true, is the sight of these animals a retrogression in time? Is there a mass-soul memory which is very faulty and subject to a great deal in the way of misinterpretation down in the Unconscious Interpretive Apparatus that we spoke about back in Lesson Two?

In religious revivals, people are often 'seized' and no longer have individual control. They go with the mob, but they call it being seized by the Holy Spirit. We hear of savages and some non-savages being seized by demons. Here is a man of high education. He writes us about a demon that is making his life miserable. It clings to his stomach all the time. He tells this story to none of his acquaintances. They would think him insane. In desperation, he writes to us. We have never seen any demons and we wouldn't know what to do about them if we did. The Christian Church doesn't pay much attention to demons because demons are not respectable at present, but Christ drove demons out of people. Nowadays you don't talk about demons, and if you talk too much about the DT's, you will be suspected of keeping bad company. You may even be somewhat suspect if you had a relative who had a nervous breakdown rather than an experience with demons.

Neptunian people often place a premium on any lack of 'respectability.' Here is a woman in her 80's who likes to get you aside and tell you in confidence that her husband's family would have none of her, because she had once been a chorus girl. There are those to whom sex holds no thrill unless it is 'illicit.' All of these people are born under Neptune afflictions, so often Mars-Neptune afflictions. We see a pattern repeated many times where a young girl from a very wealthy family is always involved with criminals and people from the underworld. Here are four cases of such girls. Each has the Sun conjunct Mars in Pisces, the sign of Neptune. Each finds it difficult to have interest in sex unless it can be regarded as illicit. There is even a thrill to having an illegitimate child. The thrill seems greater if the girl cannot be sure of who was the father.

It is important to realize that in all cases of emotional abnormality, or what we call emotional abnormality, there is a pattern. The individuals did not invent these ideas. There are too many with the same ideas, just as there are too many alcoholics who see animals. Taking these four girls born with Sun conjunct Mars in Pisces, the pattern of their lives and of their behavior is almost identical. These four all happen to come from very wealthy families. Here is one who came from a poor family. She is more or less of an invalid. We know little about her, but we do note that she suddenly overcomes her health problems when she has an opportunity of 'going out' with some man other than her husband. Concerning the other four girls, none of them have any interest in men on their own social level. They seek men from a lower or foreign world. They feel 'at home' with these men, despite the fact that they are so completely different from the kind of men they may have met 'at home.'

These girls all followed a pattern. It seems to have been more or less of an unconscious procedure. They followed their feelings, but their feelings followed the pattern. In doing so, is there any difference between these girls and the bees who build their rooms in the shape of hexagons? Or the snowflakes that freeze in the shape of hexagons? The girls and the bees saw no other way. It seemed the natural way. Had they known more about nature, they might have seen many other ways. They might have been saved from much grief. One of these girls recently died from an overdose of drugs, although the official report called it pneumonia. They all follow a certain pattern, because they are sentimental. Sentiment is a peculiar something. It can take you to strange places.

There are businessmen with plenty of money who just can't resist the opportunity of making a dishonest dollar, of putting something over on someone. They have good lawyers, and they stay out of trouble usually. But they have a yen for something that is just a little bit illegal. We greatly increased the consumption of alcohol when we made it illegal. We call a man insane, or we call him a criminal when he is following a pattern he knows nothing about. The pattern dominates his feelings, and he follows his feelings.

Does this pattern have a purpose, and if so, what is that purpose? To learn the answers to such questions, it is necessary to view things in the perspective. Stand well back and take another look. Another characteristic of Neptune is socialism in its many and varied forms. Socialism aims to bring those on the lower level up to those on the higher level, possibly to drag the higher level down somewhat to meet the lower level. The aim seems to be to equalize things, even if the result is quite often contrary to the aim. The FSD and the FSDR are trying to protect the family pattern as it has been. In the extreme, this can lead to incest, but when the SSD becomes involved with the FSD, there seems definitely an attraction between races. Who can always say who is lower and who is higher? A man with Mars conjunct Sun in Pisces married a full-blooded Indian girl. One of the girls mentioned above, daughter of the wealthiest family in one particular state, was known to have a number of affairs with Negroes. When Neptune becomes involved in sex matters, the inclination seems to be to go to the very opposite extreme from incest. Go so far away that there is no possibility of touching a gene of one's own family. If you are an Englishman and you marry a Chinese girl, this would accomplish such an objective. Meanwhile, royalty will play closer to incest, marrying cousins, etc. Either extreme is often frowned upon by respectability. The mother and father of the boy or girl who marries into a Chinese family are likely to be a bit unhappy.

Below the border in Mexico, life is more Neptunian. All the races intermarry until it is difficult to distinguish between the Spanish, the Indian and the Negro. No fixed lines are drawn except in some circles, and the rules of these circles have no effect upon the populace as a whole. A girl is protected from men until she is married, and then she is on her own. So long as she has a husband to give a name for her children, little concern is shown as to whose children they might be. Almost everyone belongs to the church with no feeling that the rules of the church are to be considered as binding.

Neither socialism nor communism were invented by anyone named Marx. The pattern was in nature. The Apache Indians were more communist than the Russian Communists. However, their brand of communism or socialism included individual freedom. No Apache ever went to war involuntarily. Conscientious objectors were respected for their views. We Americans are a lot like the English. We feel honor bound to force our views, customs and religion on all other races. We have already prejudged almost everything. How many people are there in Chicago who do not believe that their city is the second largest in the western hemisphere? How many would know that Mexico City, which had 630,000 population in 1900, is now larger than Chicago?

Every astrological principle involves a pattern of nature. The SSD involves such a pattern. We know too little about it. To know more about it, we must study all forms of illness, insanity and crime. Astrologically, they all have to do with the same pattern. They may involve something far in the past. We don't know. However, the first thing a psychiatrist does is dig into your past. Freud went back to the ideas of the ancients when he began looking for patterns and symbols in dreams and in human behavior. The future possibilities of psychiatry would appear almost unlimited as it may be expected to increase the scope of its frame of reference.

Neptunian people are often accused of dishonesty and falsehood, but a lot is dependent upon our definition of both honesty and truth. There is no question but that Neptune involves much in the way of misinterpretation, but the pathological liar may be telling what he believes to be the truth, while a lot of our accepted orthodox truths should be classified as pathological lying. They are merely interpretations based on prejudgment or prejudice.

Here is an elderly Neptunian lady who was always seeing things, and she believed them to be precognitive. She saw gold beneath the surface of the ranch, hidden, buried gold. She supervised while her husband and a son dug a hole the size of a swimming pool. They found no gold. These visions came frequently, but there was no evidence that any of them were precognitive. One day she told us of such a vision. She had been watching a road at a certain point when a car had plunged off the road over an embankment. Daily, she was expecting a car to plunge over this embankment. We were reminded of her 'vision ' five years later when, under the influence of alcohol, her husband was killed as his car plunged over the embankment at this very point. This lady was filled with visions, but insofar as we know, this was the only one that ever came true. Were most of them misinterpretations?

Let us avoid extremes. It would be untrue to claim that orthodoxy is either all right or all wrong, but orthodoxy is a fact that comes into being. Neptunianism is also a fact that ever challenges the wisdom of orthodoxy. When there is too much of a concentration of wealth, Neptunianism is out to scatter it to the masses – legally or illegally. When royalty gets closer and closer to incest, there is always an un-respectable member of the family born to have scandal with a servant or a commoner. The great trouble with orthodoxy is that it degenerates into habit and becomes a substitute for thinking. At that point, Neptune is ready to have a heyday.

We see Neptunianism flourishing in certain groups, in places like Greenwich Village, in colonies of artists, perhaps in Hollywood, and often among groups classifying themselves erroneously as intellectuals. Neptunianism oddly produces artists, and the greatest of actors and actresses. They actually become the personalities they portray. A man is often viewed as insane when he begins to take on the characteristics of Napoleon.

If we view some of the 'crackpot' socialistic ideas that brain trusters were thrusting upon us in 1933, we discover that they could not have been too bad, because they have now become a part of orthodoxy itself. Sacrifice is a part of the Neptunium principle. Cells in the human body will sacrifice their individuality and their bodies to become a part of the wall that is to heal a wound. When gasoline is poured into an anthill and ignited, ants will dash into the flames and become completely consumed in their effort to save the queen.

We see the Neptunian individual sacrifice everything that would be endeared to another in a struggle to follow some hidden pattern that is never even seen by the individual. We merely place it all under the head of sentiment.

We have asked that you stand well back and view Neptunianism in the perspective. When you do this, you will see that individuals are sacrificing themselves and everything the rest of us hold dear. We see that reward comes in the form of illness and imprisonment, loss of individual liberty and loss of an independent place in the world. Yet, so often, when we study the trend of events many years later, we can see how a purpose was served. The men who get most involved in international diplomacy are often the most Neptunian type of men. Most international organizations are Neptunian. It would appear to be an effort to supersede family and nationalism with something more universal. It is not the Aquarium who talks about the brotherhood of man, as so many writers, usually Aquarians like Evangeline Adam, have told us. The brotherhood of man idea is strictly Neptunian – not Aquarian. Evangeline Adams actually had Pisces as the ascendant of her chart. Here is another Sun-in-Aquarius astrologer who wrote in like terms, but he had Mars in opposition to Neptune. Pisces can visualize one world where all share and share alike. It is interesting to note that this Neptunian pattern tends to supersede family by also advocating that there be a sharing of mates as it is quite common among the Eskimos. If we are to understand Neptunianism, we must look beyond geographical and racial borders. We must look beyond the habits and conventions of any one people or of any one species. It is something we know very little about. Yet it is one of the most effective forces with which we must deal every day.

We have had our share of Neptunianism in the world of astrology over the last hundred years. It wasn't the astrology of the ancients. The Neptunian astrologers were a mixed up, confused group. They were sometimes arrested for 'fortune telling.' They were not people of a scientific viewpoint. There was nothing scientific about them. Some of them might cheat a little to make a prediction look good. They wrote for astrology magazines, and few of their predictions came true, but let us look at the overall effect. They were sentimentalists. They followed their intuition – what seemed right to them. Surely they were more right than the reactionary astronomers who were endeavoring by every fair means or foul to load the public with falsehoods, telling the public that the astronomers had disproved astrology at a time when not one astronomer who had investigated the subject had ever condemned it. These were the same astronomers who were offering their own dogma in the name of Sir Isaac Newton without his consent. Whatever else we may say about the Neptunian astrologers, we owe it to them that they kept the flame alive. Were it not for them, the rest of us might have had nothing to investigate. Even if their presentations were colored with emotionalism, or out right imagination, they did keep our interest alive, and they gave us a starting point from which to begin our own investigations.

We might make a serious error if we conclude that this mysterious Neptunianism has no good purpose. When viewed from a narrow, momentary vista, we are apt to condemn it, but too often its beneficial effect may actually lie centuries ahead. It is a part of Nature herself. We do not know enough about Nature to condemn any of her subdivisions. The stupid man may be following a design that we know nothing about. We know nothing about too much.

There often appears to be no common sense where Neptune is concerned. It never seems to make sense during one century, but perhaps it makes sense over a number of centuries or over millions of years. We have spoken only about the so-called negative aspects of Neptune. What about the so-called favorable aspects? What about the man who becomes greasy with oil millions? The earliest book on Neptune connected it with oil. That was the book of Elizabeth Aldrich, an astrologer with an uncanny ability to predict the future accurately. At the one time in his life when Neptune trined the Sun and Mercury in the writer's chart, two odd things happened. He could write poetry by the yard, and he made money out of oil, it just seemed to happen that way. At no other time in his life could he even tolerate reading poetry. He was not living in that rhythm. It was too slow for him.

Under a strong and so-called favorable influence, one man makes money out of oil. Oil is millions of years old. Another man may make a success with a popular band, but are not most popular bands actually appealing to something primitive within us? Are they not reviving a bit of the savage? Is it not an expression from way back somewhere? We are left with the impression that Neptune has to do with some rhythm that is very, very old. Perhaps we are being Neptunian ourselves in allowing such a statement to creep into these pages, for after all we positively do not know.

Neptune has also been identified with spiritualism. Neptunian people are often found contacting or trying to contact the spirits of the departed. Isn't that a form of retrogression, endeavoring to bring back those you knew yesterday. Like those who investigate such phenomena as haunted houses. We often find them supposedly contacting spirits of hundreds of years ago. Here is an old lady who constantly claims to be in contact with the spirits of such people as Pythagoras. That's going back 2500 years. Let us pay no attention to whether or not there is any truth to what this old lady tells us, but let us observe the pattern that exists in all of these cases. Let us note that the interest is not in the future but far, far into the past. These people are trying to live yesterday. This seems to be true of the negative Neptunian aspects, but the negative aspects deal with the past, while the positive aspects deal with the future. Nevertheless, Neptune itself seem to have some connection with something way, way back.

Strange things happen when some people go into trances, but observe how, in the majority of cases, there is an endeavor to arouse the past. Certainly, our physical bodies – through heredity and evolution – have a contact that goes far into the past, and Neptune seems to be in some mysterious way involved with these things. It may also be observed that people who practice trance phenomena as mediums very often degenerate into ill health. We find Neptune associated with the problem of ill health. In many instance good health is dependent upon one's ability to digest the past and get on with the future.

We must be very careful about making any positive statements in connection with these health views, because the research to back them up has not yet been accomplished. Nevertheless, we cannot help but observe that we can bring about a great change in the well being of a client by merely asking questions. The questions are always carefully designed to allow the client to digest the past in order to go on with the future. Here is a lady who arrives in a depressive state. She is frustrated, because the things she wants from life never happen. What does she want? What does she want to do? She tell us what she wants to do and we ask why she doesn't do it. Her reasons are not very deep reasons. They are rather superficial, and so we insist that she find better reasons. There must be better reasons. Otherwise, she would go right ahead and do it. From here on, there are two possible courses which she might take. She may go ahead and do what she wants to do, or she may discover that she never really wanted to do it at all. She had convinced herself that she wanted to do it merely because she believed there was something to prevent her from doing it. In either case, the physical change is the same. As one who has seen the light, her face lights up. There is facial expression in a face that appeared like putty a few moments earlier. There is a smile, and there is sparkle in the eyes. Also, there has been a mental change. While we have been talking, a plan for the future has developed. Now, she knows what she does want, and she has every intention of getting it. Her mind has left the past behind and its absorbed only with the future. She is happy because she has a happy outlook. People with a happy view of the future seem to be healthy people, while people with an unhappy view of the past seem to be unhealthy people. Even people with a happy view of the past seem to be less healthy than those with a happy view of the future.

The principle involved here would appear to be that bad health seems to have some connection with an undigested past, although we do not know to what ratio of illness this might apply, any more than we could tell you the exact ratio of all illness which might be psychosomatic. The problem is seldom on the conscious level, however, for it is deep within the subconscious, where the Unconscious Interpretive Apparatus has usually been responsible for misinterpretations plus erroneous conclusions which are based on misinterpretations. Ron Hubbard has used the term 'necessity level.' Take the woman who loves her child and realized that the child is in danger. She must act in order to change the future from what it will be if she does not act. She reaches the necessity level. Her feelings about the future of the child outweigh any feelings she may have about her own illness or her own welfare. The child is more important. She 'forgets' her own illness. It is no longer a part of her consciousness. She acts, and she changes what the future would otherwise have been. Of course this would not supply arms and legs to act to a person who had all limbs amputated.

We are constantly asked to recommend good books on medical astrology. There are no such books in print, and those that are out of print are hardly worth recommending. They contain a lot of very basic errors. What we need is a monstrous research program. We must first identify and classify each type of illness according to the kind of planetary pattern to which it belongs. When we do this, we will have a much broader understanding of illness. We can practically say that it will be possible to express an illness in the form of a mathematical equation involving the human dynamics. We may find that we have to begin classifying illness into three basic types – individual illness, family illness and social illness, involving the corresponding dynamics. Our own experience has led to the belief (perhaps premature) that the most difficult illness will be found to be social illness, but even this maybe cured by allowing the patient to see just how he can successfully fit himself into society.

Of course we must be able to reach the patient. In the case of mentioned clients, these people were anxious to be reached. They were willing to pay good money to be reached. There was no reluctance to talk about their problems. They like to talk about their problems and about themselves. They are only too happy to tell you anything you want to know. Other people who regard the matter as very personal, something they do not care to discuss with anybody, must solve the problem for themselves or find some other method.

Next, it must be realized that therapy is not our business. We have no time for therapy. That is the work of the physician. But, if we can help the physician to understand a particular illness as a mathematical equation, then he can employ his own methods to make whatever adjustments may be necessary to bring about good health. The problem is merely to make the body want to behave. We must be alert to notice that illness usually seems to serve some purpose. It may not be a good purpose, but the subconscious must be brought up to the conscious level where the patient can understand what is going on.

Fear is often involved. The patient may fear the worst, and for that reason, he may not want to know what is going on in the subconscious. In that case, the fear factor must be overcome, but we have found that this can often be accomplished by not allowing the patient to know what is going on. Don't allow him to know that any attempt at therapy is taking place. Just ask questions. Let him think you are curious. Most people do like to talk about themselves. Ignore whether what they are telling you is truth or untruth. Most people will want to be polite, particularly if they don't know you very well. They are apt to have more outward respect for someone they don't know very well. Through questions, you can help them to tell the truth to themselves, and that is what really counts.

One such client repeatedly used the expression, 'Well, I didn't mean just what I said.' We would always ask him what he did mean, and he would start over again. His new explanation always proved just as futile. He perspired a bit, and it was obvious that he was concealing anger. However, he was fighting a terrific battle within himself, for he was going through a violent re-evaluation of his own past life. When he finally left, he looked anything but cured, but one hour later he telephone. He wanted our approval of a plan that had developed in his mind within that hour. We gave our approval to the plan, and there has been nothing wrong with this man since. He was rid of a problem that had been constantly with him for twenty years. He had digested the past, and the past was gone. It no longer had any hold on him. After all, you know that your mind does not function well when you have indigestion, and it doesn't seem to make any difference whether it involves food indigestion or emotional indigestion. Emotional indigestion seems to be one of the principle causes of illness, but particularly mental illness.

We are forced to include all crime as illness, often a form of mental illness. The man who is in prison has had difficulty fitting himself into society, or perhaps difficulty in merely fitting himself into a family. It may not have been his fault. Society may not feel that it owes each man a living, but it would do itself a favor if it would realize that it is brewing trouble for itself when it shirks it responsibility and leaves the individual to shift for himself. Most men like Hitler, Stalin or Mussolini were at some time neglected or ignored by society. The man who is neglected by society may harbor a grudge. He may grow very powerful, and when he does, it is society that suffers. Just count the men, women and children who had to die because of the trend of development of these men. One of man's most powerful traits is his desire to imitate. We beat children to control them, and in doing so, we teach them that might makes right. We train men to kill other men for war purposes, but we expect them to be mild at all times except when they are killing our particular enemies.

Although it may be an individual who gets sick. we must not lose sight of the fact that it is society that is often at fault. In fact, it is society itself that is sick. What shows up in the individual is merely a symptom of what is wrong with society itself. It is difficult for society to change its habits. It is sick as long as it clings to hypocrisy and dogma. We cannot afford to spend money on better mental institutions and better research, but we can spend any number of billions on war and preparation for war. We can spend any amount of money to keep tomorrow like yesterday, but we are afraid to have it different and better. Fortunately, this has not been the attitude of some of the big corporations, but recent years have also been bringing men into public life who are willing to change things, too.

Yet, how far have we advanced? Suppose that tomorrow we were to ask the government to appropriate a few million dollars for a broad statistical investigation into astrology. We could expect violent opposition from astronomers, physicists, the church, and various organizations, organizations all interested in keeping tomorrow like yesterday. If we are going to do the job, we have got to do it by ourselves. If we are going to have the rest of the world benefit from our work, we are first going to have to re-educate the rest of the world, including the people who run and teach in universities and schools. Society itself is sick, and it is more difficult to cure society than to cure the individual.

There IS a philosophy behind Neptune and it is worthy of study, for until we understand it, we are going to have problems. The strongly Neptunian individual secretly, subtly and deliberately opposes organized society. The fault is not all on one side. There is plenty wrong with organized society. One of the worst illnesses of modern society is its so-called 'respectability.' Even cattle are herded but twice a year, but humans are herded every day. They are told what to wear, how to act, and where to be at a given time. If an individualist wants to survive as an individualist, he must become an employer instead of an employee. The Neptunium person may survive by working against society, by being on the other side, like the old-time bootlegger who became mighty popular so long as he wasn't caught. One of the greatest evils of respectability is that it is just plain phony. Many of these persons who have found their way into Neptunian difficulties were first impressed with the phony-ness of respectability. At that point, they showed more intelligence than those who were not so impressed. However, the first inclination is to be respectable on one side and not on the other – to live a double life and have double standards. Being respectable on one side and not on the other is something that leads to conflict within the subconscious. Any attempt to represent yourself, either to yourself or to the outside world, as something you are not leads to inner conflict which can ultimately manifest as some form of illness. It is even more dangerous to misrepresent yourself to yourself than to the outside world.

Mercury-Neptune aspects can lead to mental confusion. Venus-Neptune aspects can lead to social confusion, romantic confusion, setting up the criminal as a god, etc. Mars-Neptune aspects can lead to emotional and particularly sex confusion. Jupiter-Neptune aspects can lead to philosophical, religious and educational confusion. Saturn-Neptune aspects, often worst of all, can lead to physical confusion within the body itself, financial confusion, and bad health. The direction that Uranus-Neptune aspects may take is largely dependent upon other factors in the chart, but they are usually accompanied by a great deal in the way of nervousness and restlessness. Pluto-Neptune aspects may often be associated with efforts that are so broad that they become impossible. This is mainly true of the so-called negative aspects of which sloppiness is also characteristic. The so-called favorable aspects of Neptune are creative. They seem to furnish artistic expression. They may produce the musician, the poet, the artist and the actor as well as the salesman. There is rhythm, and they make life a lot easier. Even the so-called favorable aspects, however, are apt to have a tinge of the negative qualities we have already noted. A good Neptune likes to live an easy life of luxury. We find it tuning into society as it finds it, and taking personal advantage of all of its weaknesses. A good Neptune can be the biggest asset of the Psychologist. It can be very helpful to the physician. A good Neptune is an artist. It is what we would call the bedside manner of the physician, the fitness of the advertising man or the salesman. He is fitting himself into society whether he believes in it or not. He probably doesn't.

A good Neptune in a chart seems to give the individual the ability to recognize life and society for what they are and to take advantage of them. The fisherman has learned that fish like worms, but he puts the worm on a hook. It is possible that the symbol of Pisces, with its two fish, should have a hook there somewhere. One of the great difficulties of the negative Neptunian conditions is that whatever is organized break down. There is disintegration. There is sloppiness, a lack of neatness and order. A condition of decay sets in, and this seems to be the pattern whether the problem concerns society at large or cells within the human body. It almost seems that when we insist upon living in the past, a condition of decay sets in. An old person has more past to live in. There isn't much for a child to remember. His view is always forward.

Whenever you run up against negative Neptunian aspects, you must be on the alert for health problems. Organization breaks down. There is chaos. This can apply within the cells of the human body, or it can apply to a person's thinking. The emotions can be all mixed up. The medical world is spending millions of dollars for research, while ignoring the most important facts of all. These facts are being ignored for the sake of 'respectability.' We must be wrong in order to be respectable. With all of the research we have seen to date relative to cancer, Dr. George Crile, Jr., points out that the death rate among physicians themselves, due to cancer, is just as high as among laymen who neglect the signs of cancer. We are very jealous of methods that repeatedly fail. We hang on to them for security. We do not dare let go. 'Something' might happen. Thus, our efforts are bound to be hampered until society has been re-educated. We must accomplish this ourselves in our own way. We must bypass the orthodox educational institutions and build a new institution to a better pattern. This can be done, and it is our intention to do it. Orthodox educational institutions are living in the past to a great extent. We must not allow this to disturb us. We can go on without them. We can build the future while they are living the past.

LESSON SIXTEEN

SEEDS OF MENTAL ILLNESS

In prior chapter, we discussed some of the problems involving the Social Survival Dynamic. All such problems are pathological to some degree. It is merely a matter of what standard is accepted. Where does sanity end and where does insanity begin? When the ISD or the FSD get too far out of hand, society classifies the result as crime, but when the SSD gets out of hand, society often rates it as mental illness or insanity. In all cases, it is a matter of the individual being unable to control the dynamic forces that come up from the unconscious, because he knows nothing about them and does not understand them. There are times when whole groups of people lose control. To a certain degree, society itself is pathological. Advertising copywriters, orators, demagogues and some evangelists make their appeal to the pathological element within society. A large ratio of people never say what they think. They say what they think will make other people have a higher regard for them. We know an astronomer who publicly condemns astrology because he thinks that is what other astronomers and those he works for expect him to do. Yet, on the second floor of his home is a hidden library containing nothing but astrological books. He buys all the astrology magazines. He studies and employs astrology constantly. He proudly disclosed his astrological library to the writer because he thought the writer, being an astrologer, would have a higher regard for him.

Most of our own experience to date has been, not with the insane or pathological, but with the semi-pathological. You find it almost everywhere. Here is a lad who could be considered very close to the pathological. He has many mental and emotional problems. He drinks a good deal in order to escape them. He does wild things. He bought one of the first jeeps to be sold to the public after World War II. He amused himself all day Sunday by driving wild through the neighborhood, not over conventional thoroughfares, but over curbs, across people's lawns and gardens, and incidentally doing a good deal of damage. There were not too many complaints, because no one could quite understand what had happened or what it was all about. A few thought it was good clean fun. After all, nobody was killed. He talked like a child. He acted like a child, and he could think of a lot of very silly things to say which would probably seem funny to many children.

Anyway, he worked for an advertising agency, and he thought of something very silly to say about a product of a client. The agency decided to give it a whirl. It didn't mean anything, but when everybody got to repeating it, it was so ridiculous and suggestive that they all started laughing. Soon, we were all hearing it over radio and seeing it in ads. It kept repeating itself in the minds of housewives, and it seemed to have a certain rhythm. Sales began to mount and then skyrocket. The agency had discovered a genius. He was made vice president, and his salary was jumped from $4,000 to $25,000. The lad is still very much on the pathological side. He has more emotional problems today, but he has more money to pay for more damage. It is possible that we are overlooking our best advertising talent by not combing inmates of mental institutions? In the late 20's, just before the crash in the stock market, two young men had an automobile company. They were playboys. They got around. They were artistic. Their cars had a smooth design. They appealed to those who like a sports car. On the stock exchange, the stock was spectacular. It could jump from here to there at any moment, and often did. It appealed to the speculator. It attracted attention, as did the cars.

A very wealthy and elderly man, looking on from the sidelines, decided that here was progress. This company should be good investment. Whenever the stock would dip, he would buy in and accumulate more of the stock. One afternoon, a Park Avenue friend invited him to a cocktail party. He arrived, but the party got out of hand. Two wild Indians arrived and went berserk. Some of the sedate ladies had part of their apparel torn away. Furniture was wrecked, and the place was almost a shambles. No one could bring things under control.

'Who are those two idiots?' the elderly man asked of his host.

'Why, one is the president, the other the treasurer of X-Motors,' the host replied.

The elderly man hurriedly left, reached his broker on a phone, and ordered him to liquidate all of his holdings in X-Motors on the opening of the market on the following day. Oddly, they don't make that automobile any more, and modern youth probably never heard of it. Naturally, X-Motors is not the real name of the company.

Joe Cook was one of the most popular vaudeville actors of three decades ago. He had a very amusing skit. From the stage, he told an amusing story about four Hawaiians, As the story proceeded, it kept leading further and further away from the starting point. Since it was told with great excitement, this was not clear to the audience, but it was still exciting, and the audience listened, awaiting the ultimate climax, or to find out where the story was going. At the outset, Cook had announced that he was not going to imitate four Hawaiians, and offered to explain why he was not going to imitate four Hawaiians. Thereupon, Joe explained how his grand father's farm had originally been on the site of the theater itself. He talked about his grandfather, friends of his grandfather, drifting further and further ways, until the entire audience had completely forgotten about the four Hawaiians or the beginning of the story. Suddenly, Joe stopped, and told his audience, 'and that, ladies and gentlemen, is why I will not imitate four Hawaiians.'

The effect was terrific, because until that moment, everyone had completely forgotten about the Hawaiians.

We will find a similar technique if we read the speeches of Franklin D. Roosevelt. His action was quite frequently the opposite of that promised, but unlike Joe Cook, he never reminded his audience about Hawaiians. He always went on to something else. Unfulfilled promises were always completely concealed behind exciting new promises. The average man in the street can become a hero worshiper of a clever, colorful crook who can keep from getting caught. He honors the names of Jessie James, Billy the Kid, etc. The Westchester County police arrested such a man who was wanted from California to New York. He was very polished. By adopting a false name, he managed to be received into the homes of the most wealthy. He would case the house, and later return to pilfer it of its jewels, etc. One of the arresting officers told the writer, 'Honest, he is the swellest guy. You'd love him.'

Cochise and Geronimo, the cruelest of men, are now honored as heroes. They were not understood. Give us time to forget our pain, and we will glorify Hitler and Stalin in our history books in the same manner. We will explain that they were never understood. The principle purpose of the law is to protect the wealth and property of people who have wealth and property, but almost everyone worships a Robin Hood who will take away from the rich and give to the poor. Give us time, and we will make Robin Hoods out of Stalin and Hitler.

If we are going to understand the Social Survival Dynamic and its functioning, we must realize that society itself is, to an unknown extent, mentally ill. Here is a psychiatrist who had a 'nervous breakdown'. Let's see what happened. He was a gentle soul. He hated war. He did not want to become a party to it. He became a conscientious objector. He was slapped in jail, and when his freedom was returned to him, he was never the same. There was a conflict within his unconscious, a conflict that involved his conception of justice and righteousness. Society had placed him in jail to teach him a lesson, to teach him to mend his ways, to become a good citizen and go out and kill people when commanded to do so. You are normal in society when you do what you are told to do and soothe your conscience by explaining to yourself that there was no other way.

The warden of a Federal prison shook his head and told us, 'They are not punished while they are here. They are punished after they are released. They can never fit themselves back into society. There is no place for them.'

There are many varieties of insanity, and we are not authorities on these many kinds, but it is only the extreme cases and the violent cases that are considered pathological. There is a little bit of the pathological in everyone. In the actual pathological cases that we have observed, we have noted many cases where the 'disease' appears to have been brought on by a conflict resulting from the individual's inability to fit himself into a society that he considered filled with injustice. There was an attempt to escape from an unjust world which amounted to a retreat within the individual's self. It was more peaceful there. 'Reality' was left behind. Mental crackups come when people are under very strong Neptunian, aspects, and when people are under very strong Neptunian aspects, they get sentimental. The sadist is often extremely kind and loving to animals. One day, we picked up a magazine and read a very humorous story by Shane Miller. The theme of the story was that the people in mental institutions are the only normal people, and that it is society that is insane. The hero of the story met a man of great wisdom who imparted great truths to our hero, until two men in white uniforms arrived and led him gently back to the institution from which he had escaped. We probably enjoyed this story more than you would because we were present at its conception. Early one morning, we accidentally ran into Shane Miller at the corner of 57th Street and Seventh Avenue in New York. Neither of us had breakfast, so we entered a restaurant and had it together. We jokingly discussed the inconsistencies of society, until Shane said, 'This gives me an idea for a story. I'm going to claim that the only sane people are the insane people,' We laughed and that was the end of the matter until we ran into the story in a magazine.

We have earlier stated that Neptune doesn't appear to make sense. We might also say that insanity doesn't make sense, but would we be right? The pathological liar is quite common. You don't have to go to an insane asylum to find him. He might be a very successful real estate salesman. You might find him as the top man in an advertising agency. Industry boomed when the men with Neptune in Cancer became old enough to start selling. Of course, all the men with

Neptune in Cancer did not become good salesmen, but many of those with afflicted Neptune's in Cancer became crack salesmen. They also became crack drinkers, and drinking and selling were closely allied.

Study the pathological liar carefully, and you can learn a great deal. You will find that his lying conforms to a pattern that he knows nothing about. It's base is probably an unconscious fear. He may, and probably does, believe everything he tells at that moment when he is telling it, but he may wonder about it later and wonder why he told some of the things he did tell. He doesn't know, but there is a reason, and when you dig into the subconscious, you will find the reason. If you can help him to know the reason, he will no longer be a pathological liar. When children lie, their parents beat them, and the conflict with the injustice of a pathological society begins. The child may itself become pathological. It is having forced down into its unconscious the belief that might makes right and that the only right is that of might. Laws are made by adults, and consequently, you can go to jail if you beat an adult but seldom for beating a child. If the child reported a beating to police, he might take home to his parents where he would get another beating. We can recall cases of children who would never dare tell their parents that they were beaten at school by a teacher, because if they did the parents would beat them again at home for getting beaten by a teacher at school. There seems to be nothing in the law that guarantees a fair trial or any other kind of a trial for a child – only for adults. If a man beats his child, it is assumed that the child deserved it, but if he beats this man who lives next door, he is regarded as a criminal and can receive a jail sentence. This is intended to teach him a lesson, not to beat big people, just little people. However, the law does definitely draw a line. Don't kill the child. Under any conditions, that's murder. The politician can stir up votes in some sections of the south by talking about white supremacy. He can stir up votes in other sections of the country by taking the opposite view. Hitler stirred up votes by vilifying the Jews. Some physicians complain about women who want an operation over the advice of the physician and will go to the quack in order to get one. All of these things are evidence of disease in society itself. All of these things are the result of the survival dynamics gone wrong. The important thing to realize about mental illness is that there is a pattern in the background. There is a reason. There is conflict. Some people can become pathological merely because they have consciences and cannot understand the pathological society into which they are supposed to adjust themselves. This is often where an inner conflict begins, and then it gets out of hand. The mild may become violent.

We have talked with some very prominent judges of criminal courts. We have heard them pass severe sentences on people who did not deserve them, because it was what was expected of them, and we have questioned these sentences in later conversations with the judges. One judge said, 'Look, you're on the sentimental side. We don't make the laws. We just do what is expected of us. Forget it, and let's have a drink.' Of course, the drink would let him forget it, or at least help in that direction. We questioned the evidence in another case, and asked the judge how he could justify himself if he had sent an innocent man to jail. 'I'm only human,' he said. 'I have to handle a lot of cases, and I have to make some kind of a decision based on what things look like. Do you expect me to get my decision from some higher all-knowing power? There is a job to be done and we have got to do it.'

It is interesting to us to observe that many of the judges we have known in the eastern part of the country were heavy drinkers and heavy gamblers in hours when they were not on the bench. We have seen less of that in the west. It is all a part of the pathological side of society itself. You will get along much better with society when you realize that it is somewhat pathological. It won't give you as many problems when you understand what it is, when you realize that society itself is the patient, and that it needs to be treated like a patient. You have to be gentle with a patient. Nevertheless, it can be very amusing when you stand aside and view society in the perspective. It can help greatly when you decide to get along with society without actually becoming a part of it. Then you are free to do your own thinking, instead of allowing your thinking to become a mere reflection of the group thought. It is very easy to get caught up in group-thinking, to accept conceptions because they are generally accepted.

Here is another judge. He was a very good judge, a very fair one. He had the Sun conjunct Saturn in Pisces. He was quiet, seldom expressing an opinion of anything when it wasn't necessary, but he was always observing. You never heard him offer an opinion about anyone in politics. One Sunday morning, we stopped in to see him at his home. We discussed certain important political figures. He cut loose. These were some of the most respected citizens we were talking about, but underneath, their principles were of a very low and selfish nature. The judge wouldn't discuss these folks ordinarily. They were powerful and a wrong word uttered about them could cost him his job. This morning, the judge told us the truth about these people in confidence.

About eight years passed. We moved west, and then one

day there were headlines in the papers. Mars had been stationary in Pisces for six months. Something had happened to the judge. He had gone haywire. He had swindled some people out of $150, 000 and said that he lost it all at the racetracks. We were surprised because we regarded the judge as one of the most honorable people we had known. We looked further. Who were the people swindled? Here were the names. We knew them all. They were those same political figures who were enjoying respected places in the community, but who were using those places to practice every type of legal deviltry. Something had happened to the judge. He became a swindler, and he is now resting in jail. We might say he cracked up mentally, but note the pattern. He had punished the men that others had no power to punish. They were too strong politically. The judge sacrificed himself. This is a typical Neptunian story. It is the strange sort of thing we run up against when we deal with very strong Neptunian configurations. Over the years, there was something that always puzzled us about the judge. We always wondered about that Sun-conjunct-Saturn in Pisces, the sign of Neptune. We had never seen it manifest. It was something hidden in his nature that we could not detect, but it finally came to the surface in a drastic manner. As this is written, the judge has not been tried, so we do not know the final outcome.

If all the other children believe that it is fashionable to break windows, it is very tough on the one child who does not want to break windows. The other children will jeer him. If he wants to be a part of this society, he must break windows. Adults are like that too. If you are going to be a part of a society, you are supposed to adopt its habits. When in Rome, do as the Romans do. If you are going to live in New York, unless you dress like other people in New York it will be assumed there is something wrong with you. It may be common for women to wear shorts in one community, but in some other community, she will be arrested. No matter how insane the standards of society may be, you are supposed to follow them. When people are under negative Neptunian aspects, they often find social customs distasteful. They retreat within themselves, and when they retreat far enough, they seem to lose contact with what we call reality. If we can't reach them, if we can't call them back, we consider them insane. Their behavior begins to be abnormal. However, if your observation is alert, you may soon see that their behavior is following a very definite pattern. Whatever injustices the person may do to others, he is quite likely to believe that he is the victim of just that type of injustice. He tends to inflict upon others the very injustice from which he believes himself to be suffering.

When under very strong and negative Neptunian aspects, it is very common for a person to accuse other people, and when you probe you find he is accusing the other person of his own conduct. This conduct comes up automatically from his own subconscious in the form of compulsions. The pattern of that conduct is within him, but he sees it or suspects it in others. In California (while Mars was in Pisces) two women kidnapped a third woman and left her for dead on the desert. Following this, they appeared at a police station and reported they had been kidnapped and left in the desert. They informed the police that they suspected a certain woman and her husband of being behind the kidnapping. They named the woman they had left on the desert for dead, but she was not dead.

Here is a man who sat up nights dreaming about his employees plotting against him. He suspected everyone who worked for him. Honest employees would take little of that and they soon left. He kept the other kind. They would steal from him, but if they would confess he would not discharge or prosecute them. He would become closer to them and apologize for them. This did not show up in his chart except for an excess of Cancer and Scorpio, but his wife had Mars exactly on his Neptune. They both became alcoholics. Yet, he always prospered financially. Periodically, the man would suffer form fraud or theft, but these were elements that he was continually manufacturing within himself and then projecting into the outside world. He never surrounded himself with honest men. He appeared to be afraid of honest men. He didn't feel at home with them. When he left for the office, one of his private detectives was waiting to take over and watch his wife while he was gone. At the end of the day, he had to have a complete report on what his wife had been doing all day.

A certain pattern of behavior originates in the mind of the person with heavy Neptunian afflictions, and he sees that type of behavior in all other persons. He can see no honest people in the world. For him, they never exist, and if one comes along he will find a way of getting rid of him. He sees the same pattern everywhere in the outside world, but he never becomes conscious of the fact that the real pattern is not out there but within himself. He believes his wife guilty of adultery because why wouldn't she be if she had the chance? To have the opportunity means guilt. In the extreme, this sort of thinking may not be common, but in its milder forms, we find it everywhere. A certain pattern of thought bombards the mind of the individual and he is unable to escape it because he does not understand it.

Quite often, a client sits on the opposite side of our desk. He tells of his experiences. He has been repeatedly victimized. He

Lesson Sixteen

wants to know whether astrology can't offer some explanation as to why he is always being victimized. Investigation reveals that none of these things ever happened. He is the person who is repeatedly swindling people. The stories that he tells are not about things that have happened to him. He is playing the part of the people he has actually swindled. He is telling us what he has done to others. He is telling the story of his own victims. He is playing their role. However, it took us a long time to discover or believe one thing. The man actually believes the stories that he tells. He is not consciously deceiving us. Things take a peculiar twist done in his subconscious. He actually believes that other people have done to him all of the things that was done to others, and he is suffering from those acts. This is a strange inverse working of the golden rule. It becomes a form of self-punishment. He is being punished by his own past. There are Neptunian people who never tell the truth. When the truth makes a good story, they have to think up one that would seem more logical to them. A great many such stories of such people have been told to us by a certain district attorney who is always hesitant about prosecuting a rape case. He is always fearful that the man may have been framed. One case had been thoroughly investigated by the police, but he was not satisfied. He sent for the girl and asked her to tell him personally the whole story from the beginning. He heard the details of rape out on the desert. Finally, he questioned her on a detail that had not been filled in.

'Well now, all of this happened out on the desert a considerable distance from town. When this was all over, what did he do? Did he drive you back to town?'

The girl started to reply, 'Well first, we went out for coffee...'

Now, the District Attorney really probed. Finally, the girl broke down and explained the real story. Her husband had been out for the evening. She had made a date. She did not get home till 4:00 A.M., and found herself panic-stricken when she faced her husband. She had to think fast. She told her husband of an awful experience, of how she had been raped. The trusting husband immediately called the police. She had to follow through with the story because she could think of no other way. The victim was the man who was about to be tried. The police had failed to see through the deception of her story.

Another girl had been found tied up on the desert but near the road where her screams attracted attention. She told a similar story of rape, but under questioning ultimately broke down and admitted that she had arranged the whole thing herself, having a boyfriend tie her up, because she wanted to make her husband jealous.

All such behavior involves something akin to the pathological, and it is always related to Neptune, its nodes, Pisces or the Sixth House. The pattern varies depending upon how these factors are involved with what other planets etc. You must not be impulsive about concluding that all Neptunian cases work this way. Don't conclude that a person is guilty because of a Neptunian condition in his chart, because strong Neptunian charts will attract the pathological. Oppositions of Neptune do this, and Virgo, being opposite to Pisces, can often attract the pathological. The same can be said of strong Mercury conditions or of 12th House conditions, because the 12th is opposite the 6th. Mercury has been described as the Messenger of the Gods, which is quite false unless we have some very wicked gods. It is not the nature of Mercury to tell the truth unless it is very well aspected, but this does not mean that the individual willingly falsifies things. He is merely automatically telling what he thinks he is expected to tell. If he is expected to lie, or if he thinks he is expected to lie, he will lie. The man or woman who wants attention may do almost anything to get it. During the Hauptman case, following the Lindbergh kidnapping, the writer spent many months working on the case for a magazine. The case itself was hysteria. Neptunian people everywhere seemed to sense that Hauptman was not guilty. They came in droves and offered all kinds of information to anyone who would listen. One woman 'confessed' that her husband was the real kidnapper. Ellis Parker, famous New Jersey detective who solved many crimes, had Sun in Virgo. He was approached by a man who claimed to have contact with 'the gang' and offered to gain the return of the child. Parker was convinced that he had a man who was member of such a gang. Wanting to get at the real criminals, Parker captured this man, took him across a state line (which was illegal) and tried to torture the truth out of him. As a result, Parker himself was convicted of kidnapping and died in prison.

We constantly face unreliability when we meet up with negative influences of Neptune, but to understand that unreliability we must face the fact that it has a pathological base. Neptune is somewhere in every chart. The person who has a good moral background and training is less apt to fall victim to Neptune, but there are wide exceptions to this rule. We have forms of religion which are themselves bordering on the pathological. People follow their compulsions and justify them by claiming they were driven by higher forces, when they mean lower forces. Although they did not understand the dynamics with which they dealt, it is probable that the devil was originated to represent the lower forces while the higher forces were associated with God. Following this conception through, it relates the devil to the past and God to the future.

Whenever you contact a chart having an overabundance of Neptune, an excess of planets in Pisces or the 6th House, be alert to the possibility of pathological conditions. They may not show up in early life. They are more likely to show up when the individual is under severe strain, when there is fear and insecurity. They often show up when a woman is going through the menopause, but they are most likely to show up when the chart is experiencing very strong Neptunian transits which add to the natural conditions. Violence is more likely to show up if Mars, Pluto, Scorpio or Aries are strongly involved in addition to the Neptunian conditions. There are many insane or pathological people who are not violent. Here was an elderly man who was harmless and was never confined, but he spent his days crawling around the floor peeking out windows, waiting for the Germans to attack. He always knew that the Germans were going to attack at any time. This was between World War I and World War II, and during peace times. He died before World War II.

The pathological always involves Neptune, but there is no tendency toward violence unless the Family Dynamics are involved. The violence always has some hidden family situation as its base. That is one thing that the psychiatrist or psychologist must dig out. However, the chart of birth will save him tremendous time because it will show him exactly where to look, what to look for, and after that, therapy is his business.

The sneak thief may not be violent, but remember that fear is usually present in the subconscious where crime or mental illness are involved. Hidden fear is the motivating force. It is behind the compulsion. There is insecurity. Theft may involve lunar factors with Neptunian factors, or Saturn factors with Neptunian factors. Deep, deep in the subconscious, however, is that primitive fear of starvation which still exists as a motivating force in a world of plenty. The past is still here.

The neurotic person can often be very convincing, and no one may suspect pathology. This person may gain a big following. He may be very successful. His neurosis may catch on like a song. It may become very popular. He may be very entertaining, and people will go along with almost anything when it is entertaining. Look at the modern newsstand. Publishers have long ago learned that if you want to sell magazines, don't try to educate people. Entertain them. That has been a problem for the most sincere editors of astrology magazines sold on newsstands. The public is not seeking truth. It is seeking entertainment. There is a phase of pathology involved in that.

It is unfortunate that a book called 'The Psychology of

Suggestion' by Boris Sidis is long out of print, and we can't even locate our own copy which we prized for years. This book gave the best history of mob hysteria we have ever found. Crusades, financial bubbles, religious revivals and other mass movements have really been of a pathological nature. Some smart people rode the crest of a pathological wave, recognizing it for what it was and making fortunes. Others believed that black was white because it made them temporarily happy. It entertained them and gave them illusions about the future which kept them happy until the bubbly burst, until they again faced reality. The neurotic always retreats from reality into a world of unreality, and it is quite easy for the mind to accept unreality. The mind is misinterpreting all the time in order to accept unreality.

You will meet the person who will tell you that there seem to be no honest people in the world. This person never associates with honest people. He trusts no one. He fears honest people and keeps away from them. The real dishonesty is within himself. The honest man would disarm him and make him uncomfortable. He can associate only with dishonest people, because he can associate only with people with whom he has something in common. In order to like people, you have to have something in common with them, and this all works on the subconscious level.

As we have told you before, the way to learn astrology must finally be to watch it work. When you see it work, you understand it, but you understand it better after you realize how it works on the unconscious level. In presenting this course, one of the principle things we are doing is to make it unnecessary to spend years investigating various illusionary conceptions of astrology which have never worked. We have seen a good many students study some of these systems and wonder what was wrong with themselves, because the systems would not work for them. The better astrologers often refer to these systems as Neptunian astrology, because the pathological has crept into 'systems' of astrology than of truthful astrology, and that seems true throughout the world. Neptunian astrology can sound very convincing until you try to make it work, We note some of this Neptunian astrology in a book that associates the light of the Moon with intelligence, the dark of the Moon with ignorance–very poetical, but in no way related to facts. Ultimately, you must learn more about the mathematics of statistics, because statistics is a means of discovering what is true and what is false. Our powers of observation can be very faulty until we have trained them, so as to prevent our wishful thinking from seeing something that is not there, and you must realize how easy this is. Just as the neurotic person sees what is not there physically, the neurotic astrologer sees a poetical astrology that bears little or no relation to reality. Again, it is a matter of unconscious misinterpretation.

You have seen people who can't stop talking. They never listen. This is a typical Neptunian characteristic as are all forms of nervousness. It involves the difficulty of trying to fit one's self into society. It is the poor functioning of the SSD or the SSDR, more likely the SSD. Take a woman who can't stop talking (but there are plenty of men also). Her conversation is very likely to include much in the way of scandal, much of which may never have happened. What she is telling about others is quite likely to be all the things that she secretly wishes to do herself. Perhaps she suppresses these desires, but it is necessary for her to get them out of her system in some way. Let her talk long enough and study the pattern that her conversation follows. You are likely to discover that all of the people she talks about do about the same scandalous things. Upon the slightest opportunity, she is living her desires by attributing them to others.

The professional astrologer will find himself dealing with many of these people. The value they place upon the astrologer will be dependent upon his ability to listen. They want to talk. They love to talk about themselves, but quite untruthfully in many cases. It is probable that all physicians meet up with the same people, for they usually have many psychosomatic difficulties. What they need is a probing into the unconscious. They need to be shown what is happening on the unconscious level. Although psychiatry may be needed, the astrologer had the map of the unconscious in his hands. If the astrologer is also a psychiatrist, he has the map and he is ready for therapy. Although the majority of such cases may not be classified as pathological, astrologically, they are the same thing in a mild form. They are Neptunianism expressing itself. They involve the individual's inability to fit himself into society. In many cases, they compensate for their lack of human companionship by collecting pets. Many of these ills will disappear when the individuals can take to really intellectual interests, when they realize that there is something greater they can cling to in the purely abstract realms of fact.

Another phenomenon that appears to have some connection with Neptune, although we have very little data on the subject, is epilepsy. The epileptic loses consciousness, twists and crumbles to the floor. There follows a convulsion and the whole body trembles and shakes. In one instance involving a woman in her 30's, the woman appeared to go through all the motions of the sex act, although this would be quite untrue of other cases. Here is an odd case involving convulsions in a dog. The first seizure was only partial, and the dog came out of it upon hearing his master's voice. Although the dog had no previous seizures, frothy saliva had been running from the dog's mouth periodically for a week. It's master had been petting it. Fixing its gaze on the floor a few feet in front if it, the dog acted exactly as if it had seen a snake. It acted like an animal about to plunge into an epileptic fit until its master began talking to it. It obviously recognized the voice, but did not appear to see its master, but gradually returned to normal. About ten hours later, its master came upon the dog going through a convulsion, but when spoken to, again the dog appeared to recognize the voice, came out of the convulsion and tried to find the voice, but showed no signs of recognizing the master visually. Five hours later, the dog had a third seizure, after which it did not recognize its master at all and would merely bark at him and retreat as an attempt to approach was made.

In the cases we have observed, which were too few to pass judgment upon, epileptic seizures occurred when the transiting Moon was in opposition to the natal Sun. In other words, the individual was at the bottom of the Lunar Cycle. (The top of the Lunar Cycle is when the transiting Moon crosses the natal Sun. The bottom of the cycle is when the Moon reaches the exact opposite point in the zodiac.) In the case of the above mentioned epileptic dog, no birth date was known, but the dog was born in April 1956, which would suggest Sun in Aries. The Moon was in Libra at the time of the first seizure, which would be the bottom of the Lunar cycle. In fact, it was in opposition to Mars, which was at 26-Aries (1/22/57). Mars was approaching the opposition to Neptune. This strongly suggests that the dog may have been born on April 16th, 1956, which would place Mars on its Sun at the time of the first convulsion. If this be true, the natal Sun would be square Uranus and opposite Neptune. In a human, we know that this could involve a health liability. Sun-Neptune afflictions always give some liability to ill health. In the case of the dog, it had medical treatment immediately, and its condition improved as soon as Mars got away from the 26-Aries position. Diagnosis showed that the animal had a disease known as hardpad.

LESSON SEVENTEEN

PROGRESSIONS, TRANSITS AND HORARY ASTROLOGY

There are two schools of astrology which have been rather antagonistic toward each other, those who follow 'progressions' and those who follow 'transits'. First, let us explain what progressions are. There are many schools of progressions. Progressionists do not agree among themselves, but we will refer to the system employed most widely in this country and that which was taught by Llewellyn George. This school assumes some relationship between two time elements which appear unrelated otherwise, a day and a year. It assumes a relationship between a revolution of the Earth around the Sun and a rotation of the Earth on its axis in relation to the Sun.

It is the assumption that if you were born at 10:17 A.M., on June 16th, 1905. A chart drawn for 10:17 A.M., on June 27th, 1905 would indicate phases of your life during the year following your eleventh birthday. The movement of the planets during the first day of your life would have a relationship to the first twelve months or year of your life would have a relation ship to the first twelve months or year of your life. The ascendant and cusps of this chart will change at the rate of about a degree a year, although this can vary. The movement of the cusps in relation to planets are called primary progressions and the movement of the planets in relation to each other are called secondary progressions. However, if the system of Llewellyn George is followed, you will have all these progressions in each chart. George was not an exclusive progressionist, because he employed both progressions and transits. Transits are merely the relationship of the planets now to their birth position.

About the year 1930, Sidney K. Bennett (Wynn) opened war on the progressionists, and his magazine came forth with a headline stating that progressions do not work.

An explosion occurred around his head, because the majority of astrologers in the USA did not agree with him, and he was attacked from all quarters. It is regrettable that the two groups of people could not get together and test their view scientifically, but the debate was too emotional for that. Each side protected their ideas like their children, and astrologers of one group were not to be seen where there were astrologers of the other group.

In his original attack, Wynn had given an example in his own life. He had been hit by an automobile and spent many weeks in a hospital as a result. Everything in his life changed, and he maintained there was nothing in his progressed chart to indicate an accident at that time. Actually, Wynn had overlooked something. He had not checked progressed planets against progressed planets but only progressed planets against natal planets. For the year in question, his progressed Mars was in opposition to progressed Saturn, and if one were to consult the texts of Llewellyn George for the aspect he would find that just that sort of a condition was predicted. This was pointed out to Wynn by the writer and published in THE NEW YORK ASTROLOGER, a student publication that existed at that time. Although Wynn admitted an oversight, it did not alter his view of progressions because the whole idea of progressions was ridiculous to him. From here on, for the next 27 years, the writer has remained silent on progressions. Nevertheless, for that length of time he has continued observing. To say anything for or against progressions during the last 27 years would have been to make enemies on one side or the other. The progressionist and the transitist have hardly been on speaking terms, although it is probable that most progressionists of today use both progressions and transits as did Llewellyn George, so we should probably say that the quarrel is between the progressionists and the non-progressionists.

We cannot ignore the fact that there have been many students who have adopted progressions because they claimed to have found they work, while there have been many other students who discarded progressions because they claimed to have found they did not work. Thus, we have confusion. The witnesses do not testify to the same thing. What witnesses are we to believe?

Throughout these 27 years, while the writer has been known as a transitist, it might be noted that he has never published an actual opinion relative to progressions. He has never said YES and he has never said NO, but there comes a time when one must speak, and in putting out this Course on astrology, it becomes impossible to ignore the matter of progressions. Actually, we have seen progressions work and we have seen them fail to work. In essence, what we should say is that they have not worked accurately.

In 1926, when first studying astrology in the form of the work of Llewellyn George, we looked ahead, and we read up what was supposed to happen to us a long time hence. According to George, the writer might become the father of a child after he was 40, when progressed Venus reached his natal Sun. At the time of making this study the writer was 24 and a child had been born in that year. It is interesting to note that he had no more children until after he was 41, when his only son was born. However, the birth was off by several years. That is typical of the writer's experience with progressions. He found that they worked but they did not work at the right time. There were broad inaccuracies. In some cases, they worked very accurately, but in most instances, they did not. It is not the writer's nature to impulsively toss this sort of evidence out the window and merely say that progressions do not work. There is nothing unusual about this kind of evidence. We find it everywhere in science. Scientists are always finding something that appears to work one moment and not the next. They keep digging until they find out why. One of our greatest scientists, Charles F. Kettering recently said, 'From the time he goes to school, a child is taught that it is very dangerous to fail.... The inventor fails 9,999 times and if he succeeds once he is in. The one time you don't want to fail is the last time you try. Just the minute you get satisfied with what you've got, the concrete has begun to set in your head.' (Quoted from Collier's, October 26th, 1956.)

    The writer never used progressions in advising clients during all of the years of his professional practice, because he found that he could not depend on their accuracy although he could depend on the accuracy of transits. Nevertheless, he has always kept an open mind. Where there is smoke, there might be fire. We will later discuss what might be wrong with progressions and how they might possibly be found to work with accuracy. First, however, let us take up the claim of some that progressions are ridiculous. How could the planets on the 23rd day after your birth have anything to do with the 23rd year of your life? This question is based on the assumption that astrology is a causal phenomenon. We have held that it is not, and when you stop assuming that it is, new avenues open up to you. There is the possibility that progressions might involve some form of mathematical expression, and abstract cosmic design whereby there is a relationship between rotations and revolutions of the Earth. We do not know. It is merely a possibility. If progressions work inaccurately, we should not toss them out. We should investigate more thoroughly. We should try and find out why. The first automobiles did not run very efficiently, but we did not throw out the whole idea, although there were many people who advised doing so. Progressions in the right hands might turn up something we do not yet know.

    One of the great difficulties with many progressionists is that they are fatalistic in their attitude and they work with an expected precision that does not exist. They try to calculate an aspect such as one of Mars-Saturn down to an exact day when accuracy does not even appear to be to an exact year. Some progressed aspects would be of very long duration, and would not apply for a specific event to occur on a certain day. When the writer was a child, progressed Mars moved over his natal Sun, and that interval was certainly accompanied by a couple of years when he was always getting hurt through falls, etc. There was no other similar period in his life. The opposition of progressed Mercury to Uranus in his chart coincided with his editorship of the Long Beach (N.Y.) Sun, as a youngster, which resulted in a spectacular editorial campaign against political corruption in Nassau County, which in turn lead to a state investigation being ordered by Governor Alfred E. Smith, and this ultimately led to conviction of many public officials and the end of a political regime. You will realize that many enemies resulted. Immediately thereafter, Mercury crossed the writer's 7th natal cusp, and he was married for the first time, while visiting in Palm Beach. When progressed Mercury reached the conjunction of Neptune in his chart, he began writing for astrology magazines. During the years when progressed Mars was squaring his Jupiter, he went through a period of terrific gambling losses. In fact, almost anything he did business wise lost money, but fortunately he was very young. He was coming out of his teens. Things were more than tough when the progressed ascendant reached natal Saturn. When the progressed ascendant reached natal Jupiter, he moved from New York to Arizona and began a new era.

On the other hand, many of the most important events of his life were accompanied by no significant progressions. Now and then, however, we have a case that baffles us, and we turn to progressions to see what they might show. Here is a lady who is seized with pain in the middle of the night, is rushed to a hospital and goes through an emergency appendectomy. Mars was exactly on her natal Sun and Pluto, but it had crossed that point once every two years of her life with no operation necessary and without any similar ailments. Why did it happen this time? We turn to progressions, and we find that her progressed Mars has reached her natal Sun, so that the transit of Mars was over a progressed Mars conjunct her Sun-Pluto in Cancer. Such cases might be coincidence, but are they?

It has been our experience that transits work to natal cusps of houses computed in the plane of the Earth's orbit [ed. Equal House] and not to the cusps of houses computed in accord with the Placidian system. The progressed chart is computed in the Placidian plane, but the planets are then placed in the chart in the plane of the Earth's orbit, which is mathematically incommensurable. What would happen if the planets were re-computed in the same plane as

Lesson Seventeen

that in which the chart is drawn? Insofar as we know, this has never been tried, but there is some hint that Johndro was experimenting with such a system prior to his death. We are not sure. This would entail a very complicated set of recalculations. The question is, would progressions work if they were correctly calculated? They are not correctly calculated at the present time, because you can't take planetary positions from an ephemeris calculated in one plane of space and apply them to another plane of space [Placidus]. That is what the progressionists are doing now.

There is no question in our minds that the progressionists are partly in error, but we hesitate to say they are ALL wrong. They may be partly right. They may have something unperfected that could be perfected. To determine the answer to such a question will require a lot of research and a lot of money, money that is not available at this time, but we feel that we should all keep an open mind on the subject until such a time as such research is within the realms of possibility. **It is our advice to the student to stick to transits insofar as every day practice is concerned, but to experiment with progressions or anything else as much as you like, AFTER you have mastered transits.** We hope the student will avoid any dogma. The great difficulty with most of those who have taken part in the battle for or against progressions is that they have assumed a dogmatic stand on one side of the question and have failed to penetrate further. Each side has been unable to listen to arguments on the other side. If that is not where progressions end, it is where progress ends.

If a progressed chart is drawn in the Placidian plane, and then the planets are computed in that same plane, the planetary positions would vary considerably. What is the possibility that the astronomical error in the erection of these progressed charts equals the inaccuracies that we find in the timing of progressions? In other words, what is the possibility that transits work in the plane of the Earth's orbit (which is the plane of the zodiac) and that progressions work in the plane of the Placidian system? We have similar phenomena in mathematics all of the time. The whole idea of computing a chart in the plane of the Placidian system and then insert in the planets according to the zodiac is unsound. If you draw a chart in the Placidian system, you should forget the zodiac, because it is in a different plane of space and would have no application in the Placidian system. The two systems cannot be employed together. You have half of one thing and half of something else. It is as if a person was to dress like a man on one side, like a woman on the other. You can compute mathematically in the decimal system or you can compute in the duodecimal system, and the results will be the same, but you can't use the two systems at the same time. You have to use one or the other. In the decimal system, 2 X 8 equal 16, but in the duodecimal system, 2 X 8 equal 14. However, 16, in the decimal system means exactly the same thing as 14 in the duodecimal system. In the decimal system, 16 means 10 plus 6, while in the duodecimal system, 16 means12 plus 6.

Transits merely involve the relationship of the planets today to the date of birth. After birth, you retain the greater part of the characteristics with which you were born. A study of your chart, as it related to the planetary positions of today, is a study of how you fit into the circumstance that exist today. Just as your birth date had characteristics, today has characteristics, and they are different, although some of them might be similar. Neptune has been entering Scorpio as we have been writing these lessons. None of us are old enough to remember Neptune having been in Scorpio before, because it takes 165 years for Neptune to go all through the twelve signs. None of us can base our judgment of Neptune-in-Scorpio on personal experience, but we can judge it analytically. We know that Neptune represents the SSD and that Scorpio represents the FSD. We know that the Social Survival Dynamic. What would ordinarily be the sympathy of the SSD is overcome by the jealousy and fear of the FSD. On the unconscious level, the family wants to survive in its same old form. There is fear of any new pattern. There is fear of injecting new blood into the family stream. In extreme cases, the inclination will be toward incest. We see the effects in the south where the segregation problem is accented. Among the whites, there is fear that segregation will involve a mixture of blood. The Negro demands his birthrights, and some of the whites are afraid to grant them for fear that the past pattern of the family might not survive. This will work elsewhere than in the south, and it will work in other ways. Races will want to protect their patterns and customs of the past. Families will want to protect their own. Neptune subdued in Scorpio will not help the spirit of the brotherhood of Man, because family and racial patterns will be very strong, and this will apply throughout the world. Races can be more cruel to each other, and families can be more cruel to each other.

There will be other transits. The power of Neptune in Scorpio will be strengthened or weakened by other transits. When Mars goes into Pisces for a short while, this will balance off, because then Mars, representing the FSD will be in Pisces, representing the SSD, and each principle will be, to some extent, under the domination of the other, but watch out when planets gang up in Scorpio, as they will at times, because then the effect of the FSD will become even more pronounced and powerful. From the unconscious will come the compulsions that demand greater survival for the old family pattern. As Neptune in Scorpio forms aspects to planets in the charts of millions of people, the FSD will do everything in its power to manifest. This may create a great many strange developments in a great many places and in a great many families. It will be likely to increase racial feelings and racial prejudice. It is probably having a great deal to do with the situation in the Middle East as this is written, but Neptune's total stay in Scorpio will be about 14 years.

This will be a good place to bring forth another controversial phase of astrology that is known as Horary Astrology. The theme of Horary astrology is not unsimilar to that of a crystal ball. There are various textbooks on Horary astrology, and it has been our experience that none of the rules in them really work. Horary astrology is more or less a form of divination. When a client came to Evangeline Adams, she erected a chart for the moment of the interview, placed the client's birth planets in this chart, and gave her interpretations from the chart. Her interpretations were usually very good, but we doubt that the chart had anything in particular to do with the interpretations. The indication was that Evangeline Adams was psychic. A crystal ball would have done quite as well as the Horary chart.

The spring of 1957 issue of Tomorrow Magazine contains as interesting article by Dal Lee speculating on some astrologers whose interpretations may be more psychic than astrological.

Some astrologers often use a Horary chart to try and find the answer to a question that is proposed. When the Lindbergh baby was kidnapped in 1932, astrologers of this group all over the country erected Horary charts. They all chose different moments to erect the chart, because they did not hear about the kidnapping at the same time. They all came up with different answers.

Many years back we studied the textbooks on Horary astrology very carefully. We collected over 3000 Horary charts that pertained to questions involving the future. We kept these charts until the answer to the question was decided by time, and then we checked to see how closely the rules worked. It was our finding that the rules didn't work at all. We forgot the old methods of Horary astrology.

Yet, on the other hand, we have often made good use of such charts in another way. The charts show the transits to the natal chart at a given time. There will be other transits in the future. In a great many instances, a question can be answered by noting what the planets are going to do next, but this could hardly be termed Horary astrology. A neighbor came into see us one day. She was very upset. An aunt had been very ill for some time. A look at the patient's chart showed heavy Neptunian afflictions, including a transit of Neptune over natal Saturn. These were to become worse within a few days, because the Sun was to conjoin Neptune on her Saturn. The neighbor wanted to know what the future held. In our mind, we calculated the date when the Neptunian afflictions would reach a maximum. Then we gave ourselves a few days leeway, set a date, and said that if the patient could successfully pass that date, her condition would improve. The patient died two days prior to the date set. This could not be considered a Horary answer. It was merely a notation of when conditions would be at their worst. The question remained as to whether the patient could make the grade.

It is entirely possible that some people possess a psychic sense that allows them to unconsciously select a time when a Horary chart will give an answer according to some set of rules, whatever set of rules the individual is employing, but this is hardly to be considered astrology in the sense it is being taught in these lessons. Many times, a single aspect will give you the answer to a question. If a woman had Mars right on Uranus in her chart and asked us, 'If I leave my husband now, can we patch things up later?', we should say NO. If you take action under bad Mars-Uranus afflictions, you burn your bridges behind you, and there is no going back. It's just that we have seen that sort of thing happen again and again.

In *A New Experiment In Astrology* published in 1938, we offered what we then termed a partial system of Horary astrology, but if we are to stick to the old meaning of the term Horary astrology, then the system could not actually be considered as Horary astrology. You may find people who are seeking buried treasure or who want to find a way of beating the horses, and they may want your help. We never even consider such cases. It is a negative way of living. The world is full of grand possibilities for those who will follow a constructive course, and to those people, astrology can be very useful, but why try to help a person living a negative existence to live a more negative existence. You won't be doing him a favor. Lots of people go looking for gold for amusement, but if they really expect to find it, they are taking the matter too seriously. There is more money in a new invention. You can read all kinds of books about the early search for gold in Arizona, but the facts are that today, with the most modern mining methods, there is only one commercially operating gold mine in Arizona. Its complete find for 1955 was $20,000, and the men working could have made more money if they worked as carpenters. The big mining companies do not even look for gold.

They look for copper. They find small quantities of gold here and there, but they cannot be annoyed looking for it. They consider it merely as a by-product. It holds little interest for them. By modern methods, they sometimes take down a whole mountain, and if there is any gold, they'll find it. Nevertheless, there are still long-bearded prospectors roaming the mountains of Arizona, ever in search of that great find, but they just like to roam. They wouldn't be at home in a community. It is a lot of fun, for one who likes roaming.

There was an astrologer in New Mexico a few years back who advertised himself as a specialist in Horary astrology. From a Horary chart, he decided that oil was to be found on a certain property. He invested his every cent in the project. He talked clients into joining and investing more money. After drilling operations were complete, he committed suicide. There wasn't any oil. The Horary chart didn't work. It is our advice to forget the old rules of Horary astrology unless you are a psychic, and in that event you could do better to get yourself a crystal ball and forget astrology all together. The rules of Horary astrology might throw you off. There are no rules that go with a crystal ball. Nevertheless, if you discover one new principle, we won't have a closed mind.

Visitors are often quite surprised that we do not maintain a greater astrological library than we do. It is a little foolish to load yourself up with books filled with rules that do not work. The majority of books on astrology were written by people who knew little about astrology from actual experience. They read other books by other people with little knowledge on astrology, and in that way qualified themselves to write more books by people who knew little about astrology. If a New York publisher wants to publish a book on astrology, he merely seeks somebody who can write a thrilling book. He does not want to know whether the rules in the book work. All he wants to know is whether the book sells. In some cases, the worst books on astrology have been good sellers. They have been Neptunian. They appeal to the pathological element in society. Don't forget that the books that sell best are those that are pure fiction. Society is far more interested in reading fiction than fact. Just compare the sale of fiction with non-fiction. Nevertheless, there is hope, because as the ratio of educated people increases, the sale of non-fiction increases also. We are actually developing a taste for more factual material.

We have stated that there are many schools of progressions. It is probable that many students have investigated progressions, found that they almost worked, and began making changes to try and make them work better, with no better success. One astrologer writes, 'One system seems to work in one case, another system in another case.' Is this not merely telling us that results are not wrong but are inaccurate. However, it would seem that every new system holds just as many inaccuracies, and the system that we have suggested for investigation, erecting the chart in the Placidian system and also computing the planets in the plane of this system, might prove just as faulty. We do not know. It is merely a mathematical suggestion, which may or may not have merit.

Some systems attempt to use a degree for a year, but a degree of a circle has no factual foundation. It is a purely arbitrary, man-made standard of measurement, like a foot. We know of no real basis for dividing a circle into 360 parts. It is supposed that this was agreed upon because ancients believed that there were 360 days in a year, but this is probably some of the fiction of modern astronomy. The Aztecs had a more perfect calendar when it was discovered than the European astronomers did. The ancients knew more astronomy than we think they did. Their knowledge was lost long before the birth of Christianity. How much was lost in the burning of the great libraries of Alexandria and China, and how much was lost long before that is unknown. At any rate, we have no reason to believe that a degree or 1/360th of a circle has any meaning or significance. It is merely a handy way of measuring something, just as a foot-ruler is a handy way of measuring something so long as everyone is employing the same length foot-ruler.

On the other hand, we have found the next figure of the 144 divisions of the zodiac of definite value and significance. We currently divide the zodiac into 12 parts called signs and we divide the horoscope into 12 parts called houses. All of our evidence seems to indicate that this division has a factual foundation. It works, and astrologers have clung to it for centuries and centuries. That part tested by RCA Communications Inc., in its independent research also seems to stand up.

Astrologers have also employed what they call decanates or 10 degree areas. **Such an area is 1/36th of a circle. We have never found that these areas stood up as entities in themselves**, and there does not appear to be any mathematical reason for them. Thirty-six is merely 3 X12 or 6 X 6. However, **we have found significance in the square of 12**, dividing the circle into 144 parts or 12 X 12. This has been done by others, but we have never found the interpretations accompanying such division to be correct. We have found, for example, that the Sun in one part of a sign has characteristics not found when the Sun is in another part of the same sign. The key to this is another symmetrical pattern. This pattern appears on the next page. Each is divided into twelve equal

Lesson Seventeen

areas of 2 1/2 degrees, making up 144 areas, 144 being the square of 12, or 12 X 12.

One much used system begins each sign with a pure type of sign. The first 2 1/2 degrees of Aries is the Aries division of Aries, the next 2 1/2 degrees the Taurus section of Aries, etc. We never found that this system worked. Instead, we begin Aries with Scorpio. *We are substituting survival for non-survival.* The first 21/2 degrees of Aries will be the Scorpio division, the next 2 1/2 degrees the Sagittarius division, the next 2 1/2 degrees the Capricorn division, etc. This gives us an interesting mathematical pattern that is perfectly symmetrical. The last 2 1/2 degrees of Aries will be the Libra division, and Taurus will begin with a Libra division, so that the end of one sign is always joined to the next sign by the same sub-sign. The last 2 1/2 degrees of Taurus will be the Virgo division of Taurus, and the first 2 1/2 degrees of Gemini will be the Virgo division of Gemini. [ed. This pattern of 144 zodiac divisions follows the pattern of Hellentistic Planetary Order which is the foundation of sign rulership. The Greeks called it Dodecatmoria. Jyotish astrology uses this same 144 divisions that are called Vargas, one of which is the Divisional 12.]

Zodiac Divided by 144 (12x12)

We often find some very Neptunian situations, which are not explained otherwise when the Sun is between 17 1/2, and 20 degrees of Cancer, the Pisces division of Cancer. There will be such a point in each zodiacal sign. In Aries, it will be from 10 to 12 1/2 degrees. In Taurus, it will be 12 1/2 to 15 degrees, in Gemini 15 to 17 1/2 degrees, etc. You will see above how Cancer fits in next. This is something we spotted way back in the early 30's, but we have never published anything on it, although we have been using it since that time. You will see that it is merely one more step in figuring out the design in the solar system. However, it might be interesting to note just how we came upon the idea.

There is a very interesting book on the characteristics of the degrees written by an Australian named Isadore Kozminsky. [ed. Kozminsky was a well-known Jewish occult and esoteric author, reputed to have been a leading member of the Hermetic Order of the Golden Dawn. 'Zodiacal Symbology and its Planetary Power'] Sidney K. Bennett prized this book very highly, and he once reprinted the whole book serially in this magazine. One day, Bennett brought the book, well marked up, to the writer. He was fascinated. 'There must be a key to this fellow's interpretations,' he said. 'You will note that this division of this sign definitely has the characteristics of Mars in it. I have marked some of these divisions with the planet that seems to be the key. See what you make out of it.'

The writer marked up the divisions further and finally noted that all the pieces fitted together. All we had to do was to fill in the missing pieces of the puzzle with a symmetrical design. However, the catch that Kozminsky was using degree areas, and the 3rd degree of a sign was part of one division and part of another. We had to make an allowance for this discrepancy, but when we had finished doing so, we had a perfectly symmetrical pattern. The big question is, how did Kozminsky gain the original interpretations, which appeared so authentic in most cases. For the answer, we will have to ask him. It is his claim that he wrote the interpretations psychically. They just came to him. In other words, the author wrote the book, unknowingly, to a mathematical pattern, which he did not know to exist. For that reason, he followed convention and divided the zodiac into 360 parts instead of 144 equal parts. The result might have been even more interesting had he started out with 144 equal parts. This brings up another interesting question. Nobody has ever been able to explain psychic phenomena, extrasensory perception or precognition, because it defies time and space, as has been proved in laboratory experiments at Duke and other universities. What is the

Lesson Seventeen

possibility that these phenomena merely involve unconscious tuning into abstract, mathematical, cosmic design? This would explain everything with one swoop. In the abstract world, there is no time and no space. Neither time nor space can exist except by relativity.

The above is one more instance where our own discovery of design in the solar system was stimulated by something that was actually started by Sidney K. Bennett, and we might never have hit upon the answer had we not been fortunate enough to know him. We began by taking pot shots at each other in two opposing magazines when we were both a lot younger and wound up very good friends. In fact, the greatest element of the writer's own success in the astrological field was his ability to gain the co-operation of his competitors. Without the help of his competitors, he would never have gotten into business, and without the help of his competitors, he would never have stayed in business. Competitors can be very valuable to one if his FSD is not so strong that it excludes them as members of his family. When you have no competitors, life can get very dull.

A new question arises. If the zodiac can be divided into 12 parts, and then can be subdivided into 12 X 12 or 144 parts, can it now be divided into 12 X 12 X 12 parts? This would be 1728 sub-sub parts. It is an interesting question, but we have not had time to investigate its possibilities. We mention it, because it might have possibilities and we hope it will give somebody something to do, just as Sidney K. Bennett gave us a lot to do in our earlier days in astrology. Another question that arises and has never been tested is this. If the zodiac can be divided into 12 X 12 parts, can an astrological house be divided into twelve parts, each of which would be 1/144th of a circle. [ed. Jyotish astrology had divisional charts but they divide the houses differently. The Second House is divided into two, the Third House is divided into three parts, the Fourth House is divided into four parts, the Fifth House is divided into five parts, etc.] We do not know, but the thought may give somebody else something to do. There is lots to do. It might prove much more interesting and successful than trying to find a system of beating the horse races or than searching for gold in mountains where gold is very scarce. If the medical profession can't cure your wife of cancer, gold isn't going to do it either, but there is always a possibility that more knowledge might. Gold is only a medium to get other people to work for you, and you can often get people to work for you by merely getting them interested in what you are trying to do.

Coming back to progressions, our conclusion is that they are inaccurate. We do not claim that the idea of progressions is wrong or that there is no foundation for them. We suspect that there may be. However, the progressionist will have a difficult time trying to make them reasonable if he sticks to a causal hypothesis. We think it breaks down. Reconsidering astrology as merely mathematical expression re-opens the door to progressions. They might involve a mathematical pattern, and if they do, there is nothing strange about them. There are stranger things throughout mathematics and nature. We have not yet found any mathematical relationship between rotations and revolutions of the Earth, but there might be one, and if the progressionists can develop the fact that there IS, then they will have made the greatest scientific discovery of the age. It would open up the possibility that there is also a mathematical relationship involving all the motions of all the planets. Thus, although we have found progressions inaccurate a good part of the time, our own investigations lead us to the suspicion that we might make a very serious error if we were to throw them away altogether.

In working with transits, so long as the natal chart and the planets are in the same plane of space, you have a relatively simple matter to deal with. Astronomical tables are accurate. You know where the planets are. You are not dealing with two different things at one time and trying to make two things fit together that do not fit together. If there are two roads from New York to Boston, you cannot travel over both of them simultaneously. You have to make up your mind which you are going to take, but you might take one going and come back the other way. If one is going to use progressions one must make up his mind in what plane of space he is going to calculate. We have tried the plane of the zodiac and the result is inaccuracies.

[ed. **Divisional Chart:** A vital part of the Hindu Vedic system, where additional charts (the 16 *varga* charts) are erected. Based on fractions ("divisions") of each sign, each varga gives light on a different side of the character. This ancient system strongly influenced John Addey, who went on to devise the Harmonic Chart system for Western astrology in the 20th Century.]

LESSON EIGHTEEN
THE STATISTICAL AND
THE ANALYTICAL APPROACH

From time to time, in the field of astrology, there has been criticism of the statistical approach, claiming that astrology is something beyond statistics and that it cannot be approached statistically. Most such criticism has been leveled by people who knew little or nothing about the subject of mathematical statistics. They were unqualified to deal with the subject. However, we are going to refer to a very interesting editorial which appears in the May-June, 1957 issue of 'ASTROLOGY GUIDE' Magazine and is written by Dal Lee, its editor.

Editor Lee brings up some points about statistics which should not be ignored, but first, let us discuss mathematical statistics in a general way. The history of mathematical statistics is most interesting and intriguing. We might say that it began with Pythagoras when he taught the Triangular Numbers. That was 2500 years ago.

There are infinite series of triangular numbers, and the whole theory of mathematical probability is all wrapped up with them. Yet, in his day, Pythagoras was laughed at for teaching them, because they appeared to have no utility. Why learn numbers that wouldn't make money? The great curse accompanying history of mathematics is the way that it is taught in schools, colleges and universities, to make money, and the result has been that most people have run away from what could be their greatest comfort and pleasure in life, enjoying the beauty and symmetry of the universe and life itself. They seek money to buy happiness which they never find, while they could find directly what they are really seeking if mathematics was differently taught.

Let us give you the beginning of a table of triangular numbers. First the table at the top of the next page, and then we will explain it.

SERIES

NUMBER	1	2	3	4	5	6
1	1	1	1	1	1	1
2	3	4	5	6	7	8
3	6	10	15	21	28	36
4	10	20	35	56	84	120
5	15	351	70	125	210	330
6	21	56	126	252	462	792
7	28	84	210	462	924	1716
8	6	120	330	792	1716	3432
9	45	165	495	1287	3003	6435
10	55	220	715	2002	5005	11440

We have given the first ten numbers in the first six series of triangular numbers. Both numbers and series go on to infinity. The first column to the left under the word 'number' gives the integers themselves and numbers or identifies each figure in each series. The second column, under the figure '1', is known as the first series of triangular numbers.

This first series is the sum of the integers. In other words, 55, the last number given, is the 10th number, and it is the sum of the integers form 10 down to 1. If you add all the integers from 10 down to 1, you will get 55. The third column, the second series of triangular numbers, its the sum of the first series, or the numbers in the second column. The 9th number is 165, which is the sum of the first nine figures in the second column. Each series is the sum of the previous series. You will also note that any number is the sum of the number above it when added to the number to the left of it. For this reason, you can make up such a table very easily and very quickly.

If you write $^5T_4$, you mean the 4th triangular number in the 5th series. You use a **T** to indicate triangular, the number above and to the left to indicate the series, and the number below and to the right to indicate the number in that series. If you take any problem of the nature where you can ask, 'How many ways can you take **r** things from **n** things?' The answer always has to be a triangular number. Consequently, a table of triangular numbers will give you a quick answer to any such problem if you have a formula. (You don't have to learn this.)

Such a formula can be written thus:

$$^nC_r = T_{(n+r)-r}^{r-1}$$

The above is the writer's own formula. You can also write:

$$^nC_r = \frac{n!}{r!\,(n-r)!}$$

The last is the conventional formula, but the first is much more simple if you have a table of triangular numbers. The 'C' stands for combinations, and when you write ^nC_r you mean, 'How many ways are there that you can take **r** things from **n** things.'

Thus, if anybody had the first of the above formulas, he could have the answer to any problem involving combinations by consulting one of the tables of triangular numbers made up by Pythagoras about 500 B.C., but folks didn't know that for a long time.

Later, Omar Khayyam, using these numbers developed the binomial theorem, which is taught in high school today. The binomial coefficients are the same triangular numbers.

We are not trying to teach you mathematics or the binomial theorem here, and you don't have to know any of the above to handle this course. We just want to illustrate how far back the foundation of the theory of mathematical probability goes. Later, in the gambling houses of Europe, more complicated problems in probability arose and the gambling house keepers were interested in beating the public. So, they began hiring mathematicians. When the mathematicians were paid salaries, they were able to devote time to the matter. Unconsciously, the losing public was contributing to the development of mathematicians. Later came life insurance companies, and they hired mathematicians, today called actuaries, who developed the theory of mathematical probability further. A new science of mathematical statistics grew up in Europe. It crossed the ocean to America late. It did not reach the United States until the 1890's when Dr. Irving Fisher, an economist of Yale University, began teaching the first class in statistics in his department of economics. It was taught at Columbia University under the Department of Psychology. It was very strange that originally statistical mathematics, was taught in universities of our country in almost any department except in a department of mathematics. The result was that mathematical statistics was taught by many people who were not mathematicians at all, and many books on the subject are questionable.

Next came the decision of Franklin D. Roosevelt to build an atomic bomb. This decision was one of the most momentous things that ever happened from a mathematical viewpoint, because playing around with the atom was strictly a matter of mathematical probability. This time, just about every available mathematician in the country was put to work by the government in order to beat Hitler to the atom bomb. A terrific advance in mathematics resulted. Still, progress has always come when people wanted to make money or when they wanted to kill other people. They were not seeking the beautiful.

There are thousands of people calling themselves statisticians who are not mathematicians. We must distinguish between the popular and the mathematical meaning of the word statistics. In Wall Street and many other places, statistics merely means fact collecting, while in the mathematical sense, the word involves the whole calculus of probability, which is a most involved branch of mathematics. One deals with all sorts of mathematical points having such names as 'standard deviation', 'probable error' etc. If one would really know more about the theory of mathematical probability, he might study some of the formulas in 'An Introduction to Mathematical Probability' by Julian Lowell Coolidge, published by Oxford University Press. However, a fair knowledge of mathematics is necessary before even approaching this volume, but it was written by a mathematician and not by a mere fact collector.

In the early 30's Dr. Rhine, of Duke University set out to prove or disprove whether there is such a thing as extrasensory perception. He consulted the very best mathematical talent in order to keep his experiments within the limitations of good mathematical procedure. His results were positive, and when he announced them, he was attacked by the materialists, the behaviorists and a swarm of old-school psychologists. Each came forward with criticism of Rhine's statistical procedure. Then, a bomb fell in their midst, because the mathematicians of the country stepped in themselves. In open convention, they proclaimed Rhine's mathematical procedure in good form. However, they did not say they believed in extrasensory perception. They did not say that Rhine's results proved extrasensory perception. They merely said that his mathematics were correct. Nevertheless, this was enough to send the pseudo-statisticians back home. They were not going to argue with any real mathematician. That was like biting the tail of a tiger.

Lesson Eighteen 261

One of the principal points we want to drive home is that most persons calling themselves statisticians are actually pseudo statisticians if we speak in terms of statistical mathematics. A characteristic of the mathematical statistician is that he will never say that something is proved. He will only say that the odds are **x** to **y** that it is so. You'll never be able to pin him down more than that. This has been a part of his training. He never claims to know anything except to a mathematical degree, and he states that in figures, not in opinions. He never seems to have an opinion on anything, and he may irritate you for this reason, if you really want opinions. To him, all proof is but relative proof. The public likes opinions. The public wants to know, 'Who do you think will win the next race?'

Statistics and the laws of mathematical probability are constantly employed to 'reach' what is not apparent to the eye, not understandable to the mind. Great discoveries have been made by the statistical method. If you have a gambling wheel that is off balance and improperly centered, 'in all likelihood', the numbers on one side of the wheel will turn up more than the numbers on the other side of the wheel. The gambler wants to know whether his wheel is properly balanced. It is up to the gambler to form his own opinion.

You toss a coin 25 times and a head turns up 25 times. Does the coin have a head on each side? They layman will probably say YES, but the mathematician will say, 'There is one chance in 33,554,432 that this result was due to chance.'

The strange thing about the mathematical theory of probability is that although it is employed to try and prove things, no one has ever proved the mathematical theory of probability insofar as its usefulness in discovering causes is concerned. There is no final way of deciding whether the result was due to chance. As Mr. Lee says in his editorial, there is nothing definite. You can spend years studying the accumulated data on this subject, and in the end, you will find no final answer. There are many yardsticks, but they are all relative. In the end, we must consider all proof as relative. You can point out vast numbers of insurance companies that have made millions of dollars relying on the mathematical theory of probability, but we can point out other, forgotten insurance companies that failed while relying on the theory of mathematical probability. In the early 30's the two biggest surety companies in America went into bankruptcy, because statistics of the past completely failed to predict the future.

A scientist in the field of cycles recently consulted the top mathematical authority in the USA on a problem of this kind. He tried to tie him down. The mathematical authority could furnish a mathematical evaluation which did not say YES and did not say NO. 'How then, can we know whether the results are due to cause or chance?' The answer was, 'From there on, you just have to use common sense.' It is generally stated that statistical laws work only for large samples. In our early dealing with this subject, we wanted to know, how large is a large sample. We could find no answer. There was no dividing line. Nobody could tell us. It was just a matter of 'common sense'. Small samples were statistically unreliable, but we soon found that large samples could also be statistically unreliable. We also found that there seemed to be no rule that samples could not and did not violate.

Mr. Lee has his own views and they are very interesting. However, one example cited in his editorial was of great interest to us. He points out that out of 29 of his writers, 11 have last names that begin with the letter H. This is extraordinary. In fact, it is fantastic. Just to have a comparable or control group, we selected the names of the first 29 persons who registered for this Course. We found that just one had a last name beginning with H.

Thus, what do such results mean? It would ordinarily be passed off as coincidence, but as Charles Fort once asked, 'What if it isn't coincidence?' We will consider another possible answer shortly, but first, let us consider another such case. One of our own students gives a good example. In 1938, he bought a new car. His license tag was C-15306. Each year, he was given a new number, but in 1957, when he obtained a new tag, the number was C-15306. Since the number preceded by C run up to about 65,000, there was one chance in 65,000 each year that he would obtain that number again. Since his number changed 9 times, this would make the odds against this being due to chance about 7,000 to 1. Pretty good odds. Anyway, people usually say that this is coincidence.

In trying to build up a doctrine of materialism, the 19th Century dogmatists cast all these things aside as coincidence, but the average individual has experienced so much coincidence in life that he knows there is something operating that neither he nor the world of science knows about, and as a result, he turns to God. We have always been interested in finding an answer to coincidence. We don't think it is coincidence.

Twenty years ago, we encountered something similar to Mr. Lee's example of his 11 out of 29 writers whose last names began with H. We tabulated the birth dates of all the persons listed in WHO'S WHO IN AMERICA, but we tabulated 5,000 cases at a time, so we could see how well the result from one group of 5, 000 compared with the next group of 5,000. This meant that each group involved

Lesson Eighteen

a different section of the alphabet. Frankly, the comparison was pretty bad. If one group of 5,000 indicated one thing, the next group of 5,000 indicated something else. In the end, we just had to lump five such groups together and accept the over-all results. One group showed statistical significance of another quality. We were spending a good deal of time with Dr. Clyde Fisher, an astronomer, who was then Curator of Astronomy at the Hayden Planetarium and the American Museum of Natural History. Dr. Fisher had a novel suggestion. He said that the first letter of a person's last name might have some connection with his hereditary background. Names that began Mc would include a lot of Irish, names that began Mac would include a lot of Scotch. Perhaps different nationalities and different races respond fascinated by Mr. Lee's example of 11 of his 29 writers having last names that begin with H.

A die has six sides. Thus, we say there is one chance in six of tossing a three. Dr. Rhine tells us that if people really want to throw threes, three will turn up more than any other number. This means that a man's feelings can affect the tossing of the die in a manner of which he is completely unconscious. Nevertheless, mathematically speaking, when the die is cast, the odds are 5 to 1 that you will not throw a 3. That does not prevent you from throwing a 3.

How many people do you know who ever won a daily-double at race track? One of our students won three daily-doubles in one week. Her ascending sign is Aries. It has been our experience that Aries people have better luck at gambling than the other 11 signs.

What is coincidence?

There might be an answer to this question, and the answer might be furnished by one word, DESIGN. The other day, we received two letters that said almost the same thing. They came from two different parts of the country. Each contained a check for $24.00 which is a very odd amount for us, and we could go forward or backward several months and find no other checks in the amount of exactly $24.00. On that morning, there were about 60 letters in the mailbox. These two letters were in the middle of the stack somewhere, but they were together. There were NO other letters between them.

We often find a person in whose life the same type of event occurs again and again, and a type of event that just never occurs in the lives of other people. Here is a man into whose life there came many romances, but just before a new romance was introduced into his life, a pet always dies. This seems to have been apart of the pattern of his life. It wouldn't work for any other person, but it worked that way for him. Then, there was the much written up man who was struck by lightning seven times and survived all seven occurrences.

Now, if we turn to the greatest of all sciences, mathematics, we find that the greatest discoveries like those of Kepler in the three laws of planetary motion were not made by statistical methods. They were made by some religious person who was seeking a design in the universe and found it. I could arrange 1024 coins into a mathematical design in such a way that there are exactly 512 heads and 512 tails. You could start at one end and tabulate heads and tails, come out even, and nothing in your tabulations would reveal the design. Yet, a mathematical formula is a design. The two given earlier are designs. It matters not what figures are employed to represent **n** and **r**, the design is always there. The only reason science works is because nature is filled with designs.

It is not coincidence that editor Lee's editorial and our Lesson on statistics come out at the same time, because we have been arguing and discussing these matters with the editor for years. We worked side by side on a publication 25 years ago. These problems are not new to either of us. We have discussed them before.

In a prior chapter, we disclosed a design in the solar system. We showed that statistically, **the odds are 653,183,999 to 1 against this design being an accident.** Our common sense tells us that these are pretty big odds. However, we do not merely have those odds to back up the design. This design made analytical interpretation possible. Analytical interpretation had been attempted before, but the results were not satisfactory to us, because the wrong 'house value' had been applied to both the planets and the zodiacal signs.

When we asked students to analytically interpret Venus-in-Capricorn, we selected a number of persons we knew well who were born with Venus-in-Capricorn. We wanted to see whether new students could correctly describe these people. The results were beyond our expectations. They were far better than we expected.

The key to the whole matter involved the fact that when Venus is in Capricorn, the Family Non-survival Dynamic Guide is under the domination of the Individual Survival Dynamic Reactor. Students were able to work this out for themselves, and they found the right answer without recourse to statistics or thousands of cases.

Just as a mathematical formula is a design, a horoscope is a design. It IS a mathematical figure. It cannot be interpreted other than as a mathematical figure. It can be construed as a formula where a particular individual or entity is concerned. More important than finding out that people with Mars-Uranus aspects have difficulty going through an entire life with one partner, is to determine why. These people do not appear to be scheduled to go through life

Lesson Eighteen 265

with one partner. The design of their lives is along different lines. Religious training may cause some of them to conform more to the overall pattern of society at large, but should it be this way? As Mr. Lee points out, things may be different for one individual than for the mass as a whole. The number of people who are to be killed in automobile accidents next Sunday may not include you, but your own recklessness might have something to do with that.

In other cases, we have opposed efforts to knock down the statistical approach where astrology is concerned, but that was when the people who were opposing the statistical method knew nothing about the statistical method. We do not oppose the statistical method of gathering material now, but we do point out that it may not be the only, or the best method. Analytical interpretation offers a much shorter more efficient and more satisfactory method.

Let's have a comparison of the two methods. Euclid proved that there is no limit to the prime integers. One person might try to prove this by going higher and higher to see whether he could find any place where prime numbers end. Euclid employed a very simple proof. He pointed out that if you multiply all known prime numbers together and add 1, you have a number that cannot be divisible by any known prime. Therefore, it is either prime itself or divisible by some larger unknown prime, and in either case, there must be some prime integer larger than any known prime. We can call this an intellectual approach to the matter, and our own system of analytical interpretation falls in the same category. It is possible to reach a correct conclusion without recourse to statistics, but statistics can then be introduced for greater verification as well as for further personal and self-satisfaction. You can see your own conclusions constantly verified.

A further advantage of analytical interpretation lies in the fact that it can explain the exception to the rule. Elsewhere, we used the horoscope of Elvis Presley as an apparent exception to the rule of Venus-in-Capricorn. Actually, it is only an apparent exception to the rule, because Elvis had to express not only Venus-in-Capricorn, but Venus square Uranus, Saturn in Aquarius, Jupiter in Scorpio, etc. Yet, Elvis could not get away from the fact that he was born with Venus in Capricorn, and he did have the characteristics of this configuration peculiarly and necessarily combined with those of Venus square Uranus, etc.

At this point, we seem to agree with editor Lee in his contention that the statistical approach is filled with possible pitfalls, and no matter how large a sample of cases you may have, your conclusions can still be wrong. His quotations from Darrell Huff are very appropriate.

We feel that a better astrology of the future must be based on analytical interpretation, that the statistical approach will never furnish as great a degree of perfection, that you can accomplish many times as much in a fraction of time.

It makes a difference when we consider astrology as a matter of mathematical design rather than as a causal phenomenon. If it was a causal phenomenon, then the statistical approach would be more appropriate. If, like mathematics, it is a science of abstract cosmic design, then the statistical approach is not always the right one. Mathematicians do not use the statistical approach to prove mathematical theorems. You can offer an infinite amount of statistical proof to show that Fermat's Last Theorem is true, but this kind of proof is unacceptable to the mathematicians. They are still trying to find absolute proof. Fermat is supposed to have had this proof, but it appears to have died with him. No other mathematician has yet been able to rediscover this proof. [ed. Proven in 1997] Yet, none of them question that Fermat had found it.

No astrologer ever put as much effort and labor into statistical investigation of astrology as the writer has, and we have certainly learned a great deal through this kind of investigation, but after all these years, we are forced to admit that the statistical approach does not always appear to be the best approach. However, we did not draw this conclusion until after we had formed a better approach. This analytical approach would never have been possible without their formation disclosed in the chapter Design in the Solar System, which is probably the most important lesson in this entire Course. It is the key to everything else.

Design may be the ultimate explanation for cycles. If we consider the day-and-night cycle, it conforms to earth motion as related to the Sun, but the best authorities inform us that you can take random numbers, and they will disclose cycles, because no cause for such cycles is know, they have been called pseudo-cycles, but this may be an improper term. Even such cycles may be a matter of abstract cosmic design. We did a lot of research in connection with random numbers many years ago. Our interest was only in whether these numbers were odd or even, and what kinds of runs of consecutive odd or even numbers we ran across, whether they conformed to the expectancy indicated by the mathematical laws of probability, etc. Our experience was quite extraordinary. We couldn't help but note that we came across the longest run of consecutive odd numbers during a total eclipse of the Sun.

In view of the fact that TIME is merely a matter of how

things relate to each other and otherwise non-existent, you may begin to see how time and design fit themselves together. Both past and future are largely a matter of our present conception of them, and our philosophical outlook alters both. 1000 tosses of a coin might contain an approximately equal number of heads and tails, but there might also be a design. If cycles can be found in random numbers, the indication is that they are not exactly random but contain a design. Is there such a thing as random or such a thing as chance? The further we go, the more indication we find that we must ultimately give a negative answer to this question and say that nothing happens by chance, and that nothing is random, because all action is controlled by the design of the unconscious, perhaps by Jung's collective unconscious.

We cannot ignore the fact that the greatest progress over the centuries was made by mathematicians who believed in design and tried to find it. This applied to such men as Pythagoras, Khayyam, Copernicus, Kepler and Newton. Newton made it clear that he did not consider gravitation a causal phenomenon but a mathematical design. The planets do not plunge into the Sun, nor are they thrown off into space. They remain as part of a design. The speed with which one planet travels has a definite relationship with which another planet travels. Everything fits into a design, but followers of such men as those mentioned above have always misrepresented the original views in order to make them conform to their own inferior views. Always remember that the men who write about and interpret the views of other men like Newton are not the people who made the discoveries. Always note that textbooks avoid mentioning that each of the above mentioned men was an astrologer. This will help you to see how the plot of materialism has been hatched and how we have been led away from design. Yet, we may surmise from reading ancient religious documents that number was to be found everywhere in their work. We have done little to detect what these numbers mean. Nevertheless, we find that mathematicians and religious persons have had something in common in that they have been seeking a cosmic design. Religious leaders were called prophets. Prophets are supposed to predict the future, and this no longer seems strange when we realize that time is non-existent except as a medium to describe the relationship between or among objects or things. So long as there is change, there is time, and when change ceases to exist, time must cease to exist also. A man would not grow old unless his body changed. Note that the words we associate with time, such as change, are also associated with Uranus, Aquarius, the 7th House and the opposition aspect. Then note that the 7th House involves our relationship with other people, change in our relationship with other people, such as marriage or divorce.

The horoscope is the design of a particular life. That life has to involve change, and in that way it involves time, which we will call a mere by-product of change, an invented medium for expressing change. Although the individual is born with the heavens forming one design, that design is constantly changing, and of necessity he lives through many designs which always have a relationship to the original design.

If you photograph 1000 people with Sagittarius on the ascendant, we have no doubts but that you would find a similarity of design in their faces as related to people born with other zodiacal signs rising. Nevertheless, each of these people would have a different hereditary background which would also have to show up in his face, and no two of these people would look exactly alike. If you happened to include one giraffe among the 1000 individuals, his hereditary background would be so different from the rest that you would have great difficulty finding Sagittarius in his features. On the other had, if all the 1000 individuals were Irish, it might be easier to detect Sagittarius rising. A high ratio of the Irish have the appearance of people with Taurus or Scorpio rising, and by some method, astrologers of the past have associated the Irish race with Taurus, just as they have associated the Germans with Taurus, the English with Aries, the French with Leo, etc. Some of these associations may be right and others may be wrong, but certainly the Germans do portray the characteristics that we find in Taurus and the personal appearance we find in Taurus rising. However, Taurus and Scorpio can often be similar in appearance, and the Irish are noted for impulsiveness, emotionalism, and liking to fight, which would fit Scorpio better than Taurus. Such conclusions are highly speculative, however. Nevertheless less, racial influences are just as important as astrological designs. A race is a design.

One of the great difficulties in employing statistical principles in testing astrological samples lies in the fact that you cannot get 1000 or 5000 cases that are exactly alike. You can't even get two cases that are exactly alike, and as soon as you begin to increase the size of your sample, you decrease the similarity of your cases. As a result you are bound to reduce the statistical significance.

Another important factor is found in the fact that you tend to live the horoscopes and designs of people with whom you are closely associated. When you are married, the partner's chart will have a great deal to do with your life. There will be things that happen which never show up in your own chart. This is particularly true of the

Lesson Eighteen

opposition aspect. One partner reacts to the opposition aspects in the other partner's chart. It can be seen that here is something that could never show up statistically, because it is not in the native's own chart. When you are under strong Uranus aspects, you can have a great deal to do with influencing the lives of other people. This is something that could not show up statistically unless you had the charts of all the people to whom individuals were married. You probably realize that you can be one personality while with one person and another personality when with another person or persons.

It would be a mistake for us to suggest that anybody abandon the statistical approach. It definitely has utility. It was this statistical approach that enabled us to discover the Lunar Cycle as it relates to the individual. It was the statistical approach that led us to discover that humankind are more unstable when the Sun or Uranus is conjunct or square to the Lunar Nodes. We have discovered many things astrological through the use of the statistical approach. We have also been able to disprove some of the older claims of astrologers to our satisfaction through the use of the statistical approach. Therefore, it would seem that there are some things you can reach very easily through the statistical method, while there are other things you might reach through the statistical method and not through the analytical method.

Another drawback to statistical procedure lies in the fact that when you are dealing with an individual horoscope, you must really know that person very well in order to see in just what manner he fits the pattern of the horoscope. We might say that we know a great deal about Dwight D. Eisenhower, but we know almost nothing about him in comparison with those people who live with him and see him every day. All of our information about him seems to be second or third hand. Even when a client sits across from us at our own desk, there is not time to become intimately acquainted. We have to take his word for a lot things, and he may not be supplying us with an accurate report. A woman often lives with a man for many years and still has a lot to learn about his personality. There may be hidden departments that she has never encountered. In fact, there may be many hidden chambers of her own personality that she has never encountered.

If statistics are employed in the manner habitual to advertising agencies, Wall Street, politicians, etc., as Mr. Lee points out, they can be used to prove or disprove almost anything, but we must point out that these people are statisticians in the popular and not in the mathematical sense of the word. A mathematical statistician is a highly trained individual, master of the mathematical theory of probability, the calculus of probability, which is one of the most complicated and involved branches of mathematics. In higher mathematics, numbers are no longer employed. Everything becomes a matter of design, and designs are portrayed by symbols. One single symbol can imply a very long and complicated set of calculations. The same applies to astrology. The procedure of erecting a horoscope and portraying everything by symbols that only the trained When the astrologer writes ♀ ☌ ♅ ♈ the symbols for Venus conjunct Uranus in Aries, he implies what it might take pages to write out for the laymen. With one symbol like a calculus symbol having few numbers or more symbols above and below it, the mathematician means to add all the numbers in a particular series of numbers from one point to another point. If he writes 100! it means multiply 100 by all lesser numbers down to 1.

That is why, when he gets into complicated problems, the mathematician requires an electronic calculator to handle the detail that he merely writes out in symbol form. The same applies to the astrologer. He can erect your horoscope in symbol form, but after that is done, you might spend the rest of your life writing out all the things that those symbols can actually mean. It is very important to realize that astrology is not a causal phenomenon that it is actually a branch of mathematics, and it can be approached exactly as mathematics is approached. The methods that have been successful in the field of mathematics are also successful in the field of astrology. Thus, it is not difficult to see why, down through the centuries, the men who rated first in the field of mathematics were also the astrologers themselves. All the pieces fit together. When we deal with astrology, and when we deal with mathematics, we are dealing with one and the same thing. We are dealing with the abstract cosmic design of the universe and everything in it, including life itself.

LESSON NINETEEN

ASTROLOGY AT WORK

According to Ernest Jones, his biographer, Dr. Sigmund Freud, was born at 6:30 P.M. on May 6th, 1856 at Freiberg, Germany. We have selected this moment for discussion because of the terrific impact made upon society by an individual who was born at such a time. A chart of the heavens for that moment is reproduced on the next page.

Another chart has been offered as that of Freud in other astrological literature, giving a 9:00 AM birth time, but we had to reject the chart at the start. We are depending on his biographer plus the fact that one look at a photograph of Freud will display all of the facial characteristics of Scorpio rising—not Cancer.

This chart shows Scorpio on the ascendant, with its ruling planet, Mars in Libra near the 12th cusp of the chart. At the outset, we find Scorpio, representing the Family Survival Dynamic at the Ascendant. We find the sign of sex as the beginning of the chart. Next, we find Mars in Libra, where it is dominated by the Family Non-Survival Dynamic Guide. If we turn to the right-hand side of the chart, we find Pluto, Sun, Uranus, and Mercury in Taurus, the last three within the 7th House, Pluto almost at the cusp of the 7th. These four bodies are dominated by the Family Survival Dynamic Reactor.

Mars-in-Libra is disposited by Venus in Aries, where it is dominated by the Family Non-survival Dynamic. Venus is conjunct the Lunar Node, and it is disposited by Pluto in Taurus.

Out of 12 factors, 8 are in signs that pertain to family dynamics. Four are in signs involving social dynamics, and not one factor of any kind is in a sign that involves Individual dynamics.

Under these circumstances, it becomes quite clear why sex dominates the writings of Freud. With four bodies in Taurus (FSDR), there was hidden a great deal in the way of fear of the consequences of sex, and yet, both family survival and family non-survival factors are powerful. Freud was aware that not only are there consequences of sexual expression, but there are consequences of sex when it isn't expressed. In sex, he saw an all powerful force that has to go somewhere. You can't lock it up in a box, because it expands and it will ultimately blow the box apart.

In this chart, the Sun is conjunct Uranus, and Uranus is conjunct the node of Mars (sex again), and Uranus the planet of unorthodoxy. An astrologer cannot look at this part of the chart with so many family factors without concluding that before he became a doctor, Freud did some great suffering relative to matters that pertained to sex. Just the mere matter of associating with other people, with all of those 7th House planets, would be a very deep problem to Freud. This is evidenced by the couch technique, which for a long time became standard practice among the early psychiatrists. Freud always had the patient lie down on a couch and relax, while Freud sat at a point above the head of the patient, where the patient could not see him. This technique originated because it made Freud uncomfortable to be watched. He didn't want the patient to look at him. He couldn't stand people staring at him. He was timid. It was Freud's job to diagnose the patient and he didn't want this interrupted by the patient and he didn't want this interrupted by the patient diagnosing him.

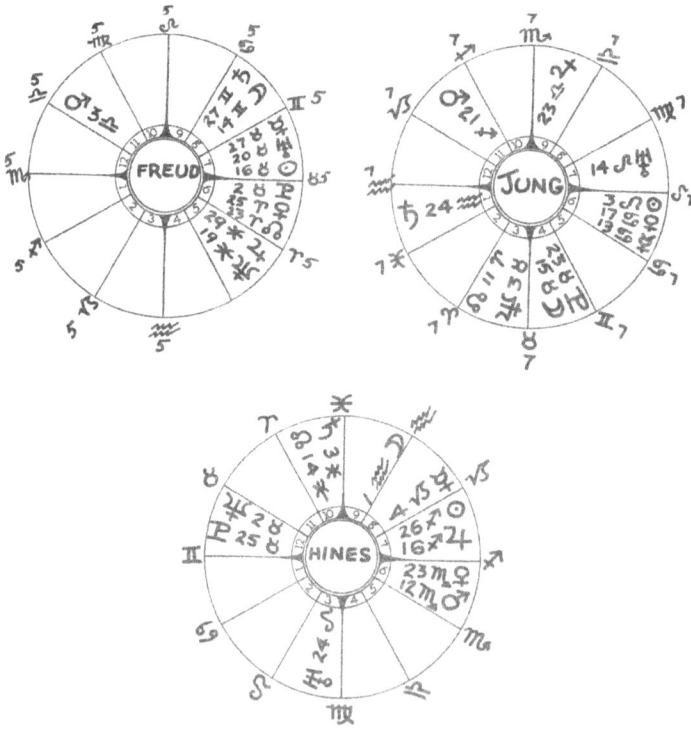

***Natal Charts of Sigmund Freud,
Carl Jung and Jimmy Hines**

Freud and Jung in 1909

Freud in 1885

Freud 1921

It is doubtful whether Freud ever dealt with any patient who had a more sexually explosive chart than his own, but there were reactors–four planets in Taurus (FSDR). It seems quite reasonable that in studying the sex lives of other people and in writing long technical books about his findings pertaining to sex, Freud was finding an indirect and safe method of expressing his own sexual complications. In reading his books, one should realize that Freud is writing about no patient he ever encountered quite so much as he is writing about himself. The doctor was bound hand and foot by the ropes of sex. He couldn't break away from them. They were his life and his consciousness. It is to be believed that all this caused a great deal in the way of inner suffering, but the scientist in him broke through and investigated.

We can trace this chart and its factors to a certain point, and we are left in mid-air. The Ascendant is disposited by Mars in Libra. Mars is disposited by Venus in Aries. Venus is disposited by Pluto in Taurus, while Pluto, Sun, Uranus and Mercury are ALL disposited by planet 'Y', ruler of Taurus, but we do not know the location of 'Y' either at the time of Freud's birth or now. *[ed. Eris could be planet Y at 5 Pisces for Freud]

Jupiter and Neptune, representing the SNSD and the SSD are both in Pisces, where they are dominated by the SSD. If Freud was not as conscious of the SSD as his student, Dr. Carl Jung, it was sure operating through him. Revolutionary as his views and books may have been at the time when he wrote them, Freud was dominated by something that went back thousands of years in history. His new technique became the interpretation of the symbols found in dreams. If this was new, it was new only to a modern world and particularly to the modern medical world. The art of dream interpretation was older than the Old Testament. Even savages interpreted dreams and their symbols. In taking this road, Freud was only joining the mystics.

However, Freud's mystical interpretations were extremely limited. He saw but one kind of symbol. To him, all symbols were sex symbols. If you dreamed of a staircase, you were heading up a genital canal. If you are the fellow who built the Empire State building, you were just kidding yourself because in reality you were just trying to have a bigger male organ than your competitor. If you dreamed of almost any kind of an object, it was the male sex organ in your unconscious and if you dreamed of any kind of a cavity or a room, that was the female sex organ. Reality consisted of only objects and 'no objects'. Objects were male sex organs, 'no objects' were female sex organs.

The effect of Freud's work was terrific. For the first time a

Lesson Nineteen

new generation of physicians discovered that Man had emotions and thoughts as well as a physical body, that sex was not only in the body but in the mind. Having been badly beaten down by religious dogma which maintained that nobody would go to heaven if he ever thought about sex, a public began reading Freud. It became permissible to mention sex in a voice above a whisper. Society began letting loose its inhibitions.

Only because he had a medical degree did Freud escape being condemned to the ranks of the outcast mystics. Without this degree, he might have been burned at the stake as a he-witch. His medical achievements BP (before psychiatry) were so great, however, that medical men opened their minds and began to experiment. With his Moon and Saturn in Gemini, the German doctor opened up a whole new frame of reference.

It must be noted that although sex factors dominate the chart of this extraordinary man, his chart is full of restraint. All of those Taurus planets represent restraint, and that Venus is sextile to Saturn. Here is a chart completely filled with explosive factors, like his Sun-Uranus conjunction and his Uranus on the node of Mars, but there is restraint, and because there is restraint, this great sexual force becomes channeled into great work and study and a new day is created, a day of psychiatry.

We had psychologists before, but men like William James were not psychiatrists. A psychologist was soon rated below a psychiatrist. The medical profession took psychology right away from the psychologist. Freud was a medical man and full of sex and vinegar. He did what the churches had fought against. He made sex respectable. He cleansed people of the sins the churches were busy creating. The remarkable thing seems to be that no religious war followed.

We have pointed out elsewhere that when you see a Big Book of a non-fictional variety, it is usually written by some Fixed Sign person. Freud had a Fixed sign on the ascendant (Scorpio) and he had four bodies in a Fixed sign (Taurus) in the 7th House. The physician created his own family. He created it to a new pattern. His new family was made up of his students. There was Scorpio jealousy. Although he was a great scientist and a more-than-great physician, his students belonged to him. In place of an old dogma, he had partially created a new dogma. Although he had created a new frame of reference, he was jealous of that frame of reference, and he did not want it subjected to competition by other new frames of reference. The FOR was sex, and the new school could have all the liberty it might desire so long as it would stay within the barbed-wire enclosures of sex. A man of Freud's accomplishments may be excused for any such weakness. It is too much that we expect him to display all the virtues.

The German physician may be excused if he considered himself unfortunate in having two students like Jung and Adler, for these men listened to Freud and then looked around to see what else they might hit upon. They bent over and managed to penetrate through the strands of the barbed-wire enclosure. Although they were still convinced that sex had come to stay, they were not as deeply absorbed in its complications as their teacher. Jung went so far as to talk about the spiritual and the soul. He studied ancient symbolism involving non-sexual factors. He studied astrology. He studied the symbols of astrology. Long before Freud, the ancients had two symbols for sex. One was a scorpion, the other an eagle. They were supposed to express two extremes of sexual manifestation. In his jealousy toward his runaway students and his exclusion of them from his family circle, he displayed his scorpion characteristics, but in his great work, in his efforts to free his patients from the wrong one of what Aldous Huxley refers to as the antipodes of the mind—from Hell-the wings of the eagle were spread. From his high perch, he can now look down upon a changed world where many of its imaginary sins have flown away with the mist. We must not forget that when Scorpio is jealous or when it is vindictive, these are only outer manifestations of inner suffering. We cannot look at this man's chart without being conscious that he was a man who suffered. It was not necessary to nail him to any cross. He was nailed to a figurative one within himself. Even in his life work, he had to go down some of those stairs into a lower world where sex manifests in its worst form, where it becomes gross and vulgar. Yet, his was not a gross and vulgar chart. His Mars was in the refined sign of Libra. Before leaving this spectacular man, let us not overlook that he had two planets in the literary sign of Gemini, where their manifestation might have been more superficial had they not been fortified by the determination and stability of those four bodies in Taurus. Freud had passed his 17th birthday by two months on July 26th, 1875 when across the border at Basel in Switzerland, a child was born at 7:20 P.M. This child was to become one of his students. He was named Carl Jung. This birth data is taken from the back of a book called 'THE SABIAN SYMBOLS' by Marc Edmund Jones.

Had Freud studied astrology and had he been able to completely overcome the scorpion side of his nature, he would have realized that Jung was born at the exact top of his (Freud's) lunar cycle, and here was a philosopher who could have been of much greater help than Freud ever realized. Jung's chart is also given on the same page. [ed. Jung's Moon is conjunct Freud's Sun and Jung's Sun conjunct Freud's 10th cusp.]

There are no planets in Scorpio, the sign of sex.

Mars the sex planet, is in Sagittarius at the cusp of the 11th house. Jung has two planets in Taurus, and he has the Ascendant square to Freud's Sun and Uranus in Taurus. Since we have already emphasized the breaks or separations and estrangements that are brought about through Mars-Uranus conditions, it is not difficult to see why these two men broke off. [ed. Jung's Sun on the Fourth cusp and square Freud's Venus and Pluto.]

In many ways, this chart is just as extraordinary as that of Freud, but the pattern of the two charts is completely different. The genius of Aquarius is at the ascendant, but just beneath it is the restricting Saturn, although it is still dominated by Uranus because it is in the sign of Uranus, Aquarius.

Jupiter is in Libra at the 9th Cusp, giving all the qualifications of the philosopher, but the saddest part of the whole story lies in the fact that despite his many other accomplishments, Jung never became a mathematician. He has the ability to understand mathematical principles, but he is beating all around the mathematical bush without knowing it. He sees patterns and designs, but nowhere do we find evidence that he is conscious of the fact that they are mathematical patterns and designs. With his Sun square Neptune, he is somewhat swallowed in mysticism, and he never actually sees the pattern of the whole. He has nothing in Gemini to make him a literary man, and he is noted for his inability to express himself. He has a lot to say but doesn't know how to say it.

Jung has never received as great attention in America as in Europe. The scorpion reaction of Freud to Jung is carried on to a great extent by psychiatric followers of Freud. Jung gains a far greater following in Europe. There are those who are against his views because he was once a Hitler appointee. Many in the fields of psychiatry and psychology have no desire to broaden their frames of reference, and to become interested in Jung is to broaden one's frame of reference. Little interest has been shown in the fact that he never treats a patient unless he can see the patient's horoscope. In fact, the first published work of Jung's use of astrology did not appear in either America or Europe but in an interview published in a magazine in India.

An Aquarian ascendant plus Sun and Uranus in Leo makes Jung a progressive, but Saturn so near the ascendant is a great limitation. He tries not to travel too far ahead of society and his colleagues. His work is restrained. His writing difficulties may have much to do with his Neptune-in-Taurus in the 3rd, the literary House, squared by the Sun, which rules the 7th House. Because Jung investigates many realms that are unknown to orthodoxy, it is more than difficult for him to find a language that orthodoxy would understand. He employs many words, but they have to be picked apart word by word in every effort to make them clear. You may read several paragraphs of Jung and have no conception of what he is talking about. He fails to get his words to form clear pictures. His words are quite likely to portray mist and fog. Freud was a mystic, but Jung writes like one, while Freud didn't. Some other physician would stay away from so many mystical subjects, but Jung takes journeys outside of everybody's barbed wire entanglements. You may find him playing with Yoga or Tarot cards. His work lacks not only limitations but form. He takes in a great deal of territory. He goes far beyond the 'respectable'. These are characteristics of Aquarius and Leo, but with Saturn close to the Ascendant, he is ever in contact with the orthodox world that lies behind him. Yet, when you catch up with what he is doing now, he is doing something else again. Freud never tried to catch up with him. He was content to remain within the security of his sex. Jung could see other motivations than sex in Man. He was curious. He had great respect for the ancients. He tried to delve into things into which they had delved. Nevertheless, his contributions have been many. He gave us introverts and extroverts, and note that he is a combination of both, Sun and Uranus in Leo (extrovert) and Mercury and Venus in Cancer (introvert). More than Freud, he is living years ahead of his time, and it is very likely that the day will come when he will gain more attention than Freud. There is a good deal of dogma to Freud's work. Jung is more open-minded. Yet, the extent of Freud's open- mindedness, where his own work was not concerned, is demonstrated by a letter written by him and published in the winter 1957 issue of TOMORROW Magazine, wherein, he told a Dr. Nandor Foder, that the pranks of a so-called poltergeist were a strain on a man who 'is unwilling to believe in supernormal happenings'. In case you don't know what a poltergeist is, it is a spook who is also a juvenile delinquent, going around knocking on doors and walls at night just to keep you awake and scare the pajamas off you. Harry Truman was bothered by one when he lived in the White House, and some thought it was Abe Lincoln or some dead Republican. Others say that Eleanor Roosevelt can tell you quite a bit about them.

    With Mars in Sagittarius, in the 11th House of his horoscope and well aspected by both Jupiter and Saturn, it is unlikely that sex

Lesson Nineteen

was ever any kind of a problem to Jung. It was a problem to Freud and he had to stay with it.

There are thousands of things in these two horoscopes that we will have no time nor room to talk about. The student can find much for study, but it will be helpful only to the extent that he becomes familiar with the lives and work of these two men. The same with other charts of famous people. If you can know the charts and know the men or women, you can learn much by seeing how the men lived within the pattern of their own charts.

Jung's Saturn so near the Ascendant would have worked quite differently had it been in some other zodiacal sign. It would then have offered a much greater restriction. His sense of duty would never have allowed things to stay as they are. The direction finder is always aimed at something in the future.

Very important is the square of Sun to Neptune in Jung's chart. Elsewhere, we find that this aspect makes a person very sensitive, sensitive to things that other people know nothing about. Women with this aspect are often classified as immoral, but in the past, the word immorality has been applied to mean the conduct of anyone who may think for himself or herself. If you do not follow the rules that have been set up by mentally inferior people, you are apt to be classified as immoral. The person with this aspect senses things. Such things may not be interpreted correctly, but they are sensed.

We see definite evidence of this aspect in Jung's new term, 'the collective unconscious'. This term was a daring innovation, but evidence of the need of such a term was everywhere, while all orthodoxy wore blinders to avoid seeing it. No one could have read the work of Boris Sidis at the beginning of the century, at a time when Jung was only 25 years old, without sensing the collective unconscious, unless one had been rigidly trained not to sense anything outside of a biased textbook. Why did army horses stage stampedes in different countries on the same day? It could not have been Communist agents at work for there were no Communist agents at that time. Neptune represents the Social Survival Dynamic, and we find it working overtime through Jung. He has proved to be a man without mental limitations, and he has had so much territory to explore that he has displayed what astrologers have long associated with Neptune. He has displayed a great deal of chaos in his thinking. We have found him investigating the ancient wisdom of the Chinese as well as that of the Hindus. To the occidental, he has committed the great sin of becoming aware of the teachings of the Oriental's. He has shown the psychologists how to become 'aware' to what they have been unaware. In view of this chart, with its Aquarius rising,

Uranus near the descendent, Sun 11 degrees away from Uranus, we are forced to view Jung as a man of the future rather than a man of the past. He is far ahead of his time. It will take future generations to interpret what he has been talking about, or what he has been trying to write about.

For some time, we have suspected that planet 'Z' is now around 20-Pisces. We wish to emphasize that we may be all wrong about this, and we want any student to consider any such thought with the very greatest skepticism. However, if the motion of the planet in this part of its orbit happens to be approximately one degree in three years, it would mean that in the first house of Jung's chart, Saturn is conjunct 'Z' in Aquarius, and if this happened to be true, we would have an excellent explanation of Jung's difficulty of expression, because 'Z' would be the literary planet more than Mercury. His difficulty of expression is certainly not indicated by his Mercury, for we find it conjunct Venus and sextile to the Moon. His difficulty in writing has not prevented him from writing many books, but people do not understand them. He doesn't create good word pictures. His own statement is that he can't write, that he has difficulty explaining his own thought.

However, although we have been impressed by certain evidence leading us to believe that 'Z' may be in Pisces and that it may be moving at a rate close to one degree in three years, we can't place too great emphasis on the fact that this evidence must not be considered as tangible. It is all right for the student to play around with this possibility, but we urge against any conclusion unless the student's own experience tends to confirm any such conclusion. Since we have stated that we believe the planet may be around 20-Pisces at this time, we must date our remark as of April 13th, 1957.

If we are wrong in our suspicion as to the present location of this planet, and if students take our suspicions seriously without confirmation, then our remarks could be very detrimental, and we do not want to take the responsibility for misleading anyone.

We find another limitation in this chart of Jung. Although Jupiter, representing the SNSD is well placed in Libra and well aspected by Mars and Saturn, it is exactly square to the nodes of Saturn. It is important to note the great difference between the charts of Freud and Jung. In Freud's chart we have the great overemphasis on family factors and sex is the motivating family force. In Jung's chart, we find great emphasis on individual non-survival factor, which prevents him from tying himself down to one thing. We do not find the insecurity in his chart that exists in the chart of Freud, although there are some factors of insecurity. He still has Mercury and Venus in Cancer, and he has Neptune, Moon and Pluto in Taurus. Had it not been for these three Taurus planets, it is doubtful whether he would ever have been tied up with Freud in the first place. He has Pluto on Freud's Neptune, the Moon on Freud's Sun, and Pluto between Freud's Uranus and Mercury. Thus, we do see good reason for his original association with Freud, but his Leo-Aquarius factors had to send him on his own explorations and had to develop his own individuality. It is quite likely that his Neptune on Freud's Pluto contributed a great deal to Freud's reaction to Jung's independent course. Freud seemed to feel that he had been betrayed. He was bitterly disappointed with both Jung and Adler. When they didn't remain as his children and loyal followers [ed. Freud's Pluto conjunct Venus], he wanted no part of them. It was all right for Freud to open up a new frame of reference, but it was not right for his students to do so. As so often happens with the sign Scorpio, the attitude is quite likely to be, "Don't do as I do. Do as I tell you to do."

The most occupied zodiacal sign in these two charts combined is Taurus. There are 7 factors in Taurus. This is as many as in the last six signs of the zodiac, and there are no factors in the other two Earth signs, Virgo and Capricorn. However, we must not associate this with the fact that they are both psychologist, because as we have pointed out in a number of different places, people who write long books of a non-fictional variety are quite often those with an excess of planets in Taurus. This does not apply to people who write short material like magazine articles. Planets in Gemini seem to be more useful in this connection.

Freud has no planets in Sagittarius, sign of social revolution, the SNSD, while Jung has Mars in Sagittarius. We might think of Freud as having brought about a type of social revolution until we realize that the principal part of his work, dream interpretation from dream symbols, was as old as the hills. Actually, all he ever did was confine the old conception down to one thing—sex. The ancients had seen dreams as prophetic. Freud excluded all this from his thinking. Compared with all other views on the interpretation of dream symbols, Freud put his mind in one groove and stayed right there. To anyone who has explored greater possibilities as to the interpretation of dream symbols, Freud was in a rut, a sexual rut. Yet, there is reason to believe that his actual views may have been much broader than any ever published. If his work may have appeared radical, we must admit that he succeeded in one thing magnificently. He stayed within the limitations of what his colleagues in the medical profession have been willing to accept. He didn't tell any of them about his views on any poltergeist phenomenon. Had he written one book along those lines, he might have been condemned to the world of the damned. With his four planets in Taurus and his Scorpio ascendant, he was practical. The medical profession had heard of sex before. It had even encountered it. His books were written at a time when society was ready to climb out of its pit of sexual hypocrisy, and they were well timed. They would have been received differently in the year 1850. Those people who were celebrating prohibition and the roaring 20's, or at least many of them, were ready for Freud. They were ready to be told that sex might be a human dynamic rather than a sin. It was a relief to get rid of a guilt complex. Even people who were going to church on Sunday felt better about what they had done on Saturday night.

The third chart on the same page is that of a man who both Freud and Jung might have found interesting for study. His name was 'Jimmy' Hines. You may not know much about Jimmy Hines unless you come from New York. He died recently (in 1957), and his death stimulates us to include his chart here. He was born on December 18th, 1876, time unknown. How can we find out when he was born? Jimmy had a protruding nose. Evangeline Adams called it the bird-beak-type nose. Its profile was more of an equilateral triangle than other people's noses. A line from the bridge to the tip of the nose is more nearly equal to a line from the tip to the upper extremity of the nose. Experience will teach you that this type of a nose is associated with the sign Gemini. There are no planets in Gemini in this chart. Under these circumstances, we have a key, and we gamble. We try a chart with Gemini rising. Because we do not know what degree of Gemini might be rising, we start with the first degree and see what happens. The result is interesting, because we find Saturn close to the 10th Cusp. Of Saturn in this position, astrologers from way back have said that the person will rise to great heights, only to fall, Napoleon and Mussolini had the planet in this position. Jimmy Hines was one of the greatest political powers in the United States, but he wound up in Sing Sing prison. It was his conviction that made Thomas E. Dewy governor of the state of New York.

Whether Jimmy was a criminal or a great humanitarian was all a matter of what you chose as your frame of reference. Like his father and his grandfather, Jimmy was a blacksmith, but they all had a flare for politics. Officially, Jimmy never rose higher than a District Leader, but he was the top man in Tammany Hall, if not officially. The top men were all there only because Jimmy put them there. There was a hard and a soft side to Jimmy. He was soft spoken, even tempered. He could afford to be, because physically, he could lick his weight in wildcats, and everybody knew it. He was sympathetic, and anyone in trouble could go see Jimmy and get help. All his life, he did favors for people, and his group of friends grew and grew. To Jimmy, these people were all a part of his family, and they could bring their friends to get help from Jimmy. The bosses of Tammany Hall did not want Jimmy around. They were very powerful. They couldn't overthrow him in his district because the people there wanted him and voted for him. Strong arm methods were employed. They would drive him out, but when thugs were employed to dispose of Jimmy, they turned up beaten to a pulp, and Jimmy did it alone. He didn't like Boss Murphy of Tammany, and because Murphy was backing Al Smith for the presidency, Hines backed Roosevelt, and is generally credited as being the man who threw the final weight to effect the nomination of FDR. Once in Washington, Franklin Roosevelt began building up the real power of Jimmy Hines. Patronage did not go to Tammany Hall. It went to Jimmy Hines, and little by little, Jimmy became the real boss behind Tammany.

During Prohibition, Jimmy was a friend of all the big bootleggers, and when Prohibition went out, the bootleggers had to go somewhere. Some of them became labor leaders under the New Deal. Others went into the numbers racket. If you lived in New York and you were in Democratic politics, you were a member of Jimmy's family or you were not. Being a member of Jimmy's family was the only credential you needed. If you were a member of this family, you had security. You could always get help. If the police got after you, Jimmy would tell them to leave you alone, and then he would tell you to behave yourself. If somebody sued you, Jimmy would phone the judge and tell him what his decision was to be. The bookmakers were all on Jimmy's side too. One bookmaker had a very luxurious apartment on 72nd Street, where from 3 to 7 PM, the biggest stockbrokers, the highest judges, the biggest people in politics, used to drop in. Beautiful women, most of them married, also dropped in. The favorite drink was an Alexander, for the bookmaker made the best Alexanders in New York. The apartment was filled with power, Alexanders, romance, and sex until 7:00 PM, and then everybody became respectable and went home to his or her own spouse. It was all in the spirit of fun and everybody had a good time. All of these people were friends of Jimmy Hines. If you had a lawsuit against you, here was the place to talk it over personally with the judge. If he wasn't there, they'd get him there. The judge would sip an Alexander, slap you on the back, and tell you, 'Don't you worry about a thing.' If you were invited to this apartment, you were a family man or woman, because you were part of the family of Jimmy Hines, and real family people stick together. Note Jimmy's family planets, Venus and Mars in Scorpio, Neptune and Pluto in Taurus.

Jimmy was a religious man. He went to church on Sunday. He was bringing about his own social revolution (Sun and Jupiter in Sagittarius). He never hurt anybody if he could find another way out. He was kind, sympathetic and compassionate. He fed the poor. He helped out those who were in trouble. He had his own ideas and conceptions about morals. He spent thousands of dollars entertaining children. Nobody in Washington was more important if some kid on the block wanted to talk to Jimmy. The kid's problem came first.

First came the Seabury Investigation, but Seabury didn't go after Hines. He questioned him and then described him as a lovable scoundrel. But, Tom Dewey was a young Aries man. He was ambitious. He became District Attorney and saw the governorship ahead. How else could you get there more quickly than to 'get' Jimmy Hines. Criminals were called in and blackmailed. The way not to be prosecuted was to squeal on Jimmy Hines. Some of them tied Jimmy with Dutch Schultz and the numbers racket. Dewey got an indictment, but the judge, for there had to be a judge, declared a mistrial and the case was over. It would have been the end but for the determination of Dewey. There was a new trial, and a new judge. The jury brought in a verdict of guilty. After all, Uranus had gone almost three quarters of the way around the circle since Jimmy was born, and it was now in opposition to Jimmy's Mars. He was convicted in January 1939. Uranus was stationary at 13-Taurus. Jimmy's Mars was 12-Scorpio. This was the end of Jimmy's family. Outside the courthouse, the streets were filled with people, awaiting the verdict. After it was announced, word reached the street that he had been acquitted. This was an error, but cheers went up. The crown was in a frenzy of excitement. Jimmy heard their cheers. He thought they were cheering his conviction. He was a confused man. Tom Dewey went to Albany and became governor. Jimmy Hines went to jail. However, you couldn't break the power of Hines by putting him in jail unless you put all of his friends in jail also, and there were not enough prisons in the country to house Jimmy's friends. Now, Dewey was the political power. In New York State affairs, he was just as much of a dictator as Hines had ever been, but there was the possibility of trouble in that jail cell. Power is more important than justice to most politicians. Even in jail, Hines was dangerous, and they knew that Hines was tired of sitting in jail. At first the Parole Board would not consider letting Hines out, but then a better idea came along. Hines, under the right conditions, might be less dangerous politically outside of jail than in. Hines was given a conditioned parole. He was allowed to leave jail so long as he stayed out of politics and did not mix with politicians or public officials of any kind. That way, he would not be dangerous to the new political powers, not near as dangerous as he was in that jail cell. Jimmy walked out of jail, moved to Long Beach, Long Island. He finally dies in the Memorial Hospital there. Meanwhile, the racetrack scandal broke out in the Dewey administration, and the Democrats regained their power anyway. They elected a Democratic governor of New York State. Dewey had tried to reach the White House, but he couldn't beat Harry Truman. How is a student to interpret this chart? Is it the chart of a criminal? Do criminals have a special type of chart? The answer is NO. It's all a matter of your frame of reference, but people with Saturn in Pisces often get themselves into plenty of trouble in one way or another, because they have a different idea of what is right and wrong from a lot of other people.

* Editor's note on Eris discovered in 2005, the same size as Pluto.
* Alternate birthdata for Carl Jung is 6:52:40 UT at Kesswil, Switzerland with 0 Aquarius Asc. The current birthdata for Freud gives city of Pribor, Czech Republic with 10 Scorpio Asc.

LESSON TWENTY

THE SECONDARY CHART
[ed. SOLAR PARTS CHART]

In presenting the 'Secondary Chart', we offer our own term for a product of the ancients little used by astrologers of today, dropped because of the inclination of modern astrologers to attempt to fit their work into the dogma of a fiction-loving academic world endeavoring to blend everything into a causal hypothesis, and audaciously and perhaps criminally labeling the package 'Science'. There has been the unfortunate attempt to fit into a world where every effort has been made to reach a truth by locking one series of errors into another greater series of errors.

It is not too unusual to hear an astrologer make reference to the 'Pars Fortuna' or 'Part of Fortune', with no particular conception of what such a thing might be, and without making any particular effort to find out. Like house cusps or sign cusps or aspects, the Pars Fortuna is a mere mathematical point and only one of a whole series of mathematical points. It is a tiny part of a pattern. It is as significant as the last numeral on an automobile license tag, which will classify it as not belonging to 90 percent of the automobiles, but it will not identify the car insofar as the other ten percent of cars is concerned. The Pars Fortuna is a single point in the Secondary Chart ed[Solar Parts Chart], just as the Moon is a single point in the horoscope of birth.

Let us assume that you have a natal chart before you, and let us assume that you have all the planets stationary to each other by some means whereby you can move them all at once without moving the signs of the zodiac or the houses, but you move the planets within the zodiac and within the houses. As you move one body, you move all bodies, and you move them all an equal distance when you move one. If you had the planets on a separate piece of paper that would turn, and if you had the planets and the degrees between the planets accurately drawn to scale, this would be quite easy.

(Editor: This is a confusing description. Please read notes and charts at end of chapter.)

Now, you move or twist all the planets as you might move or twist a radio dial. Let us say that you are 'tuning', so to speak. You twist the dial until the Sun coincides with the Ascendant. You stop there and all the other bodies have fallen into place. This is a Secondary Chart. You have maintained the original planetary pattern. You have not changed that, but you have adjusted it to allow measurement from the Zodiacal position of the Ascendant instead of from the Zodiacal position of the Sun. This was a procedure followed by the ancients thousands of years ago, and such an operation furnishes us with a simple proof that the ancients were employing astrology as pure mathematics, and if their procedure was unsound, then it is just as unsound to employ algebra, because an algebraic equation is a mere pattern of an abstract principle, and the Secondary Chart is a mere pattern of abstract principle. When a child is taught that 9 X 9 equals 81, it makes no difference whether the truth is applied to horses or cans of preserved peaches; the abstract truth is there. It is something that can be applied in a material or any other kind of a world, and we do not hesitate to argue if someone claims that just because 9 rows of 9 horses total 81 horses, that does not prove that 9 rows of 9 cans of preserved peaches total 81 cans of preserved peaches. If the Moon happened to be 120 degrees west of the Sun in the original birth chart, it will remain 120 degrees west of the Sun, but now it will be exactly on the Cusp of the Ninth House, because the Ninth House Cusp is 120 degrees west of the Ascendant and the Sun has been moved to the Ascendant.

In the birth chart, the Moon was not at the Cusp of the Ninth House, but because in this Secondary Chart, the Moon is at the Cusp of the Ninth House, this mathematical point becomes attuned to transits. The position of the Moon in the Secondary Chart is that which we have called the 'Pars Fortuna' or 'Part of Fortune'. The fact that we have already associated the Moon with the Individual Survival Dynamic and with money should be sufficient to explain why the ancients called this point the Part of Fortune.

There will be a similar point in the Secondary Chart for each of the planets. If Jupiter was 35 degrees east of the Sun in the natal chart, it is now 35 degrees east of the Ascendant or right in the middle of the Second House of the Secondary Chart. If the original chart had 13 degrees of Libra on the Ascendant, we now find Jupiter at 28 degrees of Scorpio. Remember that we do not change the natal Ascendant. We do not change the degrees of the Zodiac on the House Cusps. We merely change the planets within the chart. By this means, the ancients set up a whole series of mathematical points in addition to the regular planetary positions.

Unfortunately, it is impossible to determine these additional points that make up the Secondary Chart unless the exact time of birth or the exact degree of the zodiac that is on the Ascendant at birth is known. If your ascendant is in error by one degree, then all of these mathematical points will be in error by one degree. However, the experienced astrologer will discover that these points furnish an excellent means of further checking the time of birth, because, once they have been reliably established, **transits to these points appear every bit as important as transits to other factors in the natal chart.**

Little or almost no work or research in connection with this Secondary Chart has been accomplished in modern times, and it is doubtful whether the student can go very far with research except in those cases where there can be some degree of certainty about the ascending degree of the chart. If the student feels certainty about his own ascending degree, then there will be an exciting bit of experimentation ahead. If the chart is correctly timed, then a whole new realm of transits is opened up for inspection. By the time the student reaches this lesson, there will be a good deal of familiarity with the author's writing, thinking and style, and the student may be interested in noting that his Secondary Chart places Mercury at 21-Sagittarius, where it will be conjunct his natal Uranus at 20-Sagittarius.

When you are satisfied that your own birth time has been established correctly, insert the secondary positions into that same chart in red or a different colored ink, and see what happens. The results will often prove startling, because *important conjunctions or other aspects between secondary and natal positions can occur for a particular time of day that will not exist for any other time of day, and stupendous differences can exist for persons born less than an hour apart.* The above mentioned conjunction of secondary Mercury and natal Uranus would not apply for any persons born at another hour of the same day.

Allow us to emphasize that the Secondary Chart is an almost unexplored matter insofar as modern astrology is concerned. Nothing could offer more definite proof that the ancient astrologers were not causalists. They were mathematicians. Astrology was a study of mathematics, geometrical principles and functions, strictly a study of abstract realms. This is something a mathematician can grasp. Mathematics is pure abstraction and astrology is pure abstraction. Both are keys to the cosmic design of life itself.

We think we have progressed, and we have to some extent, but when we view the last 2500 years, progress has been blind perpetuation of dogma. We are only beginning to seek freedom from the chains of politically organized religion and academics. It may yet take many years, but when actual enlightenment comes, when it is finally realized that astrology is mere mathematical expression, there is bound to be a terrific impact, for astrology itself opens the door to unlimited realms of mathematical knowledge.

It has been our experience that when the true natal chart has been satisfactorily established to allow consideration of the Secondary Chart, a completely new phase of things is opened up. The value of the natal chart has suddenly been doubled, for half of the whole (If this is the whole) has been previously and subtly concealed. A great deal more of the design has been revealed.

More important than anything else, insofar as this Secondary Chart is concerned, is the fact that it opens up a whole new realm of thought. If we can measure in terms of patterns to this extent, how far can such a principle be carried? Please realize that from here on this conversation must be considered as purely speculative, but let us assume that a person was born with Mars 90 degrees east of Saturn. Can we consider that for the life of that person, Saturn is ALWAYS symbolically 90 degrees west of Mars? This would mean that as Mars transits the heavens, insofar as that particular individual is concerned, figuratively speaking, a symbolical Saturn is always traveling 90 degrees behind Mars, and as Saturn transits the heavens, a figurative Mars is always traveling 90 degrees ahead of it.

This would mean that the pattern of the birth horoscope works in many different ways, but the pattern always remains the same. This is the sort of thing that happens throughout mathematics. It happens in physics, in biology and in psychology. Put steel filings on a piece of paper and place a magnet beneath the paper. A pattern forms, a design, a mathematical design. The steel filings obey a design. Biology always obeys designs, and the psychologist is ever observing patterns and designs that thoughts, emotions and behavior follow. The formations of minerals obey design. Snowflakes obey design. Everything obeys design. Life obeys design. Snowflakes obey design. Everything obeys design. Life obeys design. [ed. Fractal geometry by Mandelbot and Phi, the $\sqrt{5}$, in living beings.]

Although arithmetic was formerly regarded as a very simple branch of mathematics, it has become one of the most involved and complicated since the introduction of number theory by Fermat. During centuries of history of math, there was the inclination to emphasize Euclid and forget Pythagoras as a mystic. There are no greater mystics than the more advanced modern mathematicians. Thus, today, interest in Pythagoras among mathematicians has been revived. Pythagoras was a great mathematician 2500 years ago, but he though in terms of design. To him, numbers were designs. The triangular numbers were numbers out of which triangles could be formed. Thus:

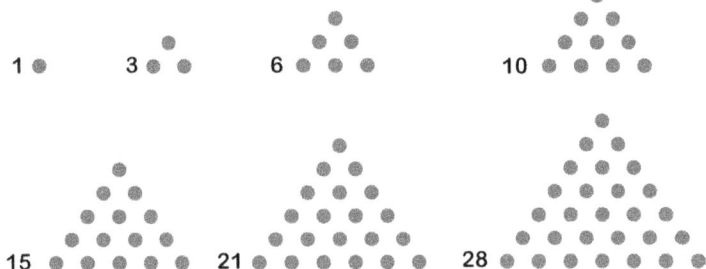

Then, there were the squares were, and squares were designs, portrayed as follows:

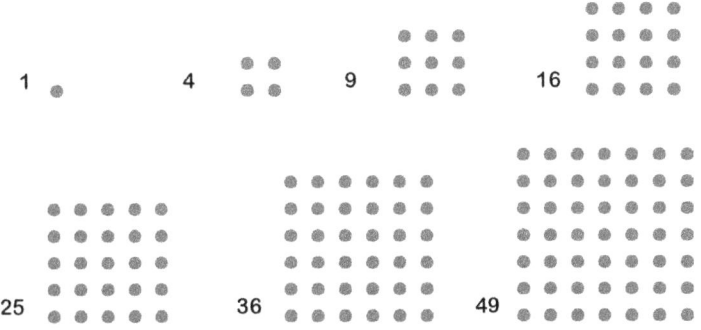

Triangular and Square Numbers

Note that any two consecutive triangular numbers, when added together equal a square, which means that any square is the sum of two consecutive triangular numbers. Note also that if you set the smaller triangular numbers on the larger triangular numbers, in layers, consecutively, you form a tetrahedron or 3-sided pyramid, while if you do the same with the squares, you form a 4-sided pyramid. Today, the mathematicians deal with all sorts of these series of numbers. The pentagonal numbers have very interesting characteristics. They are numbers that can be formed into 5-sided designs. By playing with these designs, the mathematician makes all kinds of discoveries, and he then finds counterparts of these designs everywhere in nature. It was Euclid who said, 'God geometrizes'. The whole universe is put together according to geometrical design. The ancients knew this, but we have been living through 2500 years of dogma, during which time our academicians and religious leaders forgot the ancients. The ancients saw geometrical laws working in the heavens and on Earth, in the macrocosm and the microcosm. They told us, 'As above, so Below!' That's where astrology came in. They applied their designs to the solar system as well to the lower world, and realized that by watching the laws of nature function in the upper world you can know how those laws function in the lower world. The ancient astrologers were mathematicians and the ancient mathematicians were astrologers. There were no astronomers. They came later as the illegitimate children of the rape of astrology by the Church.

The great mathematicians of today live in another world. Few people understand them. They talk in symbols and language that others do not understand. They reach a point where they leave numbers behind and talk in symbols, each symbol expressing some broad principle of the abstract world. It was in this way that they reached the secrets of the atom. They have merely been traversing the same world where the minds of the Greek mathematicians moved about. Remember that it was the ancient Greeks, who originally conceived the idea of the atom. Billiard balls do not fit together into a solid. There is space in between the balls. The ancients did not think along those lines. They know all about geometrical designs in three dimensions. They knew, for example, that twelve-sided objects having a pentagon for each side would fit together into a solid. We do not exactly know just how they conceived an atom, and our modern scientists do not know what an atom might look like if they could see one. They know only how the atom functions mathematically, and they can visualize from there, but they keep changing their views as to what an atom is like. Only recently, they have discovered what they call 'strange particles', something new about the atom that they didn't take into their previous visualization.

Whether we are dealing with astrology or some other science, progress seems dependent upon the discovery of the secrets of design. It all seems a matter of discovering the cosmic design of the abstract world. In the Secondary Chart, we have a great secret that has been passed down to us by the ancients. It is a very useful chart, disclosing many things which cannot otherwise be disclosed, but what we must grasp is not just the method of erecting such a chart. We must realize the vast possibilities that it opens up to us. It produces entirely new means of astrological measurement. It illustrates that we can employ geometrical astrology patterns for purposes of measurement. We find that the natal horoscope is filled with invisible things we knew nothing about.

Consider the case of identical twins born 16 minutes apart. The ascendant would differ in the two charts by about four degrees.

Lesson Twenty

The planets, even the Moon, would be in practically the same zodiacal positions, but the secondary position of these planets would all vary by four degrees, like the ascendant and house cusps. If Mars hit secondary Uranus by transit in one chart, it would be a number of days before it would reach secondary Uranus in the other chart. Thus, while transits to the natal positions would be identical for the two twins born 16 minutes apart, they would not coincide where the secondary planetary positions were concerned. In the case where two people were born 12 hours apart, the secondary positions would differ by roughly 180 degrees.

When we stop to realize that astrology is a mere study of abstract mathematical design, the greatest possibility of all opens up for us. *That is the indication that the greatest mathematical secrets of all, as they relate to all branches of science, are actually hidden behind the curtain of the astrological chart. Figure out the truth here, and you are likely to find it elsewhere.* Yet, you have to stop thinking in terms of cause-and-effect where astrology is concerned, because until you do, you will not be likely to thing in terms of mathematical design or in terms of cosmic design. Any study of number theory will prove helpful in getting away from a causal hypothesis. When we leave this over-ripe hypothesis behind insofar as astrology is concerned, then there is no reason why we should not find the mathematical key repeated in many places. It is no longer unreasonable to find a mathematical pattern in the horoscope, and it is no longer unreasonable if we should also find it in the palm of a person's hand. [ed. Divination using fractal geometry.]

Our experience has often indicated that the female mind more easily grasps the conception that things can fall into a mathematical pattern without the need of any causal factor. Perhaps that has been one of our difficulties. For thousands of years, we have tried to convince ourselves that the male mind is superior to that of the female. All the dogma of the last several thousand years has been brought to us by the male. It is only in our own time that we have allowed women to vote. They were not regarded as sufficiently intelligent to vote fifty years ago, and even the writer can remember hearing men argue the point. The first election where women were allowed to vote was anticipated with great apprehension. Most of the first women voters voted only as their husbands directed them. A good wife obeyed her husband because he knew best. The interest of women was supposed to be limited to housework and babies.

The husband belittles his wife if she believes in palmistry, one of the oldest beliefs on Earth, but for the palm of a hand to hold the key to a mathematical pattern that is expressed in many places is no more irrational than to believe that all snowflakes freeze with six sides.

In many cases, what we have termed a woman's intuition has merely been her ability to think in terms of patterns, and in principle these patterns are no different from mathematical patterns. They can be patterns of abstract reality, and although the woman can also be wrong, this can apply to the mathematician. It is possible for him to make an error somewhere. He may not have grasped a pattern accurately, and the woman may not have grasped the pattern accurately.

In 'The River of Life', by Rutherford Platt, we find a biologist thinking in terms of abstract patterns. Platt is not limited in his thinking by an academic status. He works as an advisor to Walt Disney. He speaks of the 'bee animal'. Since we are accustomed to thinking of a bee as an insect and not an animal, this requires a bit of explanation. His language and his use of the term 'bee animal' helps to get his views across. He does not regard the bee as an animal. By 'bee animal', he means the abstract pattern of the whole hive. He refers to the whole swarm as an animal. He compares individual bees to individual cells of a human body, pointing out how individual cells sacrifice themselves for the welfare of the body as a whole, and demonstrating a parallel where individual bees do likewise and are automatically sacrificed in the interests of the swarm as a whole unit, the bee-animal. We might refer to this as work of the Social Survival Dynamic if we were dealing with the human pattern.

If we think of the whole unit as the bee animal, then we find that there is a pattern. We can go from hive to hive and we find that all bee animals behave in a similar manner. In all bee animals, there is one queen bee. Other female bees never become queens because they are fed on pollen mush for only two days, and after that they are fed on nothing but honey. The queen is fed pollen mush for her entire life because pollen mush is necessary to develop her sexually. The other girl bees do not develop sexually. The behavior of one bee animal is exactly the same as the behavior of another bee animal a thousand miles away. There is a pattern, an abstract pattern, and all bee animals behave in accord with this abstract pattern. Just as all cells of a body behave in accord with an abstract pattern, members of a society behave in accord with an abstract pattern. Whether we deal with mathematics, genealogy, biology or atoms, we find that behavior conforms to abstract patterns. This principle applies to the behavior of minerals as they form themselves into crystals. It applies to the behavior of cells in the human body. It applies to the behavior of bee animals or ant animals. It applies where there is life and where there is no life. It applies to the pattern of thought of a particular individual. One person is conventional and another is unconventional because that was the pattern of birth.

Since the very beginning of this Course, it has been obvious that women have been able to grasp the overall pattern of our discussion more readily than men. In many cases, they appear to have less in the way of mental blocks. Often the individual with little education grasps things better than the person with a well-rounded education. This conforms with Charles Kettering's statement that the greater a man's education, the less apt is he to become an inventor. This does not argue that education is not a requisite. Instead, it points out the weakness and evils of an educational system which teaches people to memorize rather than to understand.

Whether you are to study astrology or mathematics, it is important to learn to think in terms of abstract patterns. Such thinking is a shortcut. You become familiar with a pattern where it applies in one place in nature. You get to understand it, and then you meet up with that pattern again and again in far removed places where there is no possible material connection. In the horoscope, the relationship of all planets to each other becomes a pattern. It is like a brand. All of the automatic behavior of the individual conforms to this pattern or brand. This does not mean that the individual, through understanding of his own automatic behavior, cannot begin to behave consciously according to a design of his own conscious making, and when he does this, he is discovering his own powers of free will and employing them to replace his own automatic behavior. The behavior of the bee animal is automatic. Otherwise, it would not be exactly the same as the behavior of all other been animals wherever found. Despite the well organized civilization in which individual bees live, they appear to have done nothing about developing free will. Even the queen herself is a slave to the interests of the hive. All queen behave in exactly the same manner. When it is time to do so, the queen leaves the hive followed by a swarm of males who follow her high into the air. Ultimately, one catches up to her or she allows one to catch up. At this high altitude, the queen has her one taste of sex. This completed, she kills the satisfying male. He has served his purpose as far as the interests of society are concerned. It is now his fate to die. There is no longer a need for the other male bees. They are driven from hive or killed. If they are not killed, it is their fate to starve to death. The queen returns to the hive. Her sex life is over. Never again will she have romantic contact with a male. This one act of sex has done the job well, and so long as she is fed pollen mush, she will continue to lay eggs. Her duty to society is to lay eggs.

Perhaps we have gone far afield from the Secondary Chart, but it is necessary to understand why the Secondary Chart can be an abstract reality and become as important as the natal chart itself. It is necessary to understand why transits to mathematical points can become as important as transits to points which were actually occupied by material planets at the time of birth. Of course, this is no different than transits to house cusps, because house cusps are mere mathematical points. It is no different than transits through signs of the zodiac, because the division of one sign from another is a mere mathematical point. We begin with the planets and from them arises a whole superstructure of abstract mathematical points. A whole 'society' of mathematical points ultimately becomes a mathematical pattern. We have to give a name to the whole society of mathematical points, and just as Platt invented a term for the bee animal, the ancients invented a word for the whole mathematical pattern, and they called it a horoscope.

Realize that if a person is born with the Sun exactly on the eastern horizon, so that half of the Sun is above the horizon and half the Sun is below the horizon (Mountains do not count), then the Natal Chart and the Secondary Chart are one and the same, because the Sun and the Ascendant are one and the same. By the time the Sun is one degree above the Ascendant, the Natal and Secondary Charts have parted by one degree. All of the planets, like the Sun, have moved one degree westward (as the Earth turned eastward), but in the Secondary chart, they have not changed, but this is only insofar as their relationship to the Ascendant and house cusps are concerned. It depends upon what you are employing as your frame of reference. If you employ the zodiac as your frame of reference, then all the secondary bodies have moved forward in the zodiac by one degree. In other words, in relation to the Ascendant and house cusps, all the Secondary planets will remain as they were at sunrise, but in relation to the zodiacal signs, all the planets will move forward in the zodiac as the Sun rises. (Of course, this will be slightly altered to the extent that the planets will have some additional motion of their own during the day, but this is slight. It can be great where the Moon is concerned.)

We have tried to explain this Secondary Chart from a number of different points of view in order that the student may understand it instead of being dependent upon any memorized formula. However, if you want a formula, all you have to do is take the natal chart, measure the distance, east or west, of each body from the Sun and insert it in the Secondary Chart that same distance from the Ascendant. If Mercury is ten degrees west of the Sun, insert it ten degrees west of the Ascendant, etc. This should be simple enough. If your birth time is in error by ten degrees on the Ascendant, then all the secondary positions will be out by ten degrees. You can check transits to the secondary positions. You may find out that they do not work accurately. They may work early or late. This is your key. Constant checking of transits to the secondary positions of the planets in your chart will enable you to correct your time of birth just as constant checking of transits to your house cusps will do the same. When you have the chart exactly right, you will find that all transits to all of these mathematical points will click with precision.

Realize that the planetary pattern in the Secondary Chart is exactly the same as the planetary pattern in the Natal Chart. The relationship of any material planet to all other material bodies is exactly the same in both charts. If Mars was 132 degrees east of Jupiter in one chart, it is also 132 degrees east of Jupiter in the other chart. All we have done is to twist the planetary dial exactly as we twist a radio dial when we are tuning the radio. A small twist of the radio dial may bring us music from New York instead of music from Chicago. If twins are born four minutes apart, all the secondary positions of the second twin have been altered by approximately a degree. Yet, the natal planets can be considered as exactly the same in both charts insofar as the zodiac is concerned.

In closing, let us come back to a short discussion of this difference between the male and female ways of thinking. Our experience with male and female students has been extremely interesting to us and should be interesting to all. We have had a whole series of female students who, after starting this Course, suddenly developed an appetite to know more about mathematics which, up until that time, was repulsive to them. These students are also now studying mathematics and enjoying the study to the full. This tendency has not been near so apparent among male students. This might be accounted for by the fact that on the average our female students have more time. In addition, many of our male students are engineers and already have a mathematical education beyond that of our female students. Nevertheless, we cannot escape the fact that our female students have responded with far more enthusiasm to the whole idea that we live in accord with abstract cosmic design and that both astrology and mathematics are mere studies of abstract cosmic design. We cannot escape the conclusion that female students respond readily to the idea of thinking in terms of abstract patterns, while male students are ever clinging to a more materialistic conception of things. It would appear that our lady students have found it easier to break away from old frames of reference, from old thought patterns.

Yet, we must also point out that male students with a mathematical background grasp these views much more rapidly than male students without that mathematical background, and we actually do have male students who have begun the study of mathematics anew and with new enthusiasm for the subject. Among both sexes, there have been signs of a completely new outlook on life, and this we like. Nothing has proved a greater reward to us than those letters coming from some students who state that the Course has altered their whole viewpoint on life for the better.

Notes from Editor, Naomi Bennett:

The secondary chart was discovered by Carl's long term study of the arabic parts for over 30 years. Finally in 1957, he realized that the arabic parts could be extended by calculating a new arabic part for the ascendant too. From this one mathematical point, the Secondary Chart was conceived and drawn up for the first time. For over 20 years, astrologers had guessed that Carl had a Leo personality, yet there are no planets or dominance in Leo. When he drew up his own secondary chart, 9° Leo was on the Secondary Ascendant. He knew he was onto a major discovery. On the facing page is his primary chart and his secondary chart.

Note that all the planets retain their relative positions to each other and stay in the same houses. However, the signs and degrees have changed. All the planetary positions in the secondary chart equal the following arabic part names and formulas.

Natal Planet	Arabic Part Name	Formula/Secondary Chart
Moon	Part of Fortune	Asc + Moon - Sun
Mercury	Part of Commerce	Asc + Mercury - Sun
Venus	Part of Love	Asc + Venus – Sun
Mars	Part of Passion	Asc + Mars – Sun
Jupiter	Part of Increase	Asc + Jupiter – Sun
Saturn	Part of Fatality	Asc + Saturn - Sun
Uranus	Part of Catastrophe	Asc + Uranus - Sun
Neptune	Part of Treachery	Asc + Neptune - Sun
Pluto	Part of Organization	Asc + Pluto – Sun
Ascendant	Part of Self Day	Asc + Asc - Sun

(I personally re-name these parts with their planet names to remove the stigma of names like treachery, catastrophe or fatality)

Lesson Twenty

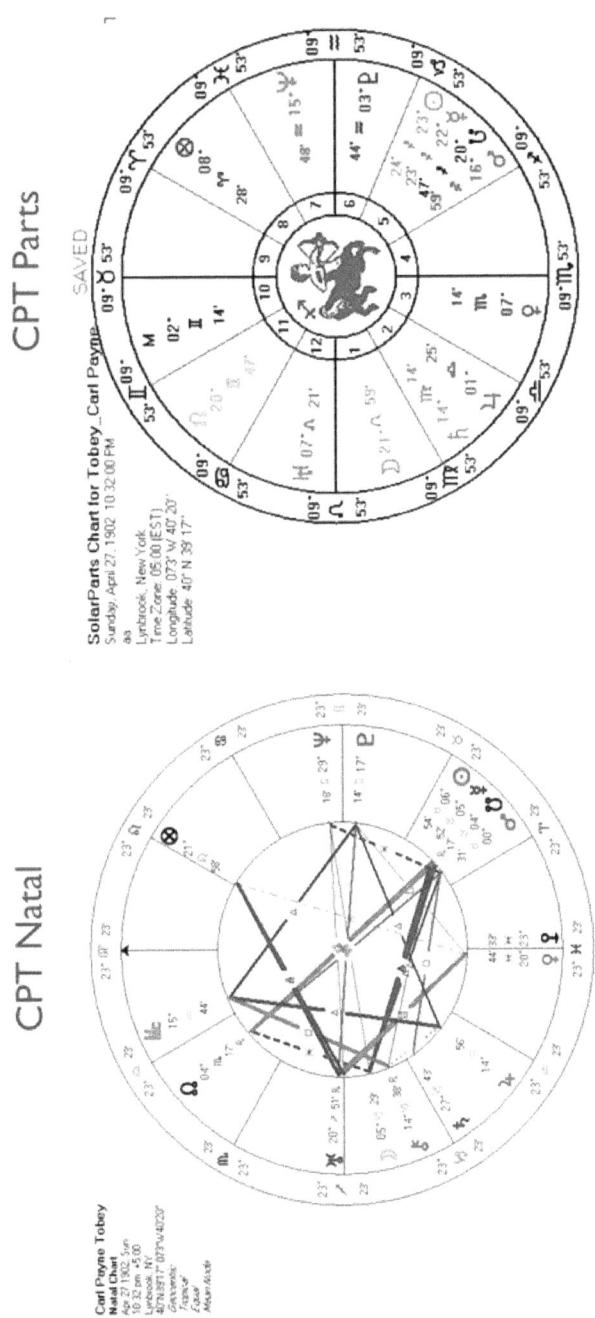

Carl Tobey Natal and Solar Parts Chart

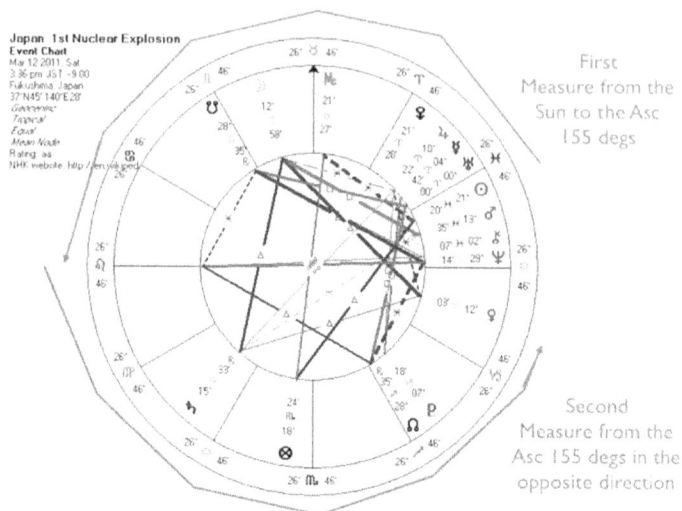

Solar Parts Measurement of Asc - Sun

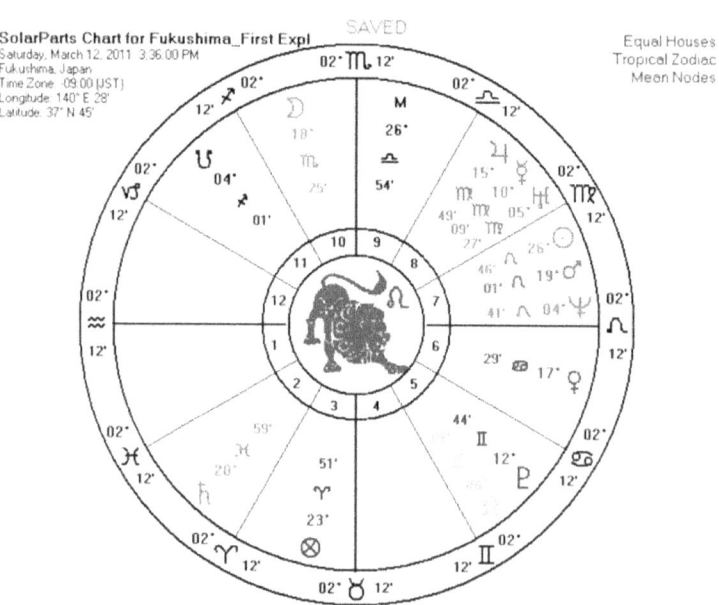

Solar Parts (Secondary) Chart for Fukushima

On the bottom left is natal chart for the Japan's Fukushima Nuclear Explosion in 2011. This is a visual diagram that shows the basic measurement of solar parts. The important measurement of all the solar parts is the relationship of the movement of the Sun to the Ascendant, Asc - Sun. This is the critical angle that creates a solar parts chart.

Uranian Planetary Pictures are very similar to arabic parts and Robert Hand's Greek Lots are also calculated in a similar manner. However, **Carl's discovery of the Secondary Chart is the only technique where the parts can be drawn into another horoscope and analyzed against the natal just as transits can be compared against a natal chart**. Since most astrologers think with visually with a round horoscope, this is a major aid in analysis. It reveals hidden, unexplained facets of an event or personality that didn't make sense from the natal alone.

Currently in 2014, Solar Fire Gold software calculates arabic parts but this software will not draw the secondary chart. The Arabic parts editor does allow new parts to be added to the software. John Halloran's Astrowin software fully supports CPT's secondary chart since 1996. I advised him on the calculation and because of Rob Hand's discovery of the important of day and night birth sect calculations of Greek Lots, I had Halloran produce the Secondary Chart as a Solar Parts Chart and a Lunar Parts Chart based on whether the natal chart had the Sun above or below the horizon. After two years of experimentation, **I believe that only the Solar Parts chart is valid** but more observation is needed to be absolutely certain. David Cochrane's Kepler software also calculates CPT's secondary chart (See following page).

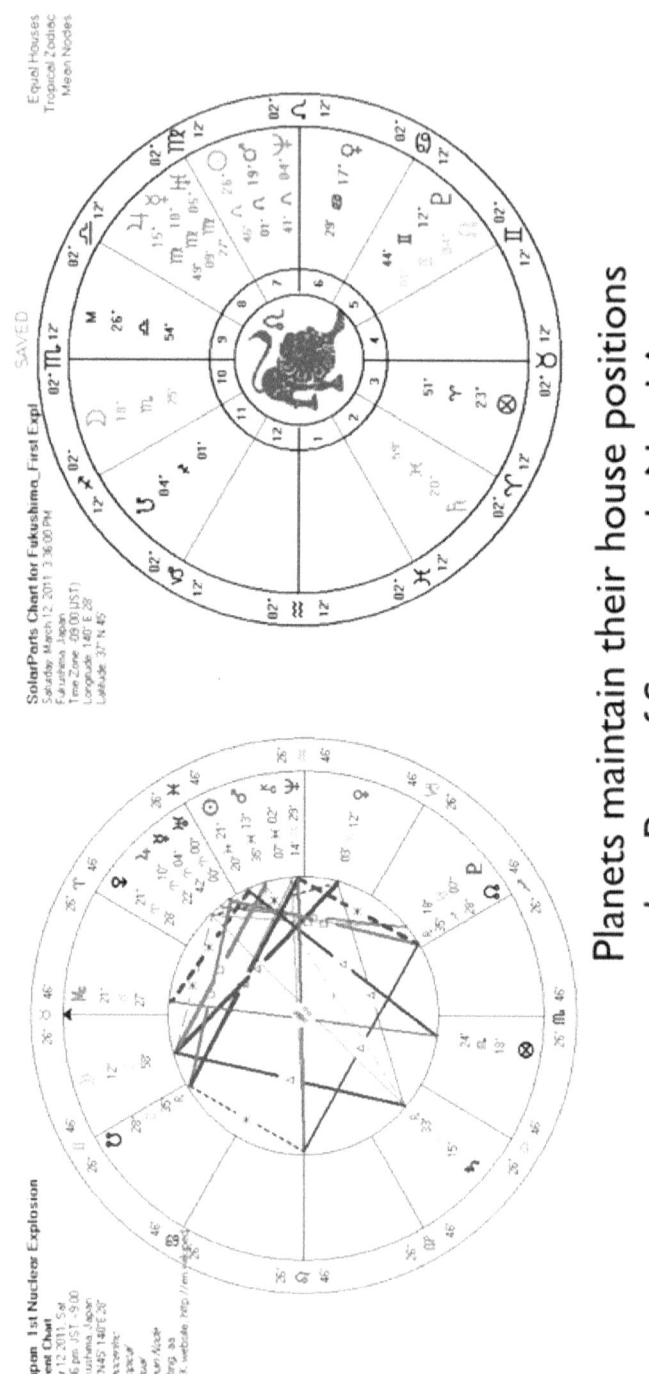

LESSON TWENTY-ONE
HUMAN RELATIONSHIPS

The only real freedom is found in solitude, but solitude is not insurance of freedom, because in solitude the average person is thinking in terms of the outside world. The great seers and religious leaders would go into the mountains to peer within, and the mathematician finds his greatest truths within himself. The work of the creative artist comes from within, to be imitated by others. Most of the population spends all its time imitating. There are but a few creative souls. However, the majority of the work that an astrologer is called upon to perform deals in human relationships, and that brings us to comparison of charts. Boris Sidis, the psychologist, once head of the New York State Pathological Hospitals, was of the view that as you increase the number of people in a group you lower the average intelligence. They start imitating each other. They begin conforming, and the intelligence level continually drops. That would be to say that if you would be intelligent, be alone, and think for yourself.

By the time that an astrologer can read charts, he should also be able to compare charts, for the procedure and basic principles are the same. One person is born with Mars conjunct Uranus, while another is not, but if the second selects a marital mate with Uranus at the same zodiacal degree as his Mars, he will take on the same characteristics as the first man who was born with Mars conjunct Uranus. *Associating with other people is one way of completely changing your horoscope and your life.* It can often be the means of shortening one's life, or it might be the way of accumulating fortune and a life of ease. If you are working with enough people, you are no longer an individual. You are like a one cell in a biological system or body. You must, from that time on, obey the plan or pattern of that group, which may be a very unintelligent plan. You become a slave to the group unless you can be sufficient of a leader to alter the pattern of the functioning unit. In this, few people succeed, principally because they never try. It is easier to copy, imitate, and accept the will of the majority.

People think they want freedom, but they do not accept it because of their fear of insecurity, whereas there can be no real security without freedom. Real scrutiny is found only within one's self, for without freedom there is no vital force, and without vital force there is no security. A man may cling to his boss for reasons of security. He may do all of his dirty work, but in the end the boss can and will fire him when he is no longer of value to the boss.

When you have handled person relationship problems for thirty years, you will realize that most human relationships that hang together are based on fear and insecurity. The marriages that last longest are not based on love but on insecurity. People live together because of their fears. They fight like tigers. They irritate each other, but not enough to overcome fear of insecurity. They don't dare live alone. There are marked exceptions to this, but they are few. The most important thing we should strive for is human relationships that are not based on fear of insecurity. We are obsessed by the idea that we must accept what society thinks about human relations, and society is stupid, knowing little or nothing about such matters. We copy. What do others do? What did Moses say? What did he tell us we must do?

What is there to indicate that Moses was any more intelligent than Jim Smith? True, he was a leader, but how intelligent a leader? In what field of knowledge did he excel? Why are we so dull as to accept his word as that of God? Have his rules ever worked? Have they cleared up the problems of society or human relations? Most decidedly they have not. Have they given happy marriages? They have not. Are we to underestimate the intelligence of God to the point that we accept the rules of Moses as the level of intelligence of God?

If you are to solve human problems, you must toss all these obsolete rules to the dogs and start thinking for yourself. Throw them all out and start from the beginning. What do YOU think? What do you HONESTLY think? Start there.

People put up a front. A marriage may appear to be a very happy one from the outside, but when wife or husband consults an astrologer, the other side of the story comes out. Each may even try to convince the other that he or she is happy. Unhappiness may be a deep inner secret, something one tries to keep to one's self, but there it is. The fact is that close and intimate relationships become a strain. They lead to all sorts of ailments. Conceal your true inner feelings and put up a front for relatives and the public, and you get one form of illness or another. Sex becomes merely a means of easing a tension. Alcohol becomes the anesthetic to dull the pain.

Are there no happy marriages? Yes, there are, but these are the ones where individualism is allowed, where intellectual interests predominate, where individual creativeness is allowed to exist, and where mates are not dependent on each other for security, where neither party is draining the other of vitality and life.

Square aspects develop the greatest emotionalism and introduce the factors of family survival. Mars and Scorpio, Taurus and its ruler, wherever it is, would do the same. Trine aspects introduce creativeness, sextile aspects intellectuality. The conjunction will depend on the sign occupied, as well as the planets involved. The opposition aspect introduces change of one form or another. The semi-sextile and quincunx aspects develop insecurity.

One of the great problems of marriage as we know it is that it subdues individualism, for one party or both. It is better if we respect each other's right to individualism, and that we develop our own individualism. Some conjunctions, most sextiles and trines, and some oppositions will help this process along, but more so when Fire and Air signs are involved rather than Earth and Water signs. We refer to 'some' conjunctions and oppositions, because combinations between Saturn and Neptune are seldom if ever beneficial. Change is one of the unrecognized necessities of life and good health. That is why vacations are sometimes helpful. The marital institution often does not recognize the necessity for change. You are supposed to have a steady job for security reasons. You are supposed to own your own home as soon as possible. That will keep you in one place, tie you down, keep you busy making repairs, and help life to become stable, monotonous, boring, routine, frustrated and unhealthy. Children might help you to break out of the rut if you don't subdue them by beating their brains out. Children have youth and are born with a lack of knowledge of conventions. They are not yet ready to settle down in the tomb. Oh yes, if it is what is recognized as a good secure marriage, you also make certain to buy a cemetery lot, for isn't that the most appropriate place for such a marriage?

A good astrologer has to listen to the client. It is well to let him or her get it all out of the system first. That is why it is also good to tolerate 10-page, single-space letters.

If someone wants to get married, first try and find out why. You'll get some pretty good answers on this one. Probe a little. Don't accept the answer, 'Because I am in love.' That is seldom the case. The young girl is often seeking freedom from her parents. Next, she must seek freedom from her husband. One lady tells us that her deceased husband always came home and tossed his salary in her lap. She would like a man to come home and toss money in her lap. Many people get married because that is what you are supposed to do. They accept the least of all evils insofar as they are able to estimate in advance. Many people are lonesome and need company.

This is a terrible affliction, for they have never discovered their own inner selves and probably never will.

Some people get married because they want to raise children, and this seems to be the one lofty and only legitimate reason for marriage. If both parties are interested in the development of the children, that keeps them from getting in each other's way. Without the desire to have children, people would be better off to live together as long as they want to, and go on their way when it becomes too monotonous, as it usually does. They could still be individuals, without all that complete frustration.

Aside from children [Aries and Pluto], the next loftiest reason for marriage is an appreciation for beauty [Libra and Venus]. When two people can help each other to see the beautiful in the design of nature, there can be mutual happiness. A young client put this very nicely. 'When I see something beautiful, like a beautiful sunset, I like to share it with someone.' That helps when the other person has an appreciation for beauty, but many people have none. They may bluff along, but their aesthetic sense has never been developed. This could apply to many of our modern artists who see only the grotesque, and portray it. They are not lifting anyone up. They are dragging them down.

If you want to judge the effect of one personality on another, merely take the first person's chart and insert the other person's planets in that chart in another color of ink. Read them just as if they had been there at birth. There you have it. It is as simple as that, but first, you must be able to read a birth chart. Reverse the procedure, and do the same with the second chart. Practice on cases you know well. You will find a lot of explanations for things. Try it out on all the marriages you know.

Uranus aspects are often most prominent in bringing about divorce. The divorce rate increases to the point where some people are alarmed. They are alarmed because people didn't used to get divorces. What's wrong with people nowadays? People didn't used to ride in automobiles either. What's wrong with automobiles?

Marriage is supposed to have been much different years back. People didn't get divorces. There was never any quarrelling. That was because the man was king in his home. The wife did not argue. It was her role only to obey. If she didn't, she got it. There were some restrictions. There is still an old statute in Connecticut which says that a man can beat his wife only with a stick the size of his thumb. This was a great advantage to fat men. Their wives behaved. However, this would seem to indicate that the wives may have been quite sturdy, when a man couldn't handle one with his fists. He needed a club.

There is no foundation for the belief that we must think of marriage as a holy institution. It is a man-made institution. Its original purpose was to make certain that children were supported by fathers and would not become a burden on society. It was also a way of supporting women who were supposed to be the weaker sex. Women were property, and we have always protected property rights first. In some places, women were purchased as property. In others, parent paid dowries to get men to relieve them of their daughters and support them. Holy matrimony has always been a pretty cold-blooded economic affair. Our modern hold on matrimony is less cold-blooded.

The complexion of marriage within the last fifty years has changed greatly. Girls are educated now. They vote. They take jobs. They smoke cigarettes and drink cocktails. When the wrier was a boy, there was a woman in the community who drank beer at home. No one woman in the community of 2000 people never spoke to or mixed with her. She was isolated from all except her husband and three sons. This was but two miles outside the limits of the City of New York. It was whispered that any woman who would take a drink was a prostitute.

Human relations have changed. They will change more. Rules and regulations will change as people become enlightened. However, we must review these matters if we are to consider human relations astrologically. We must start with no misconceptions. We must realize that one of the worst obstacles involving human relations is the outmoded conception that we battling to maintain. We must realize that up till now some form of selfishness is the foundation upon which most of our conventions are built. We must realize that hypocrisy and frustrations have been accepted as virtues. It was long accepted that you put up a front. But what you did behind closed doors was all right. There is the old story, told many years ago, of the elder Morgan of Wall Street calling the younger Morgan on the carpet for having been seen out with a woman, not his wife. The younger Morgan is supposed to have pointed out to the father that he was doing nothing that the father was not doing except that the father did it behind closed doors. The elder man is supposed to have replied, "Young man, that is what closed doors are for."

Younger people are facing the facts of life. Doctors, psychologists, psychiatrists, lawyers, judges and welfare workers are facing the facts. They are no longer viewing marriage as a holy institution, but we still have to protect children.

One of our greatest aims should be to stimulate greater

freedom in all human relationships and allow people to get rid of their fears, conscious and unconscious. The girl with a good job is more careful in the selection of a mate than the girl who is trying to get out from under the pressure of the retarded conceptions of her parents. Marriage is not likely to be happy when it is a form of escape from something. Good Uranus aspects between charts provide liberalism and relationships which grant greater freedom and individualism.

When Neptune gets involved in marriage, there are strange results. If the aspect is an unfavorable one, there can be that which we call scandal. Scandal is that which is contrary to accepted standards, that which is not looked upon as 'holy'. Dr. Worden, one of our students, has stirred up considerable discussion about Neptune and its sex factor, which has opened up a new conception of sex as embodying the entire water triplicity of Scorpio, Cancer and Pisces, which also means Mars, Moon and Neptune. Neptunian people have different ideas about marriage, some very unselfish ideas, but scandalous according to almost any standards. The idea that marriage should be based on unselfishness is more than society could bear at this time. It is more acceptable that it should be based on passion rather than upon compassion. *We find passion in Scorpio and Mars, compassion in Pisces and Neptune, and the profit motive in Cancer and the Moon.*

The Cancer type of marriage can be a financial success and can supply ample frustration. The Scorpio type of marriage can supply passion, jealousy, lots of fights, personal injuries and sometimes murder. The Pisces type of marriage can supply unselfishness, compassion, sympathy and scandal. All can supply children. The ancients described the Water signs as fruitful.

Jupiter will always help any relationship because it leads to education and social revolution, something we need badly. It leads to enlightenment. This is true of Sagittarius, but watch the point of Venus and Uranus nodes in Sagittarius and Gemini. They alter things. They become more involved. Favorable aspects between Jupiter and Neptune, but particularly the conjunction between charts, are excellent. They lift things. Mars-Jupiter combinations are passionate but harmonious. They ultimately contribute to great liberalism, although jealousies may have to be passed through at the start.

Pluto-Aries indications lead to greater independence. Saturnian combinations lead to the greatest of all frustrations plus every kind of hypocrisy, the same for Capricorn. Venus and Libra will stir interest in beauty, art, music, good clothes, and at the highest point in the abstract.

Lesson Twenty-One

I have always been customary to look to the 7th House where marriage is concerned. This is justifiable because the 7th House will help to describe the person who attracts you. The sign it is in will be important too. The sign on the cusp of the 7th will be important, as well as the condition of the planet that rules the 7th House. However, let us not stop there. After a while, unless you have very stimulating aspects, marriage will become a routine affair including budget and economic discussions. The gilt wears off. What was previously interesting is less interesting when you see it all of the time. Of course, if you have Saturn in the 7th or Venus in Capricorn, you may suffer and bear it. Venus conjunct Saturn, or Mars conjunct Saturn would help along the same lines. The important thing is that once marriage has become a matter of routine, it no longer has any relationship to the 7th House. It shifts to the 8th and becomes a Saturnian affair itself. But, if you had one or more planets in the 7th House at birth, there are bound to arise new interests. You will be attracted to the new again, unless the planet is Saturn, Mercury or "Y" (ruler of Taurus)*. These would tend to tone things down and keep them on the conventional side.

Seventh House factors, and these are to include all opposition aspects, but particularly those between charts, tend to introduce third parities. Unconsciously, a husband may introduce the very men to whom his wife is naturally attracted. Of course, it works the other way too. Signs of the zodiac occupied by the planets involved are always important, because the Earth signs will always try to keep things on a practical basis. The woman with Saturn in her 7th will be attracted to those she meets through her husband, but only from a point of view of duty. She will serve them but she wouldn't be likely to have an affair with them. Other planets can produce different results. An opposition of Venus between charts will very often produce adultery.

Venus was long known as the goddess of love. It all depends on what you mean by love. Venus seeks the beautiful where she can find it. She knows nothing about monogamy. Never heard of it, in fact, unless she happened to get involved with Saturn. Venus enjoys beautiful women or handsome men wherever she finds hem. She is social. She is refined. She desires beauty everywhere, in art, in the human form, in music, in clothes. Her personal interest is not really in sex, but she will go along with it. She will try to refine it and raise it above any taint of the gross or vulgar. It is Mars that can be gross and vulgar. Venus is not passionate. She can love many if there is the beautiful. She is seeking something higher, much higher, something few people ever understand. It was an astrological chart that first caused the writer to begin to delve more deeply into the nature of Venus an Libra, the sign it rules. Why had he awakened with the complete solution to a mathematical problem that had never entered his head before? A whole flock of planets were in Libra. The whole think was nothing but a matter of balance. The ancients had symbolized Libra with the scales of balance. Everywhere in nature there is balance until we, ourselves, tip the scales. In the solar system the centrifugal just happens to balance gravitation, although the centrifugal and gravitation are merely names for something science doesn't really understand any more than it understands electricity or atoms. Balance is everywhere in nature, if you but open your eyes to see it, but without a good Venus, or a developed Venus you will neither see nor understand it. Kepler's laws of planetary motion, design, balance, are all represented by Venus. Venus can make a good mathematician. Everywhere in mathematics, there is balance. With the equal sign, you form a mathematical equation. It is only an equation where there is balance. Kepler and Newton understood balance. The great mathematicians all understood balance. They all described mathematics as beautiful. A beautiful woman is one with balanced features. What does this have to do with the goddess of love? What does it have to do with love? The young man who had to have someone with whom to share beauty. When people can share beauty, they are in love. Love, and 11th House matter, not of the 5th or 7th, as so many supposed, the 5th being the 7th of the 11th, the 11th the 5th of the 7th. This is different kind of love. There is no passion. It is a love of beauty and of sharing. The 11th was the House of Friends. Those are friends with whom you can share beauty, even if you are married to one of them. Here is the acme of human relations, the sharing of the beauty of the universe and everything in it. Everything runs according to mathematical laws, even human dynamics, the solids, the crystals, the hexagons, the snowflakes. Even the wild mob in Little Rock, Arkansas, is obeying a mathematical pattern. It erupts the first time, after Neptune enters Scorpio, when the Sun conjoins Mars, ruler of Scorpio. Snowflakes obey geometrical laws. Bees obey geometrical laws, while the mob of Little Rock obeys geometrical laws.

Where do we find the highest expression of love? Strangely in the Family Non-Survival Dynamic Guide, strongly suggesting that the whole family relationship needs to be revised. The whole basic principle of the 'family' relationship is to pit group against group—the Hatfields and the McCoys—race against race—the whiles against the negroes, the Arabs against the Jews. Big mechanized wards belong to Pluto and Aries. Smaller family or racial wars belong to Mars and Scorpio. The Little Rock mob erupted when Neptune reached Scorpio and when the Sun conjoined Mars.

Under any circumstances, the education and philosophy of the individual is to be considered important. These are something others cannot take away from you. They are not like money. You can be drained of your money or your nerve force, but you can't be drained of your education and philosophy. We might add religion to these, but in a broad sense, they include it. The person who puts these above money and the grosser considerations of life is protected against many things. He doesn't gravitate into the same kind of relationships that he might otherwise.

We must not forget the Ascendant of a chart. For a planet in one chart to be at the ascendant of another is one of the most important possible factors. If the planet be either Venus or Jupiter, the results are excellent, unless the Ascendant itself or the planet involved is badly afflicted.

As we have pointed out elsewhere, Mars-Uranus afflictions between charts can hold possible strains, dangers and broad changes. Mars-Neptune afflictions can hold the worst in emotional disturbances. Mars-Saturn afflictions are frustrating. Either of the last two combinations can result in ill health, Mars-Neptune, like Saturn-Neptune afflictions can often lead to some form of neuroticism or metal illness, as well as to other forms of ill health, which are probably mental and emotional at their base.

Without going into all the details that we have covered, it is simplification to say that good aspects help a marriage or partnership, while negative aspects hurt it–all this on the unconscious level. Under any circumstances, creative and intellectual aspects will give you a lift, while insecure and restrictive aspects will drain our vitality and do away with what we might call your divine protection.

It is important to realize that marriage, as we know it, or as the churches know it, is not holy matrimony. It isn't holy when it costs money for a license and to pay the minister to make it acceptable. These are the business aspects. The drive-in chapels give the best rates. The big churches are for people in the higher brackets. All ceremonies help marriage to become more of a fetish. There are so many business aspects, wedding gowns, flowers, cocktails, fancy food and all that sort of thing. Rings appeal to the savage and the mercenary qualities in people. A big diamond sure shows a girl must have gotten something worthwhile. In a pinch, she can always hock it for a small part of its cost. Wedding presents, the loot, and a tomb to store it away. People actually seek these things as a part of marriage, and forever after, they have to tie themselves to the people who presented them.

The marriage that is made in heaven is the one that helps folks discover heaven within themselves, beauty within themselves—the one that helps them to contact the abstract within themselves. When they discover these qualities within themselves they can reproduce them in the outside world. This is no different in process from a partnership of two engineers, where the engineers utilize abstract mathematical principles, abstract natural law and engineering principles to erect a perfectly balanced, well designed and beautiful bridge.

You cannot build a happy and successful marriage on low and gross motives as a foundation. If people understood the higher principles, they would not want to. People do not understand the higher principles. If they did, the marital institution would not be what it is today. Marriage would be too personal a matter to submit to government or social intervention or supervision. Certain groups are allowed to perform marriages. They get paid for it. Put together your own group. Form some new religion, and you can perform marriages. Just become a minister of your own church and you are in business. Somewhat ridiculous, is it not? Isn't a marriage actually too personal a matter to take in all these outsiders? Nevertheless, it has to be done for now. Otherwise it isn't legal (Saturn). As things stand now, in a great ratio of cases, marriage is a means of a woman gaining support, a solution to her economic problems. This is her way of earning a living. It is an accepted method. If the marriage proves unbearable for both parities, some honest minded women will gladly walk out and ask no further compensation, but a large ratio will want payments indefinitely continued in the form of alimony.** In most places society goes along with this idea because of a purely selfish motive. There is the fear that the woman may become a burden to the state or to society itself. In most states, a judge will grant temporary alimony without listening to any evidential phases of the case. Legal authorities make it plain that this is because of the fear that society itself might have a responsibility in the woman. Community property laws in many states are quite equitable. In some, any profit that has been made since marriage occurred is split equally, and each party is again an individual and on his or her own. Whether going into or out of marriage, the whole thing is put on an economic basis. One of the boring things about marriage, as we know it, is that it is merely a branch of economics. [an 8th House/Saturn matter]

Let us suppose that you are a lofty spirit wanting to rise in the intellectual and perfectly designed world of the abstract, and let us suppose that you are married, and that you find another member of the opposite sex who can lift you in that new world. You are likely to be suspect. There might be sex up there somewhere. There are apt to be jealousies. If there are not jealousies, society is going to suspect all parties involved. It must be some strange cult like those to be found in deepest Africa. Society condemns what it does not understand, and it understands little. It will have to go back a few thousand years into the deep dark past and consult Moses.

Marriage should bring intellectual benefits to both parties. Otherwise, it may be too much like breeding cattle. When there is no longer mutual intellectual benefit, what is left but frustration and death, the Saturnian variety of death. Is it then unwise to seek the help of Uranus in seeking change? Is that disgraceful? Are we to progress or go retrograde? Are we going on to create a better future, or are we going aback, down the backward scale of evolution, maybe down to monkeys or fish? The future holds hope for the creative mind. The past holds frustration. Which way are we going?

Marriage often holds a purpose. Most any human relationship can have a purpose. The purpose of one marriage may be fulfilled in a year. Perhaps another takes a lifetime. When the purpose of a marriage is served, should the remainder of life be taken up with the funeral procession and the mourning? Should the wails echo night after night? Should life be a perpetual funeral? Should it be made up as a salad of frustration? Where there are children, they must be provided for. They must be educated. They should have love and affection. They should be guided, but can these things be successfully accomplished in a home that is a tomb?

Marriage is not the only human relationship. There are business relationships. Nobody blames a man for switching jobs, bosses or corporations when he can better himself, although even this was not always the case. A man was once looked upon with suspicion if he changed jobs too often. He wasn't steady or stable. He couldn't stick at one thing. The first question asked was "Why did you leave your last job?" If you answered that it was because your former boss was a big, unethical pirate, you wouldn't have much chance of getting a new job, because no other big unethical pirate would want to hire you. To be a businessman in those days, it was pretty well recognized that you had to be a big, unethical pirate. That isn't so long ago. Forty years would do it. All the big unethical pirates have not departed yet.

The marriage institution has not been handled like other human relationships, because of the factor of children. This was justifiable. It can't be handled just the same. You can't quit children like you quit a job, although children often do plenty of suffering under the present setup. It is odd that the 5th House, which represents children (Aries) is in opposition to the 11th House, which represents the higher phases of love and friendship (Libra). Yet, the opposition need not be considered as unfavorable. It brings change. We can't have improvement without change. Ultimately, we should be able to deliver from the abstract world a more perfect design for marriage. The present one is quite faulty. We can't find perfection in anything molded to that design because the design is defective.

As an overall policy bent on the improvement of human relationship, we should look for help from Venus, Jupiter, and at times Uranus. Perhaps we should also look to "Z", ruler of Gemini which we suspect is about 20-Pisces in 1957 and progressing at the approximate rate of a degree in 5.3 years. Our suspicions might be wrong, but we appear to get more and more verification for this suspicion as we continue research on the subject.***

Let us repeat something we said at the outset. If you are to solve problems of human relationships, toss the obsolete rules to the dogs and start thinking for yourself. Toss out everything and start from the beginning. What do YOU think? What do you HONESTLY think? Don't be swayed by us anymore than you think you should. Don't let Moses do your thinking for you, but don't let us do it either. Insofar as astrology is concerned, we think your experience will bear out the astrological conceptions we have presented, but don't stop here. Don't allow our views to become Saturnian crystallization in your mind. Go on from here. Let Uranus, Venus and Jupiter work for you too. Utilize your own God-given intellectual qualities. Improve on our conceptions wherever and whenever you can. We are not like Moses. We are not telling you that this is the word of God. That expression is merely a crutch. The word of God can be misinterpreted and probably always has been, except in the case of those who have discovered beautiful mathematical design in nature, mental and emotional as well as physical natural laws, for these are truly the word of God.

Two years have elapsed since we began writing this Course, and with this 24th lesson, we have completed the originally outlined design. We finished at 10:30 pm MST on September 24, 1957 in Tucson, Az. Sun, Mars and the Moon are all in Libra. With the exception of three of the lessons, they were all written with the Moon in Libra, in order to catch that abstract cosmic design. Jupiter was in Leo when we started, but it is in Libra as we finish.

Lesson Twenty-One

Editor Notes

*Eris was discovered in 2005 outside the orbit of Pluto and is the likely candidate for rulership of Taurus.
**Alimony is uncommon in 2015.
***Eris, possible ruler of Taurus was at 8 Aries in 1957, in 2015 it is at 10 Aries.

LESSON TWENTY-TWO
A SUMMATION UP TO HERE

When we began writing Lesson I, less than ten students had registered for a forthcoming course. As we begin Lesson Twenty-Five, after a gap of six months between the writing of Twenty-Four and Twenty-Five, 360 students are taking the course. If correspondence with the students has not run into tons, it seems that way. Yet, nothing could have been more interesting nor more exciting. Some students traveled so fast they were almost ahead of us. Some bogged down and we want to take up the matter of why.

One student asks this question:

'When you draw up a chart, what is the first thing you look at? This would depend upon what we were looking for. You must bear in mind that one chart could be a life-long study for you. There will always be something more to consider. What we would look at would depend upon what we wanted to know. If a sex problem was involved, we would first look at the condition of Mars, Venus, Sun and Moon in the chart. We would want to see in what signs they were placed and the aspects to these planets, because this is very basic. We would go on from there.

If a health problem were involved, we would first want to see what kind of afflictions there were in the chart. We would want to see in what signs they were placed and the aspects to these planets, because this is very basic. We would go on from there.

Of course, there is this difference. Every time we look at a chart, we have a reason. That may be different with the newer student. He may merely have drawn up a chart to see what it looks like. Under those circumstances, he may not have a good starting point. Nevertheless, he has some relationship to the person involved, and that will probably give him a starting point. Perhaps it is the chart of the President of the United States, and perhaps he just wants to know what kind of a president he is going to make. In that case, there is a life-long study, and you can start anywhere.

Quite often, someone writes in and asks, "Would I be good in the study of astrology?" What do we look for?

We like to see Air Signs occupied, because the Air Signs are intellectual, meaning that they can better visualize the abstract. We like to see a well-aspected Neptune for the practitioner, because there is sympathy, understanding, and the ability to understand other people's subjective problems. We like to see the Fire Signs occupied because they help one to let go of dogma and old, faulty ideas and conceptions. We like to see a good Jupiter because it gives the desire to gain greater knowledge and wisdom. One of our best students has Moon conjunct Jupiter in the first house. She never stops asking questions, but she went through the course like a rocket and already holds down the job as editor of one of the astrology newsstand products. Quite often we are asked, 'Why don't you just select the students who would make the best astrologer, having the best charts for it'?

Our reply is, 'Would you teach people to read only if they have good charts for it?' We have to teach all people to read. It would be a lot easier for those teaching if this policy was not followed, but we have to teach all people to read. The writer has Sun, Mercury, Mars, Moon, Saturn and the lunar nodes in Earth signs. In his early days, visualization of the abstract was most difficult. He flunked algebra in his first year of high school. Yet, he proved that such a problem can be overcome. He went to the other extreme. However, during his first year studying astrology, an astrologer told him, "You find it very difficult to grasp anything connected with the abstract. You think in terms of the material, but if you can break the barrier, you are the very person who will master the abstract and bring it down to Earth where it will be useful." The writer never forgot that statement. He carried it around with him. That is one reason why he wants to help the Water and Earth signs to break the barrier, because when they do, they will be the most practical of all in what they do with their abstract knowledge.

There is nobody who isn't helped by knowing how to read. There is nobody who cannot be helped by knowledge of astrology. One thing that our experience has brought home to us in no uncertain terms is that people with Capricorn planets have the most difficulty in visualizing what we are doing, but these people should take hope from the fact that the writer himself has two planets in Capricorn. In early life, they were responsible for a lot of frustration, but we broke the barrier there too. It can be done! Principally, you have to learn how to let go of things. If you are standing, holding onto a telephone pole, you have a choice. You cannot walk up to street without letting go of that telephone pole. Some people won't let go of some old relationships. Some people just won't let go. They always fear the consequences. The Earth signs is actually the engineer. He may not be the one who discovered the principles that make it possible to build a cantilever bridge, but he is the fellow who applies the principles and builds the bridge. Perhaps he doesn't remember any of the formulas, but he knows how to look them up in a book and apply them. Nevertheless, too often, the Earth and Water signs can see only one road, when there are many roads.

Back to the question of what we look at first. If we had no definite thing we wanted to know, we would probably look at the Ascendant first. We would look to see the sign and house position of the planet that ruled the Ascendant, and we would want to see what aspects were affecting that point. We would be particularly interested in any planets that were near the Ascendant. This part of the chart would have to fit what we saw with our eyes.

A lady just entered the office. She stated that according to her birth time she had Gemini on the Ascendant. We looked again. Gemini on the Ascendant is almost sure to give what is sometimes called an inquisitive nose, one somewhat shaped like a bird's beak, it protrudes. This can be altered by planets near the Ascendant. Mars was in Gemini, but this person didn't look like Mars either. She was very reserved in manners and appearance. She was stocky. Her neck was short. These were all physical characteristics that we associate with Taurus rising. Before saying so, the writer put one question to her. "Would you consider yourself stubborn?" She laughed and then said, "Well other people think I am."

That satisfied us. Taurus is the sign before Gemini. Her birth time, like most birth times, was probably recorded late. She had all the characteristics of Taurus rising. She had no planets in Taurus. There wasn't anything else in the chart to give this appearance.

Next, we would turn to the position of the Sun and Moon in the chart. We would study them by sign and house position, and always remember what we have told you before. **The sign conditions the planet and what the planet rules or represents, but the planet conditions the house and what the house rules or represents.**

Now we turn to Mercury. It can be a key to the mentality, not the intellectuality, but how a person unconsciously things and goes about things. Here is the chart that has Mercury in exact opposition to Neptune. There is mental confusion. The person is apt to see what never exists for other people, 'little people,' ghosts, or he may hear voices. There is danger of psychological difficulties. He should always guard against the possibility of a nervous breakdown.

The next chart has Mercury exactly square Saturn. There is the danger that he might become a depressive. When he is down things can look mighty bad. Pessimism can take over. He will become very critical. If he gives in to this psychology, or if somebody doesn't help to get him out of it, his depression will become a mental block that will completely blind him to all opportunities. He will interpret everything as bad news. If he gets one piece of good news, he may go too far in the other direction. He may become overly optimistic but only temporarily so. Depression will soon take over again.

Venus will give us a key to the kind of people a native of a chart likes, the kind of people of both sexes to whom he is naturally attracted. Earlier, we asked each student to write an interpretation of what Venus-in-Capricorn means. We had some wonderful interpretations, but some had trouble in grasping the idea of analytical interpretation. Let's go into this interpretation a little now.

Venus is the symbol of the Family Non-Survival Dynamic Guide. By itself, it is trying to attract to members of the opposite sex for the purpose of having children and improving the family strain. How will it go about this? In what way will it improve the family of the future over the family of the past?

Capricorn represents the Individual Survival Dynamic Reactor. Capricorn is always concerned with possible consequences. It always fears possible consequences. It is trying to contain the Individual Survival Dynamic. It involves the same insecurity found in Cancer, but it fears the consequences of allowing the Individual Survival Dynamic to manifest openly. It fears starvation. It will accept frustration rather than take chances. It's ideas of improving the family is to be attracted to people who have money or wealth. It wants to marry into a family of better financial standing. Venus-in-Capricorn will marry for money and prestige rather than for love. Unconsciously, of course, it is more bent on improving the financial status of children-to-be than in improving biological design. Orthodoxy is to be accepted. It is better not to marry or to have no children than to have them starve. Social customs must not be violated. The parents and the ancestors must be respected. The wife with Venus-in-Capricorn will submit to the wishes of all in-laws in order to be accepted and a part of that family. Frustration is a key word. It is subconsciously believed that this is the safe way.

We so often find men having Venus-in-Capricorn married to professional women, teachers, doctors, stenographers, etc. It is not hard to see why. These women can earn their own way. They are not to be regarded as burdens. It is financially safer to marry such women. The economic side of the picture is always foremost. Marriage is intended to improve the economic situation for the family of the future.

A woman with Sun in Pisces and Venus-in-Capricorn complained about a daily astrological column that told Pisces people to do what they wanted to do on a certain day. She considered this an immoral bit of advice, because to her, to do what she wanted to do meant to hold a sex orgy. The lady was in her 70's. All of her life she had lived a life of frustration, but when somebody told her to do what she wanted to do, she was shocked, because, to her, this meant to hold a sex orgy. As Dr. Worden has pointed out in the Student Forum, Pisces is the female side of the sex principle. The pattern of the lady's inner self is thus revealed by her interpretation of the advice, "Do what you want to do."

One student writes in, "How do you conclude that Venus-in-Capricorn equals Saturn in the 11th House?" We have covered this point, but it is very important, because it is the basis of analytical interpretation.

You must remember that when a planet is in a zodiacal sign, the sign conditions that represented by the planet, but when a planet is in a house, the planet conditions that represented by the house. In other words, **planets in the houses operate the reverse to planets in the signs**.

In Capricorn (8th), Venus (11th) is subdued by Capricorn or the Saturnian principle. In the 11th House, Saturn (8th) subdues everything represented by the 11th House, and causes one to be attracted to Saturnian people. You must remember that while the zodiacal sign conditions that represented by the planet therein, the planet conditions that represented by the house it is in. Let us have a table to illustrate this point where Venus is concerned:

Planet	Sign		Planet	House
Venus	Cancer	=	Moon	Eleventh
Venus	Leo	=	Sun	Eleventh
Venus	Virgo	=	Mercury	Eleventh
Venus	Libra	=	Venus	Eleventh
Venus	Scorpio	=	Mars	Eleventh
Venus	Sagittarius	=	Jupiter	Eleventh
Venus	Capricorn	=	Saturn	Eleventh
Venus	Aquarius	=	Uranus	Eleventh
Venus	Pisces	=	Neptune	Eleventh
Venus	Aries	=	Pluto	Eleventh
Venus	Taurus	=	"X" Eris	Eleventh
Venus	Gemini	=	"Y"	Eleventh

You can make up a table for each planet on the same basis. Note that the zodiacal sign mentioned to the left of the equation is always ruled by the planet mentioned to the right of the equation. These tables could be made up in another way.

Planet	House		Planet	Sign
Venus	First	=	Sun	Libra
Venus	Second	=	Moon	Libra
Venus	Third	=	"Z"	Libra
Venus	Fourth	=	"Y" [Eris]	Libra
Venus	Fifth	=	Pluto	Libra
Venus	Sixth	=	Neptune	Libra
Venus	Seventh	=	Uranus	Libra
Venus	Eighth	=	Saturn	Libra
Venus	Ninth	=	Jupiter	Libra
Venus	Tenth	=	Mars	Libra
Venus	Eleventh	=	Venus	Libra
Venus	Twelfth	=	Mercury	Libra

In other words, when the student has learned the meaning of Venus in Capricorn, he does not have to learn the meaning of Saturn in the Eleventh House, because the meaning is the same as Venus in Capricorn.

To some extent, a conjunction of Venus and Saturn would be similar to Venus-in-Capricorn or Saturn in the Eleventh House, except that the whole configuration would then be dominated by the additional factor of the zodiacal sign they occupied. Any aspect between Venus and Saturn would carry some of the qualities of Venus-in-Capricorn or Saturn in the Eleventh House.

These factors enable you to make short cuts in learning astrology. If you know how to multiply 47623 by 85905, you can multiply any other two numbers. You follow the same system of multiplication. Any abstract principle applies anywhere anytime. Neither time nor space is a factor in the abstract world. When you study cases of people with Venus-in-Capricorn and compare their characteristics, you can go right on and compare people who have Saturn in the Eleventh. For example, here are two girls who married into wealthy families and whose husbands later inherited money. One has Venus-in-Capricorn, the other has Saturn in the

Eleventh House. This does not necessarily mean that all girls with these configurations will marry into wealthy families. There will be other factors in the individual chart to consider. In some cases, there may be no marriage. Here is a lady who was born with Venus conjunct Saturn in Capricorn in the Seventh House. Three times she married. Three times her husband died. Three times she inherited relatively small amounts of money. She was very fatalistic about this. It was fate. She told this to Nick deVore, the astrologer. He burst out laughing and said, "Why you wouldn't consider marrying a man unless he was on his last legs." There is also the additional factor that such a person can be so psychologically and emotionally dependent on the partner that the partner's life may be shortened from strain.

Going back to our tables, although the principle on one side of the equation is exactly the same as on the other side, there can be the differences that in the case of the planets in the houses, expression can be more outward and more physical. Venus in the First House can have more affect on personal physical appearance than Sun in Libra, where the expression lies deeper. Yet, the principle is identical.

A common question asked by student is, "What happens when one aspect in a chart indicates one characteristic and another aspect represent just the opposite characteristic?" We often run up against this. One tends to offset the other where physical expression is concerned. One day, the native may express one side of the nature, while on another day the other side of the nature is expressed. The transiting planets can be the factor that will upset the balance, but in addition, the native will have an inner conflict, and a stress pattern can develop. We think of a man who had Venus conjunct both Saturn and Uranus. He was married five times. On one day he would look forward to some new love. On another day he would burst into tears about an old love. If Venus by transit was involved with Uranus, he would be looking forward. If Venus by transit was involved with Saturn, he would be looking backward. On one day he saw virtue in the future. On another day he would see virtue in the past.

One student writes, "Will you give me a step-by-step procedure for predicting my own future?" That question seems to almost automatically assume that the future is fixed and that nothing can change it. The student may not mean it that way. We might re-word the question as follows, "Will you give me a step-by-step formula for approaching the abstract pattern of the future as it relates to me?"

The writer would usually start with the outermost know planet. You can experiment with the theoretical position of "Y" and "Z: as published in the Student Forum if you want to. Otherwise, you can start with transiting Pluto and come in to Mercury, Sun and Moon. Take them one at a time. In each case, the first thing to determine is what, if anything, a given planet is doing to the birth chart being examined? Is it in aspect to planets in the chart? Is it crossing a house cusp?

The slow-moving planets are more important because a greater interval of time is involved in the crossing. A stationary planet is more important for the same reason. The slower the motion of a planet, the more likely are you to observe an outer manifestation.

Next, the more planets that are involved the greater result may be expected. For example, two planets at a cusp are far more important than one, and this could possibly operate on a geometrical rather than on an arithmetical basis. That is, two planets might be four times as important as one, because four is the square of two. Three planets might be nine times as important as one, because nine is the square of three. As yet, a method of division these that would determine whether this geometrical importance might exist has not been developed. It is interesting to note, however, that RCA research into the connection between planetary configurations and terrestrial magnetism brings out the same conclusion s that we have made. The more planets involved in a configuration the greater results may be expected where terrestrial magnetic displays are concerned.

If slow moving planets are in aspect to each other, that means that if one of these planets is on a cusp of the horoscope, the other planet is also on a cusp. This becomes far more important. Allow the writer to take a case from his own life. In 1925, Uranus crossed his Fourth cusp at 22 Pisces. Neptune crossed his Ninth cusp at 22 Leo. Jupiter crossed his Second cusp at 22 Capricorn. Saturn opposed his natal Sun. The writer was only 23 years of age. He was in the insurance business, but he also owned a weekly newspaper on Long Island. Most of his clients were large corporations. During the first six months of the year, he lost 16 such accounts through death of individuals or bankruptcy of corporations. Don't forget that in Capricorn, Jupiter is under the domination of Saturn. The newspaper was discontinued because of lack of funds. The situation appeared to be desperate.

In June the writer met Lewis J. Selznick, pioneer of the motion picture business, father of David and Myron Selznick. Selznick was putting together a group to start a motion picture city of the east in Florida. A private car was to leave with the party on June 30th. The writer was extended an invitation to go along—all expenses paid. He was told that he would have to accept or decline within 24 hours.

There was a mental struggle. However, he decided to go. On the train, he met David O. Selznick for the first time. At Jacksonville, he met Myron Selznick for the first time. Myron had come directly from California to Jacksonville joining the rest of the party there. At Jacksonville, we were the guest of Mayor John Alsop. We lingered for a day, arriving in Miami on July 4th, 1925.

First, note that with Jupiter in Capricorn at the Second cusp, the old business was failing. With Neptune at the Ninth, the writer was traveling. Neptune has always been associated by astrologers with the moving picture business. Neptune has also been associated with booms and financial bubbles. The Florida boom was reaching its apex. With his family, the writer had moved from Long Island to New Jersey on May 31st. Uranus had actually crossed the writer's Fourth cusp (home, real estate, etc.) and at that time the new home was purchased by the family. Sale of the old one followed in July. Here was a change of residence, but within a month, the writer left for Florida, not to return. For the next year, he lived in hotels.

Broke in June, in July, the writer purchased a half million dollars worth of real estate near Olympia, north of Palm Beach. This was accomplished with the money of three new partners who did the financing. In August, he had an opportunity to take an $80,000 profit, but his older partners voted him down.

In September, although it took a year for folks to admit it, the Florida boom had reached its apex and was on the way down. About that time, the writer met Marjorie Daw, motion picture actress who later married Myron Selznick. It was Marjorie Daw who first interested the writer in astrology. Here was one of the greatest turning points in the writer's life. This meeting with Marjorie Daw resulted in the writer beginning his investigation of astrology in April 1926. Here was Neptune at his Ninth House cusp, ruling religion, science, travel, etc. His whole conception of religion and science was altered by these events. Until that time, he had been somewhat of an atheist, or perhaps agnostic would be the better word. Despite the fact that astrology was in a very chaotic and Neptunian condition at that time, the writer began to see the beginning of a pattern, and from then on, he was hard to work, and that the supposed mathematical laws of probability were open to serious questioning.

1925 was a busy year. In October, the writer was married. Still fascinated by the so-called element of luck in life, he lost $1,200 in a poker game on the night of December 31st, 1925 and January 1st, 1926. He lost a total of $3,000 during the week. Nothing would go right. WHY? It was important to fine out WHY. It was necessary to find out WHY. Everything was closing in again.

At some other time, a fellow might not listen to such claptrap. But, there was that night in January 1926, when Marjorie Daw,

Myron Selznick and the writer sat up most of the night arguing. Marjorie claimed that astrology had the answer. She related personal experiences with astrology that were hard to believe. Well, noting else was working. Florida was getting ready to fall apart. People were leaving and going back north. Later the banks began to fail. Jupiter was now in Aquarius. On April 15th, 1926, the writer gave up and headed back for New York. Jupiter hit 22 Aquarius, the writer's Third natal cusp, and he bought about every book on astrology that Brentano had to sell.

What should the writer do now? He looked to his own horoscope to find out and decided to go back to writing, but to investigate astrology and write about it. Some of the next six years were very frustrating ones. Who would buy an article on astrology? There were no astrology magazine except little ones with a hundred or two hundred circulation, and they didn't pay for articles. Nevertheless, writing for nothing was better than not writing at all. In the winter of early 1932, with Jupiter on his Ninth House cusp, and Saturn on his Second cusp, the writer sold his first article on astrology for $25.00. It was the beginning. There had been many other business ventures during that six year interval, and at some times the writer was handling very large sums of money in the stock market, but his one aim was to write on astrology, and any other matter was secondary and temporary.

The real point is, look at 1925. The pattern of the past fell apart, but it was necessary to go on with the future and not live with the past. Had it not been for the so called bad luck of 1925, it is doubtful whether the writer would ever have been steered into astrology, although some other similar period might have brought it about, but there was Marjorie Daw with an answer at just the right time.

The next point is, getting back to our starting point, it is multiple planetary aspects that get results, whether they are good or bad, whether you interpret them as good or bad. Multiple aspects mean that things happen. Things might not have taken as spectacular a course had not Uranus been at the Ascendant at the time of birth, or had not Jupiter, the writer's ruling planet been in the sign of Uranus, Aquarius.

"All right," says an imaginary student at this point, "when you see and calculate the transiting aspects, how do you know what is going to happen?" An excellent question! Here again, the same principles that we have discussed before will apply. You have to start with simple cases and build up.

Let us say that transiting Venus goes over natal Saturn in

your chart. What sign is Venus in? Let's say it is in Capricorn to make it more Saturnian. Venus represent, among other things, social matters, associations with the opposite sex, etc. it also represent symmetry, art, mathematics. It isn't likely to have much to do with mathematics if you have no interest in mathematics at that particular time. Social matters are more likely to be involved. It could attract you to an older person, perhaps an older person of the opposite sex. It could cause you to seek 'maturity' in others. An old friend might turn up. It might be accompanied by the death (Saturn-Eighth House) of a friend (Venus-Eleventh). However you may be able to see no visible effect whatsoever, because usually the aspect is over very quickly. It can make a big difference if a lot of other aspects are operating at the same time, or if Venus happens to be stationary so that the aspect lasts a considerable time, giving other planets more opportunity to come along.

Instead of transiting over Saturn, suppose it is going over natal Uranus. The effect would be the reverse. There would be no interest in old friends, no interest in so-called maturity. Interest would be in the new and different. There might be vital and instantaneous attractions to newly met people, perhaps a member of the opposite sex. There is interest in life, younger people, not old ones. Instead of attraction to an older person, it would be more likely to be a dynamic or younger person.

You always have to consider other factors in the chart. A Venus transit over natal Uranus would not have the same effect if the person had Venus in Capricorn, Venus conjunct Saturn, or Saturn in the Eleventh House at birth. You have to compare conflicting actors and weight them in your mind.

In all interpretations, you must consider the positive and negative factors, considering Fire and Air Signs, the planets ruling them, and the odd houses (First, Third, Fifth, Seventh, Ninth, Eleventh) as positive, and the Water and Earth signs, the planets ruling them, and the even houses as negative. Always associate the positive factors as involved the future, new beginnings, patterns of the future, etc., while considering the negative factors as involving the past, attachments to the past, undigested factors of the past, that of which people are unable to let go. Emotional problems always involve the inability to digest the past, or inability to let go of it. Most health problems involve the same thing. However, whenever considering a health problem or an accident, try to find the purpose that is being served by the accident or the illness. Some purpose (not a good one) is being served.

Studies outside the field of astrology have indicated that

accident-prone people may not appear to be the cause of their accidents. The other fellow often appears to be the one who makes the mistake. Things just happen to accident-prone people, but they happen again and again. Let's look at a case that comes up at this moment. It is in a letter. No birth data is given, but let us just look at the circumstances. A man has been an economic failure for years. He can't get along. He starts across the street. A taxi is coming. He stops. The taxis stops and the driver motions him to cross. The pedestrian does so. For some reason that no one has ever been able to explain, not even the taxi driver, his foot pushed the accelerator. The car shot ahead and struck down the pedestrian. The taxi driver admits fault. The taxi company accepts responsibility. The pedestrian finds a way of making some money.

The illness of a woman is often an unconscious means of getting the attention and pity of her husband. People wait on her. The healthy person wants to be independent, does not want others giving assistance. Others welcome this help, and get sick. The person who refuses the help of others is often opening the door that will bring forth the vitality that will overcome disease and open up the mind. Disease is more apt to take hold when you give in to it. And it is less apt to take hold when you do not need it to accomplish some objective. All of these statements are relative, of course. There are many unknown angles to a such discussion. After being in the filed of astrology for more than 30 years, however, it is impossible not to observe these things. It would be the writer's judgment that perhaps he has been able to help the most people over the years when he has been able to convince them that they should let go of the past and go on with the future. The average person who is having economic problems is hanging onto something from the past and won't let go. It is perhaps an unexplainable fact that the moment they let go of the past, opportunity appears ahead of them. The person who can find no opportunities in life is usually a basically insecure person. He is hanging onto something because his subconscious has ignorantly identified it with security. Rob Hubbard [Church of Scientology] would say that he has an engram. An engram is an erroneous equation that has been accepted as fact by the subconscious. It may say, 'Mother=Security,' in which event, the intellect is blinded by the equation. Here is a woman who, at the age of 60, becomes seriously ill because her mother died. Life without a mother is unbearable, because the mother is still subconsciously identified with security.

One was very young. He was the writer's then 8-year-old son. He had been watching many western movies, and for a year he had been pestering his father to move to Arizona. Nevertheless, for the writer, it was letting go for the past and the opening up of completely new horizons. His thinking became clearer. Mental blocks were removed. More of the abstract world was visible.

This principle goes much farther. Society's greatest handicap is its inability to let go of the past, its insecurity. It is afraid to throw away its old textbooks. The most insecure people of all are its educators. They become school teachers because it seems a safe way to make a living. They want to be assured that they can't lose their jobs for anything short of first-degree murder. They want social security. They bow to whomsoever happens to be the momentary authority. They teach what the recognized authorities want taught. They question nothing except the new. It seems restful not to have to change anything, not to have to face change. Society hangs on to the old religions. Nothing about them is to be changed. There must be faith in the old. Until recent years, the Chinese and the Japanese worshiped their ancestors. The Japanese emperor is supposed to be the direct descendant of the Sun god. Christians and Jews turn to the commandments of Moses. It was a long time ago that those laws were originated, but they are still looked upon as wisdom. Orthodoxy constantly fights anything in the way of change and improvement. Orthodoxy is insecurity. They are one and the same thing. We have an insecure man like Martin Gardner, in his book, *Fads and Fallacies in the Name of Science*, classifying men like Thomas Edison, Nicola Tesla, Luther Burbank, Roger W. Babson and Ron Hubbard as pseudo scientists who didn't stick to orthodoxy. It would have been more secure to stick to kerosene lamps. Gardner tries to discuss Charles Fort and his writings, tries to classify him as a pseudo scientist, finally admits that Fort may have been right, but then tells, us, 'but that sort of thing is dangerous." It might be well to read this book, just to see how far orthodoxy and insecurity can go, but after you have read the whole book, go back and read the dedication, and you'll have the answer to the whole book. You will see that a very insecure person wrote it. The dedication reads, "To my Father and Mother." There you have the answer. Here is a man who is completely unable to digest and break away from the past. He is still thinking in terms of his father and mother.

LESSON TWENTY-THREE

WHAT IS THE ABSTRACT WORLD?

It might be well to explain how the title of this lesson came about. In reading letters from students for two-and-a-half years, the writer realized for the first time that there are a great many people who do not know what the word abstract means. During that interval, the writer also had it brought home to him that even in the field of mathematics, which is complete abstraction, many persons teaching mathematics do not have any clear conception of what this word abstract means. Outside of certain fields of endeavor, a very large ratio of the academicians do not have a clear conception of what the abstract world implies.

About six months prior to the May 1958 convention of the American Federation of Astrologers, the writer agreed to speak at this convention. Ernest Grant, Executive Secretary of the AFA wrote and asked him for the title of his talk, so that it could be listed on the program. Because of the afore-mentioned facts, he selected the title, 'What Is the Abstract World?' He had not given the matter too much thought, and didn't attempt to. The talk was scheduled for the afternoon of May 27th.

For a week prior to that date, an assistant wanted to know what this talk was to be about, and the writer replied that he would decide that when he stood on his feet to deliver the address. Until that moment after a very flattering introduction by Howard Duff, the writer had no plan. The talk was delivered extemporaneously. Much of what he said is already familiar to our own students.

A few weeks later, Ernest Grant again wrote and asked for a copy of the talk for publication. This was impossible. Only in a general way does the writer know what he said. Yet, many people came to the writer later to ask further questions, which brought about the realization that this was a subject upon which much more should be stated.

It should be realized that when we speak of the abstract world, we speak of abstract, verifiable truth, not some product of the imagination. In the field of art, among some artists, the word abstract is employed in connection with products of the imagination that have no counterpart in nature nor in the abstract world of truth. There IS a world of abstract truth. It is a verifiable world. It is the world that is explored by the mathematician. A mathematical theorem is an abstract truth. This does not mean that some scientific theory is an abstract truth. Most such theories fall by the wayside as we learn more. Although some consider them useful and necessary as a temporary bridge toward progress, they are often mental blocks. You must realize that much of Einstein's work is to be considered as theory rather than as abstract truth. Time and more facts might prove some of it wrong.

We must distinguish between abstract truth and all other realms of knowledge. A very large ratio of what is taught in school, colleges and universities must be excluded when we talk about abstract truth. Let us supply an example of abstract truth. We supplied one earlier when we discussed the Pythagorean theorem. Let us select a relatively simple one. We can say that no matter how many numbers are multiplied together, the result will not be divisible by five unless one of those numbers is five or is divisible by five.

Suppose you were given 100 numbers, told to multiply them together and see whether the answer is factored by (divisible by) five. This would be a lot of work. It isn't necessary. Just check each of the 100 numbers and see whether any one of them ends in 5 or 0, which would mean it is factored by five. If it does, the answer is divisible by 5. If it does not, the answer is not divisible by five. On the other hand, no matter how many numbers you multiply together, if one of them is five or if one of them is divisible by five, the ultimate answer has to be divisible by five.

This is a very simple truth and one that you should be able to understand. If you don't grasp it, merely try a few numbers and see whether you do not understand why. You can readily see that if you multiply five by any one number, you can divide the answer by five, because you are merely reversing the process. If 5 x 7 = 35, then 35 divided by 7 = 5. No matter what number you multiply by 35, the answer must be divisible by 5. For example, if we multiply 35 by 9, we get 315, and we can divide 315 by 5 to get 63, which is merely 7 x 9, the two numbers we had already multiplied by 5.

To some of you, this may seem very elementary, but the most involved and complicated looking mathematical theorems are just as simple truths once you have grasped them.

When you free yourself of emotionalism and mental blocks, all sorts of abstract truths may become apparent to you. The genius is usually a person whose mind starts wandering in these abstract realism, where he is likely to discover all kinds of short-cuts. Some people have to make material counterparts of abstract things in order to understand them, but in time these people can overcome this as

Lesson Twenty-Three

things become clearer to them.

Nevertheless, it is possible to make mistakes here as elsewhere. You might write out a theorem that you think is true, but you may have overlooked something. Theorems have to be proved analytically.

Let us take a classic example of analytical proof. There was the question as to whether there is any limit to prime numbers or whether they go on to infinity. A prime number is one that cannot be divided by any number other than 1 and itself, like 3, 5, 7, 11, 23, 31, 101. Euclid furnished proof that prime numbers are unlimited and go to infinity. How did he do it?

In effect, he said, 'Let us assume that there is a highest and last prime number, and let us multiply that number by all lesser prime numbers. We will have an answer that is divisible by every KNOWN prime number. Let us call that answer X. Now we will add 1 to that number. This new number (x plus 1) cannot be divisible by any of the known primes by which we have multiplied. Therefore, it is either prime or divisible by some other unknown prime, and our assumption that there is a last prime, or any limit to primes, is unfounded.'

Let us simplify this. This rule would work anywhere toward infinity, but let us apply it in a little way. Let us assume that we know of only three primes--2, 3, and 5. Multiplying these together (2 x 3 x 5), we get 30. We add 1 and we have 31.

Since 30 is divisible by 2, 3, and 5, the next smallest number that will be divisible by any of these primes is 32, because we would have to add one of these primes to obtain such a number:

$$30 \text{ plus } 2 = 32$$
$$30 \text{ plus } 3 = 33$$
$$30 \text{ plus } 5 = 35$$

We have two gaps, 31 and 34, but 34 can be filled in by 30 plus 2 plus 2 or 2 x 17. 31 is either prime or divisible by some unknown prime.

Here we have an absolute proof of something, but it is purely abstract truth and has dealt with nothing but abstractions.

Suppose we had gone about it another way. Suppose we had just gone along testing each number to see if it is divisible by any smaller number. This would be a slow and laborious process that would never end, because there would always be another number to test, and this would go on to infinity. This shows you the advantage of analytical proof.

We simplify everything when we tell you that the abstract world is a world of design. It is invisible design, invisible to the eye but not to the mind. The abstract can be contacted only with the mind. Mathematics is merely study of the design of the abstract world. A mathematical theorem is merely a design. The great mathematicians have always called these designs beautiful. They have experienced the greatest pleasure and ecstasy mingling with them mentally.

From a material viewpoint, in astrology, aspects, houses and signs are non-existent, for they are complete abstractions. There is nothing material there. They are all mere mathematical points, but mathematical points are vital in many sciences.

It is important to realize, fully realize, that nothing ever happens in the material or physical world except in strict accord with the design of the abstract world. An airplane will never fly unless it is built in accord with certain abstract principles. A gasoline or an electric motor runs only because Man has discovered certain such principles and is employing them. After you discover these principles, you can employ them. Next, you must realize that there are certain things that you may have feared all your life which could never happen to you because they are not in accord with the abstract design of the universe.

Seeing into the abstract world is merely the development of a habit. Many people never learn to see into the abstract world. There is a barrier that has to be broken, but once broken, you are in. All truth is before you at all times if you will but look at it, because it is there in the abstract

Now, here is a great difficulty. People attempting to look into the abstract world see inaccurately or see what is not there. Imagination distorts everything, and they see the abstract as you might see yourself in one of those fancy, curved mirrors in an amusement park. You have to be an accurate observer even in the abstract world. That is why mathematicians check each other. If we all look into the abstract world and observe accurately, we must see the same thing. The accumulated knowledge of mathematics is merely what has been verified by accurate observation. Mathematicians are hard-boiled. They do not accept anything without rigid proof. They are the most accurate observers on Earth.

One of the greatest mathematicians of all time was Fermat. He was prolific in discovering mathematical theorems. In fact, he discovered them so fast that he did not bother to write down his proof. All but one of them have been proved by other mathematicians since his death. That one is known as Fermat's last theorem. [Andrew Wiles discovered the proof in 1993]

Considering a, b, and c as representing positive integers (whole numbers—not fractions), Fermat stated that a^n plus b^n cannot equal c^n when **n** is greater than 2.

The Pythagorean theorem shows us that a^2 plus b^2 can equal c^2. We know of an infinite number of such cases such as 3^2 plus 4^2 - 5^2. On the other hand, we know of no case where two cubes made out of positive integers will equal another such cube. Fermat wrote that he had discovered a 'beautiful' proof of this theorem, but that he was too busy to write it down. Nobody has yet been able to find any over-all proof since Fermat's death, although thousands of people, at various times, thought they had it, but others found errors in their mathematical reasoning. That shows how rigid mathematicians are in checking each other.

Stop and realize that with their analytical type of proof, all mathematicians throughout the world are able to agree as to whether any accepted theorem is true or false. Russian politicians may disagree with American politicians, but Russian mathematicians never disagree with American mathematicians as to whether something is true or false. In this respect, see how different we find the world of religion, or the world of any lesser science than mathematics. Even in physics, some proof may be statistical. It is not as reliable as the analytical proof of the mathematicians. Because something has always happened in a certain way is not absolute proof that it always will. No matter how many times the Earth has turned on its axis, that is not proof that it always will.

The theologist speaks of the Will of God and the cosmic plan, but does he know anything about them? We are told about mythological figures of the past, mysterious people who knew all and talked with God, but the great mysteries are not unfolded in any religious writings. They are being unfolded by the scientists backed by the mathematicians. Let us face it, the mathematicians are closer to God than the churches. They have penetrated into God's plan, while the churches are still struggling with the mental blocks of dogma. We call the Russians atheists because they do not accept our religious dogma and our cultist, but God seems to favor the Russian scientists as much as our own. They go further with less. Both the Russian scientists and the American scientists are closer to detecting the Will of God than any of our religious authorities. The best evidence of this lies in the fact that they are changing the world while the churches have been holding it back for centuries with the theme that they already know, or that God will reveal everything in time. If he does, he will reveal it through the scientists, not through the churches. The scientists have conquered the air. They have given us air travel, while the best the church has had to offer is imaginary angels, sort of a cross between a human and a bird.

We are led to believe that the church is needed to teach us morals, but what does the church know about morals? The problem of morals is merely the problem of emotion and human feeling, and these feelings are merely the blind expression of human dynamics, which should be studied exactly as we study physical forces. We conquer physical forces merely by understanding them, learning more about them. We must do the same with human dynamics. The churches themselves have never been able to conquer or understand the emotions, as is evidence by the many religious wars. We see further evidence of church morality in mass prayer for the destruction of the enemy. What greater form of quackery or outright fraud can we find than the promise, for a consideration, of being 'saved?'

We must be very frank and tell you that we have had some students fall by the wayside merely because they insisted on mixing astrology with religion. They take to reading the bible. They forget reality and turn to a world of the imagination. There is much astrological symbolism in the bible, but it has been translated from one language to another by persons who knew nothing about astrology, and its utility has been lost. That is not the way to learn astrology, nor would it be the way to learn mathematics. At best, what is left of the bible is a nebulous document. You don't have to accept mathematical theorems on faith. No one ever asks you to. In fact, it is against the rules to accept them on faith—not everywhere, not in some universities—but among good mathematicians. You have to understand them.

It is true that a great many institutions have taught mathematics through memorizing. This is like memorizing the Ten Commandments. We don't learn by memorizing. We have to understand. Nobody ever became moral by memorizing the Ten Commandments.

The one point that we must drive across to you is that there IS an abstract world. It is a world of invisible design, but one you can see with your mind. It is the design upon which everything material is dependent for its form. It is also the design upon which all human behavior is based. Real happiness is merely knowing about this world and conforming with its design. Misery is the result of seeing the abstract world inaccurately and substituting products of the imagination. That is why we must ever be critical and on our guard against accepting anything that is false, particularly against allowing the false to by-pass the conscious and become accepted in the sub-conscious, from where it will have its own automatic effects upon our behavior.

Nothing has held astrology back more than having people accept astrology on faith. Untruths have been injected and have been re-taught and perpetuated for centuries. It is our objective to make our students critical and hard-boiled about accepting anything they cannot prove to themselves.

When you study the abstractions of astrology (houses, signs, aspects, secondary charts) you are studying the abstract world. When you study mathematics, you are studying the abstract world, except that there are many bad teachers who cannot get this across because they do not know it themselves. To go on and keep learning more and more about the abstract world can prove your greatest pleasure, but more than that, it can give you more and more control over nature. That is what it is doing for science. Compare what science has accomplished in the last hundred years to what was accomplished with religious dogma during the two thousand previous years. This process could be speeded up a billion fold. If we don't do it, the Russians may. They have already come a long way, and they did it with no religious dogma. From far behind us, they caught up to us. It is fortunate that this has made us more conscious of the defects of our educational system.

When we selected the name, the Institute of Abstract Science, we had in mind far more than we have yet been able to reveal. In our world at this time, we have to overcome the fact that society itself makes itself an obstacle. It is our plan to teach more about the abstract world. To do this, we will ultimately launch an entirely new type of a course of mathematics, one that you will understand. The matter has already been under discussion and in the embryo stage for two years. We hope to make it a reality within the next year. We must all know more about the abstract world. Even better health lies in a better understanding of the abstract world, for ill health is merely the non-conformity to abstract truth. Society would have no money problems if it knew more about the abstract world. It could produce whatever it desired. We must let go of other things. we must let go of false gods, and we must plunge into this abstract world, because it IS the will of God.

The more a student of astrology knows about all other science the better, because they all fit together into one. They are all, in their finality, a reaching into the abstract world. Much that is not science has been taught in the name of science. Nowhere do we have a better example of this than in the dogma of the world of organized astronomy, which has often been just as erroneous as any religious cult.

There is nothing in these words that is aimed at the principle of religion, but as we have pointed out elsewhere (Editorial, 'Where Do Science and Religion Meet? – Student Forum, Vol. 1, No.1, May 1957), the road to both science and religion should be through knowledge and intelligence, not through dogma or emotionalism, and the road to one should be the road to the other. Atheism can be considered a dogma just as much as some religious cults. In the mathematical world and in the astrological world, we do find design, and greater knowledge of that design is the key to the conquering of the universe, but not if we are going about it without regard for the interest of others.

Everything depends upon distinguishing the true from the false. If something is 5% true and 95 % false, we must learn about the 5% and toss out the 95%. As a student, you must continually test cases and see astrology at work. If you can find defects, you must expose them.

Astrologers of the last few centuries have not been too scientific. The majority of astrologers of today are not scientific. Instead of learning by their mistakes, they strive to conceal them. Principally, they conceal them from themselves.

A contemporary astrologer recently called on the writer. He outlined what he claimed to be a law of astrology. The writer pointed to a mathematical error upon which his whole superstructure was built. He said, 'But it works for me this way.' He still had faith in the system because he was afraid to let go of it. It didn't work for him. He was merely trying to convince himself. At one point he said, 'But you can't expect me to throw out everything I have learned!'

Yes, **he can make no progress until he has thrown out what he has learned, because what he has learned is untrue.** The great problem with the whole world today is that it has learned so much that is untrue. The next difficulty is that insecurity will not permit people to let go of their untruths. Our best students have usually been new students because they did not have to discard so many untruths. A large percentage of old students are completely unable to part with the dogma they have absorbed in the past. We condemn the Russians and accuse them of teaching untruths, but it will take them longer to catch up with us in this respect than it will take them to catch up in science. The Russians had an advantage in that they did not have to conform to our many varieties of dogma. Unless we are willing to toss out our untruths, let go of them, the Russians and the agnostics will reach God before we do.

The word abstract actually means non-material. The abstract needs no material counterpart for its existence, but the material world exists only in conformity with abstract design. The imagination is not abstract truth. Tt is merely a misunderstanding or a distortion of abstract truth. It is merely a misunderstanding or a distortion of abstract truth. The abstract world never changes, but the material world changes in connection with abstract law as portrayed by the mathematics of the solar system. Right there we have the whole story of astrology. We have the peculiar factor of growth, the mystery of growth. Even growth conforms to abstract law, but the law is permanent. Here, it is wise for us to pause and go back to Kepler and see just what he did that gave him such a place in history.

Kepler was a good mathematician. He studied design everywhere. He believed that the solar system was a design, a functioning mathematical unit. At that time (born December 21st, 1571), it was not known that planets, moons, satellites, comets and other free bodies in space travel in ellipses. For this reason, planetary positions never seemed to quite fit predictions. There was a chaotic factor that nobody could explain. The planets appeared to have a certain independence. They went along doing what they were supposed to do, and then they didn't. Kepler knew that everywhere in mathematics, there is design. Therefore, he was convinced there had to be design in the solar system. If he could find this design, he though he could explain the odd behavior of the planets. He worked on the matter for many years, meeting failure after failure, at times becoming very discouraged and falling into fits of depression.

His argument was that God's world was a perfect cosmic design if you could grasp the design. He believed in a cosmic scheme of things. He was an astrologer. All astrologers of old believed this. He finally found an answer by assuming and testing the possibility that planets travel in ellipses. This gave him his answer. Next, he found that planets sweep out equal areas of an ellipse in equal intervals of time, which explained speed variations. He also found that there was a fixed and definite relationship between the speed of a planet and its distance from the Sun. By learning how long it took a planet to go around the Sun, it was possible to calculate its mean distance from the Sun. By studying irregularities of planetary motion, it was possible to compute the eccentricity of the ellipse.

This changed everything of astronomy and made accurate calculations of planetary and other positions possible. All of this occurred only because Kepler thought in terms of abstractions, abstract mathematical designs. The astrologer thinks in terms of abstract mathematical design. The horoscope is an abstract mathematical design. It has no material counterpart other than the life of the individual. There are no material signs of the zodiac, no material houses in the heavens, no material aspects. These are all pure abstractions. They are all part of the abstract world.–just like numbers are a part of the abstract world. All of these things are non-material, but they are very, very real, and upon them the material is dependent.

We can express the number 24 in many ways. We can say that it is 2 x 12, 3 x 8, 4 x 6, 13 plus 11, 14 plus 10, 15 plus 9, 16 plus 8, 100 - 76, etc. In this way, we could go on to infinity describing what 24 is.

The square of 100 is 10,000. To find that out, all you have to do is keep the 1 and double the number of zeros. Suppose you want the next two squares and don't want to multiply them out. Suppose you want the square of 101 and 102. If you have the square of **x** and you want the square of (**x** + 1), all you need do is add (2 **x** + 1) to the square of **x**. In other words, since 10,000 is the square of 100, we can say that 10,000 plus 100 plus 100 plus 1 equals the square of 101.

Now we have 10,201 as the square of 101, and if we want the square of 102, all we need do is add 10,201 plus 101 plus 1 and 10,404 as the square of 102. This is like understanding the building blocks out of which something is built. If you understand the building blocks and the design by which they are put together, you begin to understand, and then you master.

Lets look at squares another way. So long as you add consecutive odd numbers to all lesser odd numbers, you get squares:

1	=	1	=	1^2
1 plus 3	=	4	=	2^2
1 plus 3 plus 5	=	9	=	3^2
1 plus 3 plus 5 plus 7	=	16	=	4^2
1 plus 3 plus 5 plus 7 plus 9	=	25	=	5^2

No matter how long you keep adding odd numbers you get square numbers. Thus, if you have one square and you want the next square, all you need do is add an odd number. What odd number? That's easy. If you want the next square after the square of 5, the odd number you add is 2 plus 5 plus 1 or 11. Add 11 to 25 and you get 36, which is the square of 6.

Thus, the whole matter is one of abstract design. You can

Lesson Twenty-Three

draw it on a graph or you can just write:

$$(x + 1)2 = x2 + 2x + 1$$

Whenever a mathematician writes out some very complicated mathematical theorem instead of these simple ones, he is merely portraying some design of the abstract world, part of the cosmic design that the theologies is seeking but never finds.

Thus, mathematics is nothing but a study of the abstract cosmic design. **Astrology is merely a specialized phase of mathematics that expresses relationships among concepts**. It is the science of what we call time, for time is merely an expression of relationships. We can only express time in terms of relationships among two or more things or concepts. The concept may be a man or a plan of the future. Quality is a matter of relationships. Thus, we can write an equation of own and we can say that where **T** equals Time, **Q** equals Quality and **R** equals Relationships:

$$T = Q = R$$

The horoscope is merely a mathematical expression of the individual. It involves Time, Quality and Relationships. The character or quality of the individual coincides with Time and Relationships among the various parts of the Solar System. It is no more mysterious than the fact that there exists a fixed relationship between the speed of a planet and its mean distance from the Sun. It is all part of the cosmic design. It is no more mysterious than the fact that the odd numbers all add up to squares if you start at one and include all odd numbers up to any given odd number. Just as there are many mathematical theorems, there are many individual designs where men and women are concerned. From here on, you obtain more complicated designs by adding these designs together, as you do when you compare two horoscopes of individuals, or when you compare the design of one man with the design of a certain moment in the future, which is what you do when you consider transits.

Thus, we repeat that astrology is nothing but a specialized phase of mathematics, but one of the most important phases yet discovered. By comparison, calculus is simplicity itself. Here is the mathematics of human dynamics as well as the mathematics of the human intellect. Here is the mathematics of human dynamics as well as the mathematics of the human intellect. In actual practice, up till now, we have as the mathematics of the human intellect. In actual practice, up till now, we have placed greater emphasis on that phase of astrology that deals with human dynamics than that phase that deals with human intellect, but this is because nearly all people are more conscious of emotion than of intellect. Our next most important step is to teach people to take a greater interest in the intellectual, which means in the abstract design of the cosmos. Physics is covering similar ground, because modern physics is becoming more and more abstract. The laws of mass and energy are being written in the form of mathematical equations. When men understand the equations and formulas, they control matter. When men understand the equations and formulas of astrology, they control themselves, their feelings and ultimately their environment.

We often hear some astrologer say that they find very little effect from the sextile and trine aspects. That is because these aspects deal with the intellectual and with the creative, and many people including astrologers have not learned to live beyond the emotional. They have never been introduced to the intellectual.

The 1st, 5th and 9th astrological principles involve the creative. The 2nd, 6th and 10th astrological principles involve the emotional. The 3rd, 7th and 11th astrological principles involve the intellectual, while the 4th, 8th and 12th principles involve consciousness of consequences of emotion.

The key to the abstract world lies in the 3rd, 7th and 11th principles studied in astrology. This means in the Air Signs. The Air Signs represent the intellect. We have called them the Non-survival Dynamic Guides. They involve understanding the patterns and designs of the abstract world. When you understand these designs, you control everything that is governed by them. And everything is governed by them.

When you go on into this world of the abstract, even if you do not realize it, you are entering the world of mathematics. In fact, you have been unconsciously entering the world of mathematics for a long time, ever since you began this course, back with Lesson One.

We speak of flashes of ingenuity and of divine revelation. These glimpses are merely sudden flashes of the abstract world. You do not have to wait for them. You can enter the abstract world deliberately and according to plan. You have been doing it ever since you began this course. There is no limit to how far you can go.

If we had told you at the start that you were on your way into the world of mathematics, you might not have been too happy about it, because most people have been taught by our lopsided society to fear mathematics. At the age of six, a child is subjected to teachers who begin instilling a fear of mathematics. They never tell the child that they can look into this magnificent world of beauty. They make it appear grotesque, uninviting, a strain. Some of our best students today are people who originally wrote in and said they wanted nothing to do with mathematics. We had to coax them into having confidence in themselves. They have been similar to a child who falls into the water and suddenly finds himself swimming when he didn't think he knew how. Fear of the water keeps many people from ever becoming good swimmers. Fear of mathematics keeps many potentially great mathematicians from ever going near the subject they would love most if they knew what it is and had no fear associated with it.

Every year, science becomes more and more mathematics. Every year, it becomes more and more abstract. The physicist thinks of matter as mass, and his conception of mass is not weight but resistance to change. He thinks in terms of mass and energy, and now he tells us that energy has mass. He writes equations that explain mass and energy in terms of each other, and next he becomes the alchemist and he converts mass into energy.

While the physicist contents himself with formulas involving mass and energy, these formulas being complete abstractions, the astrologer is involved in abstract formulas involving human emotion and human intellect. There are more abstract laws which, as yet, we know too little about. These are the abstract laws of heredity. Astrology functions in accord with these laws. The greatest of all handicaps that we as astrologers must overcome are the limitations of heredity. Our great struggle is to get away from the obsolete designs and patterns of our ancestors. This we must do. The key to this too lies in greater understanding of the abstract world. It helps, to some extent, when we express our willingness to break with our heredity, when we are willing to let go of the past and go on with the future. As Christ put it, 'Let the dead bury the dead.'

We must go on, but to go on, we must know the design. Our whole purpose must be in discovering more and more of the abstract design, more and more about the abstract world. Here is the new frontier. We must be the pioneers who go on into this new world, but we will not be traveling alone, for in every branch of science, men hurry into this new world. Their trips into space come only after their discoveries of what lies in the abstract world.

Are you beginning to have a better conception of what we mean when we talk about the abstract world? Perhaps you are still having difficulty in making the penetration. If so, don't push too hard. Relax a bit. Wait for some very good Venus aspects. Try to make the penetration then. It is Venus that can help us most in this penetration. The more you understand about your own primary and secondary Venus, the better. Venus involves these abstract designs. A little mathematics on the side will always help too. Get to understanding more about the infinite designs involved in numbers. Get to know more about the infinite abstract designs that are involved in all true branches of science. You will find that all of these other designs will ultimately have a definite connection with your study of astrology and your control over yourself and the outside world.

LESSON TWENTY-FOUR

MONEY, PART ONE

In allowing ourselves to accept the old designation of the Second House principle as the House of Money, we perhaps left too much unsaid, and this seems like an appropriate time to return to the subject of money for elaboration.

The Second House, Cancer and the Moon, relate to money only insofar as Individual Survival is concerned. There are much broader aspects involved in the study of money. In some ways, money can be related to all of the astrological principles, but first let us examine what we call money.

All being with the exception of Man survive without money. The invention of money has helped to develop our society, but let us not overlook the fact that we is far more important than money is credit. That is to say that most important of all is confidence, confidence in ourselves and in each other. Money became necessary because of people's lack of confidence in each other. It is also a help in making evaluations which might be very difficult without it.

If you and one other person lived by yourselves on a desert island, it is probably that you could get along very well without money. You could help each other. You could cooperate and trust each other. But, suppose that other person was a very selfish man who was so insecure that he had no interest in you. His only concern would be his own survival. You wouldn't be able to trust him. He would be trying to get you to do more for him than he would be willing to do for you. He would try to outsmart you. Now, would come the first need for something akin to money. He maybe the one to invent it. He may be a superbly insecure Cancer. When you do something for him, he may want to pay you half as much as when he does something for you. Now, money becomes an evil. Inequalities begin to creep in. Each time some new person comes to live on the island, things grow more complicated. Unless you watch out, this very selfish man will soon have all the money. Then he will want to lend to your and collect interest. He will lend you money to survive. He will stop working, expect you to do all of his work in addition to your own, and now you are in a rather bad spot.

Some people are more creative than other people. Those who are not creative begin to live by their wits in order to prey on those who are creative. The burdens of our money system now begin to show. There are some people who are unable to support themselves. This is an additional burden on those who can.

Charles M. Schwab, former president of Bethlehem Steel Corporation was generally looked upon as a very wealthy man. He lived in several homes which cost million of dollars. Yet, actually, Schwab never actually had any money of his own. What he did have was the confidence of other people Others believed in him and in his ability. For that reason, he was always able to borrow very large sums of money. The writer recalls a time when Schwab owned over $6 Million to Boston banks alone. Because he was able to borrow money and employ it in business, he had a very good income, but he spent this as he went along. When he died, and when his debts were paid off, it was discovered that Schwab had no money except that which he owned other people, he left no estate.

One of the greatest evils of our system is inheritance. Let's consider the original John D. Rockefeller. He made his money selling kerosene oil, and as soon as he was in a position to do so, he developed a money-making formula. He was a Sun in Cancer individual. Let us say that we have a small town where there is but one place where you can buy kerosene oil. This oil was very important because it was the only source of light other than candles. In came Rockefeller or his representatives. An attempt was made to buy out the one oil dealer at a very low price, far below value. When the one oil dealer refused to sell, Rockefeller set up shop and began selling oil across the street, but he sold the oil way below his own cost.

The local people liked the original oil dealer. They know he was a man they could trust, but after all, they were economical, and if they could buy oil much cheaper across the street, this man couldn't expect loyalty from them. He had never overcharged them, but here came selfishness. Nearly all the people were sufficiently selfish to think of themselves and their own pocketbooks first. They believed in the so-called law of supply and demand. They believed in taking advantage of a bargain. So, they crossed the street, and they bought their oil from Rockefeller. Actually, although they did not want to see their old friend hurt, they did not have enough community interest to care whether he survived or not if they were going to gain by his non-survival. They felt that self-preservation should be observed as the first, foremost and most important principle of life and its operation. Soon, there was no business for the old oil dealer. He didn't survive. He had to go out of business. Now, there was no competition. There was nobody from whom the citizenry could buy oil except Rockefeller. Up went the price of kerosene oil. It didn't stop at the old price. It was pushed far above that. Rockefeller had the community at his mercy. Whatever price he placed on oil, the town had to pay it or go without oil. The community suffered because of its own selfishness. The Rockefeller fortune grew and grew. He became America's richest man. He exploited the fact that they were too short-sighted to take care of their fellowman, the original oil dealer who had treated them justly. They had no interest in justice if they believed injustice would be to their personal advantage.

When things became sufficiently bad, along came Theodore Roosevelt and his Trust Busting Laws. Prior to that time, however, we saw how a whole community could suffer from its own greed. This is the kind of an evil that the Christina religion has often tried to overcome. The Mormons probably achieved most, because while Mormons have to contribute very heavily to the church, the church assures their economic welfare. They do not allow unlimited greed in their communities. The community interest must come first.

Men like Rockefeller were allowed to leave their assets, not to the community, not to society, but to those of their own designation upon their departure from earthly life.

Meanwhile, the landowners were developing. They had long ago developed in previous civilizations. Many of them had come over from Europe. Land was seized in one way or another, and there was no place for newcomers or the newly born to live unless they acquired land through their parent or ancestors. An unnecessary burden was placed on all poor people. They had to serve the already wealthy and do their work and live a life of frustration under handicaps. Even most of the churches could see nothing unfair about the system. They accepted it and contributed to it, because where else but from the wealthy could they gain the money to build churches?

The principle whereby the money of the deceased goes to those of his choice works a great hardship on the individual who is of poor parents. He has to work that much harder and support those who inherited money and do not have to work. The sanction of slavery was an additional evil, all working to the advantage of those already better off than their fellowman. Lawmakers always gave additional help to the man who was already in the best financial circumstances. He had prestige. He was respected because he had money. He could dictate the laws. The little fellow had no say and didn't know very much about the matter.

Strangers were not welcome in a community unless they had money. People with money were always welcome. There was always the possibility of getting some of it. Even today, the police in many a town will arrest a stranger and charge him with vagrancy if he has no money. Georgia, not long ago, would put such people on the chain gang. In effect, poor people were taught, "Thou shalt not steal." That had come down from Moses. Wealthy people didn't have to steal. They could trick people out of everything they wanted, and the law was always on their side. Trickery was legal and regarded as strictly within the confines of a good Christen doctrine. Study the Ten Commandments some time from the point of view of whom they were supposed to benefit. You couldn't steal from the poor. They didn't have anything to steal. The poor were told that all this was God's Will, this was the way God wanted it. When Moses concocted, "Thou shalt not steal," what remedy did he provide? The poor man was carefully arranged to be at the mercy of the rich man. That has been part of the doctrine from the beginning. A poor man has always been allowed to stay in his community of birth, because there he can be easily trained to submit to the dictates of society, frustrate himself, do what he is told to do and gain a pittance for his services.

There have been many changes. Compulsory education has played a big part. The wealthy still benefit because a trained man is more valuable to them. He can do better work. In spite of all these handicaps, we occasionally see a young man with charm, ambition, vitality and confidence in himself, who can overcome all of the barriers and become wealthy himself from some very insecure start. We see immigrants come into the country penniless and create fortunes within a few years, but some of them have the sharpness, the shrewdness and the selfishness of Europe. They come into a country where people are more easily fooled and tricked.

After this preliminary discussion, the point that we want to drive home deep is that money is only a substitute for confidence. It is a substitute for cooperation. If people had confidence in each other and if they were willing to unselfishly cooperate with each other, there would be no need for money. In the community of the bee or the ant, you see cooperation without the use of money. Yet, money is not an evil except where it is allowed to promote greed. In some communities, the people cooperate better than in other communities. Cooperation is at a very high ratio in Mormon communities, and Mormon communities have grown wealthy. They pulled themselves up by their own bootstraps. Let us face it. Communistic Russia has done the same thing, and now Communist China is on its way.

It is fortunate that the sons of the former industrialists, who inherited fortunes, are more liberal in their thinking, and less greedy. They have not taken advantage of their good fortune to the same degree as their ancestors. They have, in many cases, put their inherited fortunes to good use. John D. Rockefeller, Jr. is a good example. John Hays Hammond, Jr. is another. There are many others. We have more liberal laws, less controlled by the symbols of wealth. We abandoned slavery. We fight for more equal education. Many of the wealthy realize that they can't benefit the poor man without benefiting themselves. They are less insecure than their ancestors, and we must realize that greed and selfishness are merely objective manifestations of subjective insecurity. We can handle the wealthy and the greedy better if we realize they are very insecure people.

Large corporations are today spending vast sums of research in a very unselfish way, and yet, their ultimate benefits are very great. Money spent in this way supports some of our very best minds and allows them to function in a way that all society can ultimately benefit. However, even today, the majority of people do not know the advantages of possibilities of research. They don't even think about it. It is not a part of their consciousness. To a request for cooperation from any source, the average person's immediate reaction is, "what do I get out of it?" These people are more likely to contribute to a church because they believe that God may be watching them from on high, and he may treat them better in the next life, or wherever they think they are going. It is fortunate that the executives of some of our largest corporations are allowing something other than strict green to motivate their policies. They are not like the old corporations. They are becoming prolific in turning out new products to make life simpler and more pleasant. Their contributions to research are making this possible.

Great changes have taken place in the banking business since 1933. The stock market crash of 1929 wiped out a vast number of greedy people and brought into view the evils of the banking business. New laws were passed and some of the older banking practices were no longer permitted. Bank officials were no longer allowed to lend the bank's money to themselves. They couldn't lend money promiscuously to their friends and associates. Bankers were reduced to the level of other people. They could go to jail for fraud, and some of them did. Banks began lending money to the little fellow. He could buy a car and pay for it later, over 30 months. In other words, all we were doing was agreeing to have more confidence in the poor people than we had every had before. Furnishing credit to the little fellow has revolutionized the whole country. Furnishing credit to the little fellow merely means having confidence in the little fellow. Actually, there is more reason to have confidence in him. He is less insecure and he is more honest and reliable. Yet, despite the manner in which the wealthy have gained (because the purchases of the little fellow is what gave us this new business era), we have steady pressure from vested interests that would return to the old ways and take credit and confidence away from the little fellow.* The Eisenhower administration would have changed this long ago if it dared. Take credit and confidence away from the little fellow, and the rich will fall. They'll have no one to exploit.

It is important to realize that money is merely a substitute for cooperation and confidence. Actually, the people least willing to cooperate and have confidence in others are the wealthy. They want everything on the line. They take no chances. They hire lawyers. They are the least secure. Of course, there are exceptions to all such rules.

The labor unions have played a big part in improving conditions, but they have also been victimized by the greedy. When Franklin D. Roosevelt sponsored legislation to improve conditions for the workingman, as Prohibition ended, he allowed all gangsters of the Prohibition days to move across the street and become labor leaders (Neptune in Virgo).

Unconscious fear of a food shortage continues to exist on the subconscious level of society. The cosmic memory has not forgotten cold winters, little food and hard times. The result is that it is more than difficult to get cooperation in this world unless you have money. It is still quite difficult to use cooperation in place of money, because that is something people can't understand. They can't come up out of the rut they are in.

This preliminary discussion seemed necessary before we could get under way with an astrological view of money. First, we have to know what money is, and that when we talk about money, we both mean the same thing. Many of the men who appear to have money today do not actually have it, but they have credit. They can borrow whatever they need. This means that they have people's confidence. With that confidence, they are not in need of money. To one who has lived on both sides of the United States, it is quite apparent that there is a difference money-wise between the East and the West. There is no place where insecurity is as great as in New York and New England. Old European ideas continue to prevail. Although the wealthy in this western area have tried to spread their financial philosophy and have done so to some extent, there is a difference. There is not the cynicism. South of the border, this may be even more true. It is easier to do business in the West because it is easier to gain people's confidence. The stranger is more welcome.

A new innovation that provides confidence is the credit card system. All gasoline companies issue them. The Bell Telephone system issues them. Hotel chains issue them, and now the American Express Company. You can travel through 37 difference countries and not bother to carry any large sum of money with you. Airlines, steamship companies, hotels, restaurants, night clubs, filling stations, department stores and phone companies recognize your credit cards. You have what you want, and ultimately you get a bill. You can step into a telephone booth in 37 different countries, speak to the operator in code, she will dial you any other country you want, and bill you later.

This was regarded by some as dangerous. The world must be coming to an end. They were taught that you must save your pennies, be economical, doubt the other fellow, trim him whenever you can. When the writer was young, in the New York business world, sharp practices were called 'good business' by businessmen.   They were looked upon as a necessary evil. That's the way life was. You were a fool if you were actually honest. Honesty was merely something you preached to the young but not to your own children. You cleansed yourself of your week's sins by going to church on Sunday, and you sang loud enough so God could hear you and know you were there. You assumed that His bad eyesight didn't permit Him to see you the rest of the week.

We hear a great deal today about the national debt. It grows bigger and bigger. It frightens some—those with wealth. They overlook the fact that as the national debt rose, the country grew more prosperous. They overlook the fact that since a new money policy was adopted in 1933 and gold was taken away from everyone, there has never been a major depression. Prior to that time, such depressions were cyclic. But there are those who still believe in a tight money policy, and if they can get their way, we will return to a depression. These people were battling for control for the government every day. They believe that prosperity was never meant for any but the chosen few. To see everyone prosperous is an outrage. [ed. Note that this was written in 1957 and it is now a stark reality in 2008-2015 today as the world experiences The Great Cardinal Climax of 2008-2015 (term by Ray Merriman when Saturn is in Libra, Uranus is in Aries, and Pluto is in Capricorn) when the world economic crisis started in 2008 and the Arab Spring started in 2011.]

The change from the old materialism was largely due to the administrations of Theodore and Franklin Roosevelt.   The materialistic money policy went bankrupt with the stock market crash of 1929, but there is still a large body of people who would have it back. These are the advocates of a tight money policy, and they have their lawyers at work in Washington night and day. They long for the 'good old days' when the big fellow had everything and the little fellow was starving. These same people want to hold the negro down. He might become competition. In the very early days of television, the roofs of Harlem were a network of television aerials. Yet, in wealthy Westchester County, you saw very few. These people were hanging onto their money. These were the insecure people. They stick to the old policy of trying to take money out of circulation, and this is what causes depressions and bad business. The negroes of Harlem were buying TV sets, and that is what was keeping the industry alive. Money could be as free as air if people had confidence in each other. Money is merely a substitute for lack of confidence, and a very bad and ineffective substitute.

A man named Bimson came into Phoenix from the midwest. He became head of a small bank, the Valley National Bank. He had an idea. He wanted to lend money to the little fellow instead of the big one. He said "I would rather lend $500 to ten little men than $5000 to one big man." The result was that he was soon, 'the largest bank the Rocky Mountain States." Phoenix had a bigger bank than Denver. Other Arizona banks followed this lead, and this attitude became an important item in the growth of the state, which was the only state in the nation that did not experience any depression during the 1920-1933 years. Its banks did not go broke as did other banks. When you have confidence, you don't have any run on the banks.

It seems to many an odd circumstance that the more money you owe, the easier it is to borrow. If you have no credit elsewhere, people are reluctant to give you any. This is because they fear you have not learned the lesson of confidence. There are many wealthy people in the country who can't borrow a cent from a bank without collateral that will make it impossible for the bank to lose. Yet, they often lend the little fellow money without collateral. This is because they have found out that they can trust him better than they can trust a man of wealth. They know that if the wealthy man and his lawyers could find a way of trimming the bank legally, they would not hesitate to do so. This does not apply to all wealthy people because some have learn how to exchange confidence with their fellow man.

There is one more unpleasant (to some) detail that we have not reached. To operate on credit, you have to recognize that you have a responsibility to the rest of the world. You can't merely borrow money and spend it. You have to also learn how to utilize your creative abilities in such a way that they are of benefit to others. That is business. You have to face reality. You can't live entirely in a subjective dream world. If you do not have creative ability, then you will have to work for others, and help them to better utilize

Lesson Twenty-Four

their creative ability. Look around you and see the vast number of different kinds of business that exist. Study the classified section of the telephone directory. See the many and varied ways people have found of utilizing their creative abilities for the benefit of others. See the many and varied ways in which people are 'making money.'

Vast numbers of people now work for the government. Actually, this is helpful to the businessman, because they are no longer competitors of his, but they are still customers. We have built up such organizations as the Red Cross, the Salvation Army, community hospitals, etc. Yet, the Old Guard fights all this because it means taxes. Everyday, we read in the papers the statement, 'We must reduce taxes.' Many a businessman does not realize that to change back to the old system would ruin him first. Buying would shrink. He can't afford to have it shrink too much. It can mean the difference between profit and loss to him very quickly. We complain about crime, but we are unwilling spend money to do away with the cause of crime, because it means taxes. The deplorable conditions that exist in our prisons, where we continually turn young men, who have been guilty of some slight error of the rules of an ignorant society, into hardened criminals. We do nothing to help these men become good citizens, because so large a ratio of society is still of the belief that selfishness is our greatest virtue. As we have pointed out elsewhere, society is the real criminal. Those who have been labeled criminals are the victims.

Those who have acquired wealth are very often complete obstructionists to any form of progress and change. They are satisfied with their advantageous position and they fear that any change might jeopardize it. Here again is selfishness and a complete disregard for the welfare of others. Let us see what happened in Russia.

When the Communist government took over the country, there were those wealthy land owners who refused to cooperate with the new government and system. This was the same old policy that we have seen here. It was the insecure Old Guard which is opposed to everything in the way of change. It believed in the old way of life. It believes that money should be retained by the families that already have it. This group were ordered by new laws, not to pay taxes in the form of money, for the government was not thinking in terms of money, but to turn over to the government a certain amount of grain each year. In order to frustrate the new government and create a food shortage, this group did nothing toward raising the demanded extra grain. It made no payment in grain to the government. Stalin was a violent man. He took ALL the grain, left some owners to starve, and shot millions of others. It cannot be said that their policy was successful for them for they paid with their lives. The same thing has happened in Red China.

For hundred of years, it was believed that no economy was sound unless it was based on gold. The gold standard finally failed. It went bankrupt. Gold was taken out of circulation, and nobody knew the difference. Yet, there is still the Old Guard, praying for the day when we can get back on the gold standard and be complete materialists again. We still have some of the Sewell Averys.** Why can't we live and work in the same old buildings? Why do we need new ones? It is a slow process to get rid of these people in a peaceful democracy. We do get rid of them ultimately because they die. Their children are less likely to hold to their ideas. The children are more apt to go with the new crowd. We have the same kind of resistance today in the south to the civil rights program, but it is the old people who resist anything new, except in those families where the old people have been able to indoctrinate the young. Although the men they fought during the Civil War have been dead a long time, there are still a few in some sections of the south who think in terms of damn Yankees. Nevertheless, our educational system, our legislators and our labor unions are being effective in wiping out these fetishes. It is a brutal fact that because the Old Guard can never see the possibilities of a new world, they face murder as a choice in other countries. England holds to her fetishes, her conventions, her traditions, her royalty and its horse-drawn carriages, while the rest of the world watches her empire decline.

Before we consider the astrological phases of money, we must consider these other features. Your horoscope will not act the same in one country as in another. Conditions are different. In a great many cases, the principle reason why one person cannot make a financial success of his life is merely that he has mental blocks. Perhaps he has no incentive because he still believed in the old way of life.

We have had some very interesting experiences with students and their attitude toward money. Actually, the ratio of people who will not pay when they can is very, very small. The majority of people are trying to be honest. We have always been very liberal and lenient with students where their payments were concerned. If they go into financial jams, we tried to help. We extended them further credit, and when they could they paid, but it was not necessary for them to lose time in studying the course. Without a job, a fellow often had more time to study and concentrate on the lessons. His study often helped him to solve his financial problem, because he saw things from a new angle. However, we had a case of a man who worked in an automobile factory, There was a strike. He was temporarily out of a job. He wrote that financial circumstances made it impossible to go on with the course. We sympathized with his circumstances and offered help. We offered to carry him until he was back to work. This thought horrified him. He couldn't grasp the conception that if he improved his knowledge he might be able to hold down a better job and make more money. He was one of those persons who does not realize that educated people are in more demand and can get paid higher amounts for their services and time. This man has mental blocks. He has accepted as fact beliefs which are not true. They are his handicap. Instead of acting in one way or another, he has to sit down and wait. He has to wait for the old job to come back to him. What if it doesn't come back? Another man would be busy with something else. He would be making money elsewhere. It is difficult for many people to break away from their old habits. Life has become a routine, and they have no desire to change it. They fear any change in the routine. Their insecurity causes them to mistake their fetishes for security and hang on for dear life. Nearly all of the problems that people have in this world are merely the result of the acceptance of some false belief.

Another person never gets quality for money expended. The reason is that the desire for a bargain is so great that the individual doesn't investigate and doesn't understand quality. We might say that this person evaluates everything by weight and volume. One reason there has been so much quackery in astrology is because the people judge the work of an astrologer by how many pages he turns out on a typewriter. For so much money, he wants so many pages of material. Quality is ignored. The astrologer who could give him the right answer in a few words is by-passed for someone who knows little or nothing about astrology. This person seeks out the quack and thinks he is putting something over because he is getting more pages of material for less money. He is putting something over on somebody all right. He is putting something over on himself.

We see the same thing in the organized world of astrology. It has always been impossible to get the publisher who makes the most money out of selling astrological publications to spend one penny on research to improve their product. There is a complete reluctance to use scientific methods to improve the product, despite the fact that in all other fields, this procedure is the one that is building new industries and new profits successfully and is changing the world for society at large. The astrologers themselves have been completely unwilling to put anything back into astrology, to even put the efforts of those who are accomplishing something in improving astrology, because these efforts make them feel inferior. Here again is insecurity. They want to keep everything as it has always been. They don't dare put their conceptions to a true and honest test because of their fear of what the consequences might be. They refuse to face reality.

Fear of facing reality is one of the principle causes of many of the financial problems people face. One man could get help for the asking, but he doesn't ask, for he has already assumed that the answer would be no. We have asserted before that we are not interested in predicting the future but in making the future. That is why we have gone through all this preliminary discussion of money. A nationally prominent psychologist recently stated to the writer, "You seem to have found the secret of living out of your own essence." That must be our objective. When considering money astrologically, it must not merely be our purpose to predict when money may arrive more freely, but to find the secret of making money flow, regardless of what external circumstances my be. In the next lesson, which will be the second part of this discussion, this will be our aim. We want to show that almost everything in any chart can have some bearing on money matters. We can't limit money to the Second House, which is related strictly to the Individual Survival Dynamic and Man's subconscious fear that he may starve to death. There are many other considerations. There have to be considerations of money from the viewpoints of family survival and social survival. There also have to be considerations from the viewpoint of non-survival, where non-survival can bring us freedom from the many evils that have become associated with money. Many people could make more money and be more prosperous if they could just sever themselves from all the false conceptions they have accepted. Repeated failure is not sufficient to convince them they are wrong. They live in the hope that a favorable star will solve all their problems and force these failures to turn into successes.

Money involves all of your relations with other people. It involves your association with your family, and it involves your association with society at large. It involves your association with the government. It involves your responsibilities to all. All of your creative powers can have some kind of an association with money. We must not limit ourselves to thinking of money as some material thing, because the world is not run on money as a material quantity. We must think of money in terms of confidence. We must think of it, not as the essence itself, but merely as a symbol and substitute for the essence. We must cast aside the old conceptions of money. They constitute mental blocks. We must go on with new conceptions. We live in a world of plenty. There is more than ample of everything of a material nature. We live in a country that has almost everything,

Lesson Twenty-Four

but we must protect those who are wealthy. They need our help, or we think they do. We have high tariffs so that these people will not be subjected to competition. They are too weak to meet up with competition. They fear the foreign markets of less fortunate people. We cut ourselves off from trade with our neighbors. We high-hat them. Yet, we don't want those neighbors to trade with Russia or Red China. We will even give them a few handouts, but we don't want the rest of the world to progress.   Instead of allowing them to prosper and thus increasing our own prosperity at the same time, we want them to stay as they are. We want them to accept their poverty as a gift from God and not complain about it. We fear the competition of our most humble and poverty-stricken neighbors. Our comfort might be disturbed. The world is filled with opportunities that we refuse to see, because we have been taught differently.

What would happen if we began visualizing the billions of people of Asia riding in American built cars? Instead, we are beginning to ride in foreign cars despite the almost prohibitive tariffs that exist. How would the poor of Asia buy American made automobiles? They have no money. That is merely the thinking that follows a materialistic conception of money. What if we had enough confidence in these people to treat them as humans, to realize that we could help them to develop, help them to gain an education, give them the know-how so they could in return do something for us. No, that might hurt business over here.* They might get some of the gold buried in Fort Knox. [ed. This has happened since 1990 when American business started moving jobs to China and India to create a new middle class.]

Now that we have this discussion out of the way and have covered some necessary preliminaries, in the next lesson, on this discussion of money, we will be free to discuss money from the point of view of the twelve different basic astrological principles, how they inter-relate, and how we can better utilize our own creative abilities for a more sound financial outlook.

Notes from editor:

*How interesting that CPT perceived the return of greed in banking with the removal of Glass-Stiegel in 1999 by Pres. Clinton that was backed by Wall Street. Then by 2008 the USA has an identical financial crisis like 1929 that has not been resolved as of this writing in 2015.
** **Sewell Lee Avery** (Nov. 4, 1874 – Oct. 31, 1960) was an American businessman who achieved early prominence in gypsum mining

and became president of the US Gypsum Company (1905-1936). At the beginning of the Depression, he was asked by J. P. Morgan & Co. to turn around the failing Montgomery Ward and succeeded in restoring its profitability by making huge changes. In 1936, Fortune magazine said that Avery was "generally held to be the No. 1 Chicago businessman in the postwar years, however, he failed to take advantage of the demand for durable goods and did not expand Montgomery Ward, costing it prominence in the retail field.

LESSON TWENTY-FIVE

MONEY PART II

It was very important for us to illustrate that money is actually only a substitute for credit and confidence, made necessary by the fact that greed and insecurity, which are the same, are very real in the world and are factors that cannot be ignored. In calling the Second House the House of Money, astrologers have greatly restricted an astrological understanding of money. This is true of the rest of the world because society has looked upon money as the real essence when it is nothing of the kind, except insofar as society has attempted to make it the essence.

When we deal with the Earth and Water signs and the Planets and Houses representing the same elements, we deal with the effect of the past on the present. We deal with the fact that there are very powerful forces in society which want to prevent change, progress and improvement. These forces within society conduct a constant war against anything in the way of creative effort because creative efforts bring about changes. Ancestors of people now alive gained control of material wealth built up in the past. The objective is to freeze this wealth where it is, allow it to change hands only by heredity and keep as large a ratio of humans as possible in a state of servitude. In England, this was carried so far that it was regarded as a disgrace for members of certain families to work. One merely perpetuated the past, followed traditions, customs, conventions, rules, regulations and old patterns having no further utility for society at large.

It would appear that one side of society is benefited by preserving the past, by creating large fortunes and keeping money in the hands of a select few. This is sometimes called the capitalistic slant, although the word capitalism can mean many things to many people. Supposedly, the world of Labor works in opposition to this phase of things, but unfortunately, Labor soon becomes a new form of capitalism, and we have a new capitalistic group that runs Labor to confine it for its own exploitation. Actually, we have two capitalistic groups fighting each other. This is not a cut and dried affair. The lines are not that easily drawn. Within the capitalistic world, we have many progressive elements. Although the original Communism was an attempt to overcome the evils of Capitalism. [ed. Since the time of the Reagan presidency, Labor has lost ground to the point of defeat in 2015.]

We soon find that Communism, just as much as Capitalism, it often controlled by power groups having greed as their basic motives. However, Stalin's children did not inherit his empire, but during his lifetime, Stalin was more powerful than any Czar had ever been.

In occult circles, there was always much talk about the White Forces and the Black Forces. The teachings of Jesus Christ constituted a philosophy that would have overcome the evils of money had they ever been followed, but the Christian churches soon adjusted themselves to the acceptance of perpetuation of the past and became an additional factor in limiting the creative forces of mankind. As in the Capitalistic and Labor worlds, the churches are not all black and not all white. Thus, to properly understand money, we must divorce ourselves from all ideologies and come down to study the difference between Earth and Water on the one hand, Air and Fire on the other.

In L. Ron Hubbard's Scientology, he divides life into four basic parts. He uses the terms, environment, body-emotion-somatic, mind and theta. Theta is the use of the Greek letter to specify the creative, energetic self that is something apart from environment, body and mind.

Actually, Hubbard is talking about the same factors studied by the astrologers, and we could look at the two quadruplicates in the following manner: EARTH-Environment; WATER-Body-Emotion-Somatic; AIR-Mind; and FIRE-Theta.

We find the Earth-Water (Environment-Body) forces endeavoring to keep things as they are and prevent change and progress for fear that these may transfer wealth to new hands. Wealth must stay in the same hands. We might call these the Black Forces, although we must never consider them all black. Like the bones of the body, they do give us form that we might not otherwise have. We find the Air-Fire (mind-Theta) forces hard at work to change things and bring about revolution and improvement. We see these forces principally at work in the inventor, but his efforts are usually captured by the forces of capitalism in the form of patents. The whole thing is soon brought under control and a select few again have control of the new conceptions, the abstract ideas. The courts of the land are employed to keep progress under control and not allow it to go far enough afield to permit too great changes in our static wealth status. It is not considered ethical for wealth to fight wealth to any great extent. There is usually agreement, and one phase of wealth agrees to stay on one side of the street, leaving the other phases of wealth a monopoly on the other side of the street.

When Saturn reached Capricorn in 1929-1932, the country had one of it's worst depression Saturn in Capricorn. [ed. 2008

Saturn opposing Uranus and then in 2011 Uranus squares Pluto until 2015.] Saturn and Capricorn represent Earth and environment. Materialistic ideas, as they relate to money, were in full command. Confidence died. Credit died. Everything collapsed, and a new administration took over. New bills were invented rapidly, some good, some bad, but an Aquarian had become president. The rules were changed. Confidence suddenly returned. The Gold Standard was scrapped. Congress began passing bills that would lend money, which meant give credit. Business turned upward and for the next 29 years, for the first time in its history the country failed to fall into any further depressions. The cycles changed, but as Saturn again neared Capricorn in 1959, The old forces of static wealth began to regain control. The Federal Reserve Bank began raising the rediscount rate in an effort to cut down credit, principally credit to the little fellow. Many wealthy people had sold their stocks at high prices and were anxious to get them back at lower prices. This was an effort to bring down stock market prices to a point where those who had money could buy them at lower prices. It was an attempt to get these stocks back into 'right' hands.

In some circles it is regarded as a sin for the lower classes to have too much of the better things in life. It is believed that comfort will prevent people from hard labor. The better things of life are supposedly intended for the chosen few. That is even portrayed under the title of God's Will, because God loved the poor and wanted to keep them poor.

The government does not always correctly estimate where it's attempts to control money may have the greatest effect. It was hoped to bring down stock market prices, but stock prices did not immediately respond. The effect began to show up elsewhere but not in the newspapers.

During the interval from September 1958 through June 1959, the Federal Reserve Bank raised the rediscount rate four times, form 1.75% to 3.5%. That is an increase of 64.4% from the September starting point. One of the first results was that people stopped buying by mail. The mail-order business went into a severe slump. From all over the US, students of the IAS wrote in that they were out of jobs or had financial troubles. The stock market climbed. Food prices climbed. The government was succeeding in getting money into the hands of the chosen few.

NEWSWEEK Magazine (June 22nd, 1959) put it this way in describing the position of the administration: " it is better to take a chance on having some unemployment than it is to permit further erosion in the value of the dollar. People who save and do not speculate have suffered severely in recent years and savings are at the root of private capitalism.

This statement tells us a great deal. When it is believed that money is getting into the hands of little people who speculate, or take a chance, and all efforts that attempt to improve the world must be regarded as speculative, the forces of wealth are sufficiently powerful to use the US Government and the Federal Reserve Bank to cut off credit, put people out of work, and transfer money back to those who have savings. Nothing is said about public capitalism. It is admitted that this is an attempt to help private capitalism. Help to increase the value of the assets of those who have accumulated, those who already have savings from which to eat and live. Toss out of a job the man who has no savings and who must work to support his family. It is the same attempt that was made in 1929 after the wealthy had disposed of their securities at high prices and wanted to get them back at low prices. The results are in the record. As this lesson is prepared, we face two more years with Saturn in Capricorn. The question will be whether intelligence in government can now be substituted for the same old pattern that has been applied for centuries. The answer lies in the future. Meanwhile between September 1958 and July 1959, the income of the IAS dropped by two thirds because such a vast number of students who always made their payment on time suddenly found themselves unable to do so. High interest rates were being employed to try and keep the little fellow down where he belonged.

The lesson the student must here learn and understand is that all this is the point-of-view of

Saturn. It is not conscious thought on the part of anyone, actually but Saturn's effort to repeat the past, to copy. Because something was once done, it must always be copied and repeated over thousands of years. Saturn has build up a philosophy which has been embedded in society. It is the belief that we must hoard, that only people who hoard are sound. It is the belief that there will always be famines, that there will never be enough to go around, that some people must starve to death, that only the wealthy know how to handle money, that money in the hands of the wealthy know how to handle money, that money in the hands of the masses is unsound and dangerous, that money and material things are the true essence. Although Christ attempted to expose and destroy the untruth of this viewpoint, that which is described as the Christian church has perpetuated it, and it is perpetuated in all Christian countries.

This is the Saturnian, Capricorn, 8th House point of view. Remember that Capricorn and the 8th House are opposite to Cancer and the 2nd House, which has been called the House of Money. The conception that money must earn money in the form of interest is Saturnian. The US Government supposedly controls money, but actually, the government must borrow money from the Saturnian individuals and pay them interest. This is supposed to be sound policy. Those who have inherited large sums of money charge the government for the use of that money in an effort to keep money in the hands of the same people. These people do not work for their interest. The government could just print money, but this would tend to place it in the hands of the masses and reduce the value of whatever money has been hoarded. Those who do not create could not earn. The Saturnian philosophy has as its principal aim protecting the interest of those who do not create and do not work. This class must be protected. Saturn represents frozen, static wealth.

The legal profession is a Saturnian profession. It's principal aim has always been to protect the wealthy, to make laws that will keep wealth from getting into other hands. The aim of almost every lawyer is to reach the point where he can draw down the big fees that come from the protection of estates. The young lawyer must often be satisfied with a collection job, but that is still a Saturnian type of work. Undertaking is another Saturnian profession. The undertaker's job is to glorify and preserve the dead body. In past generations, the dead body of the wealthy king was even better preserved and mummified.

The Saturnian philosophy always becomes most powerful when Saturn passes through Capricorn its own sign. It gets a jolt when Saturn moves into the next sign. Aquarius, sign of Uranus. Saturn, Capricorn and the 8th House are the symbols of materialism. When the materialists gain control and power we have depressions. It is as simple as that. When the materialists have gained control of the money by selling out, we must have another depression to allow the materialists to buy back at low prices after having sold out at high prices. When the government investigated Wall Street in 1933 it was discovered that the firm of J. P. Morgan and Company owned no stock at the time of the 1929 crash in the stock market. It had sold all the stock to the public. It had bought up government bonds. It was now collecting tax exempt interest from the government. The public lost it shirt. When stocks reached low enough prices, the big interest bought them back and were ready to sell them again to the public when prices again rose. This is the Saturnian way of making money, they will work harder for less. High interest rates are the primary purpose of Saturn. The wealthy have to do less for their money. The poverty stricken have to work harder for less. If we permitted progress to keep spiraling, the poor might catch up with the wealthy, and that would be regarded as a sin. The old pattern must be perpetuated. We must continue to function in the same old way. Insurance companies and the banks of the older part of the country also function in accord with the Saturnian pattern. This has not been so true of banks in the western part of the country. In a new country that is growing, Saturnian conceptions do not have the same grip. The new state of Arizona suffered no depression with the rest of the country in the 1929-1932 interval. When the state was a territory and had no money, a mining company printed its own money, paid employees with it, and this money had just as high value and was just as acceptable as US currency. This privately printed money started the state on its way, when it could get no other kind of money. This money had confidence behind it. In the prior chapter, we discussed money principally as a substitute for confidence and credit. The Saturnian philosophy does not believe in either confidence or credit. Everything is placed on the foundation of materialism. To understand Saturn, the student must realize and understand that it is the symbol of the doctrine of materialism, and that we have not yet escaped the doctrine of materialism which had such a strong grip on society in the 19th Century.

The original Labor movement was an attempt to overcome and offset materialism and many of the men, like John L. Lewis, who have fought so hard to give the worker more for his wages, were Aquarians, ruled by Uranus. Labor made its greatest forward strides under Franklin D. Roosevelt, an Aquarian President. Labor became completely bogged down when the American Federation of Labor was ruled by William Green, a Capricorn ruled by Saturn, until the C.I.O. came into being under John L. Lewis, and the Labor movement was divided into two parts for a time, the AFA under Green and Capricorn, the C. I. O under Lewis and Aquarius.

While Cancer, the 2nd House and the Moon relate to money from the view point of greed and the fear of starvation, Capricorn, the 8th House and Saturn relate to money from the view point of frustration, interest, borrowed money, laws, the goods of the dead, etc. The 8th House is also called the house of death, Saturn the planet of death. Where these factors are concerned, children of the rich are taught to frustrate themselves, accumulate money but never spend it on pleasure. However, when the youth of the wealthy is not kept in hand, it breaks out of bounds and gets away from this principle. Money has no value to society at large unless it circulates. Saturn attempts to prevent circulation. Could Saturn ever bring society under its complete domination, the only answer would have to be death to society itself. The only end of Saturn is death. Fortunately, there are other astrological principles to offset it.

Lesson Twenty-Five

Now, let us shift over to Scorpio-Mars-10th House and Taurus-"Y"-4th House principles, for these too have association with money, as do all twelve astrological principles house principles.

We find Mars-Scorpio-10th House associated with executive ability, authority, power, force, cruelty, surgery, pain, sadism, family affairs, sex, and the Family Survival Dynamic.

Labor was originally forced on slaves in order that the privileged few would not have to do their own work. Those so privileged became the warriors. Although this has changed over the years, the principal cost of government today is the military. The principal function of the military has always been to protect land and gain more land. The military was being employed in World War I to gain more land for Germany. It was employed in World War II to gain more land for the Axis nations. Our military was used to take land away from the Indians, and later to collect interest from Latin-American countries. Large corporations could exploit these countries and the US military protected the corporate interests by moving troops and warships into Latin-American ports whenever, it was deemed 'necessary'. The British empire was built by the armies that marched in the vanguard. When a new country was captured, the king gave great areas to wealthy families of England. Generals were often so rewarded. Although we have little in the way of actual old-fashioned slavery today, we have it in a new form in that our youth is inducted or drafted into the army to protect the land we now have or to acquire new land. For centuries, we have educated youth to believe that it is an honor to go into the army, and be killed if necessary to protect the land of the wealthy interests.

The wealthy need generals to protect their interest, and in more peaceful circumstances we have a new kind of general and we call him the executive. It is his job to make the workers work, and as an executive, he has more honor than the common worker and he is paid higher wages than the common worker. His position is socially accepted. He does not have to do physical labor. He just sees to it that others do it. He watches everybody. Even Labor unions get around to having executives, and many workers are abused physically by the 'executives.' During the lives of Henry and Edsel Ford, the Ford Motor Company had its own police force to perform violence on the worker whenever it was deemed 'necessary.' Modern representatives find it less necessary to employ violence to keep workers working.

The Family Survival Dynamic often goes beyond the family in our present-day society. It becomes the Group Survival Dynamic, but not the Social Survival Dynamic. However, we see it at work in the animal world. Food, insofar as plant life is concerned, groceries etc., are associated with Cancer, the Moon and the 2nd House, but meat is something else again. It involves surgery. It is the slaughter. The animal world is subsidized and domesticated. Cattle (and other animals) are raised, often fed free, made as healthy as possible through free medical services, then slaughtered, butchered, and surgery is performed. We usually find the knife associated with Scorpio, Mars and the 10th House. We find that Mars, Scorpio and the 10th House are very important in money matters, because most people have to condition themselves to the principles represented. It is necessary for a man to get along with and please his boss. His salary, or the amount of this salary, is all wrapped up with the principle represented by the Family Survival Dynamic. Quite often, we see a man become fed up and irritable when he is under an affliction of Mars-Uranus. He revolts. Either he quits his job or the boss discharges him. In any event, his salary stops and his finances are very much affected. The history of the labor movement has many strikes occurring during Mars-Uranus afflictions. The finances of vast numbers of families were affected. The finances of corporations have also been affected. Mars plays a very important part in business and money. The employer or the executive is principally interested in improving his own family's financial picture. Labor unions have improved working conditions for the men who belong to such unions, but there are vast numbers of people who do not belong to unions. They are more at the mercy of the employer, who is bent on making as large a profit on each employee as possible. Mars is aggressive and after the money. The person with a badly afflicted Mars may be ruthless in taking money from others, whether he is the employer or the holdup man. In some cases, there is little difference. Both employers and Labor unions have been known to employ gangsters to keep the employees in line, and unfortunately, many of the Labor leaders are principally interested in the survival of their own families. This also applies to the gangsters. We think of a well-known gangster, now in jail for income tax evasion. He is worth many millions of dollars, but he constantly complains because his children are not accepted socially. He says that it is not fair to condemn his children for what their father has done. It probably isn't but he never considered the children of his own victims.

    From Mars, Scorpio, the 10th House and the Family Survival Dynamic, we cross to 'Y', Taurus, the 4th House and the Family Survival Dynamic Reactor. It is the purpose of the FSDR to contain and restrict the FSD. With these factors we associate the home, the fort of the family, land and real estate. We can't deny that a man's home is closely allied with money. If he does not own his own home, he has to pay rent to the landlord every month. If he owns his own home, he may have a mortgage on it, and he has to pay interest. If he was born of wealthy parents, he has less complications because his home was probably supplied to him free. He does not have the same problems as the person who had to work hard to acquire any kind of a home at all. **The FSDR involves the desire to accumulate land and real estate** [ed. for the family]. Avoid having to pay rent to others and make people pay rent to you. Accumulate wealth within the family. This principle involves all fixed wealth. We see 'Y,' Taurus and the 4th House principles at its best when it is constructing, building homes, factories, public buildings, hospitals, office buildings, etc. The factor of inheritance comes in strongly, because whoever accumulates fixed wealth has to leave it to someone when he dies, and he always dies. Who should acquire the wealth of those who depart and are separated from it? When we think of a man, living in his own home with his family, it seems only just that the home should remain in the hands of the family in the event of his death, but our society has become so far out of line that some men acquire many millions of dollars in property, leave it to their children, and keep society off balance. The ownership of property has largely become a game, a legal game. We have rules, and we play the game according to the rules. The rules are usually made or determined by those who have the most, because they are the ones who can afford to spend money influencing legislation. The poor man cannot spend money in this fashion.

For several years, we have been making a study of horoscopes of people who are engaged in real estate matters or have been engaged during 1958-59. We continually find an excess of natal planets in 22-23 degrees of signs, conforming to our conception that the current position of planet 'Y' is at 22-23 Virgo. We have had the opportunity to study the birth charts of many men who are investing many millions of dollars in Arizona real estate. We just never fail to get an excess of planets in 22-23 degrees of signs, meaning that their birth positions are being aspected by 'Y.' One young man who has accumulated 35,000 acres of land outside the city limits of Tucson has Uranus at 23-Pisces, Neptune at 22-Leo. He has made his purchases on those days when other planets hit 22-23 degrees of signs, aspecting 'Y.' Time will tell how profitable his transactions will be. With other people, 'Y' may mean almost life or death of the family, but with the big operators, 'Y' is merely a game that is played according to the rules. You outguess the other fellow. If you correctly estimate the direction a city is going to grow and buy land, you might make millions of dollars. As this is written a housing bill that would lower housing costs and make housing easier to obtain has been passed by Congress and the Senate, but the President is threatening to veto it, because it is not in accord with the tight-money policy of the administration. It might interfere with the game being played by the wealthy.

Thus far, we have shown that money goes beyond the 2nd House and into the 8th, 4th, and 10th. Now, let us consider the 6th and 12th, Neptune and Mercury, Pisces and Virgo.

Pisces, Neptune and the 6th House involve the Social Survival Dynamic, the one we know a great deal about, but by ratio we probably know the least about. This principle is always trying to help the lower elements of society to survive, and it reaches below the human to the animal level in a great many instances. We can divide food into three types, plant life, animal life and fish. We have associated plant life and groceries with Cancer, meat with Scorpio and we'll have to associate fish and marine life with Pisces, Neptune and the 6th House. We have never quite understood why this is, but we do seem to find three different types of food associated with the three Water Signs. Indirectly, we would also find them associated with the Earth Signs, which can frustrate themselves. Capricorn may want to put food away for a rainy day or save money on food. The symbol for Taurus is the bull which Scorpio slaughters. The great ranches of hundreds of thousands of acres where the cattle are raised are strictly Taurus. Neptune and Pisces love the sea. Our greatest fish supply comes from the ocean. We also find Neptune connected with money-making in other fields. Oil, photography, radio, TV and movies appear to have some connection with Neptune, Pisces, and the 6th House principle. There is some connection with drugs and alcoholic beverages. The writer has three friends who made millions out of oil. Two have the Sun conjunct Neptune. The third has Neptune conjunct the cusp of the Second House. We find this principle connected with illicit operations such as prostitution. The 6th House principle does not recognize laws of Saturn, based on the past, as legitimate or binding. The 6th House principle may go beyond the law. This is the Social Survival Dynamics. They are usually dictated by individuals, families and groups. Arizona is still trying to get out from under laws that were made by big ranchers, mining corporations and railroads. Horse stealing was long regarded as more serious than murder, and you have a tough road ahead if you get caught rustling cattle. Better to steal automobiles. Ranchers rustle each other's cattle, but that is regarded as somewhat legitimate. It is the stranger they are after.

Astrology has long associated the underworld with Neptune and Pisces. The underworld is another kind of a world. Society as we find it is never asked for help. Information is never given to the police. There is a lack of respect for law and order because it is regarded as the law and order of a chosen few. When Franklin D. Roosevelt became President on March 1st, 1933, Sun and Mercury were in Pisces. Mars was retrograding back to a conjunction with Neptune in Virgo. Jupiter was also in Virgo. During March, April and May of that year, Mars was never further away from Neptune than 7 degrees. New social ideas were inaugurated. Laws were passed that would put money into the hands of great masses of people. Labor unions were given greater power. Curbs were put on the exploiting powers of Wall Street. There were laws to stop rich bankers from taking the savings of the poor and appropriating them to their own speculative use.

The rich and established of the country opposed Roosevelt almost to a man. This easy-money policy would wreck the nation. It didn't. For the next 36 years, there was no depression. As this is written, with Saturn in Capricorn, the tight-money advocates are regaining control of government for the first time since 1933. The ultimate result is unknown at this time. They might yet be defeated. Saturn is the pessimist of the heavens. His policy is never to allow things to be done in any way that is not a copy of yesterday. It might go wrong. Saturn and the law usually protect those who already have wealth. Neptune is different. Neptune is always at work toward more equal distribution of wealth. When it can't be distributed in any other way, it is sometimes stolen. We must remember that money is like blood and it is of no value to society as a unit unless it is circulating. Saturn can never see what is ahead because he always walks backward, looking at the past. He cannot design the future. He wants only to protect the pattern of the past. He has no creative ability. He knows but one way, to record and copy the past. Everything must be based on yesterday. He is static wealth and he is poverty, because static wealth ultimately brings poverty.

The source of the Neptunian and Pisces abilities are a mystery to us. The mathematical scheme of astrology tells us that Neptune too deals with the past, but some very, very distant past. Not just yesterday. There is a question in our minds as to whether Neptune is not often psychically drawing from some greater civilization that may have existed many, many thousands of years ago and may have been far superior to anything we know today. Neptune doesn't seem to figure things out mathematically. It just sees or knows them. One man believes there is oil beneath the ground. He finds it there. How did he know? He is the Neptunian. We often find a Neptunian person who is a good money-maker. He is quiet, secretive, and he sees what others do not see. He steps aside and watches society. He takes advantage of its weaknesses and its mistakes, and he may do it all legally. If he is intelligent, he will do it legally. If he is not, he may take unnecessary chances with the law. Oil is millions of years old. He seems to know where it is. The reverse is true when Neptune is afflicted. Here is a man who made millions in other lines, but he wanted to make money out of oil. He has Mars square to Neptune. The writer many years ago advised him that he could never make money out of oil. He has drilled holes all over four states. They were all dry. This is a good example of how the individual can make money out of some lines of business and not out of others. If you have an afflicted Neptune stay away from oil.

The business of public relations is very much tied up with Neptune. Modern public relations involves the art of making people see your point of view and wind up being happy about it. It is a big business today.

We have stated that it is the purpose of the Social Survival Dynamic Reactor to contain the Social Survival Dynamic. Neptune and Pisces and the Social Survival Dynamic can get out of hand, just as the other survival dynamics can get out of hand. Charts of 11 persons involved in prostitution show an interesting distribution of the planets out to Saturn, including Sun and Moon and three Ascendants.

Note:

AQUARIUS	11	TAURUS	7	LEO	1	SCORPIO	6
PISCES	15	GEMINI	4	VIRGO	3	SAGITTARIUS	7
ARIES	11	CANCER	3	LIBRA	8	CAPRICORN	4

We find 15 planets in Pisces against 3 in Virgo. We find 37 in the three consecutive signs Aquarius-Pisces-Aries against 7 in the three consecutive signs Cancer-Leo-Virgo. Prostitution is an illegal occupation in all states other than Nevada. It should be noted that the strong sign here is Pisces and not Scorpio. One of the three factors in Virgo was an Ascendant, which would be wrong if the birth time given were in error. The only Leo factor was a Moon in the first degree of Leo, and if the birth time were earlier, this would be in Cancer.

There is a strong desire nature that goes with Neptune, Pisces and the 6th House factors. Virgo is intent on curbing and frustrating this in an effort to conform with what Virgo thinks society should want.

How does all this work out money-wise? Neptune can see

that if the bars are let down and people are able to want things and spend money getting them, business will be good. Neptune doesn't believe in the restrictions and curbs that limit human expression. It would prefer to have people happy spending money. The blood is circulating that way. Virgo can see danger in that. Small amounts of money are very important to Virgo. Large amounts are not understood. The pennies are carefully counted. There is a seeking for bargains. The Virgo viewpoint is to save a few cents here and a few cents there. Virgo will offer honest service for honest money. It is difficult to believe that money could be made more easily with less effort and still be legitimate. If you think in too large sums of money, it will excite suspicion on the part of Virgo.

Mercury and Virgo and the 12th House have a great deal to do with money, but usually in relatively small amount. Mercury is the trader. Get a little edge here and there. Be satisfied with that. Mercury and Virgo like to work. It comes naturally. There is no shirking it. Because they can do the work well, particularly the detail work or the accounting, Virgo and Mercury can often get good wages. They want to be paid as they go along, but are likely to accept something akin to standard wages. Neither Mercury nor Virgo would be likely to think of making a million dollars out of an oil well. There is a lack of understanding of the intangibles, of the abstractions. Money is something real and material. The real principles behind it are not very well understood. It is here and now. It is green. It will buy things. You accumulate money by saving so much a week. That is not the way any wealthy man ever accumulated his money. He doesn't live that long. He has to get it quick in some spectacular way. Life is only just so long.

Where does music come from? It can be put together mathematically. It is actually a mathematical science, but few musicians ever studied mathematics or know much about the subject. Yet, music comes form somewhere, and the most successful deliverers of music are the Pisces-Neptune-6th House people. The same signs that produce a maximum of prostitutes produce the most successful musicians. Coincidence? Is music too something that is being picked up from some far, far distant past? The bearer of the drums in the jungle! All primitive people have music. Where does it come from? Neptune brings together strange companions. Why do we find such associations as oil, photography, music, prostitutes, easy money, the great ocean, alcohol, drugs, rubber, art, the subtleties of life, secrecy, seclusion, public relations, politics, international relations, liberalism, the underworld, hospitals, mental illness—all things—linked with Neptune, Pisces and the 6th House principle?

What we are saying is that money is more than the 2nd House of any chart. It involves every house and every sign and planet in the chart. It involves everything in the chart. All beings except man survive without the need for money. For mankind, it is the blood of his environment. It is more than difficult for him to exist without money. He often does, but only when he has too. We live in a cockeyed society where money is the only real god. Men may not want to displease another god, and they may pray, but when they do, they pray for money. In our civilization, money is closely linked with emotion. People can be emotional about money. Sometimes they can kill for it. It takes emotion to kill, not always, but in most cases. Man first wants to protect himself through Cancer and Capricorn. Next, he wants to protect his family through Scorpio and Taurus. Then, he has a strange notion about protecting all beings through Pisces and Virgo. In all of these operations, money gets into the picture. Money or the lack of it is everywhere. It has never been too well managed. Men seek money for security. It never really makes anybody secure except for a fleeting moment. After that, security has escaped again. Few people listened when a young Congressman, Stewart Udall, told the government that what it needed was not a balanced budget but a balanced economy, but in that statement, he showed an understanding that few people possess. In striving for money for its own sake, in making money the essence instead of the symbol, we have a sick society on our hands. Money is something that the government prints in green. It was once believed that money should be printed only as a substitution for gold, as a symbol for gold. Money had to represent something material, because security is only associated with material things. Inner security is unknown to most people. The American people repeatedly turned down the silver standard because it was believed that it would place money in the hands of too many people. This would ruin the country. God never intended the poor to have money. People voted against that idea again and again. When in 1933, the gold standard wound up with every bank in the country closed, we were taken off the gold standard overnight. People were not allowed to have gold. They had to turn it in to the government. They just had to take the government's word for it that it was good. They had no alternative, so they took the government's word. Now, we don't even have a silver standard. We are on a paper standard. We proved that gold wasn't necessary, but we did not prove that static wealth is not necessary. We borrow back our paper money from those who have it and issue bonds guaranteeing that we will pay them interest on it, so they won't have to work for a living like other people. Russia and Red China do not bother with this formality. They just print money without bothering to support the wealthy in the style to which they became accustomed hundreds of years ago. The strange thing is that, considering from where they started, they have progressed faster than we have. After World War I, Germany had little in the way of gold, silver or money, so she just printed some and became another world threat. We are sound. We are the materialists.

Carl Payne Tobey
1902-1980

20th Century American Astrologer

April 27, 1902
10:32 am 40N39
73W40

By Naomi Bennett, April 2015

Carl Payne Tobey was one of America's prominent astrologers in this century. He was part of the group of asCPTCoursetrologers that revived astrology in the 1920's in New York City. He contributed to the American Astrology magazine, Wynn's Astrology magazine and The New York Astrologer in the 1930's and 1940's. He was the first breed of astrologers that started to use statistical research into the foundations of the subject. Grant Lewi and Carl were best friends and associates for years. In the 1950's, Clancy Publications moved to Tucson, Arizona and Lewi was their editor for American Astrology Magazine and his own magazine. Lewi unexpectedly died of a brain hemorrhage, so Carl moved to Tucson to help in the transition period after his death.

In 1955 he created a correspondence course to teach the principles that he and others had rediscovered about astrology through 30 years of experience. He had over 700 students take this course. It is unique from all others and still relevant today. In 1965, he wrote **An Astrology Primer for the Millions** and from 1969-74 he wrote a nationally syndicated astrology column in the Sunday papers that reached 10 million weekly. In 1973 he wrote **Astrology of Inner Space**. I was lucky enough to be Carl's student in 1968 and work with him from 1969-1974. I worked on editing his last book, and writing the forward in 1972. Carl's health started failing slowly in 1976, so he moved near his son. He died in San Antonio in 1980 at the age of 78. Much later I consolidated his early writings in a book called, **Carl Payne Tobey's Collected Works**.

One of Carl's best discoveries and talents was the ability to discern geometric patterns in astrology, their meaning in modern terms, and to correct the errors in current beliefs. Carl found his greatest success with new students that didn't have to give up prior teachings. Carl was an advocate of the equal house system, heliocentric planetary nodes, arabic parts and transits after long experimentation and use of many techniques. He had used progressions years ago but found them inconsistent, off in their timing and generally unreliable. Transits were more effective for him, so he dropped the use of primary directions, progressions, solar returns, etc.

He discovered why the planets were assigned to specific signs and he discovered the geometric pattern behind house rulership. In addition, he extended the use of arabic parts by calculating a new additional natal chart using traditional arabic parts that bring out hidden attributes of a personality and the timing of events.

Both Holloran's Astrowin software and Cochrane's Kepler and Sirius software programs supports Tobey's secondary natal charts (the solar parts chart) that are based on the arabic parts. Please note that I had John Holloran write into his program the issue of sect that Rob Hand has uncovered in Greek astrology in the 1990's. The secondary chart can be calculated for both day or night births in Holloran's program so it was renamed the solar parts chart or the lunar parts chart. After several years of testing, it appears that the solar calculation holds true for day and night births, sect does not function.

Carl firmly believed that astrology was a branch of mathematics, the science of design. I believe it's a branch of fractal geometry. If psychology used astrology it could lift itself from a social science to a physical science because it could be expressed mathematically, like chemistry or physics to express psychological characteristics. All of his books are long out of print by their original publishers but www.LearnAstrologyNow.com has them available for purchase.

www.ingramcontent.com/pod-product-compliance
Lightning Source LLC
Chambersburg PA
CBHW050512170426
43201CB00013B/1929